Using Proper Proof Marks

When I was ten and living in florida, I learned that dogs may not *always* be man's best friend.

I liked to discover new places, and one afternoon, while riding a ~~bycicle~~ *bicycle* on the out skirts of my neighborhood, I discovered a train station. As I was leisurely rolling by the ~~wherehouses~~ *warehouses*, I noticed three large dogs about fifty yards in front of me. Since I had a dog of my own, and he wouldn't (without a reason) bother anyone, I payed *no* attention to these Canines. But, as I got closer, the dogs started to approch me with menacing growls and barks. At this point I began to feel uneasy, so I turned around to ride in the other direction. As soon as I turned, all three dogs started to chase me and nip at my heels. I tried to pick up speed in order to create some distance between me and these ~~malign~~ creatures, but to no avail. One of the dogs sank his teeth into my leg (deeply) and would *not* let go, no matter how hard I pulled. Only when I gave a violent yank (he did) finally let go. At this point, I didn't think about pain; I only though about riding for my life.

Rewriting
Writing
A RHETORIC
AND HANDBOOK

JO RAY McCUEN
Glendale Community College

ANTHONY C. WINKLER

HARCOURT BRACE JOVANOVICH, PUBLISHERS

San Diego   New York   Chicago   Austin   Washington, D.C.
London   Sydney   Tokyo   Toronto

NOTE: This work is derived from *Rhetoric Made Plain,* Fourth Edition, by Anthony C. Winkler and Jo Ray McCuen, copyright © 1984, 1981, 1978, 1974 by Harcourt Brace Jovanovich, Inc., and *Rewriting Writing: A Rhetoric* by Jo Ray McCuen and Anthony C. Winkler, copyright © 1987 by Harcourt Brace Jovanovich, Inc.

ISBN: 0-15-576718-6

Library of Congress Catalog Card Number: 86-81637
Printed in the United States of America

Preface

The principal aim of this book is to teach writing as rewriting. It assumes that all good writing has been rewritten, and it sets out to systematically teach students not only how to write, but also how to rewrite their work. We categorize the rewriting process into revising, editing, and proofreading because experience teaches that students often confuse these three distinct stages, believing, for example, that to proofread (catch a spelling error here and there) is the same as to revise.

Rewriting Writing: A Rhetoric comes in two versions, hardback and paperback. The hardback version contains a handbook that covers familiar matters of grammar, syntax, and mechanics; the paperback is identical to the hardback, except that it has no handbook. Both versions of this text are divided into four sections, each of which emphasizes the writing and rewriting of some element of the essay.

Part I focuses on the *process* of prewriting, the back and forth movement of nearly constant revision that writers make to an initial plan. Part II covers the familiar range of rhetorical modes as helpful structures that students may use in the writing and rewriting process. Part III focuses on sentences, while Part IV emphasizes the argumentative essay, the literary paper, the essay exam, and the research paper. An appendix of proofreader's marks is included along with an explanation of what they mean. Here we have also included several students' essays along with guidelines for evaluating them.

This text teaches how to rewrite not merely by an exposition of theory, but through real-world examples of students' revisions. Indeed, its heavy reliance on students' works and models is an important feature of the book. Every point we make about writing is underscored by a student's example. Every chapter, every major section ends with a student's paragraph or essay in at least two drafts: the first, a rough draft of the work with our marginal annotations indicating its weaknesses and mistakes; the second, the finished paper with corrections and revisions made by the writer. We do this throughout the text and in our exercises, giving students ample opportunity to develop an editorially critical eye and to perfect their revising skills.

Some of the student written material used in this book was taken from *The Polishing Cloth,* a faculty-supervised collection of student essays published by Dekalb Community College, Georgia. An ambitious magazine that gives students a well-deserved outlet for expository writing done to satisfy class assignments, *The Polishing Cloth* has proven to be a useful pedagogical tool as well as a medium in which the superior efforts of beginning essayists may be acknowledged.

We are grateful to the following students for allowing us to use various drafts of their work in our book: Byron T. Barnes, John Greene, William Funsten, Gwen Ashby, Eric Ernst, Larry James, Sandra Capparell, Joann Andrejka, Gary Brochette, Norma Collins, Stephen Davey, Brict Wom Dong, Nancy Demaagd, Bryant Ewing, Anthony Gendal, Kathy Greer, Mary Lu Hauser, Robin L. Kusiak, Susan Leonard, Betty Netupsky, Suzanne Ozawa, Kathy Redman, Jjion An Thung, Jennifer Travers, Michael Wilds, and Gwen Wright.

Finally, we are grateful to our colleagues who reviewed *Rewriting Writing* in typescript and made valuable suggestions: Peter Zoeller, Wichita State University; Laura Quinn, University of Wisconsin, River Falls; and Josephine Koster Tarvers, Rutgers, The State University of New Jersey, New Brunswick Campus.

ANTHONY C. WINKLER AND JO RAY MCCUEN

Contents

Preface   **iii**

PART ONE
Prethinking and Prewriting the Whole Essay

Chapter One   Writing and Rewriting   3

Why Rewrite?   **4**
The Writing Process   **10**
The Rewriting Process   **11**
  Revising   **12**
  Editing   **12**
  Proofreading   **12**
Goals of Rewriting   **15**
Procedure and Sequence for Rewriting   **16**
  Proceed at a steady pace   **16**
  Maintain an objective stance   **18**
  Don't become bogged down   **19**
  Reread, reread, reread   **19**
  Save the original   **19**
  Follow your hunches   **20**

Chapter Two   Prewriting Strategies, Voice and Style   23

Choosing a Topic   **24**
Formulating a Controlling Idea and Thesis Statement   **25**

Using Invention   27
  Brainstorming   27
  Clustering   29
  Talking writing   30
Using Memories and Experiences   34
Using Observation   35
Doing Research   36
Organizing Your Ideas   38
  Create a model of the essay   38
  Make an outline   40
Voice and Style   47
Writing the Essay   56
  Find the right environment   56
  Expect to write at least three drafts   56
  Expect the worst first   57
  If all else fails, change your writing instrument   57
  Do the standing jump   57

Chapter Three   The Whole Essay: Purpose, Thesis,
Organization, and Logic   59

Purpose and Thesis   59
  Revising the thesis for clarity of aim   62
  Revising the thesis for unity   63
  Revising the thesis for coherence   64
  Revising the thesis for specificity   65
  Revising the thesis to get rid of wordiness   66
  Revising the thesis to suit your audience   68
  Following a thesis statement through successive drafts   69
Revising for Better Organization and Structure   71
  Organizing according to the order of importance   72
  Organizing according to space orientation   72
  Organizing according to time orientation   73
  Organizing according to logic   73
Revising for Logical Progression and Thought   82
  Avoid hasty generalizations   82
  Double check your evidence   84
  Avoid non sequiturs   88
  Avoid irrelevancies   92

PART TWO
Writing and Rewriting Paragraphs

Chapter Four   The Paragraph: Structure and Rhetorical Pattern   115

Parts of the Paragraph   **116**
Writing Unified Paragraphs   **118**
Writing Coherent Paragraphs   **120**
Constructing Paragraphs from the Thesis Statement   **125**
The Organizing Principle behind Paragraphs   **127**

Chapter Five   Narrating and Describing   133

Narrating   **133**
  The use of a consistent point of view   **134**
  The use of pacing   **135**
  The use of vivid details   **136**
Description   **141**
  Focus on a dominant impression   **142**
  *Appeal to the reader's senses through specific details and figures
    of speech*   **143**

Chapter Six   Defining and Exampling   151

Defining   **151**
  Give the etymology of the word   **153**
  Supply examples, functions, and effects of the word   **153**
  Say what the word does not mean   **154**
Developing by Examples   **158**
  Make your examples relevant   **160**
  *Establish a clear connection between your example and the point being
    made*   **161**

Chapter Seven   Explaining Process and Classifying   167

Explaining Process   **167**
  Begin with a clear statement of purpose   **168**
  Know your process thoroughly   **168**
  Work out the correct order of your steps   **168**
  *Make sure that the details of each individual step are clear and
    complete*   **169**
  *Use transitions to indicate when you are moving from one step to the
    next*   **169**

Classifying   **174**
  Base your classification on a single principle   **175**
  Divide the entire topic   **176**
  Keep your categories from overlapping   **177**
  Write approximately the same number of words on each entry   **177**

Chapter Eight   Comparing/Contrasting and Analyzing
Cause   183
Comparing/Contrasting   **183**
  Declare the bases of your comparison   **184**
  Complete the comparison by dealing with both sides   **184**
  Use appropriate transitions to stress either likeness or difference   **185**
  Organize your comparisons either within or between paragraphs   **186**
Analyzing Cause   **192**
  Be cautious about drawing cause-effect connections   **193**
  Use connectives to indicate a cause or effect relationship   **194**
  Focus on immediate rather than remote causes   **195**

Chapter Nine   The Beginning, Middle, and Ending   201
Beginning the Essay   **201**
  Begin at the beginning   **202**
  Take a stand   **203**
  Use various kinds of openings   **205**
The Middle   **209**
  Repeat key words at the beginning of each new paragraph   **210**
  Begin the new paragraph by restating the idea that ended the old   **211**
  Ask a rhetorical question   **212**
  Use transition phrases   **213**
  Use an initial summarizing sentence   **214**
  Use a transition paragraph   **215**
Ending the Essay   **217**

PART THREE

Writing and Rewriting Sentences

Chapter Ten   Rewriting Sentences for Clarity and
Conciseness   231
Rewriting the Sentence for Clarity   **232**
  Avoid mixed constructions   **232**

Use parallel constructions   **234**
Make logical constructions   **235**
Rewriting the Sentence for Conciseness   **241**
Don't repeat yourself   **241**
Don't use unnecessary words   **242**
Don't use big words   **244**

Chapter Eleven   Rewriting Sentences for Emphasis   **249**
Write Balanced Sentences   **249**
Structure Your Sentences to Be Emphatic   **252**
Write Sentences that Sound Emphatic   **257**
Vary Your Sentences   **259**
Use Inventive Diction   **262**
Appendix: Proofreading and Marking Your Drafts   **275**

PART FOUR

Special Purpose Essays

Chapter Twelve   The Argumentative Essay   **281**
The Proposition of an Argument   **281**
Sources of Proof   **283**
Testimonials   **284**
Experience   **285**
Anecdotes   **286**
Facts   **287**
Statistics   **289**
Reasoning   **290**
Logical Links   **293**

Chapter Thirteen   Literary Papers and Essay Exams   **307**
Literary Papers   **307**
Finding the theme   **308**
Summarizing   **309**
Paraphrasing   **311**
Quoting   **313**
Analyzing form   **315**
The Essay Exam   **321**
Read the question carefully   **322**
Think before you write   **322**
Organize your essay   **322**

Chapter Fourteen   The Research Paper   331
The Process of Writing a Research Paper   332
First Week: Finding a Topic   332
  Using the library   332
Second Week: Assembling a Bibliography   334
Third Week: Preparing Note Cards, a Thesis Statement, and an
  Outline   336
Fourth Week: Writing the Rough Draft   341
Fifth Week: The Final Paper Complete with a Bibliography   351
  I. General order for citations of books in "Works Cited"   352
  II. Sample bibliographic references to books   356
  III. General order for bibliographic references to periodicals in
    "Works Cited"   363
  IV. Sample bibliographic references to periodicals   364
  V. Nonprint materials   368
  VI. Special items   372
Sample Student Paper   381

Appendix   Practice Essays to Revise, Edit, and
Proofread   413

PART FIVE

Handbook

Basic Grammar   429
1. Parts of speech   429
  1a. Verbs   430
  1b. Nouns   433
  1c. Pronouns   433
  1d. Adjectives   435
  1e. Adverbs   435
  1f. Prepositions   437
  1g. Conjunctions   437
  1h. Interjections   439
2. Sentences   441
  2a. Subjects and predicates   441
  2b. Complements   442
  2c. Phrases   443
  2d. Clauses   446
  2e. Kinds of sentences   448

3. Sentence fragments   **453**
4. Comma splices   **454**
   4a. Correcting comma splices   **454**
5. Run-on sentences   **455**
6. Agreement   **457**
   6a. Subject-verb agreement   **458**
   6b. Pronoun-antecedent agreement   **460**
7. Pronoun case   **463**
   7a. Using the subjective case   **464**
   7b. Using the objective case   **465**
   7c. Using the possessive case   **466**
8. Adjectives and adverbs   **467**
   8a. Adjectives and adverbs after sense verbs   **468**
   8b. Don't confuse adjectives and adverbs   **468**
   8c. Comparative and superlative forms   **468**
   8d. Don't convert nouns to adjectives   **468**

Punctuation   471

9. The comma   **471**
   9a. Commas before coordinating conjunctions   **471**
   9b. After introductory elements   **472**
   9c. Series   **472**
   9d. Nonrestrictive clauses or phrases   **473**
   9e. Appositives   **474**
   9f. Parenthetical expressions   **474**
   9g. Miscellaneous elements   **474**
10. The semicolon   **476**
11. The colon   **477**
12. The dash   **478**
13. The period   **479**
14. The question mark   **480**
15. The exclamation point   **480**
16. Quotation marks   **481**
17. The apostrophe   **482**
18. The hyphen   **484**
19. Parentheses   **485**
20. Brackets   **486**

Mechanics   491

21. Capitalization   **491**
   21a. First words   **491**
   21b. Proper nouns   **492**

21c. Names   **492**
21d. Other capitalization rules   **492**
22. Italics   **496**
23. Numbers   **499**
24. Abbreviations   **502**

Effective sentences   505

25. Subordination   **505**
26. Dangling modifiers   **510**
27. Misplaced parts   **512**
28. Parallelism   **513**
    28a. Basic rules   **514**
29. Illogical constructions   **516**
    29a. Illogical comparisons   **516**
    29b. Mixed constructions   **517**
30. Shifts   **519**
    30a. Tense   **519**
    30b. Mood   **520**
    30c. Person   **521**
    30d. Voice   **522**
    30e. Discourse   **522**
31. Pronoun reference   **524**

Index   527

Rewriting Writing
A RHETORIC AND HANDBOOK

PART ONE

Prethinking and Prewriting the Whole Essay

Chapter One

Writing and Rewriting

Writing and rewriting are a constant search for what it is one is saying.

JOHN UPDIKE (b.1932)

At 37,000 feet the Lockheed L-1011 was flying from Chicago to Atlanta through a violent thunderstorm. Crammed into the center aisle of seats was a nervous instructor of English and, beside him, a student on her way back to school after a long weekend. Oblivious to the shuddering of the aircraft in the dark night, the student coolly took out a yellow legal pad, neatly outlined an essay, and began to write.

She was finished by the time the L-1011 had shaken itself loose of the storm and was rocking gently in the night sky seven miles above a speck of light the captain had identified as Louisville. Casting her eyes around the cabin at her fellow passengers, the student noticed the instructor watching her and struck up a conversation with him. It was plain to the instructor that she was proud of her freshly composed work and wanted to share it with someone, and since he was fascinated that anyone could even dream of writing under such nerve-wracking conditions, he eagerly accepted the invitation to read her essay.

When he was done, the instructor decided that produced under unthinkable conditions—in bad light aboard a crowded aircraft bouncing through a thunderstorm—the essay was a brilliant effort. But read on the good earth during a placid hour, it would rate at best a "C." Its main point was clear enough but supported only by weak generalizations and trite de-

3

tails. Its paragraphs seemed choppy, being held together neither by a strong narrative thread in the writing nor by smooth transitions. While the language occasionally sparkled with the personality of the writer, for the most part it was drab and obvious. In short, the essay was glib but not at all convincing.

"Do you like it?" the student asked, looking hopefully at her fellow passenger who, so far as she knew, could have been anyone from a plumber to a househusband.

Seven miles up in a stormy night sky aboard a crowded aircraft, the instructor reflected, was no place for academic criticism (prayer struck him as a better use of the time), so he said politely that it seemed like a "good first draft." The student heaved a heavy sigh at this faint praise.

"I'm in premed," she said with disappointment, putting the essay away. "I'm not a writer. It's the best I can do."

In fact, it was not her best effort, and only the belief in a mistaken theory of composing could have made the student think so. She seemed to think that writing an essay required little more than pen, paper, and fifteen makeshift minutes, even in a thunderstorm. She had made no attempt at rewriting, but had merely glanced at the finished work, made a spelling correction here and there, and then sat back radiating an expression of premature contentment. It struck the incredulous instructor, who was occasionally used to struggling for hours over a single paragraph, that a gifted writer working this way could hardly have done better. The student's essay was not badly written; but it had been written badly.

And so we come to the premise of this book, which is a simple one: if you write, you should rewrite. If you do not rewrite, you most likely will not write well. If you do rewrite, you will almost certainly write better than if you don't.

Why Rewrite?

Writers revise and edit their work for the simple reason that experience has taught that doing so will almost always make it better. You begin with a rough idea. You put it down on paper, perhaps in an explosion of inspiration. But if you then think you are done, you're mistaken: you've merely taken an exhilarating plunge on the tram down into the mine shaft. Hours of hard work still lie ahead. That is the labor of rewriting which nearly all writers who wish to perfect their work must practice.

Testimony to the truthfulness of this observation is common in literary history. Somerset Maugham, the English essayist and novelist, said of his style, which is regarded by many as effortlessly graceful, that "nature seldom provides me with the word, the turn of phrase, that is appropriate without being farfetched or commonplace." Maugham admitted that he attained the effect of ease, if at all, "only by strenuous effort." Hemingway rewrote parts of *The Sun Also Rises* some seventeen times. The French writer Colette confessed to often spending an entire morning working on a single page. Then there is this poignant anecdote by Mark Twain, a writer whose homespun prose often strikes our ear as unaffectedly natural:

> I began a story which was to turn upon the marvels of mental telegraphy. A man was to invent a scheme whereby he could synchronize two minds, thousands of miles apart, and enable them to freely converse together through the air without the aid of wire. Four times I started it in the wrong way and it wouldn't go. Three times I discovered my mistake after writing about a hundred pages. I discovered it the fourth time when I had written four hundred pages—then I gave it up and put the whole thing in the fire.
>
> —*The Autobiography of Mark Twain,* ed. by Charles Neider.

The hard fact is this: Even for the gifted, writing is neither automatic nor easy. A writer's work may read with an effortless grace, but it is wrong to assume that the style cost no effort. What you read on the page as you lounge in a cushioned chair is hardly ever what the writer composed at one sitting. Most good writing is as laboriously cultivated as any drought-stricken farmer's crop and just as dependent on ceaseless labor mixed in with an occasional rain of inspiration.

We bring this up because students, like the one on the plane, often give up too quickly on their writing. Appearing in all its polished glory, the printed page too glibly conveys the mistaken impression that it sprang untouched from the writer's pen. Some such pages no doubt have sprung from writer's pens, but from our own have come no more than one or two in decades of writing. In the more ordinary course of events, a writer begins with a very rough first draft, which is made better only after repeated stabs at rewriting. Yet many students share the universal delusion that if they cannot write a flawless essay at one sitting it means that they cannot write at all. But the truth is that writers can no more be judged by their first drafts than books by their covers. Typically, almost all first drafts are insipid and unpublishable.

For example, here is a good student paragraph. It is clearly written and carries out a sharp sense of purpose with an unfaltering touch. As an experiment, we asked the student who wrote it as part of a paper on Arthur Conan Doyle—the creator of Sherlock Holmes—to save her successive drafts for us. Here is the paragraph as it finally appeared in her paper.

From the first, Conan Doyle tried to give his characters their own idiosyncrasies, strengths and weaknesses that would make them react humanly in all their adventures. The creation of Dr. John Watson, the narrator for all of Sherlock Holmes' adventures, gives us a classic example of how he accomplished this. Watson was actually a composite of two men Doyle had known during his service in the South Seas. The first was a Dr. James H. Watson, who had been a close friend and whose slightly modified name became the character of whom Doyle wrote, "Good old Watson! You are the one fixed point in a changing age." Before lending his narrator the name of the real Dr. Watson, Doyle had called him "Orman Sacker," which he later rejected because he sensed that it "smacked of dandyism." The second person of whom the fictional Dr. Watson was made was another close friend of Doyle from his South Seas days. His name was Major Wood, and it was from him that Doyle took his physical description of Watson with, "the square jaw, thick neck, moustache, burly shoulder and indeterminate bullet wound." Although Wood later became Conan Doyle's secretary, he is remembered today mainly for the image he gave the redoubtable Dr. Watson, the most famous of narrators in the detective story.

The writer who can produce such a compact and clear paragraph on a first try without even a marginal scribble or erasure smudge deserves our admiration. But for this particular student, this was not a first try but a fourth. Here is her third draft, along with the corrections she made to it:

Third draft:

From the first, Conan Doyle's aim was to

give his characters their own idiosyncrasies,

strengths and weaknesses that would make them

react ~~realistically and~~ humanly in their

adventures. *, the narrator for all of Sherlock Holmes' adventures,* The creation of Dr. Watson gives us

a classic example of how he accomplished this.

Watson
~~This main character, who was the narrator for~~

~~all of Sherlock Holmes' adventures~~, was a *actually*

composite of two men ~~Conan~~ Doyle had ~~met~~ *known* during

his ~~stay~~ *service* in the South Seas. The first was a Dr.

James H. Watson, who had been a ~~comrade, doctor~~ *close friend*,

~~and friend~~, and whose slightly modified name

became the character of whom Doyle wrote, "Good

old Watson! You are the one fixed point in a

changing age." Before ~~borrowing~~ *lending his narrator* the name of ~~his~~

~~friend of the South Seas' days~~ *the real Dr. Watson*, Doyle had ~~named~~ *called him*

~~Watson~~ "Orman Sacker," ~~but~~ *which he later* rejected ~~this~~ because

he sensed that it "smacked of dandyism." The

second character of whom the ~~composite~~ fictional

Dr. Watson was made, was ~~a~~ *another* Major Wood, and a

close friend of Doyle's ~~in the~~ *from his* South ~~seas~~ *8 days.* ~~It~~

~~was from~~ *His name was Major* Wood ~~that Doyle~~ *and it was from him that Doyle* took his ~~famous~~

physical description of Watson with, "the square jaw,

thick neck, moustache, burly shoulder and

indeterminate bullet wound." *although* Wood later became

Conan Doyle's secretary, ~~but posterity~~ *he is* remembers*ed*

~~him~~ *today* mainly for the image he gave the ~~good~~

redoubtable ~~doctor~~ *Dr. Watson*, the most famous narrator *of s* in

the annals of the detective story.

Even the inexperienced eye can see that this is not as smooth or strong as the final copy and that it was markedly improved by the writer's scribbles. Her second draft was even worse:

Second draft:

From the first, Conan Doyle tried to
breathe life into his characters by endowing
them with recognizable personalities that would
make them react realistically in their
adventures. He tried to give them their own
idiosyncrasies, strengths and weaknesses.
Watson was originally named "Ormand Sacker," but
fortunately Conan Doyle sensed that this name
"smacked of dandyism." Recalling his own past,
Conan Doyle remembered two gentlemen with whom
he had served in the South seas. One, Dr. John
Watson, who had been a comrade, doctor, and
friend, would give his name to the narrator of
all Sherlock Holmes' adventures. "Good old
Watson! You are the one fixed point in a
changing age." The other, a Major Wood, gave
Watson his famous features, "the square jaw,
thick neck, moustache, burly shoulder and
indeterminate bullet-wound . . . " Major Wood
was a close friend Conan Doyle's while he was in

the South sea and would later serve as Conan

Doyle's secretary.

Worst of all was her original draft. It was disorganized, repetitious, occasionally ungrammatical, and entirely lacking in the clear sense of purpose of the final copy. Here it is exactly as she wrote it in a single sitting:

First draft:

From the first, Conan Doyle took pains to

bring his characters to life——not only in the

plots of the adventures, but also in their

personalities. Doyle liked to make his

fictional characters come to life by giving them

their own little idiosyncrasies, their strengths

and weaknesses. Watson was originally named

"Ormand Sacker," but fortunately Doyle decided

that this name lacked grit, or rather that it

"smacked of dandyism." So, recalling his own

past, Conan Doyle brought to mind two gentlemen

with whom he had served in the South Seas. Dr.

James H. Watson, comrade, doctor, and friend of

Doyle's——his name would be used after a slight

modification to read Dr. John Watson, as the

name that would become the cornerstone from

which Doyle would write his adventures: "Good

old Watson! You are the one fixed point in a

changing age." Although named for Dr. James

Watson, it was Major Wood's features, in general

terms, that were used for Watson's features.

"Watson of the square jaw, thick neck,

moustache, burly shoulder and indeterminate

```
bullet wound. . . . "  Major Wood was a close
friend of Doyle's while he was in the South Seas
and would later serve as Doyle's secretary.
```

This gradual reworking of a blurry first draft into crisp final copy is, very simply, the way most writers work. And if you wish to improve your own writing, it is a process you must master and practice as your own. You learn to be philosophical about first drafts, to greet them not with harsh judgment, but with hope. Before you had nothing, but now you have something, even if only a few pages. Granted they may strike you as scruffy and ill-expressed, but that is the nature of all first drafts. Now you can set about tidying up your language, clarifying your purpose, making your ideas sharper. And if anything about your prose should strike you as especially bad, that is the best sign of all. It means you are seeing your own weaknesses and can begin amending them. It is the unnoticed flaw in style—the overuse of certain phrasings, the doting over a particular construction—that bedevils all writers, not the one that can be flushed out in a single rereading.

The Writing Process

Writing is a creative process—an intellectual exercise that results in a symbolic product, be it a book, story, play, report, essay, memo, letter, or paragraph. But it is not as simple a process as learning to ride a bicycle with a definite point at which mastery is visibly and finally achieved for all time.

One peculiarity of writing is that it does not have to be done in any fixed sequence. Of course, you write always from left to right, assembling words into sentences, and in that narrow sense there is sequence. But you do not necessarily have to start at the beginning nor complete the middle before you can work on the end. Read what one American essayist and novelist had to say about the way she writes:

> "I knew why Charlotte went to the airport even if Victor did not."
>
> "I knew about airports."
>
> These lines appear about halfway through *A Book of Common Prayer*, but I wrote them during the second week I worked on the book, long before I had any idea where Charlotte Douglas had been or why she went to airports. Until I wrote these lines I had no character called "Victor" in mind: the necessity for mentioning a name, and the name "Victor," occurred to me as I wrote the sentence. "I knew why Charlotte went to the airport" sounded

incomplete. "I knew why Charlotte went to the airport even if Victor did not" carried a little narrative drive. Most important of all, until I wrote these lines I did not know who "I" was, who was telling the story.
—Joan Didion, "Why I Write," adapted from a Regent's lecture delivered by the author at the University of California, Berkeley.

What this author says about writing fiction applies as well to expository prose—that written primarily to clarify or explain. A writer can begin anywhere in a projected work: beginning, middle, or end. Indeed, often you are better off starting at whatever point in a work strikes your fancy rather than dragging yourself, pen in hand, kicking and screaming to the opening paragraph.

The writing process is also a **recursive** one. Its nature is circular and self-feeding. Professional writers seldom compose unblemished text at one sitting. More commonly they compose in increments, often pausing to read what they have just written to get ideas about what to say next. When they get stuck, as all writers occasionally do, they go back and look over what they have already written for further ideas.

Implicit in this recursive process is the notion of rewriting, restating, a continual patching of this sentence or that, this phrase, this expression. You jump from this paragraph to the start of the essay and, while lingering briefly there, find a better word, a better image, a less crooked sentence, and so make the correction.

Its symbolic nature, however, is what sets the writing process apart from any other. Whether prose or poetry, the written word is a complex symbolic stew of substance, form, style, and tone, which generally cannot be composed at a rush or done at one pass. A writer can nearly always find an idea that might have been better explained, a sentence that might have been framed more elegantly, a word that might have been more apt. So commonplace is the writer who incessantly tinkers with a manuscript that most publishers enforce a cap on changes made in page proofs, the last stage before a manuscript becomes a bound book. After this cap is exceeded (usually at ten percent), the writer must pay the cost of making any further changes.

The Rewriting Process

Writing and rewriting are inseparably part of the same process as inhaling and exhaling are to breathing. When you write you invent. When you rewrite you better your invention. The process is circular and indivisible and there is a great deal of back and forth movement between writing and rewriting as a writer struggles to express an idea. For the sake of this discussion, however, we will assume that the rewriting process is divisible into separate parts that may be conveniently labeled and examined.

Revising

Revising means making gross changes mainly to the content but also to the form of a work. This means you change not only what you say, but also how you say it. Our model reviser is the Scottish professor at Oxford who reportedly used to say to his students, "Did ye remember to tear up that fir-r-st page?" For the reviser makes wholesale changes: tears up pages, alters paragraphs, inserts material where the text seems drab or threadbare of meaning. Figure 1–1, for example, is a facsimile page of the beginning of this book showing initial revisions made to the text. As you can see, we started out with an entirely different beginning than the one we finally used. Of the some ten beginnings of this book, nine perished in the revision process.

Editing

Editing means making alterations mainly in form rather than content. Changes are made to smooth out a sentence, sharpen an expression, tone down a passage, all with the general aim of improving readability and style. Figure 1–2, for example, is a facsimile page of the manuscript of Mark Twain's *Autobiography* showing some of the writer's editing. Although Twain struck out some redundant words and inserted a clause here and there to round out an idea, little of substance was altered by his editing.

Proofreading

This is the final stage in the rewriting process. Here you read your work for literal correctness. You pore over the page looking for the misspelled word, the grammatical slip, the misplaced comma, and when you come across these venial flaws, you make the correction either by erasure or retyping. Your focus should be microscopic since your aim is to produce clean copy.

For the writer lucky enough to work with a word processor, the drudgery of proofreading has become largely mechanized. Spelling checker programs are available that can scan a text, identify misspelled words, and correct them at the touch of a key. But whether you use a computer or not, proofreading depends on your own keen eyes and judgment. No program can spot subtle misuses such as "there" in place of "their," and none can replace the writer's own sense of appropriateness for a word or expression.

Figure 1–1   Facsimile Manuscript Page of This Text Showing
Rewritten Changes

Chapter 1

If you write, you will rewrite. That is as close to a
universal law of writing as there is. A few writers, to be
sure, have been exempt from it, or so history tells us.
Shakespeare was said to have never blotted a line. Oscar
Wilde, on the other hand, boasted of having spent a morning
putting a comma in, and an afternoon taking it out. The rest
of us fall largely somewhere in between: we write and then we
rewrite, some of us more, and some of us less.

At 37,000 feet ~~on a stormy evening~~ the Lockheed L-1011
was flying from Chicago to Atlanta through a ~~shoal of black~~ *violent thunderstorm.*
~~strom clouds that violently pummelled the fuselage of the~~
~~aircraft with body blows from a giant fist.~~ Crammed into the
center aisle of seats was a nervous instructor of English and,
beside him, a student on her way back to school ~~from~~ *after* a long *g*
week-end. Oblivious to the shuddering of the aircraft in the
dark night, the student cooly took out a yellow *legal* pad, ~~made a~~
neatly
~~neat~~ outline ~~of~~ an essay, and began to write ~~it.~~

She was finished by the time the ~~aircraft~~ *L-1011* had shaken ~~its~~
itself loose of
~~way out to~~ the ~~stubborn~~ storm and was rocking gently in the *sky*
~~coacal pitch dark~~ night seven miles ~~over~~ *above* a speck of light
the captain had identified as   *Casting*
~~called~~ Louisville. ~~Casrting~~ her eyes around the cabin at her
fellow passengers, the student noticed the instructor watching

---

Why the emphasis on these stages? Partly because students often
confuse proofreading with revision. It is not enough simply to proofread
your text for grammatical slips: dusting a room is not the same as remodel-

Figure 1–2 A Page of Mark Twain's Manuscript Showing Corrections in His Own Hand

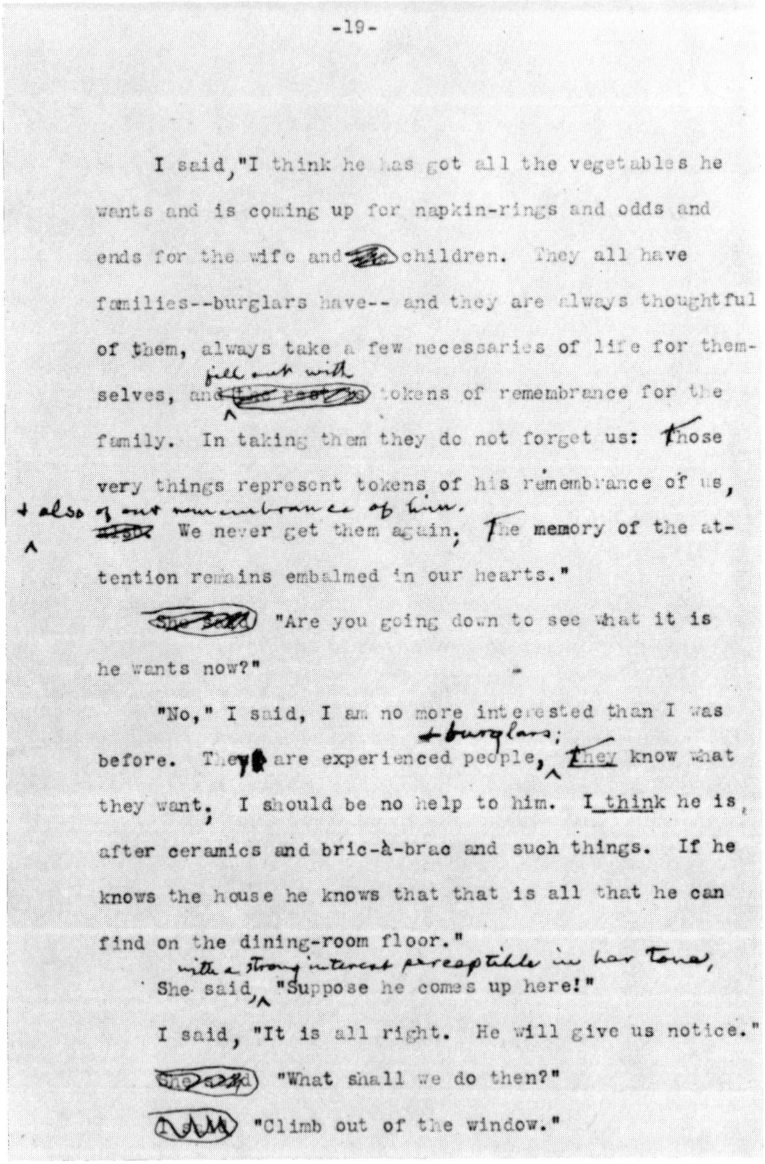
-19-

I said, "I think he has got all the vegetables he wants and is coming up for napkin-rings and odds and ends for the wife and children. They all have families--burglars have-- and they are always thoughtful of them, always take a few necessaries of life for themselves, and fill out with tokens of remembrance for the family. In taking them they do not forget us: those very things represent tokens of his remembrance of us, & also of our remembrance of him. We never get them again; the memory of the attention remains embalmed in our hearts."

"Are you going down to see what it is he wants now?"

"No," I said, I am no more interested than I was before. They are experienced people, & burglars; they know what they want; I should be no help to him. I think he is after ceramics and bric-à-brac and such things. If he knows the house he knows that that is all that he can find on the dining-room floor."

She said, with a strong interest perceptible in her tone, "Suppose he comes up here!"

I said, "It is all right. He will give us notice."

"What shall we do then?"

"Climb out of the window."

ing it. Revision requires that you make changes in the structure of the text. Editing means making changes mainly in style. Proofreading is the final cleanup. But all three are as indispensable to writing as the act of composition itself.

Goals of Rewriting

One of the arguments that regularly rage in English seminars is whether or not one ever writes entirely for oneself. Does the diarist write for anyone else's eyes? What about the secret keeper of journals who pours out heart and soul onto the unanswering page? Some say no, that all writing is done for an eventual reader. Others argue that it is just as possible to write for oneself as to talk to oneself.

However, nearly everyone would concede that expository prose is written to be read. It is the workhorse of the literary world and usually bears a freight of definite meaning and purpose. One writes expository prose to explain or clarify, to outline an idea, make a recommendation, scold a debtor, or to attend to any of the other practical affairs of life. As this is a book about expository prose, we may then lay down this ironclad principle: all rewriting is **audience directed**.

This idea is simplicity itself but easily overlooked. As a general rule, writers do not make changes in their writing for the infamous sake of change itself. They make changes for the more purposeful end of expressing their ideas better. But "better" can only be defined by the effect the writing is expected to have on its audience. It follows that you cannot intelligently write or rewrite without having an audience in mind. If you are writing for an audience of laypeople, your style should be appropriately simple and to the point. On the other hand, if you are doing a sociological paper intended to be read by a sociology professor, you should use the jargon of the trade and write in a style of suitable scientific detachment. The intended audience of a work is a writer's only yardstick for writing and rewriting it.

Let us take an example close to home: the book you are now reading. It is written to be used in composition classes attended mainly by freshmen. The need for clarity and directness we had uppermost in mind as we wrote and rewrote. We wanted to get to the point, make it cleanly, and move on briskly to the next idea. To this end, we write mainly in short sentences and with an informal diction. Occasionally, we make a stab at levity or underscore an idea with an anecdote. But mainly we attend to the business at hand and hold asides to a minimum.

Rewriting the manuscript has chiefly meant pruning irrelevancies, substituting plainer words for more complex ones, and chopping in two the occasional serpentine sentence that wiggled out during the heat of composing. This is not the only style we could have used; but it was, however, the style we judged most appropriate for the audience and purpose of this book.

In the chapters that follow, we will focus on specific matters of tone, substance, and style that writers must weigh as they address their prose to particular audiences. We will give general advice about revising, editing, and proofreading, and specific advice about treating this or that item of grammar and style. But the anticipated effect of the work on your audience is the final court of appeal for every word you write and every change you make.

Procedure and Sequence for Rewriting

Rewriting has no fixed procedure, no hard and fast sequence. Neither has writing. Creative processes tend to defy prescription, and writers and their working habits are often wildly individualistic. But we can get a glimpse of some general method in the overall madness from Figure 1–3.

Our diagram resembles a makeshift Ferris wheel or the schematic for a computer program. It tells us that writers do not march to the swift completion of their appointed tasks, but rather get there by a kind of roundabout dancing. It also tells us what we have already said: that writing and rewriting are two halves in the continual process of composing. Later, we will get down to specifics about how to rewrite your work. But for now, we will talk in generalities about the procedure you might follow in your rewriting.

Proceed at a steady pace

If writing is like eating, rewriting is like nibbling. No one ever rewrites in one big bite. In the first place, one becomes numb to the flavor after a while and cannot tell whether the fare is good or bad. Time is the only cure for this numbness. Put the work away for a day or two and go throw a Frisbee or run amok in the woods. Give yourself at least a good week to peck away at the text, to return to it periodically. When you do come back, begin by rereading it from start to finish. During these rereading sessions, use a pencil or pen and make any changes that occur to you (and they will). One cannot overstate the importance of the pause in rewriting.

In successive attempts at rewriting, the logical progress will be from the big change to the little one: from revising to editing to proofreading. But it is not necessarily always so. On your third pass at the manuscript, for

Figure 1–3   The Recursive Process of Writing and Rewriting

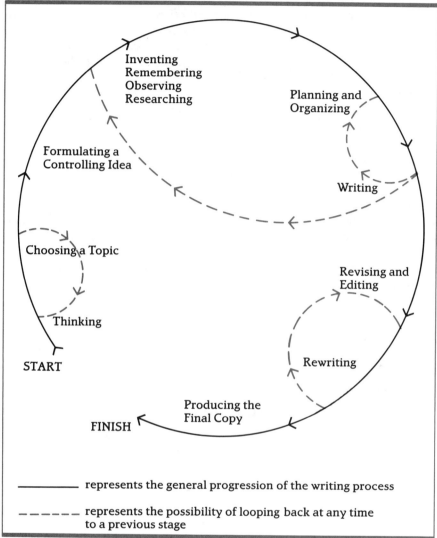

Inventing
Remembering
Observing
Researching

Planning and
Organizing

Formulating a
Controlling Idea

Writing

Choosing a Topic

Revising and
Editing

Thinking

Rewriting

START

Producing the
Final Copy

FINISH

————— represents the general progression of the writing process

– – – – – represents the possibility of looping back at any time
to a previous stage

example, you might find some glaring structural defect you had previously overlooked. If that happens, don't talk yourself out of making the necessary corrections (self-delusion is the writer's Satan for avoiding extra work). Buckle down and do what you have to even if it means starting over again from scratch (Twain did that four times).

Maintain an objective stance

It is written that "if thy right hand offends thee, cut it off." A similarly merciless precept must apply to your efforts at rewriting. Your aim is to be critical without being faultfinding, to look for weaknesses in your own prose with a cool and dispassionate eye. Admittedly, this is as difficult for a writer to do as it is for a parent to criticize a beloved child. Yet it must be done if your rewriting efforts are to be fruitful. Maintain the fiction, if you must, that you are editing not your own brainchild, but the work of a stranger.

Occasionally, you will even find it necessary to cut a perfectly wonderful sentence because sober reflection tags it as unsuitable for either your reader or your purpose. Everyone who has ever set pen to paper has had the horrible experience of watching a vivid but inappropriate image swirl down the revision drain. But if you cling too tenaciously to the fanciful over the appropriate, your work will end up blazing with the occasional "purple patch." This term, commonly defined as the occurrence in the text of an overworked piece of writing, is intended in a derogatory sense. It means that the writer has been caught huffing and puffing at the pen. Here is an example:

```
It is important to remember that poetry by

itself cannot solve all problems or cure all

illnesses.  Poetry does, however, do more than

many other forms of therapy because as Time

states, "it encourages verbalization, the life-

blood of psychotherapy."  There is no doubt that

this language of Parnassus, though it is

rarefied and scented with the dulcet tones of

the immortals--the primal rhythms of Shakespeare,

the Delphic warnings of Milton, the prurient

sighs of Sappho--can help the ordinary, troubled

soul of our time.  Dr. Peter Luke emphasized

this when he said that a poem comes from a

patient's unconscious mind and brings with it

his deepest feelings.  "Poetry and medicine,"
```

according to poet-physician William Carlos

Williams, "are the two parts of a whole."

The underlining in this paragraph—from a paper on poetry therapy—marks where the writer suffered a momentary lapse, forgot her audience and context, and got carried away with her own words. That aptness of expression must always win out over richness is the hardest lesson for all writers to learn, beginners as well as veterans.

Don't become bogged down

As you go over a manuscript, you may occasionally find a flaw in it you simply cannot correct. Perhaps there is a page or two that you know doesn't work but somehow you can't rewrite it. If that should happen, proceed to a page that you can rewrite and work on it. Keep coming back to the offending section but don't allow yourself to become bogged down in it. Often, a solution will hit you when you are working on some other part of the manuscript.

Reread, reread, reread

Rereading your work can be pure torture after a while, but it is a cleansing lesson in humility and good for rewriting. The next time around you will almost always find minor infelicities you overlooked before. It is also helpful to have a fresh pair of eyes read your work. *Peer editing*, a method of teaching English in which students working in small groups mutually critique the writing of each other, is based on the commonsense notion that two or more heads are better than one. And often they are. Get a friend to read your manuscript and make suggestions for improving it.

Save the original

Experience has taught us that it is always a sensible practice to retain unrewritten manuscript. On scanning it later, we sometimes find that we threw out the good with the bad. When we make that discovery, of course, we promptly restore the good. But if we had thrown out the old manuscript, good and bad alike would have perished.

This is especially easy to do if you are writing with a word processor. Changes are made on the screen and once the new text has been typed in, the old is gone for good. We get around this hi-tech trap by printing out a hard copy of the original and revising and editing that with a pencil. Then we go back to the screen and transcribe all our changes. This gives us new text on the screen, plus a working hard copy of the old text with our changes on it. If we later wonder why we made this change or that, we reconstruct our thinking by consulting the working hard copy.

Admittedly, this method of working is a trifle messy, since it burdens our desks with multiple scrawled-on versions of the text. Yet on those rare occasions when our eye failed us and the original was better than the rewrite, it has saved us hours of additional work.

Follow your hunches

Finally, we come to the hunch, which some may dismiss outright as mumbo jumbo. But as working writers we know that the hunch exists, for it has guided us faithfully through many a torturous exercise in rewriting.

Sometimes, for some inexplicable reason, a passage or page will strike us as simply wrong. We cannot say what offends us about it and have to grope to try and make it better. But still, something about it doesn't seem right.

If that should ever happen to you, as it has to us, we advise you to treat this feeling of dissatisfaction with respect. Your subconscious is trying to tell you something, and since it is by far a larger part of your brain than your conscious, you should listen. We always go on the assumption that if the text doesn't feel right, it probably isn't right. And in such cases, our answer has always been to rewrite until we've gotten rid of that nagging feeling. Usually, we end up with better text than we had before.

Exercises

1. Before you can practice the process of rewriting taught in this book, you need to become aware of your present methods of writing. Keep a journal on the next essay you write. Log the amount of time you spend actually writing it. Read the material on pages 13–15 and decide whether your rewriting, if any, consisted of revising, editing, or merely proofreading. Make a note of the time you spent doing each. When you are through, you should have an idea of (a) how much you rewrite (b) exactly what you do when you rewrite.

2. Find any old essay already graded by your teacher and make an attempt at rewriting it. If possible, submit the rewritten version to the teacher and ask for a trial grading. If not, compare the new version with the old.

3. In what sequence do you compose your own essays? Do you work strictly from beginning to middle and end? If so, on your next essay, try writing it as inspiration dictates rather than in strict sequence.

4. How do you react when you get stuck in composing? Do you stare at the wall or chew on the end of a pen? Try doing what professional writers do: reread what you have written from the beginning to the point at which you are stuck. Continue rereading until your pen budges and you begin writing again.

5. Find an old essay written for any science class—geology, chemistry, or biology—and compare it with one written for speech, English, or history. Is there a difference in the style and diction of each essay? What is this difference, and what does it tell you about your adaptation to different audiences? (If there is no difference, then perhaps you are stubbornly sticking to a single style rather than making an effort to adapt your writing to your audience.)

Writing Assignments

1. Take the final draft of the student paragraph on Doyle's characters on page 6, and try to improve at least two sentences of it. Compare your version with the student's and say why you think yours is better.

2. Select any paragraph from this first chapter, and rewrite it for an audience of a lower grade. What did you find yourself doing to make it easier to read and understand?

3. This is the first sentence from the prologue of *I Never Played The Game*, by Howard Cosell:

> I am writing this book because I am convinced that sports are out of whack in the American society; that the emphasis placed upon sports behavior distorts the real values of life and often produces mass behavior patterns that are downright frightening; and that the frequently touted uplifting benefits of sports have become a murky blur in the morass of hypocrisy and contradiction that I call the Sports Syndrome.

Make at least two, possibly three, simpler and easier to understand sentences of it.

4. Find one of your old essays, on any subject, and try to deliberately insert a "purple patch" in the middle of it.

5. Using one of your old term papers, try to improve its beginning by following the advice of the Scottish professor of English (page 12) and tearing up the first page. Insert a new paragraph if necessary to remake your beginning.

6. Literary style, formal and informal, changes from one generation

to another. Rewrite this brief passage in a style that would be considered appropriately formal in our own day:

> The appointment of death by the agency of carnivora, as the ordinary termination of animal existence, appears therefore in its main results to be a dispensation of benevolence; it deducts much from the aggregate amount of the pain of universal death; it abridges, and almost annihilates, throughout the brute creation, the misery of disease, and accidental injuries, and lingering decay; and imposes such salutary restraints upon excessive increases of numbers, that the supply of food maintains perpetually a due ratio to the demand.

7. Bertrand Russell once wrote:

> It is clear that for every man and every woman there is a degree of open-mindedness, which is desirable; more than this, or less than this, leads to bad results. A completely open mind is either a disease or a pretense; a completely closed mind is a useless assemblage of indefensible prejudices.

Write a brief essay either agreeing, disagreeing, or simply commenting on this opinion. Produce at least three successive drafts. Label and submit all three to your instructor.

Chapter Two

Prewriting Strategies, Voice and Style

V<sub>ery young writers often do not revise at all. Like a hen look-
ing at a chalk line, they are hypnotized by what they have written.
"How can it be altered?" they think. "That's the way it was written."
Well, it has to be altered.*

DOROTHY CANFIELD FISHER (1879–1958)

It is midnight in a dimly lit garret. Suffering a creative itch in the
soul that only the pen can scratch, a tormented writer begins to write.
Muses whisper and words of wisdom pour in a torrent from the writer's
pen while a neglected lover sulks in a corner.

This picture of a working writer is brought to you courtesy of
the movies.

Of course, it is narrow, incomplete, and gives a totally false impression. Some lucky few writers may indeed work under the goad of an other-
worldly itch, but for the rest writing is strictly a practical art done to satisfy
a superior, meet a deadline, and earn bread and board (or a grade). We do
not write in a romantic garret, but in a noisy office or busy kitchen, and
usually on a subject dropped on us from above like a brick.

Under such workaday circumstances, how do real writers work?

Choosing a Topic

They begin by narrowing the unloved subject into a liked topic. The subject is the general assignment you are given. It is usually not specific enough for you to leap in and begin writing about it straightaway. Ordinarily, it is fraught with implicit choices, like a fine menu, and requires you to whittle it down to a narrower option called the **topic**. An instructor, for example, may ask you to write an essay about an environmental problem and leave it at that. But you might as well hope to swallow a Thanksgiving turkey whole as to write about such a subject. It needs carving, paring down, portioning out. So the very last thing you will do is write. But the first thing you will do is make an acceptable topic of your large subject.

One way to do this is through a process of Socratic narrowing. Socrates, if you remember, was a Greek philosopher who taught by asking questions. His questioning was directed at erring listeners who were gradually and firmly led to the truth. You can use this questioning technique to narrow a subject down to a topic you care about.

Here is an example. Your instructor assigns a paper on some environmental problem. You sit down, pen and pad in hand, and begin the questioning:

First Narrowing

Question: What environmental problem do you care about anyway?
Answer: Hardly any. Not enough to write about, anyway.
Question: Do you care about any environmental place at all?
Answer: Yes, I do. I like Wickiup Canyon. I like to go swimming there.

Second Narrowing

Question: So what's the environment of Wickiup like these days?
Answer: Pretty terrible. The ATC riders have really torn up the surrounding landscape.

Final Narrowing

Question: So what'd you think ought to be done?
Answer: If it were my choice, I'd ban all ATCs from wilderness canyons.
Question: Why would you do that?
Answer: Because ATCs are motorized vehicles that belong on paved roads. They're noisy, smelly, and poison to the watershed.

Now you have your topic: the effects of rampant ATCs (all-terrain cycles) riding on the environment of Wickiup Canyon. Your next step is to express it in a controlling idea.

Formulating a Controlling Idea and Thesis Statement

Every essay needs a **controlling idea,** an angle or approach that the writer takes towards the narrowed topic. Whether or not the controlling idea is plainly stated or remains discreetly in the background, it is decidedly there exercising control and direction over the essay. This book, for example, is about writing and rewriting, but its controlling idea is that revising and editing are essential to the improvement of writing. Whenever we feel the itch to wander or stray, our controlling idea looms before us like a stop sign. We break off and slink back guiltily to our appointed labor.

Your **controlling idea** is the position you have taken towards your topic. Your **thesis statement** is the answer you would give, in a sentence, if someone happened by as you were reading an essay and asked, "What is that all about?" Your reply would contain a condensation of the author's main point or big idea, known as a **thesis statement**. Some essayists begin by carefully enunciating this main point in an opening paragraph, and many teachers insist that students follow this formula to the letter.

The thesis statement is your controlling idea made explicit. It is an announcement of exactly what you intend to oppose, propose, suppose, or depose in the essay. Setting down clearly what your essay is about will solidify your purpose and consequently help you write it. For example, your opposition to ATCs in the wilderness canyons must be grounded in some substantial facts about the damage they cause, the noise they make, the pollution they spread, and exactly which of these harmful effects your essay intends to document. All of this should be summed up in one thesis statement.

Naturally, the topic, the controlling idea, and the thesis statement are related as progressively narrowed parts of the same subject. A mathematician would say that each is a subset of the other. So if the subject is "environmental problems," your controlling idea must reflect a particular approach to that topic, which your thesis statement must carefully spell out. Here are four examples of a subject reworked into a narrowed topic, controlling idea, and thesis statement:

> **Subject:** Write an essay about an environmental problem.
> **Topic:** Wickiup Canyon.
> **Controlling idea:** The destructive effect of unrestricted ATC use on the environment of Wickiup Canyon.
> **Thesis statement:** Allowing Wickiup Canyon to be used by all-terrain vehicles has unleashed noise and emission pollution that threatens the fragile beauty of this lovely wilderness area.

Subject: Write an essay about a mammal.
Topic: The common shrew.
Controlling idea: The effect of its metabolism on the life of the common shrew.
Thesis statement: The shrew is a furious, reckless mammal whose life is tyrannized by its tiny body and voracious metabolism.

Subject: Medical care in the United States
Topic: Preventative medical care for children.
Controlling idea: The federal government should provide preventative medical care for children under 16.
Thesis statement: The federal government should provide free preventative medical care for children under 16 because in the long run this is the most economical way to control medical cost and ensure a healthy and productive workforce.

Subject: Foreign languages.
Topic: Techniques for learning a foreign language.
Controlling idea: Total immersion is the best technique for learning a foreign language.
Thesis statement: Total immersion in culture and everyday life is the best way to learn a foreign language since it teaches not only everyday idioms but also culture.

Do not expect a controlling idea to pop automatically onto the page once you have a topic. But after you've narrowed your topic sufficiently and before you write even the first paragraph, ask yourself provocatively: what is my essay going to be all about? What angle will I take on my topic? What point will I argue? Answer in a single sentence, then tape it to the typewriter, the wall, the CRT, or someplace where you can see it as you write. This is your controlling idea, your leash, and eventually it will become your thesis statement. (For more on the thesis statement, see Chapter 3.)

Exercises

1. Narrow the following subjects into at least two topics:

dating	public holidays
self-confidence	pets
campus politics	an important historical figure
censorship	disease
terrorism	careers
modern art	

2. Select at least two of the narrowed topics and formulate a controlling idea and thesis statement on each.

3. Find an article in any magazine whose controlling idea is implied rather than spelled out. Summarize this controlling idea in a single statement that could have served as the article's thesis.

4. Rewrite the following controlling ideas into thesis statements:
a. The idiotic content of some television sit-coms.
b. Children should be seen but not heard is generally a bad rule for child-rearing.
c. Smoking as an addictive and self-destructive habit.
d. Consumer education and its place in the college curriculum.

5. Write a paragraph clarifying the distinction between a controlling idea and a thesis statement.

Using Invention

You have your topic and a notion of what your controlling idea will be. What you need now is to generate some ideas that will make up the body of your paper. This is where invention comes in.

In its most practical sense, invention means making or devising something new. In its literary sense, it means thinking creatively or inventively about your topic. Some methodical and time-honored processes exist that writers have used to do so. Among them are brainstorming, clustering, and talking writing.

Brainstorming

This colorful word means an intense thinking session in which you generate and quickly jot down as many ideas as you can. Your aim is to throw open the floodgates of creativity and undam a raging surge of ideas. Sit with pen and paper in a place to your liking. Think intently about your subject. Make a note of every idea, every fragment of thought that swirls down the stream of consciousness. Brainstorming on the topic of stress might produce a list such as this:

```
Stress, stress, what is stress?

Anxiety

Panic

Feeling pressure
```

Needless worry

Causes?

Who knows?

pressure from job

peer pressure

high expectations

effects of stress

Can't think of any

heart palpitations

sleeplessness

biofeedback helps

vacation helps

friends are stressful

parents too

What to do?

fight stress

meditation helps

a drink can relax you

thinking too much is bad

Ban brains

do animals suffer stress?

rats do, in psych labs

monkeys go bananas over stress

I can't think

this is stressful

stress affects health

physical health

mental health, too

I wish I lived on an island

```
think about stress

THINK!

stress causes insomnia

studying causes stress

fretting brings on stress

Christmas stress

overwork

holiday stress

type A personality

Am I one?

No

This is tough

type A suffers stress

heart attacks--stress causes them

high blood pressure

Help! I can't think

high blood pressure

wanting to get good grades--that's stress

I'm stressed out on this

Think!

stress is everywhere

fight or flight response

modern life and stress
```

A list produced by brainstorming should show the aftereffects of the storm surge: it should be strewn with the debris of random, even haphazard, thinking. But as you sift through the litter, you will most likely find some promising ideas that can be used in the essay.

Clustering

Clustering is a technique for associating a large idea with its smaller and related parts. It is the diagrammatic equivalent of brainstorming, but done systematically and with more editorial control. You are trying to break down the topic into its constituent parts about which you can write paragraphs and pages. Figure 2–1 is an example of the topic "The Liberal Arts in Colleges Today" rendered in a cluster.

Clustering and brainstorming are both useful for generating ideas to be included in an essay, but they are certainly not mutually exclusive. Indeed, it is often helpful to render the best ideas from a brainstorming list into a cluster. One way to do this is to cull ideas from your list and arrange them logically under interrogatives such as "What?" "Why?" "Who?" "When?" Figure 2–2 is an example. The brainstorming list on the topic of stress is rendered into a cluster.
Your list of randomly generated ideas is now refined into a graphic outline of your essay.

Clustering teaches us an added lesson: writing is never focused on the whole, but always on its parts. We cannot write about the Pacific Ocean, although that may be our intent. What we can write about is this island or that archipelago in the Pacific Ocean. And if we cover enough islands and mention enough archipelagos, we will do justice to our ocean. Just as the sentence is made of individual words and paragraphs of separate sentences, a topic is also necessarily treated in pieces and parts, which clustering (and brainstorming) can help us find and identify.

Talking writing

Mark Twain tells this story about how talking helped him write:

> In the course of twelve years I made six attempts to tell a simple little story which I knew would tell itself in four hours if I could ever find the right starting point. I scored six failures; then one day in London I offered the text of the story to Robert McClure and proposed that he publish that text in the magazine and offer a prize to the person who should tell it best. I became greatly interested and went on talking upon the text for half an hour, then he said: "You have told the story yourself. You have nothing to do but put it on paper just as you have told it."
> I recognized that this was true. At the end of four hours it was finished, and quite to my satisfaction. So it took twelve years and four hours to produce that little bit of a story, which I have called "The Death Wafer."
> —The Autobiography of Mark Twain, ed. by Charles Neider.

Twelve years is, of course, a bit long to spend on a freshman essay, but Twain's experience is otherwise applicable.

Figure 2–1   Clustering Example of "The Liberal Arts in
             Colleges Today"

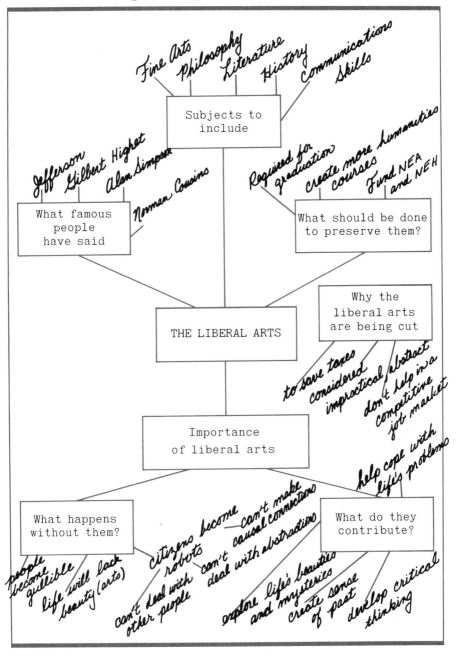

Figure 2–2   Clustering and Brainstorming Example

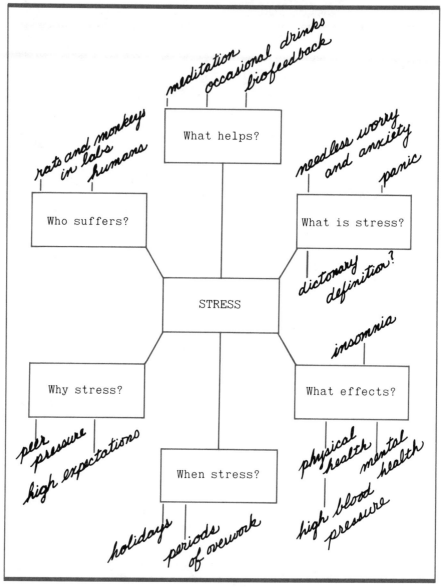

You can hold a monologue with yourself or talk about your work with someone else. For example, this exchange was overheard between an instructor and a student. The student approached the instructor claiming to be baffled by the assignment to write an essay about his hometown:

Teacher: Which place do you consider your "hometown?"
Student: Kalamazoo, Michigan.
Teacher: Was it a good town to grow up in?
Student: Oh, yes, it was. I was happy there. In fact, I think it is the best town in the world to grow up in.
Teacher: Give me one major reason why.
Student: Well, it was wonderfully . . . safe.
Teacher: How do you know it was safe?
Student: It just was.
Teacher: Give me some specific examples of how it was safe.
Student: Well, for instance, we never had to lock our houses, cars, or any-thing—yet no one ever really got robbed. We wandered freely over the neighborhood, just walking into each other's houses without fear. Little kids played in the streets without fear of being kidnapped or abducted. I had to walk a mile to school every day, but I never worried about it, not even when the snowdrifts hid me from passing cars.
Teacher: O.K. Great! You're flowing. Now, can you think of another reason why your hometown was so great?
Student: Yeah, we always had things to do, fun things! My friends always tell me how bored they were in their hometowns, but I was never bored.
Teacher: Why? Name some things you did for entertainment.
Student: Let me see. We flew kites in the vacant lot in our neighborhood. We explored all the nearby housing developments. We'd pretend to be detectives and follow an adult through the streets and write down everything we saw him do. That was hilarious. In the winter we rode sleds and went ice skating on the ponds.
Teacher: I'm sure you could elaborate even more on that, but let's move on. Give me another general reason why you liked your home-town.
Student: I liked it because I was never lonely there. Everybody played together. Sure, we had our occasional fights, but we usually got over them quickly. Actually, the adults were often just as much fun as the kids. There was an old widowed woman, for example, who lived on our street. One day she called us into her kitchen and showed us how to make an angel cake.
Teacher: So far so good. You have the basis of a good essay. Now, can you express your three reasons in a single sentence?
Student: I'll try. Kalamazoo, Michigan, was a wonderful town to grow up in because it was safe, there was always something to do, and there was always someone to play with.
Teacher: That's the beginning of a good thesis. It just needs tightening.

You can also talk to yourself about your own work, asking yourself how you really feel about this, what your opinion is about that, until you arrive at a conclusion usable as a thesis for your essay. One of the authors of this book, for example, is a great believer in the power of talking writing. When he gets stuck and is in a place where he can talk aloud to himself without fear of the butterfly net, he asks himself bluntly, "What the devil are you trying to say?" and then tries to answer himself in plain language. Often it requires only a transcription of the answer, and a deleting of expletives, for him to get unstuck.

Using Memories and Experiences

Memories and experiences are major sources for all writers. For the memoirist and diarist, they are principal sources, but for a range of other writers—from the textbook writer to the journalist—they are indispensable raw materials useful in many assignments. For example, if you were writing an essay about social security cutbacks, you might relate the story of some elderly acquaintance who suffered hardships because of them and so add a human touch to the usual parade of facts and figures. Before you begin writing, sit quietly and meditate about your personal experiences and memories and how you might use them as raw materials in an essay. Your topic may not be obviously linked to any personal memories or experiences, but a few moments of quiet thinking might uncover some relationships between the two that you've overlooked.

As living sources of memories and experiences that can add a unique touch to their essays, students frequently tend to underestimate their own value. One of the authors, for example, once had a student who labored mightily to write an essay on responsibility. Finally, at his wit's end, the student turned in a turgid recital of what he imagined were the responsibilities of surgeons, popes, and teachers. When asked about the difficulty he had had writing the essay, he said lamely that he simply couldn't relate to the topic. It came out later that he had spent two years in the Air Force as a copilot on a heavy transport helicopter and had been entrusted with responsibility for the lives of hundreds of troops. Yet not a word about this experience with responsibility had been mentioned in the essay.

Note, however, that the temptation to overemote on the page is especially strong for any writer when relating personal experiences or memories. Use these to add a piquant touch here and there, to underscore a point, or to dramatize a fact, but never in place of hardheaded arguments and evidence.

Using Observation

Observation is the source of most written details. But by observation we do not mean merely what you have seen: we mean what you have perceived—smelled, tasted, seen, touched, and heard. Some descriptions revel in the visual, and when appropriate, images based on sight alone can be powerful and moving. Here, for example, is a description of an old woman rendered in a series of brilliant visual metaphors:

> I give a sideways glance at the mirror, and see a puffed face purpled with veins as though someone had scribbled over the skin with an indelible pencil. The skin itself is the silverish white of the creatures one fancies must live under the sea where the sun never reaches. Below the eyes the shadows bloom as though two soft black petals had stuck there. The hair which should by rights be black is yellowed white, like damask stored too long in a damp basement.
> —Margaret Laurence, *The Stone Angel.*

We cannot complain about the brilliance of this description. But the typical domination of the visual in the work of beginners has the effect of rendering the world as seen through a soundless camera. Objects about us not only sparkle and glint, but also smell and make noises. If you include impressions from these other senses as well in your writing, your descriptions will be more vivid than if you merely gorge them with feasts of sight. Here is an example, the opening paragraph taken from the novel *Wolf Solent*, by Welsh writer John Cowper Powys:

> From Waterloo Station to the small country town of Ramsgard in Dorset is a journey of not more than three or four hours, but having by good luck found a compartment to himself, Wolf Solent was able to indulge in such an orgy of concentrated thought, that these three or four hours lengthened themselves out into something beyond all human measurement.
>
> A bluebottle fly buzzed up and down above his head, every now and then settling on one of the coloured advertisements of seaside resorts—Weymouth, Swanage, Lulworth, and Poole—cleaning its front legs upon the masts of painted ships or upon the sands of impossibly cerulean waters.
>
> Through the open window near which he sat, facing the engine, the sweet airs of an unusually relaxed March morning visited his nostrils, carrying fragrances of young green shoots, of wet muddy

ditches, of hazel-copses full of damp moss, and of primroses on warm grassy hedge-banks.

The key to using observations is selectivity. You cannot cram on the page every impression that pops into your head, and if you did, your work would be none the better for the bulk. What you have to do is select, with economy and premeditation, only those observations that add to the effect you are after. Here, for example, is the ritual of Thanksgiving dinner rendered negatively by an author's selective use of observations:

> Consider for a moment the Thanksgiving meal itself. It has become a sort of refuge for endangered species of starch: cauliflower, turnips, pumpkin, mince (whatever "mince" is), those blessed yams. Bowls of luridly colored yams, with no taste at all, lying torpid under a lava flow of marshmallow! And then the sacred turkey. One might as well try to construct a holiday repast around a fish—say, a nice piece of boiled haddock. After all, turkey tastes very similar to haddock: same consistency, same quite remarkable absence of flavor. But then, if the Thanksgiving *pièce de resistance* were a nice piece of boiled haddock instead of turkey, there wouldn't be all that fun for Dad when Mom hands him the sterling-silver, bone-handled carving set (a wedding present from her parents and not sharpened since) and then everyone sits around pretending not to watch while he saws and tears away at the bird as if he were trying to burrow his way into or out of some grotesque, fowl-like prison.
> —Michael J. Arlen, "Ode to Thanksgiving," reprinted in *Camera Age*, 1978.

Is this the bedrock and unshakable truth about Thanksgiving dinner? Hardly. It is merely a single view of the ritual seen through one writer's eyes. Other writers, peering at this annual holiday, would no doubt observe and record it quite differently.

Doing Research

Wide reading makes good writing. This truth has been known for years but is easier to impart as an exhortation than to teach as a lesson. If you read widely on your topic, you will almost surely write a better essay than if you write only from your own observations, memories, and experiences.

Before you write, then, do your reading. Go to the library and scour through magazines, journals, newspapers, and books on your topic. Begin with an overview of your topic found in any good encyclopedia or general reference work. Many subjects have their own specialized encyclopedias such as *The Encyclopedia of Biological Sciences*, the *Encyclopedia of Science and Technology*, and the *Encyclopedia of Philosophy*. After an overview of such works, you can make your way to magazines, journals, and even books. You can also search periodical literature indexes on general knowledge or in specialized subjects. For more on this, see pages 332–33 in Chapter 14.

One research source badly underused by students is available expert help or opinion. Most campuses are awash with specialists who are willing to lend a hand to the student researcher. A recent example comes to mind. A student of ours became interested in the problems of Afghan refugees and decided to write an essay on that country's history. We suggested that he interview a professor of eastern history on campus, who in turn gave him a mini-lecture on Afghanistan dynasties. As a result, the student settled on Mahmud of Ghazni, a great Afghan ruler of the eleventh century, as his topic. The professor was also able to direct the student to key references on Afghan history, which spared him the usual initial spade work.

Exercises

1. Brainstorm on one of the following:

The violence in motion pictures today.
The end of the sexual revolution.
Looking before you leap is good advice.
Love is often overstated in our culture.
War memorials serve a public good.
Pop music lyrics should/should not be censored.

2. Convert your brainstorm list into a cluster, using the method discussed on pages 31 and 32.

3. For any one of the above topics, jot down any appropriate personal memories or observations you think you might profitably include in an essay.

4. Write down your own personal impressions—in rough note form—of Christmas.

5. Make a detailed list of your observations of a favorite instructor.

Organizing Your Ideas

You have your topic. You've done your brainstorming, inventing, reading, and are teeming with ideas. Now you're ready to begin writing. Here we are squarely in the capricious realm of individual differences.

The truth is that some writers do not, cannot, or will not organize any piece ahead of actually writing it. One member of this writing team, for instance, never organizes before writing; the other never writes before organizing. Individual differences are obviously at work here, and it is plainly a waste of time to force anyone to use a composing method antagonistic to his or her personal temperament.

The section that follows explains various processes for organizing, but you would do well if you find and stick to the degree of organizing that matches your working and thinking style. If that means plunging headlong into the sea of disorganized notes flooding your desktop, so be it. However, you may have to reconstruct an outline later for the sake of satisfying an instructor's requirement that you have one.

Create a model of the essay

A model is a rough sketch of the major parts of your essay. Like a formal outline, it is the essay in miniature form by a sequential listing of abbreviated subtopics. But unlike the formal outline, it is constructed without strict obedience to indenting.

To make a model, you begin by writing down your thesis statement:

```
The legendary cruelty of Moslem forms of legal

punishment is in reality less sadistic than

legal punishment in our own country.
```

Since the aim of the writer is to contrast the Moslem penal system with our own and to argue that ours is the more cruel, the heart of the essay will consist of paragraphs that weigh the dissimilar penalties meted out by the two systems for the same offense. Here is the model:

```
In several Moslem countries, public flogging is

the punishment for drunkenness; however, in the

U.S. we throw drunks in jail.

In several Moslem countries, amputation of the
```

```
right hand is the punishment for theft; in the

U.S. thieves are sent to prison.

In several Moslem countries, murder is punished

by public execution; however, in the U.S.

murderers are sent to prison.

U.S. prison sentences are the ultimate cruelty

because they are indeterminate and place the

criminal in institutions filled with violence

and rampant with serious diseases.
```

At a glance, the model provides an agenda of subtopics along with a sketch of their main points. Not so obvious, however, is that it also prescribes a developmental pattern for writing the essay (for more on developmental patterns, see Chapter 4). The writer knows that this particular essay must be developed as a contrast because that pattern is implicit in the ordering of topics. Many other patterns are possible. Here is, for example, a model of an essay to be developed by classification:

```
College students can be classified according to

the forces motivating them to be in college.

First, there is the social butterfly--the

fraternity or sorority groupie.

Second, there is the student who attends because

of parental pressure.

Third, there is the careerist humorlessly bent

on acquiring a degree in a field of his or her

choosing.

Fourth, there is the dilettante who uses college

as a holding tank until something better comes

along.
```

```
Finally, there is the older returning student
who has battered about long enough to value an
education and is deadly earnest about finally
getting one.
```

Make an outline

If you were educated in the western hemisphere, chances are good that you have either been taught, seen someone use, or actually used an outline yourself. Essentially, the outline is a numbered system of indented shelves in which a multitude of topics, subtopics, and minor parts of a work may be filed.

The basic numbering system of the outline is this: main topics are designated by Roman numerals such as I, II, III, IV, and V. Subtopics are designated by capital letters: A, B, C, D, and so on. Subtopics may be further divided into smaller units designated by Arabic numerals such as 1, 2, and 3. A further subdivision may be designated by lower case letters: a, b, c, d, and so on. Here are the empty shelves of an outline:

Thesis
I. Main topic
  A. Subtopic
    1. Subdivision of a subtopic
     a. Further subdivision of a subtopic

This convention of numbering and indentation may seem fussy, but it gives a quick snapshot of the major parts of an essay.

An outline may be either simple or complex. The simplest is a one-level outline—named for its single level of entries—which is especially useful for brief and uncomplicated writing assignments. Here is an example:

```
Thesis: College students are returning to a pre-
        1960 level of academic success.
  I. They are achieving higher SAT scores.
 II. They are spending more time in libraries.
III. They are partying less.
 IV. They are spending less time on politics.
```

All the statements of the outline are extensions of the thesis, which they are intended to prove. Notice that the indenting and the parallel phrasing of the main topics make for easy scanning.

More complex assignments require outlining in greater detail, as in this example:

Thesis: Modern science and technology have had
        good as well as bad effects on our
        society.

I. Many scientific and technological advances have
   dramatically improved human life.
   A. The ability to communicate worldwide has made
      people less isolated and less provincial.
      1. National radio and television keep Americans
         in touch with each other.
      2. Communications satellites keep foreign
         nations in touch with each other.
      3. Air travel allows people to study societies
         other than their own.
   B. Effective birth contraception has given
      societies a new sense of freedom.
      1. Women are having small families in order to
         pursue professions.
      2. Men live under a regimen of sexual freedom
         less binding than that of the Victorian era.
   C. The latest advances in biomedical research have
      cured major life-threatening diseases.
      1. Virulent diseases have been curbed.
         a. Syphilis is now easily cured.
         b. Typhoid practically no longer exists.
         c. Tuberculosis is rare.
         d. Polio has vanished.
      2. Nonvirulent diseases have been curbed.

    a. Open heart surgery has replaced weakened arteries with stronger ones.

    b. Certain forms of cancer are forced into remission through radiology and chemotherapy.

    c. Genetic research is on the verge of preventing genetic diseases such as cystic fibrosis and Down's syndrome.

II. Many scientific and technological advances have endangered human life.

    A. The pollution of our oceans is a threat to human food supplies.

        1. Oil tankers and off-shore drilling works are causing oil slicks that kill fish and plant life.

        2. Sewage waste from industrial plants is poisoning our beaches.

    B. Pollution of our atmosphere is a threat to human health.

        1. Aerial sprays poison the atmosphere and destroy its ozone layer.

        2. Smog from factories and automobiles infects the air and causes lung diseases.

    C. World security is being threatened by the constant emphasis on improved nuclear arsenals.

        1. We have enough megatonnage on land, at sea, and in the air to blast mankind into oblivion.

```
  2. Competition between the USSR and the United

     States for nuclear dominance threatens

     global destruction.
```

The entries of an outline may consist of full sentences, as in the previous examples, or they may consist of words and phrases that merely summarize the intended topics and subtopics. Here is an example of a topic outline:

```
Thesis: Government service brings with it the

        penalties of media harassment, financial

        loss, and loss of privacy.

  I. Media harassment

     A. Ferraro's problems

     B. Meese's investigation

 II. Financial losses

     A. Treasury Secretary Blumenthal

     B. SEC Chairman Chad

III. Loss of privacy

     A. The Kennedy family

     B. The Reagan family
```

The choice of sentence or topic outline will be dictated by the complexity of your essay. Use a sentence outline for a complex topic, a topic outline for a simple topic.

Outlines are meant to highlight only the principal points of an essay and do not include introductions, materials, transitions, and details. One page of an outline will usually translate into five pages in the essay.

In working up outlines, the most common mistake students make is a lack of parallelism between the entries. Parallelism simply means expressing equivalent ideas in similar phrasing. Properly observed, it is a convention that makes the outline easier to read than one whose entries are randomly worded. Here is an example. The entries in this excerpt from an outline on astrology are not parallel:

```
Thesis: Astrology is based on so-called natal

        signs.
```

```
  I. Each person has a sun sign.

 II. Rising signs also play a part.

III. Signs are ruled either by fire, air, earth, or
     water.
```

Contrast this with the excerpt from the following parallel outline:

```
Thesis: Astrology is based on so-called natal

        signs.

  I. Each person has a sun sign.

 II. Each person also has a rising sign.

III. Each person is ruled by a sign of either fire,

     air, earth, or water.
```

The difference is decisive: with the parallel outline, the writer can see at a glance the sequence of topics in the essay. With the outline whose entries are not parallel, the structure of the essay is not as immediately apparent.

Faulty subordination of topics is the second most common error students commit in their outlines. The accurate outline should give equal billing only to topics of equal importance in the essay. Consider this excerpt of an outline on the consequences of divorce:

```
Thesis: Divorce has a decisive effect on the

        life of the entire family

  I. The individual marriage partners are affected.

 II. Children are affected.

III. In-law relationships are affected.

 IV. Family pets are affected.
```

It is plainly warped logic to equate the suffering of the family pet in a divorce with that of the human participants. This kind of error, however, is not strictly one of outlining, but of illogical thinking that is merely reflected in the outline.

Why are outlines so persistently popular with a certain kind of writer? One reason is that writing tends to be a grubby, involved, subterranean act somewhat akin to tunnelling. One's nose often gets too close to the ground to get an overhead view of exactly where all the digging is leading. The outline, however, shows the view from above. It points out glaring visible defects of structure, logic, and incompleteness. Here is an example:

```
Controlling idea: People own handguns for

            several reasons.

     I. People own handguns to commit crimes.

        A. Handguns can easily be concealed.

        B. Knives are also popular weapons of criminals.

        C. Handguns are lethal.

    II. People own handguns to defend themselves against

        criminals.

        A. They want to defend their homes.

        B. They want to defend themselves while

           traveling.

        C. Too often the homeowner himself gets killed.

   III. People own handguns for sport.

        A. They feel macho when carrying a handgun.

        B. They target shoot with handguns.

        C. They hunt animals with handguns.

        D. Small-caliber handguns are more likely to

           wound than to kill.
```

The underlined entries do not follow the heading under which they appear. For example, I B is not a reason for owning a handgun; neither is II C. Likewise, III A and III D do not logically follow under the main point, "People own handguns for sport." These lapses, glaringly visible in the outline, are harder to spot in the essay itself.

Exercises

1. Create a model of one of the following theses:
a. The tradition of Halloween is a waste.
b. The tradition of Halloween is an important ritual of childhood.

c. Providing women with the luxury of a fur coat involves cruelty to animals.

d. Having married couples share household responsibilities is an excellent new trend.

e. Having married couples share household responsibilities undermines the traditional family.

f. Sometimes it is rewarding to take risks.

g. Living in a big city has decided advantages.

2. Create an appropriate two-level outline for one of the following theses, using full sentences for each entry.

a. Private ranting—throwing pillows, yelling at the wall, or screaming at an imaginary antagonist—can be an excellent psychological release for pent-up anger.

b. The recent emphasis on ecology encourages a beneficial respect and love for all forms of life that will help with the preservation of our fragile ecosystems.

c. Fly casting is a demanding sport that requires patience, guile, and a respect for the most wily adversary a fisherman can stalk—the brown trout.

d. The relationship between a stepparent and child is often an ambivalent and psychologically troublesome one.

3. Find and correct the flaw in the following outline excerpts:

Controlling idea: Conspiracy theories on the assassination of public figures are frequently unbelievable.
I. They depend on hearsay testimony.
II. Crucial witnesses are usually deceased.
III. Our paranoid fears are fueled by them.

Controlling idea: The movie is an inferior, collaborative art form.
I. It often dazzles the viewer with vistas while resorting to psychological implausibilities.
II. It often resorts to *deus ex machina* resolutions.
III. Ticket prices have simply gotten too high.

Controlling idea: Travel is a broadening experience that can teach graphic lessons about foreign cultures and lands in the way that no book can.
I. Travel teaches about foreign customs and cultures.
II. Travel teaches intimate lessons on geography and history.

III. Seeing the grandeur of the Roman Colosseum teaches an unforgettable lesson about the Christian martyrs.

Voice and Style

Voice and style are regarded in some quarters as nearly the same, but we think a distinction between them is worth making. Voice is the projection of a personality on the page. It is the way you wish to be seen by a reader, the front you present to the world. Style, on the other hand, is purely a matter of word choice and sentence formation.

To some extent, we could say that voice influences style the way role influences behavior. In the role of a student, we act and talk a certain way because it is expected of us. In the role of a salesperson, we also act and talk a certain way that is likewise expected of us. Something similar is true of writing. When we write, we project a voice, a personality on the page. But it is not always the same voice or personality. In a note to Mom asking for money, we do not sound the same as in a letter formally applying for credit at a bank. If you are playing the part of a certain someone in your writing—whether the needy child or the worthy borrower—the effort is bound to influence your style.

Nowhere is the influence of voice on style plainer than in a narrative, where the writer is consciously acting out the point of view of the person chosen to tell the story (see Chapter 5 for narration). For example, guess who the narrator is in this selection:

> The blonde slunk across the room, cutting a path through the fog, drawing the sweaty stares of a half-dozen beady-eyed guys in the bar. She was built like a truck, with a cantilevered topside that gave off seismic tremors when she walked. She took a table next to mine, gazed around the room, and took in my nastiest stare with a cool indifference. I lit a cigarette and sent a smoke ring sailing toward her like a life preserver, only in this case it came from a drowning man. It had floated over to her table when she inclined her head, bit a chunk out of the ring, and spat it out on the floor. I took that as an invitation and walked over.

As any reader of popular fiction will recognize, this is not the voice of an evangelical parson, but of the hard-boiled detective. Language is working on two levels here: first, it is describing what the narrator sees—that is its style; second, it is giving us information about the narrator—that is its voice.

In writing expository prose, you might think that the writer merely has to convey information and does not, in the process, have to reveal anything about the self. But that is not how writing works. Language is a necessary part of the way we think, and our every utterance is to some extent colored by our sense of self. Sometimes, especially if we are writing from a corporate or public voice, we think it necessary to hide this self behind a public mask. For example, bureaucrats charged with writing a public document often try hard to project an impersonal voice in its language. Here is an example that was quoted by former President Jimmy Carter in 1978, during his vain attempt to get government agencies to write plainly:

> Except as provided in paragraph B of this section, applications, amendments thereto, and related statements of fact required by the Commission shall be personally signed by the applicant, if the applicant is an individual.

The style of this is plainly bad. Its single sentence is twisted like a twine of overcooked spaghetti, its language is legalistic and archaic, and it seems to say something much more profound than it actually does. According to President Carter, what it really said was this:

> If you are an individual, you must sign your own application personally.

But it says a great deal more than that. Part of what it says, however, has nothing to do with the actual arrangement of the words on the page. It has to do with its voice, which trumpets loudly to the reader, "This is your almighty government speaking, pay attention here!" What is bad about this writing, then, is not blamable on its style, but on its voice.

To some extent, all writing means playacting on paper. We project a voice or self appropriate to the audience and occasion of our writing, and this voice or self determines our style. And so we come to the nub of this argument: who is the student writer, and what is the appropriate voice for one?

It is at this point that most textbooks agree: "Be yourself," the student writer is advised. This is usually good advice, but it has mixed results with students who, on the whole, are in personal transition and generally unsure about who they are or what they hope to eventually become. Our suggestion is that you be honest in your writing voice.

To be honest means to put on no assumed airs, to imply no lies about yourself. Here is the opening paragraph of a student essay in which the student was dishonest:

```
A finally awakened probity citizenry,

concerned about pullulating urban decay, has

finally been galvanized into remedial action in

Philadelphia. This action took diverse forms
```

```
involving urban renewal programs, incentives for

business to relocate at erstwhile factory sites,

and training programs for the hordes of

transients hastily domiciled in the inner city.
```

The wrongs in this paragraph are only superficially grammatical; mainly, they are psychological. Plainly put, the writer has been caught telling a lie about himself. His voice is saying, "Listen, bub, I'm an expert on this topic, so you better pay attention to me while I tell you about it." That is what he hopes his big words will tell us. What they really tell us is that his expert posture is phony, that he is unsure of himself, and that he is burning with desire to impress. That kind of bogus voice we call dishonest.

Here is another example of it. The writer is trying desperately to sound scholarly, with vain and unhappy results:

```
The Romantic movement did not suffer

cessation or surcease upon Victoria's ascendance

to the throne, and neither were the Victorian

writers vehemently and inextricably in revolt

against it.  The chronological reckoning etched

in the history books document that the Romantic

period began in 1780 and ended in 1830, while

the Victorian period's commencement began in

1830 and terminated, but not without scholarly

contradiction and some controversial naysaying

by dissenters that rages to this very day, in

1880.  However, be that as it may, the launching

of the Romantic movement, experts and laymen

agree, began with publication of a slim volume

of poetry titled Lyrical Ballads.
```

Whatever faults this style has—and pompousness is surely among them—it is caused by bad playacting: the writer tries hard to play a role she cannot do convincingly.

For the beginning writer, then, the most sensible path to developing a good style is to cultivate an honest voice. Don't put on airs. Don't tell lies about yourself. Don't play the cocky expert. However, don't wallow in a mire of despairing disclaimers either—"in my opinion," "I think this is," "at least that is the way I feel,"—as if to apologize for presuming to think. You have an opinion; you have backing for it; you are a reasonable person with all your marbles and this is what you think. That should be the attitude behind your writing voice. If you consciously practice it as you write, the style that results will at least be your own.

But will it necessarily be appropriate for an essay? Practically speaking, academic essays should be written in either a formal or an informal style. A formal style means the use of standard diction, standard sentences and punctuation, with no fragments, slang, abbreviations, or contractions. As the bearer of objective opinion and truth, it is the style typically found in scholarly journals, and its use tends to reduce writing to grammatical exactness at the expense of personality or voice. Here is an example of the formal style from a student paper on physical anthropology:

> Brontosaurus thrived during the Jurassic
> period, which is the middle period of the
> Mesozoic era, between 190–140 million years
> ago. As reconstructed from paleontological
> evidence excavated from Como Bluff, Wyoming,
> Brontosaurus was an enormous animal weighing
> nearly twenty tons. In life it was fifty feet
> long, had a neck over thirty feet high, a
> moderate abdominal cavity, no dermal armature,
> and feet whose soles were as large as a square
> yard. That the animal was slow moving and
> unintelligent is inferred from its very small
> brain and thin neural cord.

The formal style is recommended for research papers on scientific topics, for essay examinations, for any serious academic assignment that demands accurate and objective writing. On such an occasion, what you say is more justly important than how you say it.

On the other hand, an informal style encourages writing with flair and personality—the characteristics of a distinctive voice. It is suitable for short essays written for English classes, for persuasive papers, and for assignments that ask for the colorful expression of personal opinion. Here is an example, taken from a student description of a museum exhibit of a Brontosaurus. Notice the intimacy created between the writer and reader:

```
In the middle of the museum towered the
great beast, a Brontosaurus some 190 million
years old.  It consisted of hundreds of
intricate rib bones and vertebrae propped up by
steel rods and frames, and it dominated the
other displays of dead birds and ancient
mammals.  What your eye saw was an enormous
skeleton of astonishing ugliness and
ungainliness, a whopping mistake made by God on
his first try at creation.  The tiny skull
loomed above the room on the end of a delicate
neck of intricate fish bone and seemed to sniff
the air.  With a little imagination, you could
almost feel that the beast, if it came alive,
would immediately begin munching greedily at the
tree framed in the second story window.
```

Whether using a formal or informal style, you should always practice it with consistency. An informal style should never be punctuated by stilted phrasing, nor should a formal one ever lapse into colloquialisms and slang. Generally, the second is the more common inconsistency found in student writing. Preventing this lapse is largely a matter of common sense, which we will discuss later in Chapter 5, under narration. Here is an example of what we mean:

```
The principle behind the statute of
limitations is the recognition of human
```

```
fallibility.  Evidence grows stale, facts become

blurred with passing time, and human memory

dims.  It is a piece of cake for witnesses to

testify accurately when the indignation is still

fresh and moral outrage still running high, but

it's no snap to get them to do so after the

passing of years.
```

The slang in the underlined words is inappropriate to the formality of the rest of the passage. Here is an improvement:

```
The principle behind the statute of

limitations is the recognition of human

fallibility.  Evidence grows stale, facts become

blurred with passing time, and human memory

dims.  It is easy for witnesses to testify

accurately when the indignation is still fresh

and moral outrage still running high, but harder

to get them to do so after the passing of years.
```

In establishing the voice and style of the essay, the first paragraph is obviously important. It is here that you make your beginning, find your pitch, strike the note you will use. Part of the agony of beginnings is that you are groping not only for what you want to say, but also for a voice to say it in. If there is any faltering or stumbling in your voice, it most commonly occurs in the beginning. For that reason, it is always a good idea to rewrite the first paragraph last.

Remember, too, that the writer's voice and style come from premeditation and rewriting. No passage of this book is extemporaneous since its every word, its every sentence, has been laboriously rehearsed and rewritten. Like most writers, we sound naturally like ourselves only after great exertion and pain.

Exercises

1. The following two parodies of "Goldilocks and the Three Bears" are narrated in entirely different voices and styles. The first is a parody of

J. D. Salinger's *The Catcher in the Rye*; the second, of Ernest Hemingway's *A Farewell to Arms*. After reading both pieces, answer the following questions about them:

a. How would you characterize the personality behind each selection? What characteristics of language are used to give the narrator personality?

b. How would you characterize the differences in style? Be specific. Point to differences in syntax, diction, and phrasing.

c. In writing these parodies, did the parodist mimic the style of Salinger and Hemingway in order to parody the voices of their characters, or did he imitate the voices of their characters in order to capture their styles? Justify your answer.

Dan Greenburg
THREE BEARS IN SEARCH OF AN AUTHOR

I Catch Her in the Oatmeal

If you actually want to hear about it, what I'd better do is I'd better warn you right now that you aren't going to believe it. I mean it's a true *story* and all, but it still sounds sort of phony.

Anyway, my name is Goldie Lox. It's sort of a boring name, but my parents said that when I was born I had this very blonde hair and all. Actually I was born bald. I mean how many babies get born with blonde hair? None. I mean I've *seen* them and they're all wrinkled and red and slimy and everything. And bald. And then all the phonies have to come around and tell you he's as cute as a bug's ear. A bug's ear, boy, that really kills me. You ever *seen* a bug's ear? What's cute about a bug's *ear*, for Chrissake! Nothing, that's what.

So, like I was saying, I always seem to be getting into these very stupid situations. Like this time I was telling you about. Anyway, I was walking through the forest and all when I see this very interesting house. A *house*. You wouldn't think anybody would be living way the hell out in the goddam *forest*, but they were. No one was home or anything and the door was open, so I walked in. I figured what I'd do is I'd probably horse around until the guys that lived there came home and maybe asked me to stay for dinner or something. Some people think they *have* to ask you to stay for dinner even if they *hate* you. Also I didn't exactly feel like going home and getting asked a lot of lousy questions. I mean that's *all* I ever seem to do.

Anyway, while I was waiting I sort of sampled some of this stuff they had on the table that tasted like oatmeal. *Oatmeal*. It would have made you puke, I mean it. Then something very spooky started happening. I started getting dizzier than hell. I figured I'd feel better if I could just rest for a while. Sometimes if you eat something like lousy oatmeal you can feel better if you just rest for awhile, so I sat down. That's when the goddam *chair* breaks in half. No kidding, you start feeling lousy and some stupid *chair* is going to break on you every time. I'm not kidding. Anyway I finally found the crummy bedroom and I lay down on this very tiny bed. I was really depressed.

I don't know how long I was asleep or anything but all of a sudden I hear this very strange voice say, "Someone's been sleeping in *my* sack, for Chrissake, and there she is!" So I open my eyes and here at the foot of the bed are these three crummy *bears. Bears!* I swear to God. By that time I was *really* feeling depressed. There's nothing more depressing than waking up and finding three *bears* talking about you, I mean.

So I didn't stay around and shoot the breeze with them or anything. If you want to know the truth, I sort of ran out of there like a madman or something. I do that quite a little when I'm depressed like that.

On the way home, though, I got to figuring. What probably happened is these bears wandered in when they smelled this oatmeal and all. Probably bears *like* oatmeal, I don't know. And the voice I heard when I woke up was probably something I dreamt.

So that's the story.

I wrote it all up once as a theme in school, but my crummy teacher said it was too *whimsical.* Whimsical. That killed me. You got to meet her sometime, boy. She's a real queen.

II   A Farewell to Porridge

In the late autumn of that year we lived in a house in the forest that looked across the river to the mountains, but we always thought we lived on the plain because we couldn't see the forest for the trees.

Sometimes people would come to the door and ask if we would like to subscribe to *The Saturday Evening Post* or buy Fuller brushes, but when we would answer the bell they would see we were only bears and go away.

Sometimes we would go for long walks along the river and you could almost forget for a little while that you were a bear and not people.

Once when we were out strolling for a very long time we came home and you could see that someone had broken in and the door was open.

"La porte est ouverte!" said Mama Bear. "The door should not be open." Mama Bear had French blood on her father's side.

"It is all right," I said, "We will close it."

"It should not have been left open," she said.

"It is all right," I said. "We will close it. Then it will be good like in the old days."

"Bien," she said. "It is well."

We walked in and closed the door. There were dishes and bowls and all manner of eating utensils on the table and you could tell that someone had been eating porridge. We did not say anything for a long while.

"It is lovely here," I said finally. "But someone has been eating my porridge."

"Mine as well," said Mama Bear.

"It is all right," I said. "It is nothing."

"Darling," said Mama Bear, "do you love me?"

"Yes I love you."

"You really love me?"

"I really love you. I'm crazy in love with you."

"And the porridge? How about the porridge?"

"That too. I really love the porridge too."

"It was supposed to be a surprise. I made it as a surprise for you, but someone has eaten it all up."

"You sweet. You made it as a surprise. Oh, you're lovely," I said.

"But it is gone."

"It is all right," I said. "It will be all right."

Then I looked at my chair and you could see someone had been sitting in it and Mama Bear looked at her chair and someone had been sitting in that too and Baby Bear's chair is broken.

"We will go upstairs," I said and we went upstairs to the bedroom but you could see that someone had been sleeping in my bed and in Mama Bear's too although that was the same bed but you have to mention it that way because that is the story. Truly. And then we looked in Baby Bear's bed and there she was.

"I ate your porridge and sat in your chairs and I broke one of them," she said.

"It is all right," I said. "It will be all right."

"And now I am lying in Baby Bear's bed."

"Baby Bear can take care of himself."

"I mean that I am sorry. I have behaved badly and I am sorry for all of this."

"Ça ne fait rien," said Mama Bear. "It is nothing." Outside it had started to rain again.

"I will go now," she said. "I am sorry." She walked slowly down the stairs.

I tried to think of something to tell her but it wasn't any good. "Good-by," she said.

Then she opened the door and went outside and walked all the way back to her hotel in the rain.

Writing the Essay

"Scientists tell us it is harder to start a stone moving than to keep it going after it gets started. And every writer can bear witness that the most unyielding stone is mobile as thistledown compared to the inertia of the average human mind confronted with a blank sheet of paper." So wrote Dorothy Canfield Fisher (1879–1958), a Kansas-born writer who authored several novels and some notable books for juveniles.

The blood enemy of every writer is the blank page (or its high-tech equivalent, the empty CRT screen), and if you do not already know this bitter truth, you are soon to find it out. Here are some ideas and techniques for doing what is hardest for all who write to do: getting started.

Find the right environment

Everyone who writes regularly will eventually hit upon a favorite place, time, and circumstance for writing. Find yours. Experiment with a quiet room, a noisy room, a solitary room, a crowded room. Take a notepad and walk into the woods. If that doesn't work, take a notepad and sit in an airport terminal. Sometimes, for some peculiar reason, an assignment that cannot be written here can be done there.

One memorable evening during his college years, for example, one of the authors of this book could not begin an assignment that was shortly due. His working environment (on paper, at least) was perfect: a clean, well-lighted room haunted by a graveyard silence. Noise and confusion was what finally got him going. He turned on three radios, two television sets, and the dishwasher, and composed among this racket a usable first draft which, after repeated revisions, earned him an "A" in the course.

Don't be afraid to experiment with the environment. Your aim is to do your best work. How you and where you do that is beside the point.

Expect to write at least three drafts

We have said enough about this already, but since rewriting is the theme of this book, we will say it again. Rome wasn't built in a day; few papers are penned at one sitting. Expect to do multiple revisions. You can always find something to improve in another draft. Reread your work incessantly not only when you are finished, but also while you are writing it.

Expect the worst first

Why this is so is a mystery, but the best writing invariably comes later, after you have tried repeatedly. Some have drawn the homely comparison between a writer starting to work and a baseball pitcher warming up. Neither has the best stuff in the beginning, but with persistence and practice, it emerges slowly. The fast ball begins to sail, the curve to snap down. The first sentences, composed while the brain was cold and the fingers stricken with rigor mortis, can suddenly be made fresh and lively. Themes and subthemes occur to you; phrases and apt images pop into your brain. But the road to these riches is the lonely and rutted cart track of effort and persistence. So don't be discouraged if your first sentences, paragraphs, and pages are utterly worthless. The best is yet to be.

If all else fails, change your writing instrument

Peculiar as it may sound, this works. If you find that you are sitting glued to your typewriter keyboard with nary a good word to show for all your patient mummification, switch to writing with a pen. If the CRT is as blank now as it was an hour go, try writing with a pencil.

In the beginning of any project, the computer or word-processor is a mixed blessing. Its strong suit is high-speed composing because its keys are switches which cannot jam no matter how furiously your fingers rain upon the keyboard. Yet there you sit, while the words drip out onto the screen one by one as from a leaky pot. This can be unnerving for anyone. Some writers prefer to begin composing with pen or pencil when the going is slow and then switch later to the computer, when the words and sentences are really gushing out of them.

Do the standing jump

In 1947 the West Indian–born novelist and writer, Jean Rhys, found herself hopelessly blocked. She made this entry in her diary: "This time I must not blot a line. No revision, no second thoughts. Down it shall go. Already I am terrified. I have none of the tools of my trade. No rows of pencils, no pencil sharpener, no drink. The standing jump." What she meant to do was simply plunge into the writing and do it without looking back. Apparently her prescription worked because she later published many successful stories and books, including her acknowledged masterpiece, *Wide Sargasso Sea*.

In fact, the best thing the timid or blocked writer can do is exactly as Rhys did: start writing. Don't look back. Put it down on the page. Yes, it seems terrible and inferior and you wonder how a normal human brain could hatch such utter rubbish, but put it down anyway.

The aim of all this is to get you started. Writer's block usually comes from a loss of self-confidence and a too critical eye. If you should ever suffer from it, the antidote is to do the standing jump, to leap before you look. Write away, no matter how silly it sounds. You can always make it better later.

Writing Assignments

1. Write an essay on the debate raging in some school districts about the teaching of evolution versus "scientific creationism."

2. One survey reported that the most common fear among Americans—ranked above death itself—is speaking in public. Write an essay probing the reasons for that widespread fear.

3. Write an essay on the subject of video games. Find a narrowed topic, reduce it to a controlling idea, and express it in a thesis statement.

4. Using your own experiences, memories, and observations, write an essay on the importance of self-respect.

5. "Psychic phenomena is hokum." Agree or disagree with that statement in an essay.

6. In an essay, explain the methods of prewriting, organizing, and actual composition that work best for you.

7. Write a letter to a friend asking him or her to repay an old loan of $100. Pretend that a month has passed with no reply. Write a second letter demanding payment of the debt. In a paragraph, analyze the differences in the voice and style of each letter.

8. Find a paragraph of obtuse writing—taken from any official or government source—and rewrite it in plain and understandable language.

9. Using any old letter from a family member or friend, write an essay analyzing and explaining the voice and style in which it was written.

Chapter Three

The Whole Essay: Purpose, Thesis, Organization, and Logic

There's an art of reading, as well as an art of thinking, and an art of writing.

ISAAC D'ISRAELI (1766–1848)

Why do you write essays? If "to earn a grade" is the best answer you can give, then you are likely to have no compelling sense of purpose to guide your hand. A good or bad grade is the effect of good or bad writing, but not its main purpose. Yet as a writer you do benefit from having a definite sense of purpose for an assignment—whether to enlighten a reader, argue a case, or merely blow off steam about some pet peeve. Purpose is the premeditated effect you are hoping to achieve in your writing. Its success is measured by whether or not the reader is *persuaded* to react to the written piece in the way you had hoped. So before you begin to write that first line, think of your aim, your end, your purpose as a kind of persuasion. More concretely, imagine that whatever you will be asked to write will fall into one or another of these three aims: (1) expressing yourself, (2) providing information, or (3) arguing a point. Imagine also that you are trying to do each of these tasks persuasively.

Purpose and Thesis

In Chapter 2, we pointed out that while all essays have a controlling idea, many do not express it in an explicit thesis. Here is an example. Can

59

you find a thesis in this opening paragraph, where one would be expected to occur unfailingly in a student essay?

> Now here is a strange and very likely a wonderful thing: The people who watch chimpanzees in the wild—and that has become a scientific specialty since Jane Goodall made it famous twenty years ago—say that it appears the animals practice herbal medicine.
> —Tom Teepen, "Man's Arrogance, and Humility," *Atlanta Constitution,* January 2, 1986.

This paragraph makes an observation about chimpanzees but asserts no overall point that could be called a thesis. And if you inferred from it that the essay is about the habits of chimpanzees, you would be wrong. The author's controlling idea, expressed partly by his title, "Man's Arrogance, and Humility," is to argue for the preservation of animals in the wild because of the lessons about nature that they can teach us. That chimpanzees seem to know instinctively which herbs to chew for certain illnesses is simply one example he uses to shore up this argument.

The undeniable fact is that many professional writers do not write with an explicit thesis. But all write with a controlling idea—some major emphasis that ties their ideas together into a single coherent point. It is harder to write an essay from a background controlling idea than from an explicit thesis, and many students simply cannot do it well. For that reason, most instructors follow the convention of teaching students always to use an explicit thesis in their essays. As you grow as a writer, your reliance on the formulaic use of an explicit thesis will naturally lessen. But in the meantime, stating the major point of your essay in an explicit thesis is a requirement of most composition instructors even if not widely practiced among professional writers.

For the beginner, then, the entire structure and logic of a writing assignment should spring from its thesis—from the opening statement that commits the essay to one or another of the three aims already listed. The thesis is your declaration of purpose to the reader, a manifest of the cargo contained within your essay's pages. What the reader expects to find in the essay is no more or less than what your thesis has declared will be there. Consequently, the first major efforts at revision should be directed at the thesis statement.

Besides telling the reader what you are up to, your thesis statement can also give you an editorial sense for the kind of details that should go into the essay and the kind that should be left out. Consider, for example, this thesis:

```
Moving from Vietnam to this country gave me a

wrenching sense of loneliness and isolation that

I had never in my life experienced before.
```

An essay written on this thesis will be an exercise in **self-expression**, with its details being drawn chiefly from the writer's personal experiences and memories. If you were writing on this thesis and found yourself pumping dry statistical details into the essay from the unlikely source of an encyclopedia, you should suspect that you had strayed badly from your point.

Here is a thesis of an entirely different kind:

```
Many college graduates become underemployed as

the jobs available to them require highly

technical skills never learned in colleges

stressing a liberal education.
```

The aim of any essay written on this thesis is to **inform**, to paint the picture of suffering experienced by the "many." We expect the air to be drier here and more laden with a cloud of facts and case histories. We do not expect a wealth of personal anecdotes since they would overly particularize the proof.

Here is a third thesis, which makes an entirely different promise:

```
The government should assist historical

societies to preserve our nation's graceful old

homes because the history of architecture is

written on them.
```

"Should" is a call to **argument** and implies the coming of reasons and evidence. We expect to see opponents brought to trial and refuted, to hear expert testimony, to be led by the hand of logic. Persuasion is the strongest single element in an argumentative essay, but it is also implicitly present in essays written for self-expression and to inform. If we are not persuaded by what writers tell us, we are unlikely to be swayed by their stories or informed by their facts.

Revising the thesis for clarity of aim

If you could know exactly how your writing would affect a reader, you would be a writer of unparalleled ability. But no writer completely knows that. Nevertheless, you probably have a vague idea which of the three purposes your effort comes under—to express yourself, to inform, or to argue. From formulating your controlling idea, you also know what you are trying to say in the essay. In short, you have a clear enough notion of the assignment to describe the content as well as the formal purpose of the essay in the thesis statement.

There is, we think, a decided advantage in wording your thesis statement to do both. The thesis statement that says what you are going to do while simultaneously committing you to a clear aim not only sets the table for the reader, but it also provides a menu for the cook. Here are some examples of what we mean, showing both the original thesis and its revision:

Original: Churches and youth can be incompatible.

This is an aimless thesis, an empty promise that asks no commitment of the writer and evokes no anticipation in the reader. What is the writer trying to do here? Express the self? Inform? Argue? We cannot tell.

Revision: At an early age I rebelled against the stultifying

conformity and orthodoxy of belonging to a church.

Now the thesis statement clothes the essay in the overall purpose of *self-expression*. It tells the writer what must be done while alerting the reader to what to expect.

Original: American attention has recently been focused on the

famine in Africa.

This thesis reads like a preliminary topic and has neither certainty nor intention to recommend it. A reader cannot know what to expect in an essay written about it; worse yet, neither can a writer.

Revision: The recent focus of world attention on the African

famine has resulted in three major U.S. organiza-

tions contributing large sums of money and quanti-

ties of food to Ethiopia.

The aim of this essay is now clear: *to inform* the reader of the work of three charitable organizations to relieve the African famine.

Original: Why should colleges have honor courses as part of their curriculum?

As a declaration of a writer's intention and agenda, the thesis should answer the initial question of every reader, namely, "What is this about?" It should not answer this implicit question with another question.

Revision: A truly democratic college should not allow honor classes in its curriculum because they create a subtle snobbery and elitism that belittle the average student.

Or, argument may be just the opposite:

Revision: Honor courses should be established in every college curriculum so that students with motivation and talent can be challenged to bring out their best.

Now the writer's purpose is plainly spelled out: it is *to argue* the merits of the thesis.

Revising the thesis for unity

There are many kinds and causes of bad writing, but the recipe for good writing is still somewhat a mystery. One unarguable cause of the badly written essay is the wavering purpose, which is usually found in the forked or split thesis statement. The forked thesis is one that, embodying a split proposition, tugs in different directions and threatens to sunder the essay into two irreconcilable parts.

Original: Hemingway's fictional women fall into two major categories, the nurturing mother and the bitch goddess, and his men seem to be flawed.

Two separate writing assignments are buried within this forked thesis: Hemingway's categories of women, and the weaknesses of his men. The solution to the forked thesis is either to entirely discard one of the propositions or subordinate it to the other. In the rewritten example below, subordination is used to unite the ideas of the thesis:

Revision: `Many of the flawed men in Hemingway's novels have`

`been brought to ruin by the selfishness of the`

`stereotypical bitch goddess.`

To explore the cause and effect relationship between Hemingway's male and female characters is now the single proclaimed aim of this thesis.

Faulty grammatical construction is a common cause of the forked thesis, with the writer typically asserting a coordinate relationship between two ideas that are logically subordinate. Here is an example: "Antony neglected the business of Rome *and* was a self-indulgent general." To unite this forked thesis requires a subordinating of its parts: "Antony neglected the business of Rome *because* he was a self-indulgent general."

Revising the thesis for coherence

Coherence is a word overshadowed in the popular understanding by its opposite. Nearly everyone understands what is meant by, say, "The driver of the car was incoherent and therefore plainly drunk." But it is not as universally clear what is meant by "The essayist writes with coherence."

Coherence in this sense means that the words, sentences, paragraphs, and ideas of the essay are held together not only by sequence on the page but also by logical and syntactic necessity. Sentences following one another on the page may be as sequential as ducks waddling in a row but not necessarily any more coherent. It is a writer's careful use of linking words, phrases, and repeated key terms, that makes words and sentences cohere.

Later, in the chapter on paragraph writing, we will take this up again. But for now we want to emphasize the importance of a coherent thesis statement, one that specifies the writer's purpose and agenda with the utmost clarity. Here is an actual example of an incoherent thesis:

Original: `In actuality lobbying the legislature is not always`

`unethical because of desirable political action`

`whereas most people think in terms of negativism,`

`which shows a lack of knowledge about how the system`

`works.`

The writer may have known what she was trying to say, but we have only what she has actually said, and it is a perplexing stew. Part of the problem comes from her inappropriate use of the linking words "because," and "whereas." The larger part, however, is caused by muddled thinking. Here is the rewritten thesis:

Revision: Whereas many politically naive citizens think of

lobbying the legislature as unethical, in actuality

lobbying is a practical system that often results in

desirable political action.

"Say what you think" is advice often given in rhetoric books of this kind. "Think about what you say" is, in our view, a better prescription. This means reading and rereading your thesis again and again, trying to fathom the writing through a reader's eyes. Think of the sentences of your essay as poles along which your ideas are to be transmitted like electricity. You must provide the connections, the junction boxes, the relays, the wiring. You do so by carefully linking concepts and ideas together so that they follow with logical necessity.

Revising the thesis for specificity

Every thesis will be found to have one or two pivotal words that encapsulate some essential part of your theme and commit your essay to some specific task. As an example, consider this weak thesis: "The rule of Indira Gandhi was important." The pivotal word here is "important." Demonstrating the importance of Indira Gandhi's rule is what you have committed your essay to do.

But the word "important" is too general, too spongy a term on which to base an essay. If you meant that her rule was characterized by a growing sense of Indian nationalism, or by a policy of nonalignment, you should come out and plainly say so in your thesis. Either point is discussable in itself. "Important," while it may point to discussable matters, is not.

Here is another example. A student tried without success to write an essay on this thesis:

Original: Many citizens of Communist regimes are wonderful

people.

After vainly struggling with "wonderful Communists" for a page or two, the writer then turned to the instructor for help. By "wonderful" she had meant that they were, in the main, as unideological and as self-seeking as the ordinary citizen of a Western democracy. The instructor urged her to say so in her revised thesis:

Revision: Many citizens of Communist regimes are as unideo-

logical and as self-seeking as their counterparts in

the Western democracies.

This is a discussable opinion and in the long run the human race may have cause to rejoice over the ordinariness of people everywhere, but it is hardly "wonderful." Once the thesis had been freed of this wishy-washy adjective, the student was finally able to write her essay.

Revising the thesis to get rid of wordiness

Of all the sentences in your essay, the thesis is the one that should never be wordy. If it is, you are probably confused about your purpose and should sit down and rethink what you are trying to do.

There are three common kinds of wordiness, each equally ungainly and ugly. The first is **padding**.

Original: In my honest opinion, the U.S. government should stop promoting the questionable process of affirmative action because, as can be clearly seen, it is beginning to have the reverse effect of denying school entrance and jobs to middle-class whites, who are becoming the disadvantaged minority.

The horticultural word used to describe the flaw of this sentence is *deadwood*. All introductory qualifiers such as "in my honest opinion," "it is my sincere view," "I think," "I believe" belong to this branch of bramble. If you express a thought, the world takes it as your own unless you deed it in a footnote to another writer. You do not have to say "I think" or "this is my opinion." That affirmative action is a process is already common knowledge, so it is unnecessary to further say so. The thesis is calling affirmative action into question, which makes the "questionable" superfluous. Also, it is not at all clearly seen that affirmative action is as the writer alleges: that is what the essay must make us clearly see. Here is the revised thesis:

Revision: The U.S. government should stop promoting affirmative action because it is beginning to have the reverse effect of denying school entrance and jobs to middle-class whites.

Many students tend to overqualify their opinions because of insecurity or out of deference to the instructor. Knowing your topic well is the antidote to insecurity. To express yourself plainly and emphatically insults no one, least of all your instructor, who is hoping to inspire exactly that kind of self-confidence in students. In any case, hedging in your opinions only makes you sound as if you haven't done your homework.

Repetition is the second kind of wordiness. Here is an example from a student paper:

Original: Traditionally, the southern funeral of past times was not so much a ritual comforting the bereaved, who had lost a loved one, as a reminder of man's immortality and a warning not to lose the faith or church belief.

"Past times" needlessly repeats the idea already summed up in "traditionally." A "bereaved" person is someone who has "lost a loved one"; "the faith" already contains the idea of "church belief." Here is the revision:

Revision: Traditionally, the southern funeral was not so much a ritual comforting the bereaved as a reminder of man's immortality and a warning not to lose the faith.

The third kind of wordiness is **roundaboutness**. Writers guilty of it commit the sin of circularity in their sentences. Rather than get to the point cleanly, they circle it like a merry-go-round. Here is an example:

Original: Beginning sometime between 1970 and 1980, automobile insurance companies began to impose surcharges on individual drivers who are prone to have accidents, so as to achieve some form of fairness in assessing insurance premium rates for drivers in general.

"Automobile insurance companies" could be made "auto insurers"; "individual drivers who are prone to have accidents" could become "accident-prone drivers." The phrases are not wrong, but any of them could have been more elegantly and compactly put:

Revision: Since the 1970s auto insurers have used surcharges on accident-prone drivers to achieve equity in the overall assessment of automobile insurance premiums.

Sometimes padding is done intentionally so that the essay will meet a minimum word count. But this remedy is wrongheaded and futile. If you are truly interested in your topic, if you are immersed in your sources, if you have a substantial thesis, your efforts should be in the other direction, namely, to rein in your essay before it gallops over the minimum. But if you catch yourself straining to stuff every additional word or two you can in a sentence to satisfy a minimum length, you are either disenchanted with your topic and your thesis, or you do not know your subject well. If so, you should leave off the compositional huffing and puffing and go back to thinking about your subject until you can narrow it into a topic that suits you better.

Revising the thesis to suit your audience

Every discipline, every occupation brings with it a certain cast of mind and manner of expression. For example, sensitive to the charge that their work is not truly scientific, social scientists have cultivated a writing style of postmortem detachment. The personal "I" has been largely banished from it along with the active voice and a whole train of sentient adjectives. You will rarely find a social scientist writing in a personable, familiar style, and if you do you can be sure that the author has such an impressive reputation as to be exempt from the syntax and diction demanded of lesser colleagues.

When in Rome, the old saw goes, do as the Romans do. When you write for social scientists, you must practice their way of writing, their conventions of syntax and diction. A similar caution applies to any other discipline or audience for whom your work may be intended. For example, if you were writing an essay aimed at an audience of nurses, you could freely use a medical vocabulary that in good conscience you should spare an audience of secretaries.

How to adjust your style to match your audience is a matter largely of sensitivity and common sense. Read before you write is a good rule to follow. Before you write for your sociology instructor, read one or two representative papers in the field. Pay attention to the style and diction, to whether or not the authors paint their points with colorful metaphors and images or set them down plainly. For example, this thesis would strike most social scientists as flawed:

Original: `Role playing is covering one's face with a bandanna`

`or veil and playing at being someone else during the`

`masquerade, the way I do when I sell shoes at my`

`part-time job.`

Aside from its other difficulties, this thesis strikes too personal a note and is entirely too metaphorical. Since social scientists do not write about their discipline in this way, they are unlikely to be sympathetic to any paper that flouts their literary conventions.

Revision: Role playing is the assumption of an external pat-

tern of behavior and expectations which one carries

out regardless of personal feelings and disposi-

tions, and is especially associated with occupation

and work.

Writers do not have to give readers exactly what they want, but they should observe appropriateness both in content and wording of their theses, to say nothing of the rest of the essay.

Following a thesis statement through successive drafts

The example below shows the successive rewriting of a thesis state-ment to make it sharper and more clearly expressive of the writer's purpose. It also demonstrates what every veteran writer knows: that the distance from first draft to final product is measurable only by persistence and effort.

First draft: Some countries, where class distinctions still

exist, create a bad social atmosphere.

Some countries, where *a* class distinctions still
            between the rich and the poor   in which two
exist, create a bad social atmosphere,
        sets of inhabitants are bred totally ignorant of each other.
This thesis statement does not sufficiently spell out the writer's purpose. Will it express the writer's feelings? Inform us about the effects of class distinctions? Argue against the distinctions of class? A clearer aim is needed.

Second draft: Some countries, where a class distinction still

exists between the rich and the poor, create a

social atmosphere in which two sets of inhabi-

tants are bred totally ignorant of each other.

A country that allows too big a gulf
~~Some countries, where a class distinction still~~
                    is in danger of becoming like two
~~exists~~ between the rich and the poor, ~~create a~~
countries on different planets, where the
~~social atmosphere in which two sets of~~ inhabi-
        made what they are by different breeding,
tants are ~~bred totally ignorant of each other.~~
different food, and different laws that control them.

The focus of this thesis statement is sharpened in the second draft with its emphasis on the gap between the rich and the poor. But the writer is still not committed to a specific structure.

> **Third draft:** A country that allows too big a gulf between the
>
> rich and the poor is in danger of becoming like
>
> two countries on different planets, where the
>
> inhabitants are made what they are by different
>
> breeding, different food, and different laws
>
> that control them.
>
> *nation*
>
> A ~~country~~ that allows too big a gulf between the
>
> rich and the poor is in danger of becoming like
>
> *separate*
>
> two countries on ~~different~~ planets, where the
>
> *formed*
>
> inhabitants are ~~made what they are~~ by different
>
> *fed by*   *controlled by*
>
> breeding, different food, and different laws⊙
>
> ~~that control them.~~

The third draft gives the essay structure by limiting the writer to three effects of the gulf between rich and poor: breeding, food, and laws. But the statement could still be further tightened.

> **Final draft:** A nation that allows too big a gulf between the
>
> rich and the poor is in danger of becoming like
>
> two countries on separate planets, where the in-
>
> habitants are formed by different breeding, fed
>
> by different food, and controlled by different
>
> laws.

In this revision, "nation" is substituted for "country," restricting the discussion to formal political entities. "Separate planets" emphasizes the idea of gulf between rich and poor. Repetition of the past participles—"formed," "fed," and "controlled"—gives the statement coherence and symmetry.

Bear in mind that some thesis statements will require many more revisions than are shown here. We do not mean to suggest that you limit your rewriting efforts to three or four passes. We often make a dozen or more passes at our own passages before we are satisfied with them.

Exercises

1. The following thesis statements are poorly written. Correct their flaws in a revision.

a. Terrorism is often poorly handled by various agencies.

b. The compact disk player (CD) is flooding the consumer market.

c. People on vacation try to avoid a heavy intellectual fare when they read.

d. Francis Bacon is a controversial modern painter.

e. During its final phase, the Roman Empire declined rapidly, and the Christian church quickly took on a dominant role.

f. In my opinion, writing with a computer, although some people might find it useful, will only hasten our spreading dependence on high technology while weakening some of our hard-earned literary skills.

g. Bilingual education may win some short-term gains whereas being offsetted heavily by the divisiveness too many languages can be blamed even in a pluralistic society such as our own.

2. Choosing three topics from the list that follows, compose for each a thesis statement free of all the errors discussed so far in this chapter:

a. body consciousness

b. wilderness preservation

c. private versus public education

d. fads or fashions

e. a major government scandal (anywhere in the world)

f. promiscuity in our society

g. the developing nations

h. the effects of romantic love

Revising for Better Organization and Structure

The structure of an essay is often implied in its thesis statement, which can be worded to commit the writer to a certain organizing pattern. Here, for example, is the first paragraph of a student essay:

```
Like most people I love to eat and eat and

eat.  If I had just one wish, it would be to be

able to cook. Being able to cook my own meals

would keep my stomach full, my body healthy, and

my bank account in the black.
```

The structure of this essay is implicit in its thesis: it will be based on a pattern of enumerating the effects being able to cook will have on this student's life. The first would be the effects on his stomach; the second, the effects on his body; and the third, the effects on his bank account. This pattern is known as organizing by **simple enumeration** and is especially well suited for any essay that describes a process (see "Process Analysis," pages 167–70).

In planning the overall structure for your essay, then, you should first examine its thesis for any implicit organizing pattern. Sometimes simple enumeration will be the most obvious. But there are other patterns that writers can use to organize an essay, depending on the particular wording of its thesis.

Organizing according to the order of importance

> Thesis: Elderly parents have basic needs that either their children or
> society must provide.

An essay on this thesis may be organized in a pattern that presents its ideas in either ascending or descending order of importance. For example, you could cover the needs of elderly parents in this descending order:

1. Regular visits from children and other loved ones
2. Good medical care, including proper diet
3. Occasional appropriate recreation
4. Help with grooming
5. Help with housekeeping chores

The first item is, in the writer's opinion, the most important need of an elderly parent; the last item is the least.

Organizing according to space orientation

The organization of an essay may also be based on movement in space: from top to bottom, from left to right, from inside to outside, and so on. A description of a Japanese teahouse, for example, could be organized according to this spatial pattern:

> Thesis: The formal Japanese teahouse is a place of solemn ceremony
> and peace.

1. The stone path leading to the teahouse
2. The low lintel to force a humble bow
3. The starkly furnished one-room interior
   a. The mat on the floor in the middle of the room
   b. The gridiron and the teakettle in front of the mat
   c. One simple flower arrangement on the shelf at the back of the room

    d. A porcelain tea service near the flower arrangement
    e. One painting on the wall above the flower arrangement

The movement of the description is from the outside to the inside of the tearoom. Once begun, the essay should stick to this orderly flow.

Organizing according to time orientation

> Thesis: The English language traces its origins to prehistoric time and has been influenced by many cultures.

This organization is based on a chronological listing of the main points of the essay. The lapse may be over the course of a day, week, month, year, decade, or century. For example, below is the pattern that might be used in an essay on the history of the English language:

1. Celtic influence (earliest recorded time)
2. Roman influence (43 A.D.)
3. Anglo-Saxon influence (449)
4. Norman influence (1066)
5. Influence of northern, midland, and southern dialects (1100)
6. Fixation of standard English as influenced by Oxford and Cambridge universities and by Dr. Johnson's dictionary (1650)

Naturally, once you have begun to use an obviously chronological sequence, you should stay with it consistently to the end.

Organizing according to logic

> Thesis: Taxpayers need not pay millions of dollars to support presidential libraries in order to gain the benefit of the memoirs and recollections of former presidents.

Organization by logic consists of some predictable pattern of reasoning: a discussion of cause and effect, a recounting of examples to support a main point, a listing of reasons why something should be done or not done, a series of questions and answers. For example, here is the pattern that might be used to organize an essay arguing against perks for presidents leaving office:

1. Thomas Jefferson died so poor that his personal property had to be sold off to satisfy his debtors; yet he left us a brilliant legacy of writings.
2. U. S. Grant left office with a few thousand dollars and later went bankrupt, but he wrote his valuable memoirs without the help of a presidential library.

3. Harry S. Truman typed his own letters once he left office, but these letters are now a historical treasure.

A series of examples supporting the author's overall conclusion is the logical pattern implicit in this outline.

Whichever of these organizational patterns you follow in an essay, it is helpful to either hint at or spell out your intent somewhere in an opening paragraph. Expository prose is easier to read when one knows what to expect; it is also easier to write once the writer has made a commitment in the thesis statement to some specific pattern.

The following first draft of an essay is annotated to show the thrust of the student's rewriting. A second draft is also included, showing how the student cleaned up some of the lapses in structure and organization. Notice that the revision often entailed the shifting of paragraphs or blocks of sentences that either had been misplaced or became more effective elsewhere.

Original:

What Is Piety?

move this opening paragraph to the second sentence of paragraph 3. It can be the first example in the historical sequence. Substitute a new introductory paragraph.

① In 1535, Sir Thomas More defied King Henry VIII and put his head on the chopping block because of dedication and duty to his religion. When he publicly refused to subscribe to the Act of Supremacy, which made the British king head of the Church instead of the pope, he was imprisoned and eventually beheaded. More had been admired throughout England for his legal decisions in favor of the poor, the weak, and the oppressed. One of his famous works was a treatise comforting people experiencing great tribulation. More's piety gave him the courage to obey his conscience, do his duty, and accept his tragic fate on earth. Such faithfulness to the duties owed to God is called piety.

② The word piety derives from two Latin words—piete, meaning "pity," and pietas, meaning "dutifulness." Back in the 12th century, when the word first became popular, it was associated exclusively with the first meaning, pity, but then it evolved from pity to a sense of duty concerning one's elders or family. From that meaning it eventually came to be linked primarily with religious matters, as it still is today. In our world, if a person is considered pious, he is devout and obeys the rules of his church.

③ Examples of how piety has affected history are scattered throughout the centuries. *insert paragraph 1* ⌃America was settled by men and women who were persecuted in Europe for their religious convictions. The Plymouth settlers left England for America because they could no longer tolerate neighbors who mocked them, threw bricks at them, burned their Bibles, or treated them as clowns. Their sense of duty to God and Church was strong enough to let them abandon their homeland and embark on a journey to an unknown world, where they could fulfill the dream of freely practicing their religion. An important part of the pilgrims' creed was to have pity on people in trouble and to share the bounty of their harvests with neighbors who had fallen on ill times. The Crusades and Spanish Inquisition are

move this paragraph to follow paragraph 5. It should follow the examples of true piety to indicate a contrast: piety can be counterfeit. Supply a transition for better coherence.

striking examples of piety run amuck. In both instances, the overzealous duties of those bringing "the true religion" to others consisted of torture, looting, rape, and murder—hardly pious means. These corrupt movements demonstrate what happens when duty and pity part ways.

(4) Our present age offers numerous examples of piety. For instance, the Moral Majority's quest to influence governmental policy in the United States stems from the pious belief that abortion is wrong and that youth must be kept from moral decay. Although the methods of this Moral Majority may be questioned, still the movement itself is obviously spurred on by a sense of religious duty and a concern for fellow man, which form the essence of piety.

(5) Recent Nobel Peace Prize recipients Mother Teresa and Bishop Desmond Tutu have been recognized on a global scale for their pious behavior. As servants of the Church, they both are committed to doing God's work by helping others. Bishop Tutu's fight against the injustices of apartheid in South Africa and Mother Teresa's caring for the sick and hungry children of India and other parts of the world are carried on under the dictates of the Church. As representatives of their religion, these two humanitarians are duty-bound to manifest the

doctrines of their faith. In 1985 Bishop Tutu
risked his own life by speaking out for human
rights during the bloody riots of Johannesburg.
That same year Mother Teresa selflessly
confronted the disease—ridden refugee camps of
Ethiopia to help distribute food to starving
children.

Insert the section about the Crusades and Spanish Inquisition here.

(6) Quite clearly, piety is exhibited in its
purest and most admirable form when it reveals
aspects of both its earliest and later meanings.
When a person combines pity with duty and makes
these qualities the fuel for a passionate
involvement with humanity, he or she is living
the highest form of piety.

add a statement about what happens when the element of pity is lacking.

Revision:

What Is Piety?

"And I would wish my days to be
Bound each to each by natural piety."

These are lines penned by William Wordsworth,
the great Romantic poet, who longs for piety as
a desirable character trait. On the other hand,
another noted Romanticist, Edmund Burke, warned
that "religious persecution may shield itself
under the guise of a mistaken over—zealous
piety." It seems then that piety is a Janus: it
can be malevolent as well as benevolent. Since
the term is so loaded, what are its true roots?

The word piety derives from two Latin words—piete, meaning "pity," and pietas, meaning "dutifulness." Back in the 12th century, when the word first became popular, it was associated exclusively with the first meaning, pity, but then it evolved from pity to a sense of duty concerning one's elders or family. From that meaning it eventually came to be linked primarily with religious matters, as it still is today. In our world, if a person is considered pious, he is devout and obeys the rules of his church.

Examples of how piety has affected history are scattered throughout the centuries. In 1535, Sir Thomas More defied King Henry VIII and put his head on the chopping block because of dedication and duty to his religion. When he publicly refused to subscribe to the Act of Supremacy, which made the British king head of the church instead of the pope, he was imprisoned and eventually beheaded. More had been admired throughout England for his legal decisions in favor of the poor, the weak, and the oppressed. One of his famous works was a treatise comforting people experiencing great tribulation. More's piety gave him the courage to obey his conscience, do his duty, and accept his tragic fate on earth. Such faithfulness to the duties owed to God is called piety.

America was settled by men and women who were persecuted in Europe for their religious convictions. The Plymouth settlers left England for America because they could no longer tolerate neighbors who mocked them, threw bricks at them, burned their Bibles, or treated them as clowns. Their sense of duty to God and Church was strong enough to let them abandon their homeland and embark on a journey to an unknown world, where they could fulfill the dream of freely practicing their religion. An important part of the pilgrims' creed was to have pity on people in trouble and to share the bounty of their harvests with neighbors who had fallen on ill times.

Our present age offers numerous examples of piety. For instance, the Moral Majority's quest to influence governmental policy in the United States stems from the pious belief that abortion is wrong and that youth must be kept from moral decay. Although the methods of this Moral Majority may be questioned, still the movement itself is obviously spurred on by a sense of religious duty and a concern for fellow man, which form the essence of piety.

Recent Nobel Peace Prize recipients Mother Teresa and Bishop Desmond Tutu have been recognized on a global scale for their pious behavior. As servants of the Church, they both are committed to doing God's work by helping others. Bishop Tutu's fight against the injustices of apartheid in South Africa and Mother Teresa's caring for the sick and hungry children of India and other parts of the world are carried on under the dictates of the Church. As representatives of their religion, these two humanitarians are duty-bound to manifest the doctrines of their faith. In 1985 Bishop Tutu risked his own life by speaking out for human rights during the bloody riots of Johannesburg. That same year Mother Teresa selflessly confronted the disease-ridden refugee camps of Ethiopia to help distribute food to starving children.

But piety has its dark side. Hideous crimes have been committed in the name of a distorted piety, a piety consisting of duty without pity. The Crusades and Spanish Inquisition are striking examples of piety run amuck. In both instances, the overzealous duties of those bringing "the true religion" to others consisted of torture, looting, rape, and murder--hardly pious means. These corrupt movements demonstrate what happens when duty and pity part ways.

Quite clearly, piety is exhibited in its purest and most admirable form when it reveals aspects of both its earliest and later meanings.

```
In fact, robbed of the element of pity, piety

can turn into a devilish fanaticism.  Only when

a person combines pity with duty and makes these

qualities the fuel for a passionate involvement

with humanity, does he or she live the highest

form of piety.
```

Exercises

1. Which pattern of organization would you likely use in writing on the topics below? Your choices are (a) simple enumeration, (b) order of importance, (c) space orientation, (d) time orientation, or (e) logic. Make a tentative model of each essay according to your chosen pattern.

a. From the moment that President Reagan gave his O.K. for navy F-14 fighter planes to intercept the Egyptian 737 carrying four terrorists who had hijacked the Italian cruise line *Achille Lauro* and killed an elderly American to the time that the terrorists were taken into custody, only five hours had elapsed. It is 1:00 P.M., Friday, October 11, 1985. President Reagan gives his O.K. to execute the interception. Totally blacked out and running under complete radio silence, the U.S. planes head for a location south of Crete. A command post vectors the fighters to intercept the 737. The 737 follows the lead of the F-14s into Sigonella. The terrorists are taken into custody.

b. A Mongolian "yurt" (home), such as the ones found in the foothills of the High Altai Mountains, consists of a round wooden lattice-work frame covered with canvas or camel-hair felt. The organization of the interior is dictated by the circularity of the structure.

c. There are important reasons why child pornography should be banned from bookstores and magazine stands.

d. Saving energy has several effects, from saving money to saving your life. Let us consider the effects according to how each influences human activities.

e. Some grownups believe that children should not be encouraged to read fairy tales because they are often cruel and frightening. This attitude is based on lack of understanding. In reality, children already know about evil, fear, and bogey. Fairy tales are not responsible for producing fear in children. That is in them already because it is already in the world. In actuality, fairy tales give children the clear possibility of defeating evil and bogey.

Revising for Logical Progression and Thought

Think of the house of logic as a public facility, a place of free room and board where all willing to abide by its rules can go to settle their differences. Three indispensable characteristics are required of all guests: that their arguments be *focused*, cite only *verifiable* evidence, and consist of *visible* reasoning.

To develop a thesis logically, your argument should focus unwaveringly on the supporting evidence and facts. It should not splatter your opponent's reputation over the stones, make appeals that tug at the heartstrings, or trumpet facts that are bogus or irrelevant. It should concentrate only on the available evidence, which must be publicly verifiable and therefore cannot come from the unnamed sources of journalism. Your reasoning must also show all the intermediate calculations in your thinking that led from proposition to conclusion.

Excluded from the company of this public house are those who will not live by these rules: the occultist whose knowledge is founded on an alleged secret power; the prophet who claims to be uniquely gifted; the diviner who pretends to know but cannot say how. Lacking from their modes of thinking is the public and democratic participation that is the cornerstone of all logical thought. Nothing can be hidden, concealed, masked, or disguised in a logical argument, and its outcome is never dependent on secret testimony or unique gifts. With logic, what you see is what you get.

In fact, a great deal of what makes an argument logical comes from fair play and common sense. Playing fair with the evidence, being willing to listen to the reasoning of an opponent, ignoring irrelevant issues of personality—these are traits universally associated with logic. To argue logically, you need only focus on the question in dispute, cite only verifiable evidence, and make your reasoning visible to a listener or reader.

Below are some of the common departures from logic often committed by speakers and writers along with suggestions for editing them out of your own arguments.

Avoid hasty generalizations

A hasty generalization is a rash conclusion based on too few examples, on atypical examples, or on the omission of examples that attest to the contrary. For instance, if because of a newspaper story about two TWA crashes you were to assert that travel on TWA is dangerous, you would be making a hasty generalization utterly unjustified by the scant evidence. A similar charge could be made against you for concluding that small towns such as Santa Fe, New Mexico, produce the best grand opera. Santa Fe has exceptional opera, but that distinction is unshared by thousands of other small towns. Or, if your thesis argued that Japanese students in the United States were unimaginative writers, you would be generalizing hastily since you probably have not had contact with a large enough number of Japanese students to infer any sweeping truth about their writing.

Some generalizations may be accurately deduced from a single example, especially those based on experience or natural law. For example, one fall from a tree is enough to teach a true and accurate lesson about gravity. But to lose money in one transaction in the stock market does not make that institution a den of thieves. Everyone who falls from a tree is taught more or less the same lesson by nature. But not everyone who invests in the stock market has the same experience and learns the same lesson.

Part of growing up is to come to a painful awareness that personal experience, cherished as it may be to us, is not always the best doorway to truth. It is simply our personal experience. One man might hate dentists because he was roughly drilled by an unfeeling quack. But another may have had just the opposite experience, having spent serene moments in a dental chair listening to music and being afterwards told that he hasn't a single cavity in his mouth. Neither experience teaches anything universal about dentists.

Before you make such sweeping pronouncements as "All American cars are poorly engineered," "No woman can bear as much stress as a man," or "The best motion pictures are foreign made," ask yourself how you came to these opinions and what support you have for them. If it turns out that you once owned an American-made lemon, that you once were stuck in an elevator with a hysterical woman, that you once saw a wonderfully made foreign film, be mature enough to realize that your sampling is based entirely on personal experience that, while justifying your feelings, is insufficient to proclaim a truth.

Here are some examples of hasty generalizations, followed by acceptable revisions:

Original: All commencement speakers parrot the same old advice
about gaining society's respect, finding a fulfilling career, and living an altruistic life.

Revision: Some commencement speakers parrot the same old
advice about gaining society's respect, finding
fulfilling career, and living an altruistic life.

Some commencement speakers are plainly windbags who hurl about a good deal of mush and bombast at graduation ceremonies. But other speakers on these occasions have made eloquent and memorable speeches.

Original: Since no one can stem the tide of illegal drugs

flowing into this country, they might as well be

legalized for everybody.

Revision: Unless a way can be found soon to stem the tide of

illegal drugs flowing into this country, we might as

well opt to legalize them in order to control their

use.

The idea of legalizing drugs to control them at the source has been proposed by serious thinkers (the American writer Gore Vidal, for example, wrote a perceptive essay on that very subject). Advocating this view, however, is not the same as arguing for legalization of drugs because no one can stem their influx into the country (that smacks of specious negativism).

Original: Marriage is an unworkable institution in which two

people are trapped for life by humdrum convention

and boredom.

This is clearly a rash overstatement: all marriages are obviously not bad, nor would all married people consider themselves trapped by humdrum convention.

Revision: Although the divorce rate in America remains high,

marriage is an institution that has worked well for

some people who have worked hard at it.

Double check your evidence

An argument is very much like a teeter-totter on which two propositions sit. If the weight of evidence is preponderantly on one side over the other, the balance will tip in its favor, leaving the opposing side up in the air. In judging whether or not your assertion is based on strong evidence, ask yourself these basic questions.

What is the weight of the evidence?

The weight of evidence is its sheer quantity and preponderance. The evidence of ten eyewitnesses who positively identify a bank robber is weightier than the evidence of one person who claims the suspect was home at the time minding the baby. If virtually all medical experts regard a disease as having a certain cause, their opinion outweighs the contrary claims of two dissenting experts. The idea is not to practice a slavish adherence to popular thought, but to carefully sift and weigh the evidence.

That the majority is often wrong is, as a matter of fact, the paradox to be learned from history. But that is as it should be in a society which lives by the impartiality of evidence and marches progressively closer to the truth. For example, in earlier centuries a standard treatment for disease was to bleed the victim by making a small incision in a vein and suctioning off blood in a cup. The father of England's Queen Victoria was treated with this remedy for a fever, with some 120 fluid ounces of blood being drained from his shivering body during a 24-hour period. It is still unclear whether he died from his illness or his treatment. Fever was thought to be caused by an imbalance of "humors" in the blood, which the bleeding was believed to correct. Today, medical science knows better, and therapeutic bleeding is often cited in textbooks on medical history as an example of a misguided theory that did more harm than good. No doubt some of the medical beliefs of our own day will seem just as nonsensical and bizarre to a distant generation.

Nevertheless, in the light of present knowledge, a belief supported by the testimony of large numbers of experts is more convincing than one that enjoys little or no backing. While its value is always relative to what is known and accepted, evidence is still the best available support in a logical argument. A classic example of how the weight of evidence leads to a reliable conclusion can be found in the death of Josef Mengele, the notorious Nazi concentration camp doctor. It was only after all the evidence had been carefully weighed—the dental charts checked, the bone samples exhumed and compared with known injuries suffered by Mengele—that an official consensus was reached confirming his death.

What is the source of the evidence?

Whether in a court of law, a family dispute, or a written argument, the value of a source depends on its credibility. Quoting your Uncle Louis as supporting testimony for the belief that Uganda has an atomic arsenal and is planning to attack the United States will brand your argument as empty—unless, of course, your uncle is a big shot in the CIA. (Even so, one would wonder about an uncle who would leak such confidential information to a chatty relative.) Sources stand or fall on the world's judgment of their expertise, and making this judgment is part of the writer's job.

As a beginning writer, you may feel overawed by this task. Yet it is an exercise in free thinking you are called upon to do every day. If a shadowy figure beckons to you in a parking lot and offers to sell you a gold watch for $10, you are certain to pass internal judgment on the source before plunking down the money or walking away. (If you would buy a gold watch under such circumstances, we'd like to interest you in a good used bridge.) So much of the thinking that is required by logic is simply a more elaborate exercise of common sense.

The trick in citing expert opinion is to stay with impeccable sources, the ones roosting in the pages of major encyclopedias and enjoying tenure at such recognized institutions as Harvard, Johns Hopkins, M.I.T., or Yale. A glance at the various volumes of *Who's Who* will help you get a feel for what's what. Certainly, few instructors will question articles by experts printed in newspapers like the *New York Times*, the *Chicago Tribune*, and the *Christian Science Monitor*. Reasonable men and woman also give due honor and credit to evidence culled from established magazines such as *Time*, *Newsweek*, *National Geographic*, and the like.

What is the worth of the evidence itself?

Good evidence is timely, impartial, and relevant. Annual statistics about the number of criminals released from prison in 1975 no longer bear on our own time. The racial speculations and findings of a person known to be a committed racist must be held suspect. Statistics on newspaper reporting have little relevance in an argument directed against television news. Perhaps we are all not equally equipped to judge evidence for its timeliness, impartiality, and relevance, but most of us are at least equal to the task. Can you, for example, spot the flaws in the following assertions culled at random from various student papers?

Original: The shroud of Turin proves incontrovertibly that

Jesus was wrapped and buried in it.

No scientist worth his or her salt would attach "incontrovertibly" to this opinion. The shroud does indeed have a documented history going back to 1353, and it has been subjected to rigorous scientific analysis. But the weight of the evidence does not "incontrovertibly" prove it to have been Jesus's burial garment. Here is an acceptable version:

Revision: The shroud of Turin is unquestionably an important

Christian relic; however, before it can be fully

recognized as the burial cloth of Jesus, more

scientific evidence needs to be produced.

Original: Indians are the poorest people in our country: They

die early; they live in squalor; they have no work;

they go to their graves uneducated; and no one
cares.

As an argumentative thesis statement, this assertion could lead to a provocative essay. But now it is only an assertion, not evidence or proof. Here is the kind of evidence it would need:

Revision: According to Peter Collier, Walter Daniels, and
Edwin Embree, who have written widely on the plight
of the American Indian, the American Indian suffers
one of the most serious economic and cultural
deprivations of any minority in our country. His
average yearly income is $1,500, below the poverty
level. The Indian's average age at death is 44,
much lower than that of the national average, which
is 66. The median number of school years completed
by Indians is 8, and between 15 and 20 percent have
never been to school at all. About 70 percent of
Indian housing is substandard. A 50 percent
unemployment rate is not considered high. Yet, the
government has done very little to improve the
Indian's plight.

Original: An alarming health problem in our country is the
recent growth in numbers of pre-teen youths who have
taken to chewing tobacco and dipping snuff. If
parents would instruct their children in the
religious principles set forth in the Bible, where
it is clearly stated that man's body is the temple
of God, this terrible habit could be stopped. But
going to church and reading the Bible in order to
find a pure way of life is distasteful to many

```
parents, who themselves indulge in evil

habits. . . .
```

The evidence behind this assertion is based on moral belief not hardhearted facts and figures. Evidence based on belief is no evidence at all; it is merely belief. The revision correctly sticks to relevant evidence concerning health:

Revision: An alarming health problem in our country is the

recent growth in the number of pre-teen youths who

have taken to chewing tobacco and dipping snuff.

Although these youngsters claim that this smokeless

tobacco is healthier than smoking cigarettes,

doctors disagree vehemently, pointing out that in a

relatively short span of time chewing and dipping

can cause gums to recede, teeth to loosen, biting

surfaces to be worn off, and even cancer to appear.

Some users may well require gum grafts or radical

mouth surgery. Recent medical research by the

National Cancer Institute and the University of

North Carolina points to a direct link between oral

cancer and the use of smokeless tobacco.

Avoid non sequiturs

A **non sequitur** is an assertion or conclusion that does not logically follow from the statements preceding it. For example, here is a syllogism whose conclusion is a non sequitur:

> Large cars use a lot of gas.
> Harry Smith's car uses a lot of gas.
> Therefore, Harry Smith's car must be large.

That Harry's car must be large because it uses a lot of gas is not necessarily true. Instead, it could be a *small* sports car with an engine designed for speed and performance rather than economy. This fallacy, elegantly known to logicians as "the undistributed middle term," fails to account for exceptions. A more valid version follows:

Large cars use a lot of gas.
Harry Smith's car is large.
Therefore, Harry Smith's car must use a lot of gas.

The premise of this syllogism says that if a car is large, it uses a lot of gas. That Harry Smith's car is large is admitted in the second statement. It therefore logically follows that Harry Smith's car must use a lot of gas. On the face of it, this is all very logical. But only on the face of it; for the assertion made by the premise of a syllogism could be dubious or untrue. Here is an example:

Blonds have more fun.
So-and-so is a blond.
Therefore so-and-so has more fun.

This nonsense has a logically intact look to it if we take its initial premise to be true. But is it necessarily true that blonds have more fun? In the whole world, are there no blonds who are also chronic, joyless grumps? Even if you have never met a blond sourpuss, common sense should tell you that some must exist and that having fun can bear no logical relationship to the color of one's hair. Logical propositions, even if accurately reasoned, are valid only when they are founded on assertions of truth.

Another kind of non sequitur is the **post hoc ergo propter hoc** fallacy—from the Latin meaning "after this therefore because of this." It occurs when precedence and causation are confused, with an earlier occurrence being mistaken as the cause of a later one. For example, we once saw a man angrily shoo his wife away from a blackjack table in a Las Vegas casino because he started to lose after she arrived. (He continued to lose at an even greater pace when she left, which made us wonder why he didn't stem the tide by bringing her back.) A man walks under a ladder and shortly afterwards suffers an accident, so walking under ladders is assumed to be the accident's cause.

Many medieval fears and superstitions were often founded on post hoc fallacies. A certain planetary conjunction immediately preceding the bubonic plague was taken as its cause. Much later, microbes were found to be the carriers. Ringworm was treated by washing the scalp with a boy's urine, gout by applying a plaster of goat dung mixed with rosemary and honey. Both remedies were probably based on rumors about the recovery of some fortunate soul on whom they were applied, but who would have gotten better anyway.

Here is a typical post hoc fallacy, followed by a revision for improved logic:

Original: Ever since Mayor Bryan was elected, the traffic

situation in Boom City has become intolerable. We

>   must get rid of the mayor before it is no longer
>   possible to drive in our city.

Revision: Ever since Mayor Bryan was elected, a new influx of
>   industry and people has caused an enormous increase
>   in traffic snarls and accidents. However, the mayor
>   does not seem willing to deal with the problem;
>   therefore, he should be replaced.

The second version makes the mayor answerable for the heavy traffic, not
its cause.

Faulty condition is another common fallacy of the non sequitur
variety. This fallacy is based on an erroneous "if this, then that" equation.
Here is an example:

Original: If students are allowed to question their teachers'
>   lectures or assignments, soon the whole educational
>   system will come under the rule of immature and
>   capricious students.

Revision: While students should be encouraged to ask questions
>   about their teachers' lectures or assignments, those
>   in charge of school administration cannot
>   uncritically accept all student judgments about
>   teachers since these judgments are often immature
>   and capricious.

It is a faulty condition to assume that the rule of immature and capricious
students must automatically result if students are allowed to question their
teachers' lectures and assignments. The revision more reasonably sees this
questioning as useful if done in the right spirit.

Closely related to the faulty condition is the fallacy of the **faulty
alternative**, which stews an issue down to two simplistic and equally in-
edible alternatives. To insist, for example, that a person is either against
abortion or a supporter of murder is to exclude those who regard life as
precious but approve of abortions under extenuating conditions. To argue
that recruits join the police force because they are either sadistic or have an
inferiority complex is to ignore the attractions of adventure and good pay.
Here is an example of an either/or argument:

Original: Either our government must legislate socialized medicine, or Americans by the millions will die of serious illnesses because they cannot afford hospitalization and doctor's care.

Revision: Because of the soaring costs in medical care, it is time for the government to make it possible for all U.S. citizens to have some form of low-cost compulsory insurance, such as Kaiser, Ross-Loos, or a similar form of health maintenance organization.

"Sink or swim" is the motto of those who see issues as divisible into only two alternatives. Generally, it is more prudent to clamber onto the high middle ground rather than to take the plunge with them.

Finally, there is the non sequitur of circular reasoning, also known as "begging the question." This argument "begs" the reader or listener to accept a debatable assumption as if it were already proved or disproved. This is the classic exchange of circular reasoning:

> The Bible is the word of God.
> How do you know this?
> Because the Bible says so.

In effect, this proposition asserts that "the Bible is the word of God because the Bible is the word of God." To write, "Everyone knows that prison reform is a big waste of taxpayers' money," is to beg that question, which everyone does not know. Here is another example of circular reasoning:

Original: Prostitution should be legalized because both men and women have strong sexual drives which they are now forced to unlawfully satisfy through contacts with prostitutes.

Revision: Legalization of prostitution has been undertaken in some states, for example, Nevada, with none of the consequences of moral doom and wholesale promiscuity that opponents have claimed were bound to occur.

The original argument states that prostitution should be legalized because otherwise people will break the law against prostitution.

Avoid irrelevancies

An irrelevance is any assertion or allegation that has no bearing on the issue in dispute and therefore does not belong in the argument. The **ad hominem** argument (Latin, "against the man"), which directs its venom at the character of an opponent rather than at the opponent's ideas, is the most common example. For instance, to mention that the sponsor of a mass transit bill you are against is a three-time divorcee is to engage in an ad hominem argument. Here is another example:

Original:

> Some unthinking people applaud Richard Nixon's
> foreign policy, placing a veneer on his
> diplomatic efforts in China. They claim that he
> made inroads into a renewed friendship between
> the United States and the regime of Mao Tse-tung
> by using extreme tact in upholding our American
> democracy with its attendant capitalistic system
> while also praising China for its advances in
> literacy and help for its starving millions.
> But isn't it the height of hypocrisy to engage
> in hero worship of a man who created the
> greatest governmental scandal since Teapot Dome?
> Nixon's memoirs should be taken off the shelves
> of bookstores because a President who committed
> the crimes that Nixon did should not be given
> credit for advancing a creative foreign policy.

This argument is directed against Nixon the man, not Nixon the maker of foreign policy. Here is a possible revision of the passage:

Revision:

> During his term as U.S. President, Richard Nixon
> administered a strong foreign policy, beginning
> the phased withdrawal of U.S. troops from South
> Vietnam, achieving a cease-fire accord with
> North Vietnam, and initiating strategic arms
> limitation talks with the Soviet Union.
> However, his greatest achievement in foreign
> policy came as a result of his 1972 visit to the
> People's Republic of China, where he effected a
> change in the chilled relationship between
> Chinese and Americans by talking with Mao Tse-
> tung personally and promising to have cultural
> and economic exchanges with China but not to
> interfere in its internal politics.

Another fallacy of irrelevance is the **ad populum** argument, which appeals to prejudices, slogans, and cliches beloved by the populace. The debater's views are therefore stroked with the brush of "Mom," "flag," and "apple pie," while the opposition's are tarred with "Communism," "dictatorship," and "bureaucratic red tape." Since every country has its stock of favorite virtues, ad populum arguments are appeals of cultural relativism. "Communism" carries the same diseased association in our culture that "capitalism" must have in the Soviet Union. Here is a typical ad populum argument:

Original:

> Recently the papers have been filled with
> editorials promoting the idea of clearing up the
> slum area of our city and building brand-new
> facilities for the poor. Who would bear the
> gigantic financial burden of this project? The

faithful middle class, who always end up paying

for the extravagant ideas wild-eyed liberals

think up. This particular brainstorm is

especially odious because the health and welfare

types whom these new buildings would house are

irresponsible and dedicated to the perpetuation

of crime. They will not maintain the new

buildings properly and thus more and more money

will be drained from law-abiding citizens, who

are already carrying an excessive tax burden.

Our wonderful democratic system is based on

individual responsibility, not socialistic

reform. In the days of our pilgrim fathers

every American was on his own. Big Brother was

not responsible for him. Let's keep it that

way.

Hidden in this murky ad populum argument is the issue of whether or not the redevelopment of slum areas is good or bad. The writer's side on the issue is propped up by such righteous pillars as "faithful middle class," "law-abiding citizens," "individual responsibility," "our pilgrim fathers," "every American on his own." The opposition is gored with negative epithets such as "wild-eyed liberals," "welfare types," "irresponsible," and "dedicated to the perpetuation of crime."

Revision:

Our city council is debating the possibility of

redeveloping the downtown slum area in order to

build adequate housing for people with low

incomes. While the project appears an excellent

one on the surface, certain admonitions are in

order. First, we must make sure that all

residents of this tax—supported project are
truly needy and not just taking advantage of a
handout. Second, we must establish a system of
rewards that will motivate residents to maintain
the buildings and keep them from deteriorating
into the kind of slum they became in the first
place. Finally, since the area in question has
always had a high crime rate, the police
department should organize a workable district
watch program in order to assure a safe new
neighborhood.

In the fallacy of the **red herring**, a writer or speaker introduces a luridly emotional side issue to disguise the weakness of an argument. The term comes from a ruse practiced by escaping prisoners who dragged a bleeding fish across their trail to confuse tracking bloodhounds. Many arguments on controversial issues of our day often use the red herring to disguise the trail of evidence and truth. Here is an argument containing a red herring:

Original:

The unisex clothing fashion that has been
occasionally proposed by designers is an
international attack on the nuclear family.
Traditionally, father and mother dressed
differently, were brought up differently, and
were expected to perform different roles in the
family setting. Father was supposed to go out
into the world and earn a living for his family,
while mother was expected to stay home and take
care of their children. Now comes unisex
clothing which many international designers are

```
pushing on the American public.  The fashion has
not yet caught on, but when and if it does, it
will drive a stake through the heart of the
American family.  Father and mother will not
only look alike, eventually they will become
alike. The role separation on which all families
are based will dim and then disappear.  And so
will the family.
```

Common sense tells us that fashion designers are motivated not by hatred of the family, but by a desire for profit and popular acceptance of their styles. In any event, clothes do not the person make, and it is rash to assume that the differences between the sexes must automatically vanish if they dress alike. It is also untrue that the structure of the family must be ruined if its traditional male and female roles are in any way modified. In many families today, the wife is the breadwinner while the husband is the homemaker. (One popular newspaper cartoon, *Adam*, depicts exactly that situation.) The red herring nature of this argument was pointed out to the student, who was asked to recast the paragraph's opposition to unisex clothing in more reasonable terms. In the revision, the student took a more humorous approach:

Revision:

```
Unisex clothing is sexless ugliness. Rather than
highlight the endearing differences that exist
between the sexes, this style covers them both
in the same burlap sack.  The physique of the
male, the figure of the female, are hidden under
baggy cloth.  Femininity is smothered, and so is
masculinity.  One would think that the style was
designed for an organism like the amoeba that
reproduces by fission.  But our species and its
reproductive existence depends on attraction
```

between the sexes. The female cannot go into a
hospital and split herself into two halves, nor
can the male. Thank goodness that the unisex
clothing fashion has not caught on, for what it
could do to our species not even Darwin himself
could have anticipated.

Note that it is a legitimate ploy to make a measured emotional appeal in an argument. Here, for example, is an emotional appeal used in an essay arguing for stronger air pollution laws. The student has already made a stirring factual and statistical argument for stronger mandatory control on automobile emissions. Now she winds up her paper with an emotional appeal:

There is a condition in Los Angeles known as
the "School Smog Alert." When the ozone
concentration is high enough, this alert is
issued by the public health authorities, and
schools are asked to keep children in the
classrooms and away from the playgrounds. The
oxygen they need to breathe and play is poisoned
by ozone, carbon monoxide, and traces of
cyanide. At this level of alert, older people
are warned to remain indoors and not to exert
themselves. Age has already made their lungs
liable to disease, but now the air itself has
become an enemy that would further weaken, and
even kill. The healthful oxygen they need for
life has already been inhaled by automobiles and
exhaled back into the atmosphere as poisons. Is
this the sort of world we want to live in? And

> is the convenience of family automobiles worth
>
> the bad air we suffer? On sober thought, most
>
> of us would have to say it is not.

Although such appeals can be moving if they are carefully used, they cannot entirely replace evidence, testimonial opinion, and hardheaded reasoning.

Finally, there is the irrelevance of **faulty analogy**, which asserts a false resemblance between two situations and then draws a conclusion from it. Instead of addressing real issues, the faulty analogy fusses over bogus metaphors. For example, here is a student's view of the lot of the American farmer: "The American farmers are like the Jews of Hitler's World War II concentration camps: they are mistreated, neglected, and left to survive on their own." This analogy is laughably farfetched. Hitler set out to systematically exterminate the Jews. No administration, however uncompromising its attitude toward farm subsidies, would even think of exterminating farmers. Analogies are useful in making complex issues understandable, but they seldom prove anything. Here is an argumentative statement based on a faulty analogy, followed by an improved revision:

Original:

> Teaching sex education in the high schools is
>
> like teaching a terrorist how to use explosives.
>
> Teenagers do not have self-control to prevent
>
> them from getting into trouble. Giving them the
>
> techniques for having sex will not make things
>
> better, but worse. What they need to learn is
>
> the moral discipline and restraint, and these
>
> cannot be taught or learned from a manual or
>
> textbook on sexual practices. Yet everywhere we
>
> hear that more education is the answer. This is
>
> like saying, "Give the terrorist a bigger gun.
>
> Teach the terrorist how to use the A-bomb." It
>
> used to be said that ignorance is bliss. This
>
> remains true when it comes to high school
>
> teenagers and sex.

Enough absolute differences exist between teenagers and terrorists to make this analogy ludicrously inapplicable. Note that what is wrong with this argument is not the stand it takes on sex education, but the farfetched analogy it uses to make it. The student was asked to recast the argument without resorting to the false analogy:

Revision:

Teaching sex education in the high schools is a wrong idea because it seems to show the approval of society for sexual experimentation among teenagers. Teenagers do not have the self-control to prevent them from getting into trouble over sexual matters. Teaching them the techniques for having sex and practicing birth control will not make things better, but worse. What they need to learn is moral discipline and restraint, and these cannot be taught or learned from a manual or textbook on sexual practices. Yet everywhere we hear that more sex education is the answer because teenagers will experiment anyway. That may be true, but it may also be untrue. Some experiments will occur among teenagers, no matter how little or much they know about sex. But more sophisticated experiments are going to occur among teenagers who are taught sexual techniques without at the same time being taught moral restraint.

Whether or not you agree with this, it is now plainly a more reasoned and logical opposition than before.

To sum up, what distinguishes the logical writer from the illogical one is not the presence or absence of belief, but the grounds on which belief is based. Stick to the issue, play fair with the evidence, explain your reasoning, avoid hysterical appeals, and your own writing will be distinguished by its logic.

The following brief student argument contains some logical fallacies. Study the essay, along with the editor's marginal comments. Then notice how the rewritten version corrects the fallacies.

Original:

Next to sleeping, the typical American child
spends most of his time watching television. Of
course, all of the major networks proclaim that
television can instruct these children in
amusing and captivating ways that parents and
teachers cannot. On the battlefield of
television ratings, where viewing points are the
bullets used to kill the enemy competitor,
children function as important hostages.
Programs like <u>Sesame Street</u> or <u>Mr. Wizard</u> seem
to bear out the contention that all knowledge
becomes delectably fascinating when proffered
via the boob tube. Indeed, viewed
superficially, persuasive reasons exist for
encouraging children to broaden their
intellectual and emotional horizons by watching
television. Nevertheless, subtle signals alert
us to a greater truth: Far from broadening
children emotionally or intellectually,
television contributes to their mental and
social stagnation. Here are some proofs:

First, children who watch television do not
read. The reason they do not is obvious: It is
easy to sit in mesmerized passivity while a

steady dose of cartoons, movies, or live
dramatizations bombard the child's psyche.
Watching the Pink Panther or Mickey Mouse escape
the conniving enemy by diving off a cliff or
leaping across mountain tops with aerial magic
is far less strenuous than trying to read a
child's edition of Greek mythology or American
history. Watching a program about Tarzan
swinging from tree to tree above the flora and
fauna of a phony T.V. jungle certainly
titillates the emotions of a child more than
does visiting a museum and reading the
inscriptions describing endangered animal
species in their natural habitats. But the
romance of watching television will not help the
child to become an accomplished student. In
fact, it will probably have the opposite effect   *Evidence*
of slowing down his reading skills by blunting   *needed*
intellectual curiosity and preempting the   *for*
precious time needed to develop proper reading   *this*
skills at an age when these skills are the   *assertion.*
easiest to acquire.

Second, children who watch television do
not interact socially. A child sitting cross-
legged on the carpet, munching from a bag of
chocolate chip cookies while following the
vicissitudes of Charles and Caroline Ingalls in
some episode from <u>Little House on the Prairie</u>,
is not going to want to play with little brother

or answer Dad's humdrum queries about school.
Why bother with a lackluster real family life
when one can be involved with the fictional
Ingalls, who have just discovered that an
unethical tycoon is taking over the town of
Walnut Grove? Here is the excitement of a
romanticized farm life and the glamour of youth
combatting evil powers to achieve heroism. Some
children become so entranced with television
that if a parent dares call them away from the
screen, they stage temper tantrums. Children
who no longer want to interact with family
become isolated and estranged. Families whose
main source of recreation is watching television
don't really know each other well because they
have forfeited the chance to share each other's
hearts and minds. Later on, this same kind of
isolation and estrangement can cause the adult
to suffer serious problems in relating to
colleagues and to friends. He may actually
become a social outcast. How can a child who
has spent so much time silently staring at a
T.V. screen grow into a man or woman capable of
holding an interesting conversation with a
friend or colleague? A child who watches
television is like a heroin addict. All he cares
about is his next fix. He withdraws from the
world around him and merely exists in his foggy
world of fantasies, adventures, and escapades,

evidence needed

faulty analogy between T.V. and heroin addiction

accompanied by appropriate background music.

Last, children who watch television develop a distorted view of reality. Even though this medium has the uncanny ability to catch life in crucial moments of truth, such as Robert Kennedy's 1968 assassination in the rear exit of the Ambassador Hotel in Los Angeles, it ignores truth for the most part in favor of the sensational, the romantic, or the occult. Most programs children watch teach them totally false ethical values. They may grow up believing that violence is an acceptable means for social reform or that sex is the way to personal happiness. After all, the A-Team's Mr. T becomes a hero by knocking people unconscious or by machine-gunning storefronts and factories. If violence works for him, why not for the average person? The most successful cops on Hill Street Blues are constantly seen dallying in bed with incomparably sensual sex goddesses. Erotomania seems the agenda for all their evenings. Surely a young boy watching this series will be tempted to judge the good life as one in which lust plays a leading role. A little girl who is allowed to watch Charlie's Angels may grow up believing that only women who combine perfect figures with lovely faces and brilliant minds will attract fame, fortune, and happiness. After all, everyone knows that as

ad populum argument

the twig is bent, so the tree grows. In one way
or another, most T.V. programs typically watched
by children give a slanted, biased view of life.
Additionally, many top actors and actresses lead
utterly debauched personal lives. Celebrities
like Stacy Keach, John Belushi, and Madonna—
reputed either to be on drugs, to promote
pornography, or generally to live (and, in the
case of Belushi, die) in the fast lane—should
never be allowed to appear on television, where
minors can see them and use them as role models.

ad hominem attack

Television is a double-edged sword in that
it is capable of influencing the young for bad
as well as for good. And although staring at
the tube seems far more mentally stimulating
than sleeping, there are times when for children
a nap would be better than watching T.V.

Revision:

Next to sleeping, the typical American
child spends most of his time watching
television. Of course, all of the major
networks proclaim that television can instruct
these children in amusing and captivating ways
that parents and teachers cannot. On the
battlefield of television ratings, where viewing
points are the bullets used to kill the enemy
competitor, children function as important
hostages. Programs like <u>Sesame Street</u> or <u>Mr.</u>

<u>Wizard</u> seem to bear out the contention that all
knowledge becomes delectably fascinating when
proffered via the boob tube. Indeed, viewed
superficially, persuasive reasons exist for
encouraging children to broaden their
intellectual and emotional horizons by watching
television. Nevertheless, subtle signals alert
us to a greater truth: Far from broadening
children emotionally or intellectually,
television contributes to their mental and
social stagnation. Here are some proofs:

First, children who watch television do not
read. The reason they do not is obvious: It is
easy to sit in mesmerized passivity while a
steady dose of cartoons, movies, or live
dramatizations bombard the child's psyche.
Watching the Pink Panther or Mickey Mouse escape
the conniving enemy by diving off a cliff or
leaping across mountain tops with aerial magic
is far less strenuous than trying to read a
child's edition of Greek mythology or American
history. Watching a program about Tarzan
swinging from tree to tree above the flora and
fauna of a phony T.V. jungle certainly
titillates the emotions of a child more than
does visiting a museum and reading the
inscriptions describing endangered animal
species in their natural habitats. But the
romance of watching television will not help the

child to become an accomplished student. In
fact, it will have the opposite effect of
slowing down his reading skills by blunting
intellectual curiosity and preempting the
precious time needed to develop proper reading
skills at an age when these skills are the
easiest to acquire. "A Nation at Risk," the
significant report presented to Ronald Reagan
and the Secretary of Education in 1981 by a
special task force appointed by the President to
analyze trends in education, is an alarming
analysis of how the ability to read has declined
since television came to dominate children's
lives. The report states that 13 percent of all
17-year-olds in the United States are
functionally illiterate. Functional illiteracy
among minority youths may be as high as 40
percent. Since 1960, when watching television
became the national pastime, there has been an
unbroken decline in the average verbal scores of
students trying to enter college. The report
indicates that many teenagers do not possess the
"higher order" intellectual skills expected of
them. Nearly 40 percent cannot draw inferences
from written material; only one-fifth can write
a persuasive essay. In short, learning to
become educated is a difficult, demanding
enterprise for which television viewing does not
prepare children.

Second, children who watch television do
not interact socially. A child sitting cross-
legged on the carpet, munching from a bag of
chocolate chip cookies while following the
vicissitudes of Charles and Caroline Ingalls in
some episode from Little House on the Prairie,
is not going to want to play with little brother
or answer Dad's humdrum queries about school.
Why bother with a lackluster real family life
when one can be involved with the fictional
Ingalls, who have just discovered that an
unethical tycoon is taking over the town of
Walnut Grove? Here is the excitement of a
romanticized farm life and the glamour of youth
combatting evil powers to achieve heroism. Some
children become so entranced with television
that if a parent dares call them away from the
screen, they stage temper tantrums. Children
who no longer want to interact with family
become isolated and estranged. Families whose
main source of recreation is watching television
don't really know each other well because they
have forfeited the chance to share each other's
hearts and minds. The Pulitzer Prize-winning
author, Daniel Boorstin, warns against the
"segregation from one another" caused by too
much television. He points to the fact that
with "more and more two-T.V. families, a member
of the family can actually withdraw and watch in

complete privacy," thus breaking all ties with
other people. How can a child who has spent so
much time silently staring at a T.V. screen grow
into a man or woman capable of holding an
interesting conversation with a friend or
colleague? A child addicted to watching T.V.
runs the risk of becoming a social misfit.

Last, children who watch television develop
a distorted view of reality. Even though this
medium has the uncanny ability to catch life in
crucial moments of truth, such as Robert
Kennedy's 1968 assassination in the rear exit of
the Ambassador Hotel in Los Angeles, it ignores
truth for the most part in favor of the
sensational, the romantic, or the occult. Most
programs children watch teach them totally false
ethical values. They may grow up believing that
violence is an acceptable means for social
reform or that sex is the way to personal
happiness. After all, the A-Team's Mr. T
becomes a hero by knocking people unconscious or
by machine-gunning storefronts and factories.
If violence works for him, why not for the
average person? The most successful cops on
Hill Street Blues are constantly seen dallying
in bed with incomparably sensual sex goddesses.
Erotomania seems the agenda for all their
evenings. Surely a young boy watching this
series will be tempted to judge the good life as

one in which lust plays a leading role. A
little girl who is allowed to watch Charlie's
Angels may grow up believing that only women who
combine perfect figures with lovely faces and
brilliant minds will attract fame, fortune, and
happiness. In one way or another, most T.V.
programs typically watched by children give a
slanted, biased view of life. As Daniel
Boorstin comments, "A new miasma—which no
machine before could emit—enshrouds the world
of T.V. We begin to be so accustomed to this
foggy world, so at home and solaced and
comforted within and by its blurry edges, that
reality itself becomes slightly irritating."

        Television is a double-edged sword in that
it is capable of influencing the young for bad
as well as for good. And although staring at
the tube seems far more mentally stimulating
than sleeping, there are times when for children
a nap would be better than watching T.V.

The revision has added the weight of evidence by quoting an important study and an authority on the influence of television on the lives of children. It has deleted the faulty analogy, the ad populum saying, and the ad hominem attack, replacing these with more measured commentary.

Exercises

1. Find and correct the logical fallacy in each of the following assertions:

a. The most feared disease of our time is cancer. It is a known truth that a Pollyanna personality can prevent, postpone, and cure cancer. Most psychiatrists agree that there is a strong connection between the mind and the body.

b. Benjamin Franklin once wrote that executive officers in the federal government should not be salaried lest profit and avarice become motivations for serving in government posts. What was true of Franklin's day is still true today. If only the wealthy would become senators, representatives of congress, or heads of departments, they would not be tempted to make decisions based on bribes and other temptations.

c. Old people become crotchety and selfish. Mr. Smith, the city councilman, is a terrible grouch and refuses to spend money to improve the city. It is obvious that Mr. Smith is getting old.

d. Enacting stringent teenage curfew laws will reduce juvenile crime because it provides the steps to make teenagers more law abiding.

e. There is no such creature as a juvenile criminal. As Judge Tom Clark pointed out long ago, "Every boy in his heart would rather steal second base than a car." Juveniles are capable of continuous moral improvement.

f. If we are not vigilant, the computer will force teachers out of business the way the car forced horses and mules out of business.

g. What does it matter whether or not import tariffs are economically sound? Willis Hawley, one of the original senators who sponsored the Tariff Act, was in league with labor bosses and was therefore beholden to organized crime.

Writing Assignments

1. Choose a thesis from the list on pages 45–46. Create an outline using one of the organizing patterns taught in this chapter and write an essay based on it.

2. Organize the following facts into a logical outline. If necessary, delete or add appropriate heads. Write an essay of 300–500 words based on the outline:

> Multiple-choice examinations have replaced the essay.
> Students no longer have to think.
> Homemakers no longer use creativity in housework.
> Students use calculators for simple arithmetical problems.
> Precooked or frozen food has replaced food made from scratch.
> High technology is keeping people from using creative mindpower.
> To drive a car, you just put the gear level in "drive."
> Factory workers have become like robots.
> Robots have replaced factory workers.

3. Write an essay of 300–500 words using appropriate evidence on one of the following topics:

a. Fantasies are good for one's mental health.
b. The space program has given us many useful technological spin-offs.
c. Funeral rites and customs are a rip-off for most consumers.
d. Preservatives in food serve a useful function.

4. Write an essay analyzing the logic (or lack of it) in many popular television commercials.

5. Write an essay on residential indoor air pollution.

PART TWO

Writing and Rewriting Paragraphs

Chapter Four

The Paragraph: Structure and Rhetorical Pattern

A sentence should contain no unnecessary words, a paragraph no unnecessary sentences, for the same reason that a drawing should contain no unnecessary lines and a machine no unnecessary parts.

WILLIAM STRUNK, JR. (1869–1946)

The paragraph may be a nearly universal convention of writing, but it is still subject to a wide range of inconsistent practices. Most newspapers and popular magazines use short paragraphs whereas scholarly journals and serious books use long ones. Moreover, many writers seem to paragraph for capricious reasons—to change topics, to move the discussion to a different angle, to make a transition between ideas, to shift rhythm, or even to alter emphasis. Logic dictates many of these usages, but their practice is largely based on personal style.

Given the arbitrary customs to which they are subject, it is no wonder that beginning writers are often bewildered by paragraphs. So we will begin by saying what a paragraph is not.

A paragraph is not a chunk of words randomly framed into a rectangular segment. It is not on the page mainly to relieve the monotony of a compact block of print. It is not merely an ornamental form to which all prose writing must adapt.

Primarily, the paragraph is a division of thought, a subtopic of your subject, one room in the house of your essay. The foundations of your paragraphs are laid when you break the subject into a series of smaller topics, which you will do as you map out your essay's structure. (See Chapter 3 for more on doing this.) If you paragraph badly, you are most likely failing to perceive the presence of the big subject among the fragments of smaller topics.

Parts of the Paragraph

In its simplest formulation, a paragraph consists of a topic sentence that makes a general assertion and of supporting details that prove it. The topic sentence is usually but not necessarily the first sentence of the paragraph. Sometimes it is the last sentence, and sometimes it is not even stated but merely understood.

In any case, the topic sentence should contain some discussable issue or assertion. It should not be the plain statement of a dead-end fact, such as "My eyes are blue," or you will leave yourself with nothing further to say. (A seasoned and clever writer may indeed write a paragraph on such a skimpy sentence, but it is tricky and difficult to do.) Instead, the topic sentence should contain some idea or proposition in need of support or proof as, for example, "I have always wanted to have blue eyes." Picture your reader as an impudent doubting Thomas who challenges your every topic sentence with, "Oh, yeah? Prove it!" or, "Oh, yeah? Show me!" If you have nothing to show or prove in your topic sentence then you have nothing to write a paragraph about.

The second part of a paragraph consists of its supporting details—those facts, data, evidence, testimony, and opinions that prove the assertion made by the topic sentence and satisfy your doubting reader. What you include here will depend on the topic sentence. For example, if your topic sentence was "No time of the day is more serene and lovely in the tropics than sunset" (Oh, yeah? Show me!), you must pack your paragraph with details of serenity and loveliness found in a tropical sunset. On the other hand, if your topic sentence was "My Aunt Agatha was an unconscionable witch who plagued me throughout my childhood" (Oh, yeah? Prove it!), your details must show her in the act of cackling and tormenting you.

In diagram form, Figure 4–1 shows the structure of a typical paragraph. And Figure 4–2 illustrates our conception of the essay as a building—we have in mind a Grecian temple. As you can see, its roof is the thesis statement, supported by load-bearing columns of paragraphs. The capital of the column is the topic sentence with the specific details making up the shaft. Admittedly, this is a static representation, but it gets across the idea: namely, that all of your paragraphs must support the thesis statement.

Figure 4–1   The Structure of a Typical Paragraph

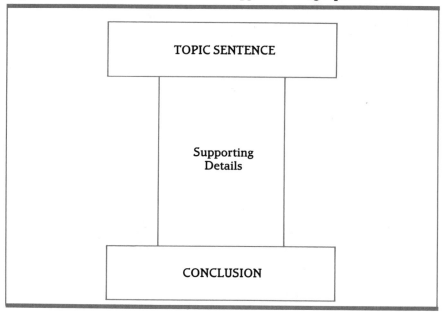

Figure 4–2   The Essay as a Building

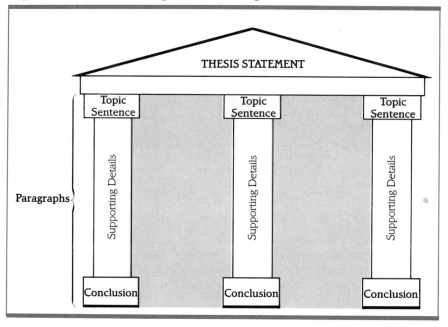

In addition to having the principal parts of a topic sentence and supporting details, paragraphs are also subject to two universal conventions of style: unity and coherence.

Writing Unified Paragraphs

The principle of writing unified paragraphs is a simple one. Plainly put, it says, stick to the point. Don't introduce irrelevant issues or details that have no bearing on your topic sentence. Here is an example of a paragraph that has unity:

A good example of this disguising of the female figure is the unique ruff of the Elizabethan era. In those days women were not satisfied with the necks created for them by God, so they began to wear the ruff. The ruff is an immense collar with ruffle piled on ruffle, starched and wired, to give the famous strangulating effect much sought after by women at court. A woman appeared to be stretching her neck like a ruffled ostrich. (These "neck braces" would have served well for whiplash had whiplash been popular then.) When looking at pictures of an Elizabethan woman wearing a ruff, one finds it easy to imagine her head being detached from her body and remaining with the collar when it is taken off at night.

On the other hand, here is a paragraph that lacks unity.

Another example of women's desire to disguise their natural appearance is the

<u>Victorian bustle</u>. Apparently Victorian women disagreed with God's construction of their rumps, so they took the Elizabethan barrel, cut it in half, and attached it to their backsides. This contraption was called the bustle, a wire cage shaped like a big bump and worn under the back of the dress. No prehistoric monster was shaped any funnier. A bustle could be as much as a foot deep, giving the wearer the silhouette of an "h." A woman wearing a bustle looked as if some little prankster were hovering under her skirt. <u>The bustle, as bizarre as it may seem, does not win the prize for the most absurd fashion. This honor belongs to the leg-o'-mutton sleeve. The sleeve was tight from the wrist to the elbow, but from the elbow on it looked like a gigantic balloon waiting to be popped. Although a leg of mutton would look flattering on most sheep, the same could not be said of the Victorian women wearing it</u>.

The last four underlined sentences break the unity of the paragraph by straying to a discussion of the "leg-o'-mutton sleeve," an irrelevance not required by the topic sentence. These details should either be dropped or the topic sentence reworded to predict them: "Further examples of women's desire to change their natural appearance are the Victorian bustle and leg-o'-mutton sleeve."

Paragraphs written with unity are more believable than those without it for the same reason that the speaker who sticks to the point is more believable than the one who doesn't. The writer whose mastery of a topic is artfully demonstrated in focused paragraphs tends to be convincing. The one who cannot make a point and stick to it tends to be boring.

Writing Coherent Paragraphs

In Chapter 3, we discussed coherence as a characteristic of a well-written essay. There we said that an incoherent essay is one whose sentences do not follow logically. Put another way, the coherent paragraph is one that makes sense; the incoherent one does not. Here is an example of a coherent paragraph:

(1) The term klutz has its origin in the Yiddish term klots, and is applied to males and females alike as an insult or reproach. (2) Basically, a klutz is someone who cannot get from here to there without a mishap occurring—without stumbling, tripping, or falling. (3) For example, the klutz is the outfielder who drops the lazy fly ball that soars overhead in a perfect arc on a clear, cloudless day. (4) The klutz has room to park but nevertheless runs into the curb, bumps into the trash can, or bangs into another car. (5) The klutz handles your prized Chinese vase only once, and then shatters it on the edge of the hearth. (6) Fathers don't want their sons to be klutzes; wives don't want their husbands to be klutzes; daughters don't want their mothers to be klutzes. (7) Klutziness is devoutly to be avoided.

In a coherent paragraph, the thread of a common idea runs between the sentences, with each one adding further to the overall meaning. The incoherent paragraph, on the other hand, is one whose sentences seem a jumble on the page. Here is an example:

Owning a home is far more satisfying than renting a place. The homeowner knows the joy and pride that accompany all the loving labor of being a conscientious homeowner. Owners can make wonderfully constructive changes to improve their properties. They can move walls, tile roofs, paint or wallpaper rooms, and even turn a spiritless square bungalow into a charming Italian villa. Expensive remodeling by renters is out of the question since all money expended brings no returns except to the landlord. Most renters leave their living quarters just the way they found them when they moved in. Homeowners experience a feeling of deep satisfaction each time they make their mortgage payments because they know that they are inching a little closer to the time when they will own their homes outright. The dream of holding the deed to a home makes working worthwhile. Each month hundreds or even thousands of dollars go into rent. The cancelled check among the stack received from the bank is the only reward. The dreary thought that next month another hunk of money will disappear with nothing to show for it plagues all renters. Every April, when income tax is due, homeowners realize a decided financial boon because all interest payments are tax deductible. Renters can claim no such advantage. Whatever money has been poured into

```
rent, disappears forever into the pockets of the

landlords, who can then claim the huge tax

benefit.
```

How can you write in coherent paragraphs? First, fulfill the promise made in your topic sentence. Follow this advice faithfully and your sentences will be held together by their focus on a common idea. Second, use the following techniques for mechanically linking sentences into a coherent whole.

1. Repeat key words or their synonyms and pronouns. These intermittently remind the reader what the paragraph is about.
2. Use transitions to keep the ideas flowing smoothly.
3. Use parallel structures to create a sense of rhythm and harmony.

All these techniques are used in the paragraph on the klutz. The term *klutz* is frequently repeated to hold the focus of the paragraph. *Basically* is used as a transition to introduce the definition of a klutz. "For example," the transition used at the start of sentence 3, tells the reader that the term *klutz* is about to be exemplified. To create a sense of rhythm and flow, sentences 4 and 5 open with parallel phrases, while sentence 6 consists of parallel structures.

Of the three techniques, modern writers are more apt to use mechanical transitions and repeated key terms over parallelism, a proportion which holds true in our own writing. Parallelism is a nice occasional touch, but it confers an air of ceremonial formality to writing. If you cannot think of appropriate transitions to use, consider the following options:

1. When an example is to follow:
   as an illustration, for instance, for example, in other words, specifically, that is
2. When a comparison is to follow:
   in comparison, likewise, similarly, also, as
3. When a contrast is to follow:
   in contrast, yet, but, although, however, nevertheless, on the contrary, on the other hand, otherwise
4. When an additional comment is to follow:
   furthermore, further, then, besides, also, and, first, second, next, last, moreover, and then, yet another
5. When a result is to follow:
   therefore, as a consequence, consequently, as a result, accordingly, then
6. When a concession is to be granted:
   admittedly, granted that, naturally, of course, one must admit, after all

7. When a summary is to follow:
   finally, all in all, on the whole, last, in conclusion, as has been stated, to summarize

Here is a revision of the paragraph on renting versus owning a home, which now ensures coherence through the use of repetition, parallelism, and appropriate transitions. We have circled repeated key terms, used a dotted line to mark parallel structures, and underlined transitions.

Owning a (home) is far more satisfying than renting a place. Only the (homeowner) knows the joy and pride that accompany all the loving labor of being a conscientious (homeowner) Let us consider some of the advantages of owning a (home) over paying rent: First, owners can make wonderfully creative structural changes to improve their properties. Owners can move walls, tile roofs, paint or wallpaper rooms, and even turn a spiritless square bungalow into a charming Italian villa. Renters cannot move walls, tile roofs, or even paint or wallpaper rooms, but must ask permission from their landlords even to change a piece of linoleum on the floor. Moreover, expensive remodeling is out of the question since the money expended brings no returns except to the landlord. Consequently, most (renters) leave their living quarters just the way they found them when they moved in. Second, (homeowners) experience a deep feeling of accomplishment each time they make their mortgage payments because they know that they are inching a little closer to the time when they will own their homes outright.   The dream of holding the deed to a (home) makes working worthwhile.   However, (renters) feel no such pride or satisfaction.   Each month hundreds or even thousands of dollars go into rent, with the only reward being a cancelled check among the stack received from a bank.   The dreary thought that next month another big hunk of money will disappear with nothing to show for the investment plagues all renters.   Third, every April, when income tax is due, (homeowners) realize a decided financial boon because all interest payments are tax deductible.   On the contrary, (renters) can claim no such advantage. Whatever money has been poured into rent has disappeared forever into the pockets of the landlords, who can then claim the huge tax benefit.   All in all, (homeowners) are winners whereas (renters) are losers.

Exercises

1. Draw a line through any sentence in the following paragraph that weakens its unity:

> In Henrik Ibsen's play *Hedda Gabler*, the major contributing factors to Hedda's confusion and inability to accept her new life with her husband are her notions of aristocracy and superiority, which she considers her birthright as the daughter of the late General Gabler. In this respect, she reminds one of Faulkner's Miss Emily, who likewise came from an aristocratic background but fell in love with one not of her own class. Hedda's father, even in death, is Hedda's controlling force. This fact is evident if one considers the title of the play. A title is often an important clue to the action and theme of a play. Consider Shakespeare's *The Taming of the Shrew* or *Much Ado About Nothing*. In both cases the title tells us what the message of the play is. In a letter, Ibsen wrote: "The title of the

play is *Hedda Gabler*. My intention in giving it this name was to indicate that Hedda, as a personality, is to be regarded rather as her father's daughter than as husband's wife." The audience is introduced to the venerable gentleman in the opening scenes of the play, and his portrait is a dominating factor of the set throughout. Indeed, Hedda's sense of security and control is seen in terms of her physical proximity to the portrait at several points in the play. Inevitably some critics tried to read into the play statements about social issues. For instance, one critic saw it as a strong attack on conformist respectability. But it really is a play about human beings and their destinies.

2. Identify the most obvious techniques used in the following paragraph to achieve coherence:

> Enormous amounts of time, money, and talent go into commercials. Technically they are often brilliant and innovative, the product not only of the new skills and devices but of imaginative minds. A few of them are both funny and endearing. Who, for instance, will forget the miserable young man with the appalling cold, or the kids taught to use—as an initiation into manhood—a fork instead of a spoon with a certain spaghetti? Among the enlightened sponsors, moreover, are some who manage to combine an image of their corporation and their products with accuracy and restraint.
> —Marya Mannes, "Television: The Splitting Image."

Constructing Paragraphs from the Thesis Statement

As we pointed out in Chapter 3, the topics into which a thesis statement may be divided are often predicted by its wording. Here is an example:

```
Like most young men I love to eat and eat
and eat.  If I had just one wish it would be to
be able to cook.  Being able to cook my own
meals would keep my stomach full and give me a
pleasant taste in my mouth, keep my body
healthy, and keep my bank account in the black.
```

It is evident from this thesis statement (underlined) not only what the writer must do, but also more or less what the topic sentences of the successive paragraphs should be. Here are the topic sentences that the writer actually used:

First paragraph: `To be able to cook like Mom would keep my`
`stomach full and give me a pleasant taste`
`in my mouth.`

Second paragraph: `Not only would my stomach be full and my`
`taste buds happy, but the rest of my body`
`would also be content and healthy.`

Third paragraph: `My life would not be the only thing on`
`cloud nine; my bank account would be there,`
`too.`

Two lessons are to be learned from this example. First, that writing an essay requires a sense of **connection** between its thesis statement and the paragraphs that are its necessary subtopics. This should seem a matter of common sense, but it is a point often ignored by beginning writers who tend to set down one agenda in the thesis and carry out another in the paragraphs.

The second lesson is that as a literary form the paragraph serves two masters. It is the subtopic of an essay; but it is also a group of individual sentences logically connected to make a single point. This single point, in turn, must enlarge on the thesis. For example, here is the first paragraph the student wrote about how being able to cook would help keep his stomach full:

`Like most young men I enjoy only one type`
`of cooking:  Mom's.  To be able to cook like Mom`
`would keep my stomach full and give me a`
`pleasant taste in my mouth.  I would be able to`
`enjoy eating a satisfying and filling meal at`
`one gorgeous sitting, instead of incessantly`
`snacking every 20 minutes as I now do.  I would`
`be able to savor every morsel of every course,`

and my stomach would tingle with happiness as
every mouthful went down. I could make all of
my favorite dishes: enchilada, lasagna, and
quiche. Of course, I would also cook all the
fabulous desserts: all the apple pies, cheese
cakes, and Danish pancakes I crave today but
seldom get. Just thinking about being able to
cook like my Mom makes me and my stomach
deliriously happy.

Notice the dual purpose served by the paragraph. On the one hand, its individual details support its topic sentence. But on the other hand, the paragraph as a whole backs up and adds to the thesis statement, "Being able to cook my own meals would keep my stomach full and give me a pleasant taste in my mouth, keep my body healthy, and keep my bank account in the black."

The Organizing Principle Behind Paragraphs

When planning what to say in your paragraphs, you can use the thesis statement to predict your subsequent topics, especially if you have cleverly worded it. But the thesis statement can do even more: it can also help you determine the abstract structure of your individual paragraphs.

The abstract structure of a paragraph is its organizing principle. All paragraphs have an organizing principle, some purposeful pattern the writer used to meld its sentences into a single unit of meaning. This pattern, known as the **rhetorical mode** of the paragraph, is the organization used to make its topic intelligible. The most common modes are **narration, description, definition, example, process, classification, comparison/contrast, causal analysis**, and **argumentation**. A paragraph developed by narration, for example, uses the techniques of that mode to organize and relate a story. Similarly, a paragraph developed by comparison/contrast uses the techniques of that mode to make clear the similarities and differences between two items.

Ideally, the rhetorical mode used to develop a paragraph should be the most natural expression of its main idea. Grasping which form of development to use in a paragraph is mainly a matter of common sense, as the following examples show:

Topic sentence: On my fourteenth birthday a tragedy hit my family that taught me the value of respecting one's elders.
Rhetorical mode: *Narration.* The writer will narrate an experience.

Topic sentence: The Statue of Liberty has a virtuous, noble bearing.
Rhetorical mode: *Description.* The writer will describe the statue.

Topic sentence: The word *gay* as applied to homosexuals has an ambiguous history.
Rhetorical mode: *Definition.* The writer will do an etymological study of the word *gay.*

Topic sentence: Women and men today are obsessed with looking young.
Rhetorical mode: *Example.* The writer will provide some appropriate examples of how women and men reveal their obsession with looking young.

Topic sentence: Improving one's reading ability involves five major steps.
Rhetorical mode: *Process.* The writer will explain the five steps in appropriate order.

Topic sentence: Literature can be divided into four genres: short story, drama, poetry, and novel.
Rhetorical mode: *Classification.* The writer will describe and explain each genre in turn.

Topic sentence: The pastime of nineteenth-century dueling was different in France than in Austria.
Rhetorical mode: *Comparison/contrast.* The writer will contrast the French and Austrian practices of the duel.

Topic sentence: Human laughter, according to the French philosopher Henri Bergson, has a surprising and simple cause.
Rhetorical mode: *Causal analysis.* The writer will cite Bergson's view of what causes human beings to laugh.

Topic sentence: All mothers should be encouraged to breast-feed their infants.
Rhetorical mode: *Argumentation.* The writer will try to convince the reader of the rightness of this proposition. (This mode of development will be treated in Chapter 12.)

In deciding by which rhetorical mode a thesis statement should be developed, be guided by your controlling idea or purpose. Ask yourself, what are the logical divisions of my thesis statement? What should I do and say first, what second? Sometimes the answer will be obvious. For example, the student who wrote the essay about longing to be able to cook developed all its paragraphs by the pattern of cause/effect implicit in the thesis. Every paragraph detailed the good *effects* learning to cook were expected to have on different aspects of his life (see pages 125 and 126).

But how would you develop this thesis statement and with what kind of paragraphs?

```
In a matter of mere years, the personal computer

revolution has gone from boom to bust mainly

because the expected usefulness of the machines

did not live up to the hype.
```

You begin by putting yourself in your reader's shoes and by asking those commonsense questions that immediately come to mind. First, what do you mean by the "computer revolution"? Your opening paragraph, then, might *define* that term. Second, what do you mean when you say that computers have gone from boom to bust? What you mean is that sales of computers have levelled off and are declining, several manufacturers have gone broke, and computer retailers have closed in droves. A paragraph organized by *example* could efficiently convey these facts. Third, you now have to account for the decline in the popularity of the personal computer, which will require a paragraph organized by *cause and effect*.

There is, as you can see, nothing especially mystifying in this process. What you are doing is asking yourself questions about your thesis statement that would logically occur to any interested reader, and then answering them in appropriately organized paragraphs. For that matter, your answer could take the form of a paragraph written in a mixed mode, where you do two or three different things at once. Be warned, however, that because the mixed mode paragraph is one of shifting purpose, writing it well requires a strong sense of transition. (See pages 120-22, for the use of transitions.) Good writers can and do write mixed mode paragraphs because they know how to move gracefully from doing one thing to doing another without leaving the reader behind. This comes with practice and experience. Beginners are better off staying with pure forms until they have acquired this knack.

The chapters that follow contain a detailed discussion of the various rhetorical modes, with explanations of the patterns and techniques behind them. (Argumentation is treated separately in Chapter 12 since it tends to be a hybrid.) Rhetorical modes can help you organize your thoughts by focusing your paragraphs, and if you should ever tumble into that "I-don't-know-what-to-say" ditch, knowing how to use them can help you to clamber out. Do not, however, regard them as absolutes into which every idea you have must necessarily be crammed or never committed to paper. The rhetorical modes are nothing more than convenient patterns for expressing your ideas and thoughts; consequently, their usefulness will vary from writer to writer.

Exercises

1. Explain what mode of development would be most appropriate for the following topic sentences:

a. In terms of expense, time, and convenience, the microwave oven is far superior to the conventional oven.

b. Let me explain the easiest way to make a kite that will, on a windy day, soar like a bird.

c. For peculiarly economic reasons, many young adults are choosing to live at home rather than venture out on their own.

d. Chicago is populated by three types of denizens.

e. I was nine years old and living in the Bronx, New York, when I learned a memorable lesson about class differences from witnessing a conflict between a commuter and a bag lady.

f. Love is an often used term whose meaning is seldom clearly understood.

g. The lobbying combination of religion and politics on some issues has produced a clear threat to certain constitutionally guaranteed freedoms.

h. My dog Napoleon is so emaciated that he can hardly walk and so weathered that he looks as if he might die at any minute.

2. The late sociologist Margaret Mead once observed: "The family is the toughest institution we have." Assuming the use of Mead's statement as a topic sentence for a unified paragraph, delete any sentence in the list below that would break its unity:

a. Families are capable of undergoing considerable change and stress without being destroyed.

b. History has witnessed the decay and destruction of numerous families—even entire dynasties.

c. Sometimes what we normally think of as destructive forces may strengthen the family.

d. Despite the present high rate of divorce, most couples want to get married (or remarried) and want to have children.

e. It is difficult to assess just how many couples will have children who are either retarded, handicapped, or socially delinquent.

f. Married couples have obviously not rejected parenthood.

g. According to a recent article in the *New York Times*, cohabitation without being married is mostly a period of experimentation before moving on to conventional marriage and family life.

h. Most women work hard to combine their careers with devotion to family life.

i. Some careers held by women make a good family life impossible.

j. At the present time, and into the foreseeable future, households with married couples directing their families remain the predominant social arrangement.

k. There is good reason to believe that the family is under siege, but it may survive.

Writing Assignments

1. Using only applicable information provided in the preceding Exercise 2, and adding your own material, write a 300-word paragraph proving that the American family is alive and well. Make sure that every one of your sentences directly supports the paragraph's topic sentence.

2. Write a paragraph in which you cite three reasons why you either approve or disapprove of one of the world figures listed below. Be sure to use a clear transition leading from one reason to the next. Also, when necessary, use transitional expressions such as *however, thus, likewise, on the other hand, therefore,* and *furthermore* to connect one sentence to the next.

a. Albert Einstein

b. Indira Gandhi

c. Eleanor Roosevelt

d. Richard Burton

e. John F. Kennedy

f. Pope John Paul II

g. Pablo Picasso

h. Queen Elizabeth II

i. Muhammad Reza Shah Pahlevi, Shah of Iran

j. Elvis Presley

k. Margaret Thatcher

Chapter Five

Narrating and Describing

What is written without effort is in general read without pleasure.

SAMUEL JOHNSON (1709–1784)

Narrating

Narration is an organizing pattern that treats experience in dynamic rather than static terms: people interact, events come to a climax, cause leads to effect, psychological impulses are satisfied. Something always happens. In its largest sense, narration includes history, biography, personal experience, travel, and fiction. Because we all have an instinctive curiosity about the capricious events and occurrences all around us, narration is probably the easiest mode to master. We want to know what happened, how, and why. Satisfying this craving has made millionaires of many otherwise forgettable novelists.

Here is an example of a narrative paragraph. In it, Jack Kerouac relates an experience he had while working as a fire lookout somewhere above Ross Dam on Desolation Peak in the Cascades:

> In the middle of the night I woke up suddenly and my hair was standing on end: I saw a huge black shadow in my window. Mt. Hozomeen (8080) looking in my window from miles away near Canada. I got up from the forlorn bunk with the mice scattering underneath and went outside and gasped to see black mountain

shapes gianting all around; and not only that but the billowing curtains of the northern lights shifting behind the clouds. It was a little too much for a country boy. The fear that the Abominable Snowman might be breathing behind me in the dark sent me back to bed where I buried my head inside my sleeping bag.

—Jack Kerouac, "Alone on a Mountaintop," *Holiday Magazine,* October 1958.

There are three important techniques of narration exemplified in this paragraph: the use of a consistent point of view, the use of pacing, and the use of vivid details. Let's look at each.

The use of a consistent point of view

Every narration is a story told by someone (or even in bizarre instances of experimental fiction, something) who speaks to the reader in a particular voice and with a certain personality, referred to as the narrative's **point of view**. For example, if you were narrating an incident from your childhood and wished to tell it dramatically, you might use the point of view of a child. This fiction would be for the sake of realistically recreating what the world looked like to you then, even though it no longer looks the same to you now. But should you begin the narrative in language such as a child might use and then suddenly switch to that of a crotchety philosopher, the effect of believability would be instantly ruined. A prime technique of narration, then, is consistency in the use of point of view. Once you have decided who the spokesman, spokeswoman, or spokesthing of your narration is and assigned he, she, or it a certain voice, you must stick with it for the duration of your story.

For example, the following passage consistently reflects the point of view of a young, uneducated black woman:

I spend my wedding day running from the oldest boy. He twelve. His mama died in his arms and he don't want to hear nothing bout no new one. He pick up a rock and laid my head open. The blood run all down tween my breasts. His daddy say Don't *do* that! But that's all he say. He got four children, instead of three, two boys and two girls. The girls hair ain't been comb since their mammy died. I tell him I'll just have to shave it off. Start fresh. He say bad luck to cut a woman hair. So after I bandage my head best I can and cook dinner—they have a spring, not a well, and a wood stove look like a truck—I start trying to untangle hair. They only six and eight and they cry. They scream. They cuse me of murder. By ten o'clock I'm done. They cry theirselves

to sleep. But I don't cry. I lay there thinking bout Nettie while he
on top of me, wonder if she safe.
—Alice Walker, *The Color Purple.*

To make your prose reflect a consistent voice and point of view,
you may want to resort to playacting, to temporarily assume the personality
or character of the figure from whose point of view the narration is being
told. Try to imagine how that person would talk, in what syntactic patterns
and with what vocabulary, and then recreate these patterns faithfully in the
language. Whatever voice you choose to hide behind—young and uneducated, or old and wise—be sure to stay in character throughout the whole
narrative.

The use of pacing

Pacing is the technique of selective focus. The well-paced narrative
focuses on the details of important events in order to highlight them, but
glosses over those events that have little or no bearing on the meaning of
the story. Here is a student's example:

By April of 1975, the victory of the
Communists became obvious. Since my family
wanted to live in freedom, we decided to leave
Vietnam forever. The decision was a highly
risky one and involved some terrifying nights in
foreign camps. Finally, after two weeks of
agonized wandering from camp to camp, we were
flown to Camp Pendleton in the United States. I
wept with relief, thinking that now at last life
would be better than it had been at the hot and
arid camps of such places as Guam. The reality
was disappointing. We arrived at Pendleton at
one o'clock in the morning. The weather was
blue cold. We were checked in by uniformed
officials who did not know our language and who

were crisply but uncaringly efficient. I was so
cold that my teeth chattered; consequently, one
of clerks handed me a thin blanket and pointed
to a tent with three military beds in it. My
mother and I huddled miserably on the bed while
my father filled out papers. A few hours later,
another official signaled us to head toward the
mess hall, where we were to eat breakfast. The
morning darkness was rendered eerie by a thick
fog. I had to walk down a steep incline to
reach the eating area, and on the way, I
stumbled over a rock and broke my leg. The pain
was numbing and put me in shock. I was no
longer hungry——just cold and afraid. One month
later, when we left the camp, I was still in my
cast.

Notice that a mere phrase is devoted to "two weeks of agonized wandering from camp to camp," and a whole month of living at Camp Pendleton is dismissed with a simple "One month later . . . ." What the writer zooms in on is the misery of arriving at camp. That event is highlighted in detail because the point of the paragraph is to narrate how different the reality of moving to the United States was from the dream.

The use of vivid details

All paragraphs, no matter how developed, are made better and more lively by the inclusion of vivid details. This is especially true of narratives. Here is an example, taken from a short story in which a young man tells how he took his aunt to a concert after she had spent 30 years running a farm on a homestead in Nebraska:

> From the time we entered the concert hall, however, she was a
> trifle less passive and inert, and for the first time seemed to per-
> ceive her surroundings. I had felt some trepidation lest she might

become aware of her queer, country clothes, or might experience
some painful embarrassment at stepping suddenly into the world
to which she had been dead for a quarter of a century. But again,
I found how superficially I had judged her. She sat looking about
her with eyes as impersonal, almost as stony, as those with which
the granite Rameses in a museum watches the froth and fret that
ebbs and flows about his pedestal. I have seen this same aloofness
in old miners who drift into the Brown Hotel at Denver, their
pockets full of bullion, their linen soiled, their haggard faces un-
shaven; standing in the thronged corridors as solitary as though
they were still in a frozen camp on the Yukon.
—Willa Cather, *A Wagner Matinée.*

This kind of vivid accounting requires minute observation of one's environment. In your own narrations, be as specific as you can. Say how things
looked, smelled, tasted. Don't be satisfied with the approximate, the hazy,
the imprecise. Say what you mean as specifically as possible, using as much
detail as you can remember.

The following is the first draft of a student narrative paragraph. In
it, the narrator tried unsuccessfully to narrate the coziness he had felt toward
a garret apartment he moved into after the breakup of his marriage:

Original:

```
    Not so long ago, I went in search of "La

Paix," the place I lived in for two years after

my wife and I broke up our marriage.  For a long

time we had been haggling over money, religion,

friends, and lifestyle.  We became increasingly

hostile toward each other, eventually reaching

the point where we could hardly tolerate each

other.  Then, one day she kicked me out into the

streets, and I went in search of a new dwelling.

I finally found a small garret on the top of a

condemned garage.  It was to be my springboard

to a new life.  Since it had played an important

part in my emotional rehabilitation, I wanted to
```

Gloss over for better pacing. unimportant to your story.

see it again. Standing on the balcony, looking
into what was once my home, I saw no connection,
no relationship, no bridge between then and now.
I was peering into the dark, uninviting interior
of an ugly substandard building——now even
shunned by winos infecting the area.
Nevertheless, I ventured inside to snoop and
mess around a little bit. I was scared spitless
that the floor might give way beneath me. It
was a hideous, dirty place. I found it
increasingly difficult to square this squalid
reality with my nostalgic remembrances. Tired
and dissatisfied, I drove to my parents' home
and sat in their backyard to mull things
over. "La Paix" had witnessed the biggest
emotional transition of my life so far. I had
hidden there for two years, writing gawd awful
poetry, trite short stories, and first scenes of
a one-act play. The place had symbolized
freedom from a restrictive, middle-class
lifestyle, and a wife I had succeeded only in
making miserable. Heck, for me it had been a
tree house with electricity or a Tom Sawyer's
island, and realizing that it was gone made me
feel like a trapeze artist who has just been
told, "Tonight there'll be no net." After a few
moments of self-indulgent, morbid introspection,
I quietly acknowledged one of life's cruel
aphorisms: "You can never go back."

As indicated by the editorial comments in its margin, the original narration was improperly paced, had an inconsistent point of view, and did not include enough vivid details. Notice the improvement with rewriting:

Revision:

>   One afternoon not so long ago, I went in
> search of "La Paix," the place I lived in after
> my wife had kicked me out into the streets
> following our stormy and unhappy marriage. It
> was a small garret on the top of a condemned
> garage--isolated, self-contained, and
> inexpensive. After christening it "La Paix" for
> "peace of mind," I had filled it with books,
> posters, classical music, and irrepressible
> optimism. It was to be my springboard into a
> new life. But that afternoon, standing on the
> balcony, looking into the spooky bowels of what
> was once my cozy home, I saw no connection, no
> relationship, no bridge between then and now. I
> was peering into the dark, uninviting cavity of
> a substandard building now even shunned by the
> winos that infect the area. I ventured inside
> as carefully as an archaeologist enters a tomb,
> genuinely afraid that the floor might give way
> beneath me. In the main cavity of the dwelling
> I noticed subtle traces of human habitation.
> The floor was littered with artifacts of a
> primitive, transient branch of humanity.
> Bottles of cheap wine lay, long empty, nested in
> beds of torn newsprint and acrid smelling

rags. Standing in the midst of what seemed several generations of accumulated filth and debris, I found it impossible to square this hideous reality with my beatific reminiscences. I began probing the heaps of refuse. Surely somewhere amongst the broken glass and vile leavings, there must be a trace of my two years of existence! I searched for over an hour—in vain. I came up with nothing except a fit of sneezes and some insect bites. Disillusioned and tired, I stood in front of a dusty shelf that had housed my books and mulled over the experience. "La Paix" had housed the biggest emotional transition of my life. For two full years I had hidden there, composing third-rate poetry, trite short stories, and one hopelessly insignificant play. This place had symbolized freedom from a restrictive, middle-class lifestyle and from a wife I had succeeded only in making miserable. It was my tree house, my Tom Sawyer's island, and realizing that it was gone made me feel like a trapeze artist who has just been told, "Tonight there'll be no net." After a few moments of self-indulgent, morbid introspection, I quietly acknowledged one of life's cruel aphorisms: "You can never go back."

The revision has improved the pacing by glossing over the narrator's unhappy marriage and by deleting the reference to his trip home. Neither incident is important to the topic sentence of the paragraph, which in this case is the final sentence: "You can never go back." Getting rid of slang expressions like "mess around," "gawd awful," "scared spitless," and "heck," makes the point of view more consistently that of an introspective, mature person looking back. The addition of vivid details also infuses some liveliness into the narrative.

Exercises

1. What kind of person are you—patient, easygoing, nervous, timid, imaginative, jealous? Choose the adjective most characteristic of you and narrate an incident that highlights it. Pace the narration to focus on details that prove what kind of person you are.

2. Using the point of view of either an old man or a young child, narrate the experience of opening gift packages at Christmas. Be sure to keep your point of view consistent.

3. Write a narrative paragraph or two on one of the following topics:
a. Experience is the best teacher.
b. when love turned to hate
c. a psychic experience
d. an awakening to books

Description

A good description lures the reader into a sensory experience of sight, touch, smell, taste by focusing on a single dominant impression and then supporting it with vivid details. For instance, the dominant impression of the paragraph below is a blinding November snowstorm in Russia:

> On the sixth of November the sky became terrible; its blue disappeared. The army marched along wrapped in a cold mist. Then the mist thickened, and presently from this immense cloud great snowflakes began to sift down on us. It seemed as if the sky had come down and joined with the earth and our enemies to complete our ruin. Everything in sight became vague, unrecognizable. Objects changed their shape; we walked without knowing where we were or what lay ahead, and anything became an obstacle. While the men were struggling to make headway against the icy, cutting blast, the snow driven by the wind was piling up and filling the hollows along the way. Their smooth surfaces hid unsuspected depths which opened up treacherously under our feet. The men

were swallowed up, and the weak, unable to struggle out, were
buried forever.
—Count Philippe-Paul de Segur, *Napoleon's Russian Campaign.*

This description of the Russian winter storm that destroyed Napoleon's invading army allows the reader to feel the icy blast of the relentless
wind, to see the sinister vagueness of the mist, to experience the mortal
despair of the soldiers facing burial in the snowdrifts. The writer, who was
an aide-de-camp of Napoleon, practiced in it the two fundamental requirements of all good descriptions: focusing on a dominant impression and appealing to the reader's senses.

Focus on a dominant impression

A dominant impression is a representative characteristic of the
whole scene that functions as the theme of your description. We do not
mean that the scene must resemble your dominant impression in every way.
No doubt there were a handful of officers in Napoleon's retreating army
who had the luxury of temporary shelter and adequate clothing to shield
them from the ferocity of the storm. But if the author had focused on these
fortunate few, he would have missed the mark in depicting the ravages of
the wintry blast on the majority of the men. What you are after in your
description is not photographic accuracy, but concentration of an overall
theme that is mainly faithful to the truth. So if you have decided to describe
the Ayatollah Khomeini as a stern fanatic, stick to that dominant impression
and hammer it home with details. The following student sample fails to do
so:

Iran's present leader, the Ayatollah
Khomeini, is a frighteningly fanatical man, who
rules without tenderness or mercy. During
interviews with the press, his piercing black
eyes send out darts of hatred, especially when
he refers to the United States as "the great
Satan." When he orders an execution——"Death by
hanging!"——he does so without a hint of
regret. His eyes mist over with gentleness and
kindness when he is caught looking at one of his

<u>grandchildren. He obviously is a strong family</u>

<u>man with a great love for his grandchildren</u>.

The underlined portion breaks the unity of the dominant impression and should therefore be deleted. By contrast, notice how this description of the German composer Richard Wagner (1813–83) is unremittingly focused:

> He was a monster of conceit. Never for one minute did he look at the world or at people, except in relation to himself. He was not only the most important person in the world, to himself; in his own eyes he was the only person who existed. He believed himself to be one of the greatest dramatists in the world, one of the greatest thinkers, and one of the greatest composers. To hear him talk, he was Shakespeare, and Beethoven, and Plato, rolled into one. And you would have had no difficulty in hearing him talk. He was one of the most exhausting conversationalists that ever lived. An evening with him was an evening spent in listening to a monologue. Sometimes he was brilliant; sometimes he was maddeningly tiresome. But whether he was being brilliant or dull, he had one sole topic of conversation: himself. What *he* thought and what *he* did.
> —Deems Taylor, "The Monster," *Of Men and Music.*

Every detail supports the dominant impression—namely that "he was a monster of conceit."

Appeal to the reader's senses through specific details and figures of speech

Specific detail is detail that is exact, representative, precise, and hard-edged. Its opposite is the generalization made up of offhanded observations and insipid adjectives. "He walked like a seaman and looked around him as though he were at sea" is a generalization. "He walked with the stooping, shuffling gait of a seafarer and squinted at everything about him as though even the grasslands and trees sparkled with the painful scintillation of the open sea" is specific. With practice, you will soon get a feel for this difference. Blurry generalizations, vague adjectives, drab details are the first to occur to any writer. Only after hard digging and searching does a writer occasionally strike a vein of crystalline images. Here is a passage from a student's essay filled with generalizations:

> The Eagle Rock Plaza is a melting pot of
>
> lonely people. Here the old people congregate

in the hope that they will find someone who will
listen to their sad tales of woe. They sit on
one of the center benches, wearing old clothes
and old tennis shoes. Sometimes, they munch on
food, and occasionally they can be seen
gratefully chatting with a younger person, who
probably reminds them of a son or daughter.
These are society's neglected citizens.

This drab description does not fulfill the promise of its opening sentence. Here is the second draft after the student received some editorial suggestions from a peer group:

The Eagle Rock Plaza is a melting pot of
lonely people. These forlorn citizens migrate
toward the center benches, where they sit in
various hunched-over positions, their wrinkled
eyes, furtively darting up and down the mall,
hoping to catch a glimpse of some scene that
will allow them to escape their empty lives for
a few minutes. For instance, they will smile
eagerly at two screaming four-year-olds fighting
over a silver balloon, or at a young man
spontaneously planting a kiss on his lover's
lips. Occasionally, one of them will lick a
single-scoop ice cream cone as if it were a
gourmet delicacy—each bite savored and made to
last as long as possible. Sooner or later, one
of the more outgoing types will strike up a
conversation with her neighbor: "Yep, my son's
in charge of the Main Street post office," one

```
might hear her announce proudly.  Or, one of the

old men, leaning on his cane, will complain,

"The rheumatism is really getting to me

today."  The plaza is occupied by the same

people every day--all suffering identical

loneliness, but too proud to let anyone know.
```

This second draft is superior to the first mainly because it uses more vivid specific details.

The vividness of a description can usually be enhanced by the use of figures of speech. Often, these figures evoke a colorful comparison, as when the young boy from James Joyce's "Araby" falls in love and confesses that "my body was *like a harp* and her words and gestures were *like fingers running upon the wires.*" Or, when William Faulkner describes Miss Emily: "She looked bloated, *like a body long submerged in motionless water,* and of that pallid hue. Her eyes, lost in the fatty ridges of her face, looked *like two small pieces of coal pressed into a lump of dough. . . .*"

Similes are comparisons openly linked by the prepositions "like" or "as." **Metaphors** are comparisons made without the use of any linking word as in the following description of May Bartram by Henry James: "*She was a sphinx,* yet with her white petals and green fronds *she might have been a lily too—only an artificial lily,* wonderfully imitated and constantly kept, without dust or stain, though not exempt from a slight droop and a complexity of faint creases, under some clear glass bell." The power of these figures is illustrated by this passage:

> She was a little woman, with brown, dull hair very elaborately arranged, and she had prominent blue eyes behind invisible pince-nez. Her face was long, *like a sheep's;* but she gave no impression of foolishness, rather of extreme alertness; *she had the quick movements of a bird.* The most remarkable thing about her was her voice, high, metallic, and without inflection; it fell on the ear with a hard monotony, irritating to the nerves *like the pitiless clamour of the pneumatic drill.*
> —W. Somerset Maugham, *Rain.*

Figures of speech can add sparkle to your writing, but they should be used cautiously and with a deft touch. The overuse of these figures, especially in straight expository writing, can make writing seem ridiculous rather than sublime. There are also some well-known dangers attendant on their use. The first is triteness. It is better to write plain descriptions than colorfully trite ones. Similes such as "white as a sheet," "hungry as a bear," or "sharp as a needle" are shopworn and no longer effective. Other examples of tired images are expressions such as "He threw in the towel"; "They swallowed it hook, line, and sinker"; "There's a fly in the ointment."

The second danger is the mixed figure of speech. Some examples of these, culled from actual student papers, are: "Into every life some rainbows will fall"; "He is a thorn among daisies"; "She tends to sweep all of the perfume of life under the rug." The effect of these twisted images is invariably comical.

Finally, be careful not to create an absurd image through the use of the wrong word or clumsy phrasing. Here are some examples: "Many problems steam throughout the city"; "In many areas of the world people bear the weight of suffrage"; "The movements of break dancing are completely uninhabited;" "Once you have climbed the hill of education, don't throw your knowledge overboard."

The following student paragraph describes the island of Iwo Jima, site of a fierce and bloody battle of World War II between American and Japanese troops. Pay attention to the editorial comments in the margin and to the changes made by the student in the revision. Mainly, what the student did in revising the paragraph was to strengthen its dominant impression, eliminate those sentences that detracted from it, and add more specific details.

Original:

needs a stronger dominant impression

Be more specific

       The island of Iwo Jima is the site where many men have died. As the wind blowing in from the sea tousled my hair, I felt myself deeply moved. Perhaps it was the sight of war wreckage all around me. Not more than three feet from me were the very bunkers that had housed the Japanese guns. These same guns had mercilessly

eliminate cliché

pounded the landing craft at point-blank range until the beach was cluttered with craft smashed to smithereens. To my right was another beach

Drop details that do not support your dominant impression.

the invasion forces attacked as an alternative. The beach was long and sloping, so it provided no cover. Fishing canoes sunned themselves

there, accenting a scene of peace and
tranquility. The Japanese had defended this
Add more details about this calm and beautiful beach with an interlocking
network of machine gun emplacements; many lives
were lost capturing the beach. No wonder I felt
odd, standing here on this plot of death. One
could almost hear the screams of a thousand
souls caught in the anguish and torment of
battle.

Revision:

Looking out over the barren, windswept
island of Iwo Jima, I stood on the pinnacle of
Mount Suribachi surveying the site where, 39
years before, thousands of men had struggled and
died for this barren speck of volcanic ash. As
the wind blowing in from the sea tousled my
hair, I felt myself deeply moved by an eerie
sense of death and foreboding. Perhaps it was
the sight of the American landing craft still
sitting there, half submerged in the shallows,
that made my knees quiver. Their shattered
hulks sat there rusting through the years since
that fateful day they had met their destruction
at the hands of the Japanese defenders. Not
more than three feet from me were the very
bunkers that had housed the Japanese guns.
These same guns had mercilessly pounded the
landing craft at point—blank range until the
beach was cluttered with wreckage and impassable

```
for the remaining troops.  To my right was
another beach the invasion forces attacked as an
alternative.  The beach was long and sloping, so
it provided no cover.  The Japanese had defended
it with an interlocking network of machine gun
emplacements; many lives were lost capturing the
beach.  No wonder I was ill at ease, standing
here on this plot of death.  One could almost
hear the screams of a thousand souls caught in
the anguish and torment of battle.
```

Exercises

1. In one sentence, state the dominant impression you might use to describe one of these items:
a. your bedroom
b. your favorite restaurant
c. your car
d. your best friend
e. the woman or man of your dreams
f. any scene in your neighborhood

2. Complete the following sentences with a fresh simile or metaphor:
a. His voice trembled like a . . . .
b. Once they were married, they got along as well as . . . .
c. The train whistled in the distance; it promised . . . .
d. For him life had become a . . . .
e. You couldn't see the barren trees and bushes in the dark, but you knew they were there—like . . . .
f. The street wound its way downhill and across the dunes like . . . .
g. I shuddered, for I barely recognized her. The passing months had turned her into . . . .

Writing Assignments

1. Turn one of the following models into an essay developed by either narration or description. Only the skeleton of the model is provided. Some reorganization of the details below may also be necessary:

a. In the eleventh grade I was introduced to the infamous and dreaded Miss Sullivan.

> She was then in her late forties and not glamorous.
>
> She had an unpleasant voice.
>
> She would stare piercingly at the class from her desk.
>
> She marked our English essays with a red pencil and returned them to us bleeding from many wounds.
>
> She always referred to us as, "Now, class . . . " and demanded, it seemed, the impossible.
>
> In the eleventh grade I hated her, but today I revere her as the best teacher I have ever had.

USE DESCRIPTION

b. One of the most embarrassing moments of my life was when . . . .
USE NARRATION

2. Write a suitably organized and developed essay of between 300 and 500 words on one of the following topics:

a. Narrate any memorable act you either personally participated in or witnessed.

b. Describe any object or place of either striking beauty or repulsive ugliness.

3. In a 500-word essay, narrate any incident that occurred within the last ten years and was important to our history and culture. (Examples: the assassination attempt on President Ronald Reagan; the space shuttle explosion of January 28, 1986, that killed seven astronauts, including teacher Christa McAuliffe). Pace your narration to make it interesting and use vivid sensory details to capture your reader's imagination.

Chapter Six

Defining and Exampling

*I*t *is very easy to persuade oneself that a phrase that one does not quite understand may mean a great deal more than one realizes. From this there is only a little way to go to fall into the habit of setting down one's impressions in all their original vagueness.*

W. SOMERSET MAUGHAM (1874–1965)

Defining

What do you mean? In composition, in debating, in nearly every effort of thinking, this is assuredly among the most asked questions. You say that this baseball player is better than that one, but what do you mean by "better"? Do you mean that he had more overall hits? That he had a higher lifetime average? That he scored more runs in his career, or was a better fielder? You argue that capital punishment is not a deterrent, but is it clear what you mean by "deterrent"?

A paragraph or essay organized by definition tells what you mean. It draws a circle of meaning around a word or term; it says what the boundaries include and what they do not. The basic procedure in defining is to place a word into a general category and then specify how it differs from other words in that same category. This is the method employed by dictionaries. Here are some examples:

Word	General Category	Difference
nightmare	dream	arousing horror
to classify	to organize	according to category
dynamic	pertaining to motion	in relation to force

In writing an essay, you should define any word crucial to your thesis whose meaning is fuzzy, ambiguous, or disputed. This especially inclues any abstract word—such as *sovereignty, intuition, communism, prejudice,* or *economy*—that can be easily misunderstood and misinterpreted. Notice how Joan Didion, the noted writer, carefully defines the word *migraine* before she gets into the full swing of an essay on this unpleasant disability, from which both she and her husband suffer:

> It was a long time before I began thinking mechanistically enough to accept migraine for what it was: something with which I would be living, the way some people live with diabetes. Migraine is something more than the fancy of a neurotic imagination. It is an essentially hereditary complex of symptoms, the most frequently noted but by no means the most unpleasant of which is a vascular headache of blinding severity, suffered by a surprising number of women, a fair number of men (Thomas Jefferson had migraine, and so did Ulysses S. Grant, the day he accepted Lee's surrender), and by some unfortunate children as young as two years old. (I had my first when I was eight. It came on during a fire drill at the Columbia School in Colorado Springs, Colorado. I was taken first home and then to the infirmary at Peterson Field, where my father was stationed. The Air Corps doctor prescribed an enema.) Almost anything can trigger a specific attack of migraine: stress, allergy, fatigue, an abrupt change in barometric pressure, a contretemps over a parking ticket. A flashing light. A fire drill. One inherits, of course, only the predisposition. In other words, I spent yesterday in bed with a headache not merely because of my bad attitudes, unpleasant tempers and wrongthink, but because both my grandmothers had migraine, my father has migraine, and my mother has migraine.
> —Joan Didion, "In Bed," *The White Album.*

If you were to reduce this paragraph to a one-sentence definition, you would see that it places migraine into the general category of vascular headaches and then differentiates it from other vascular headaches (causes blinding pain). The capsuled definition would read something like this: "Migraine is a vascular headache that is inherited and that causes blinding pain."

By emphasizing that a migraine attack is severe enough to cause chills, sweating, nausea, and a general debility, Didion also clarifies what it is *not*: the mild and characteristically common headache occasionally experienced by everyone.

Here are some other suggestions on how to make sure that your definition really clarifies the word you want to explain: give the etymology of the word; supply examples, functions, and effects of the word; say what the word does *not* mean.

Give the etymology of the word

The **etymology** of a word is its linguistic history—where it began, what it originally meant, how it was first formed. An unabridged dictionary is the best source of etymologies, which are usually provided in brackets following the word's entry. Sometimes the etymology of a word is a useful starting point for a discussion of its meaning. For example, it could be significant to find out that the word *hypnosis* comes from the Greek *hypnos*, meaning "sleep," or that the word *simple* originally meant "foolish." To explain that the root of the word *jeopardy* is the French *jeu parti*, meaning "divided play" or "even chance," is to at least show the great shift that has occurred between that original meaning and today's "peril and vulnerability." Sometimes explaining the history of an ambiguous word can help you to anecdotally define it.

Supply examples, functions, and effects of the word

Words change in meaning, fashion, or usage, and dictionaries are hopelessly behind the times in cataloging these subtle shifts. It is therefore not enough to parrot the dictionary definition of a complex or ambiguous word. You also need to show, through examples and anecdotes, the effect of the word in a living context. For instance, Marya Mannes has written an essay in which she defined the term "sophisticated man." Admitting that the term is at best illusive, the author resorts to using examples:

> Would you recognize this kind of man if you saw him across the room? I think so. He's the one talking with an attractive woman; conservatively dressed, but easy in his clothes. His hair is trimmed close to his head, but not too close. His hands are well-groomed, but not manicured. He does not laugh loudly or often. He is looking directly at the woman he speaks to, but he is not missing the other attractive women as they enter; a flick of the eye does it. For in all ways this man is not obvious. He would no more appear to

examine a woman from the ankles up than he would move his head as he read or form the words with his lips. His senses are trained and his reflexes quick. And how did they get that way? From experience, from observation, and from deduction. He puts two and two together without adding on his fingers. He is educated in life.

—Marya Mannes, "The Sophisticated Man."

Say what the word does not mean

Clarifying what a term does *not* mean can sometimes help a reader understand what it does. For instance, after a writer has defined *felony* as "a serious crime punishable by stringent sentencing," a reader may still not know exactly what kind of crime is considered a felony. One way to clarify the meaning is to say that a felony is *not* a misdemeanor, such as disturbing the peace by getting drunk, stealing someone's purse, or cheating in some small way on income tax. In her essay defining the "sophisticated man," Marya Mannes explains not only what a sophisticated man is but also what he is not:

> Now, here we come to the crux of the situation, for I maintain that a man who has never traveled in other countries and been exposed to other societies cannot be sophisticated. I am not speaking of package tours or cruise trips, but of a reasonable familiarity with foreign cities and peoples and arts and customs; an education reading alone cannot provide. For sophistication to me suggests, primarily, a refinement of the senses. The eye that has not appreciated Michelangelo's David in Florence or the cathedral of Chartres is not a sophisticated eye; nor is the tongue that has not tasted the best fettuccine in Rome or the best wine in Paris. The hand that has not felt the rough heat of an ancient wall in Siena or the sweating cold of a Salzburg stein of beer is an innocent hand. So are the fingers that have not traveled, in conscious and specific savoring, over the contours of many different women.
> —Marya Mannes, "The Sophisticated Man."

The most important principle, of course, is to keep amplifying on the definition until the term is made so clear that it cannot be misunderstood by the averge reader.

Here is an early draft of a paragraph by a student trying to define the term *envy*. Also included are the editorial comments in the margin. After studying this first attempt, read the revision to see what improvements the student made:

Original:

Envy produces nothing but pain and misery; it is a viciously destructive trait. Envy is often confused with jealousy; yet, the two terms are quite different one from the other. Envy is wanting what does not by right belong to you whereas jealousy is resenting having something taken away that by right does belong to you. Thus jealousy is justifiable whereas envy is not. The person who wants to remain psychologically healthy should purge away all feelings of envy. At the root of envy are selfishness and pride. But what envious persons often fail to realize is that when they harbor strong feelings of envy, they are destroying only themselves. Those who shoot arrows of envy at others, end up wounding only themselves. The surest way to gain victory over jealousy is to promote the welfare of the one envied. To conquer this green—eyed monster, the envious person must show good will to the object of envy.

Use examples to show differences between two terms. Give the etymology of envy. You really don't go much beyond the dictionary definition.

You need an anecdote here on the evil effects of envy.

Revision:

Envy produces nothing but pain and misery; it is a viciously destructive trait. Envy is often confused with jealousy; yet, the two terms are quite different one from the other. Envy is wanting what does not by right belong to you whereas jealousy is resenting having something taken away that by right does belong to you. For instance, a wife who flies into a rage because her husband is having a love affair with another woman is experiencing jealousy, an emotion quite appropriate to the situation. On the other hand, a woman who wants her best friend's husband for herself is feeling envy, an inappropriate trait. Consider what The American Heritage Dictionary says about envy. The roots of this word are traced back to the Latin invidere, meaning "to look upon with malice." Envy is seen as synonymous with begrudging and coveting, which all Christians and Jews are warned against in the Decalogue. The person who wants to remain psychologically healthy should purge away all feelings of envy. At the root of envy are selfishness and pride. But what envious persons often fail to realize is that when they harbor strong feelings of envy, they are destroying only themselves. An ancient fable tells the story of an eagle who was envious of another eagle who could fly better. One day this envious eagle spied a sportsman with a bow and arrow and said to him, "I wish you would bring down that eagle up there." The sportsman replied agreeably that he would do so gladly if he had some feathers for his arrow.

So the envious eagle quickly pulled out one
feather from his wings and gave it to the
hunter. The arrow was shot, but it did not
quite reach the rival bird because he was flying
too high. The envious eagle then pulled out
another feather, then another, and still
another--until he had lost so many feathers that
he himself could not fly. The archer took
advantage of the situation, turned around, and
killed the helpless bird. Here is the lesson
from this fable: If you are envious of others,
the one you will hurt the most by your envy is
you. In shooting arrows of envy at others, you
wound only yourself.

The definition uses clarifying examples, etymological information, and even an illustrating fable to explain what the writer means by envy.

Exercises

1. In a brief paragraph, define each of the following items by (1) placing it in a general category, (2) indicating how it differs from others in its class (see page 152), and (3) extending the definition to further explain it.

a. lawyer
b. red
c. hammer
d. expressionism
e. ghetto
f. pinafore

2. Using an example, clarify your definition of one these words:

a. nonchalance
b. reverence
c. desolation

3. Clarify your definition of one of the following words by stating what it is not:

a. heaven

b. platitude

c. genius

4. Supply the etymology for the following words:

a. anecdote

b. nausea

c. clinic

d. dandelion

e. lunatic

f. mediocre

g. phlegmatic

h. xenophobic

Developing by Examples

The use of examples to explain or reinforce an idea is a mode of development found in the writings of nearly every profession. Ministers use examples in their sermons to illustrate religious principle; lawyers use them to establish precedents; psychologists infer theories from specialized examples known as "case histories." Much of what we do or refrain from doing is based on the example of those who have preceded us. Selected carefully, examples can clarify a point better than any other rhetorical technique.

An example is a supportive instance of some larger point: an idea, a state, an allegation. It is not a different kind of detail, but detail used in a particular way. You are giving examples when you are trying to support some larger point by citing details that are contextual and representative of it. Merely writing "for example," does not make an example any more than writing "the fact is" actually creates a fact. Students will sometimes write "for example" and then follow it with information that is not truly an example. Here is an example of what we mean:

```
Rock and roll music is the greatest music on the

radio.  For example, the Rolling Stones are my

favorite band.  Their music ranges from hard,

solid rock to softer songs.  Rock music is the

best because you do not have to know the words

to enjoy the music. . . .
```

This is not an example, it is an expression of personal preference. Use the prefacing "for example," only when you are truly giving examples, meaning details that are representative of a larger whole, that are contextual, and that explicate it.

There are two main kinds of examples. A point may be supported either by many brief exemplifying details or by a single extended example. Here is a paragraph containing a list of brief examples:

> There can be no question about the average American's Americanism or his desire to preserve this precious heritage at all costs. Nevertheless, some insidious foreign ideas have already wormed their way into his civilization without his realizing what was going on. Thus, dawn finds the unsuspecting patriot garbed in pajamas, a garment of East Indian origin; and lying on a bed built on a pattern which originated in either Persia or Asia Minor. He is muffled to the ears in un-American materials: cotton, first domesticated in India; linen, domesticated in the Near East; wool from an animal native to Asia Minor; or silk, whose uses were first discovered by the Chinese. All these substances have been transformed into cloth by a method invented in Southwestern Asia. If the weather is cold enough, he may even be sleeping under an eiderdown quilt invented in Scandinavia.
>
> —Ralph Linton, "The 100% American," *The American Mercury* 40 (April 1937).

And here is a paragraph whose main point—that the courtship of animals often recounts the sorrowful lengths to which the males will go to arouse the interest of a female—is supported by a single extended example:

> One of the flies of the family Empidae, who had tried everything, finally hit on something pretty special. He contrived to make a glistening transparent balloon which was even larger than himself. Into this he would put sweetmeats and tidbits and he would carry the whole elaborate envelope through the air to the lady of his choice. This amused her for a time, but she finally got bored with it. She demanded silly little colorful presents. Empis had to go around gathering flower petals and pieces of bright paper to put into his balloon. On a courtship flight a male Empis cuts quite a figure now, but he can hardly be said to be happy. He never knows how soon the female will demand heavier presents, such as Roman coins and gold collar buttons. It seems probable that one day the courtship of the Empidae will fall down, as man's occasionally does, of its own weight.
>
> —James Thurber, "Courtship Through the Ages," *My World—And Welcome to It.*

Either use of examples is fairly straightforward and demonstrates the writer's grasp of representative details. Here are some other tips for getting the most out of your examples: Make your examples relevant and establish a clear connection between your example and the point being made.

Make your examples relevant

Whether brief or extended, the example must support the point of the paragraph. The following example in a student paper misses the point:

> In fourteenth–century England, a campaign
> of heresy was launched against the Templar
> knights, a monastic order formed to be the right
> arm of the Church, who were accused of sorcery
> and magic. For example, they had become
> immensely rich, since they were tax exempt. As
> a result of their wealth, they became the
> bankers of the Church and preferred living
> lavishly to going on crusades. Also, they
> acquired a sinister reputation because of the
> secrecy of their rituals and because, unlike
> other knighthoods, they supported no hospitals.

The topic sentence requires an example of the campaign of heresy against the Templars for purportedly using sorcery and magic, forbidden by the Catholic church. But instead of an example, the writer provides a general description of the Templars. Here is an improved version:

> In fourteenth–century England, a campaign
> of heresy was launched against the Templar
> knights, a monastic order formed to be the right
> arm of the Church, who were accused of sorcery
> and magic. For example, many of the old
> Templars were racked, thumbscrewed, starved,
> hung with weights until joints were dislocated,

had teeth and fingernails pulled one by one,
bones broken by the wedge, and feet held over
flames. In between torture, they would be asked
to confess that they had indulged in sorcery or
black magic, or some other form of Devil
worship.

The example now supports the topic sentence.

Establish a clear connection between your example and the point being made

Generally, an example should be given a brief introduction or preface to make its meaning clear to the reader. The following passage fails to make a connection:

Old people are referred to as "chronologically
advantaged." Stinky garbage pits are called
"landfills." People who used to be considered
crippled, are now considered "physically
challenged." Even nuclear war has been diluted
to "nuclear exchange." People seem to feel more
comfortable asking for the "powder room" than
for the toilet. It is rather amusing to
consider how often we avoid saying what we
really mean.

These examples lack an introductory context; the reader needs to be told what they mean and what they have to do with the topic sentence. Here is an improved version:

The dictionary tells us that a euphemism is
"the substitution of an inoffensive term for an
offensive term that would be more accurate."
Examples of euphemisms abound in our society.
For instance, old people are referred to as

"chronologically advantaged," as if by
eliminating the word old perhaps age itself will
vanish. People who used to be considered
handicapped now prefer to be called "physically
challenged," hoping that the new label will
encourage employers to treat them more
respectfully. Even nuclear war has been diluted
to the much less threatening "nuclear
exchange." It is rather amusing to consider how
often we avoid saying what we really mean. Most
of the time we use euphemisms because we do not
wish to offend our listeners. Thus, we prefer
to ask for the "powder room" than the toilet,
and we serve "ragout" rather than stew made from
leftover meat and vegetables.

Use these connective expressions to introduce an example: "for example,"
"for instance," "to illustrate," "a case in point is," "the following illustration
underscores this point."

Occasionally, the point of the example will be unmistakable from
its context, in which case no formal connective phrase is necessary. Here is
an example:

> A dress code signifies that school is a special place in which
> special kinds of behavior are required. The way one dresses is an
> indication of an attitude toward a situation. And the way one is
> *expected* to dress indicates what that attitude ought to be. You
> would not wear dungarees and a T-shirt that says "Feel Me" when
> attending a church wedding. That would be considered an outrage
> against the tone and meaning of the situation. The school has
> every right and reason, I believe, to expect the same sort of consid-
> eration.
> —Neil Postman, "Teaching as a Conserving Activity."

The example of not wearing a T-shirt to a church wedding needs no formal
connective because its context is so clear that the reader knows exactly what
is being exemplified.

The following student essay uses examples that are either irrelevant or not clearly connected to the rest of the text. Notice the editor's comments and the changes made in the revision:

Original:

The topic sentence should say that much litigation in the U.S. is intensely personal. At least, that seems to be the point of your details.

The United States ranks among the most

Indicate that examples will follow.

litigious countries in the world. From 1979–

1985 Mary Kling sued Los Angeles County after

the University of Southern California Medical

Center withdrew her admission to nursing school

because she could not pass certain physical

tests due to an ileostomy involving the removal

of part of her large and small intestines.

After five years of court battles, an appeals

court ruled in her favor, saying that she had

This example seems out of place with the others.

been discriminated against. A string of airline

crashes during the last few years is expected to

result in suits for hundreds of millions of

dollars in compensation to victims' families. A

Transition needed.

high school girl in New Jesey sued the school

district because she was not allowed to play on

transition?

the high school's football team. The Illinois

estate of a man who committed suicide in jail

sued the prison's architect for "breach of duty"

your conclusion is weak. say what the examples mean.

because he did not make the jail suicide

proof. People in our country love to sue.

Revision:

"I've never lived in a country where people

sue in court for such strangely personal reasons

as they do here in the United States." This is

a comment made by the British Consul General at a reception in Los Angeles. Indeed, the United States is the most litigious country in the world. Lawsuits based on what might strike a foreign observer as "strangely personal reasons" are part of our cultural sense of individuality and freedom. For instance, from 1979 to 1985 Mary Kling sued Los Angeles County after the USC Medical Center withdrew her admission to nursing school because she could not pass certain physical tests due to an ileostomy involving the removal of part of her large and small intestines. After five years of court battles, an appeals court ruled in her favor, saying that she had been discriminated against. Another rather eccentric case involved a high school girl in New Jersey, who sued the school district because she was not allowed to play on the high school's football team. In a most extraordinary move, the Illinois estate of a man who committed suicide in jail sued the prison's architect for "breach of duty" because he did not make the jail "suicide proof." These examples illustrate how Americans consider it their constitutional privilege to go to court when they think their personal rights are in danger of being abridged.

In the revision, the example of the airline lawsuit was deleted because it seemed out of place with the theme of the others. Added were an introduction, some connective phrases linking the examples to the topic sentence, and a conclusion pointing out what the examples mean.

Exercises

1. Support each of the following statements with three appropriate examples:

a. The wedding ceremony has become a sham.

b. Newspapers focus on bad news.

c. Fraternities and sororities promote snobbery.

d. Some people substitute love of a pet for love of human beings.

e. Old people can be fascinating.

2. Give a typical example of each of the following:

a. government fraud

b. words that come from people's names (Example: *Machiavellian* comes from "Nicolo Machiavelli" [1469–1527], the Florentine writer who wrote *The Prince.*)

c. a utopian society

d. discrimination

e. new slang expressions

3. Choose one of the concepts listed below. After defining it in one sentence, list some examples you would use to develop a paragraph amplifying your definition. (*Note:* If you are unsure about the concepts, look them up in a good dictionary.)

a Moorish architecture

b. euphemistic expression

c. archetypal symbol

d. Freudian slip

e. military camouflage

Writing Assignments

1. Turn one of the following models into an essay developed by either definition or by examples. Only the skeleton of the model is provided. If necessary, go to the library and find your own details. Some reorganization of the details below may also be necessary:

a. Semantics is the study of the meanings of words.

The basic principle of semantics is that every word is a symbol.

Another principle of semantics is that words have denotative as well as connotative meanings.

A third principle of semantics is that words are concrete or abstract.

USE DEFINITION

b. Some foods, long thought to be wholesome, contain unhealthy ingredients.

Carrots contain carotatoxin, a potent nerve poison.

Avocados contain the chemicals *pressor amines*, which elevate the blood pressure.

Milk contains *galactose*, a component of milk sugar that has caused cataracts in animals when given in large doses.

Shrimp contains a significant amount of arsenic.

USE EXAMPLES

2. With the help of an unabridged dictionary, write an extended definition (300–500 words) of one of the words listed below. Include an etymology of the word and examples to illustrate its meaning:

a. mediocre
b. monopoly
c. phlegmatic
d. sophistry
e. xenophobia
f. testify

3. In a 500-word essay, develop one of the following statements by using examples. When necessary, introduce the example by a phrase like "for example":

a. "It is impossible in our condition of society, not to be sometimes a snob." —William Makepeace Thackeray
b. "It is undesirable to believe a proposition when there is no ground whatever for supposing it true." —Bertrand Russell
c. "Resolve not to be poor: whatever you have, spend less. Poverty is a great enemy to human happiness; it certainly destroys liberty, and it makes some virtues impracticable and others extremely difficult." —Samuel Johnson
d. "A little rebellion now and then is a good thing." —Thomas Jefferson
e. "Property has its duties as well as its rights." —Thomas Drummond
f. "The mass of men lead lives of quiet desperation."—Henry David Thoreau

Chapter Seven

Explaining Process and Classifying

<hr>

Less is more in prose as in architecture.

DONALD HALL (b. 1928)

Explaining Process

To develop by **process** is to give a step-by-step explanation of something. The explanation may be of a concrete process—writing a research paper, hoisting a boat sail, performing a chemistry experiment—or it may be of an abstract process—how a U.S. president is elected, how a medieval Catholic atoned for his sins, or how the Japanese economy has come to be among the world's most powerful. Much of this chapter, especially those parts that explain how to write in the different modes, is developed by process.

Clearly written processes are crucial to many of the daily tasks performed in the workaday world. Yet, as anyone knows who has ever tried to follow instructions for assembling a chair, installing an electric garage door, or weatherproofing a window, process manuals are among the most bedevilling products of our time. In them, simple tasks become mystifying, ordinary jobs nightmarishly perplexing.

In spite of this widespread deficiency, the process essay is regarded by many instructors as too simple for college students. Indeed, it is the easiest essay to write if the student observes five basic steps.

167

Begin with a clear statement of purpose

In plain language, tell your reader what process you are explaining. A simple "Here are the directions for planting pansies in a clay pot" will do. Or, "Let me explain the steps involved in researching and establishing a family tree." Or, "The purpose of this paper is to demonstrate the simplest way to organize your home library." This initial summary tells your reader what to expect while providing a usefully limiting context for your explanations.

Know your process thoroughly

You should know your process extraordinarily well or you will be unable to anticipate the reader's occasional mystification. This mastery may well mean extra work, more time spent in the library, but that is what writing a clear process takes. For example, if your political science instructor asks for an essay explaining the process of a presidential veto, be prepared to consult sources other than the textbook. Aim to collect the information you need not merely to understand, but to explain as well.

Work out the correct order of your steps

Don't start too soon or too late. Begin at the beginning, assuming that your reader is a kindly ignoramus on this particular subject and badly in need of your clarifying advice. After you have found your opening, place the rest of the steps in their exact order. A practical way to do this is to create an outline of all major and minor steps necessary for a full understanding of the process. Here is an example of such an outline:

```
Topic sentence: When people fast, their bodies

                take certain steps to adjust.

    I. Tissues supplement their glucose supplies.

       A. Fat is used.

       B. The brain gets energy from ketone bodies.

   II. The body tries to protect vital organs.

       A. The metabolic rate drops.

       B. The pulse slows.

       C. The blood pressure lowers.

       D. The body's thermostat cranks down.
```

```
III. If the fast continues, the body consumes itself.

    A. Muscles are consumed.

    B. Protein reserves are consumed.
```

A detailed outline of this sequence makes either confusing the steps or omitting a step less likely.

Make sure that the details of each individual step are clear and complete

Every step in the process must be numbered and explained. For example, a process analysis of Richard Nixon's transformation from a hard-liner in the cold war with the Soviet Union to the architect of a policy of peaceful coexistence would probably list the following major stages: (1) From World War II to 1952, when he was elected vice-president of the United States, Nixon was a hard-liner who often denounced the Soviet Union as evil and dangerous. (2) From 1952 to 1969 Nixon was suspicious of Russian moves but ended the period with a changed attitude and an attempted easing of cold-war tensions. (3) Beginning with 1969 to August 9, 1974, Nixon initiated his policy of peaceful coexistence known as détente. These major stages in Nixon's foreign policy towards the Soviet Union also include some minor stages that should be mentioned. For example, the period of détente can also be subdivided into smaller stages of the SALT agreement to limit nuclear weaponry, the Paris peace talks to end the war in Vietnam, and the new trade and cultural agreements with Russia.

Similarly, a writing assignment explaining how to assemble the equipment needed for snow skiing might divide the process into two main steps, both of which would also include minor parts: (1) preparing the clothes (2) preparing the skis. Preparing the clothes means getting a waterproof parka and pants, warm gloves, a hat that covers the ears, light but warm underwear, and a pair of goggles. Preparing the skis includes getting the ski bindings adjusted, filling and waxing the bottoms and tops of the skis, sharpening their steel edges, and tending to the poles. Both the major and minor parts of the entire process should be covered.

Use transitions to indicate when you are moving from one step to the next

The easiest and simplest way to emphasize the correct sequence of a process is to number each step, either by using terms like "first," "second," "third," or by placing each step under a sequential heading such as (1) "choosing a subject," (2) "narrowing the subject," (3) "formulating a thesis statement," and so on. Clear headings can be exceedingly helpful to anyone who must follow a complicated explanation.

The following is a student process analysis of the steps involved in a "special circumstances" murder trial in the state of California. As before, we have included the instructor's editorial suggestions along with the student's revision.

Original:

In 1978 California adopted a death penalty law that requires execution or life imprisonment without possibility of parole for first-degree murder committed under what are termed "special circumstances," such as murder for financial gain, multiple or torture murder, murder by a hidden bomb, murder of a police officer, or murder to avoid arrest. Here are the steps involved in the trial of such an alleged murderer: First, the suspect is apprehended and charged with the murder. Second, a jury is chosen to listen to the testimony of the prosecution and defense and to find the defendant either guilty or innocent, and, if the defendant is found guilty, to decide whether "special circumstances" were involved. Third, if the defendant is convicted of murder with special circumstances, then the jury must decide whether to impose the death sentence or life imprisonment without the possibility of parole. Fourth, the law requires that in determining punishment, jurors must make a judgment concerning the aggravating or mitigating

This step — apprehending and charging and is not part of the trial (as announced in your first sentence).

elements affecting the crime, being bound to
impose death if aggravating circumstances
outweigh mitigating ones. In presenting its
case for mitigating circumstances, the defense
can bring up anything, from the defendant's
tragic childhood to mental illness or drug
addiction. Finally, the judge pronounces the
sentence. (Appeal) of a death sentence to the
California Supreme Court is automatic. If the
California Supreme court affirms the sentence,
the defendant may appeal to the U.S. Supreme
Court. If that route fails, the defendant may
go the route of habeas corpus proceedings, where
any issue not raised before can be brought up.
Aside from the courts, the governor may commute
a death sentence. It is no wonder that most
murder trials go on for years, completely
ignoring the U.S. Constitution's call for a fair
and speedy trial.

the appeal is not part of the trial either.

Revision suggestion: reorganize essay into three phases of bringing a murder suspect to justice. Revise the topic sentence to include ① arrest, ② trial, ③ appeal. If needed, add substeps under each heading.

Revision:

In 1978 California adopted a death penalty
law that requires execution or life imprisonment
without the possibility of parole for first-
degree murder committed under what are termed
"special circumstances," such as murder for
financial gain, multiple or torture murder,
murder by a hidden bomb, murder of a police
officer, or murder to avoid arrest. The task of

bringing a murder suspect to trial and seeing
that justice prevails is long and complex. The
entire process moves in three stages: The first
stage consists of the <u>arrest</u> in order to set a
court date. The second stage consists of the
<u>trial</u>, which in itself moves in phases: First,
a jury is chosen to listen to the testimony of
the prosecution and defense and to find the
defendant either guilty or innocent, and if the
defendant is found guilty, to decide whether to
impose the death sentence or life imprisonment
without parole. Second, the law requires that
in determining punishment, jurors must make a
judgment concerning aggravating or mitigating
circumstances, being bound to impose the death
sentence if aggravating circumstances outweigh
mitigating ones. In presenting its case for
mitigating circumstances, the defense can bring
up anything, from the defendant's tragic
childhood to mental illness or drug addiction.
Last, the judge pronounces the sentence. Now,
the final stage, the <u>appeal</u>, begins. Appeal of
a death sentence to the California Supreme Court
is automatic. If the California Supreme Court
affirms the sentence, the defendant may appeal
to the U.S. Supreme Court. If that route fails,
the defendant may go the route of <u>habeas corpus</u>
proceedings, where any issue not raised before
can be brought up. The last appeal is to the

governor, who may commute a death sentence.

Each of the three stages mentioned usually takes

months and years to become final. It is no

wonder that most murder trials go on for years,

completely ignoring the U.S. Constitution's call

for a fair and speedy trial.

The original version was badly organized because it did not stick to elaborating on the key word *trial* in the topic sentence. Since the paragraph dealt with such topics as apprehension and appeal, which are technically not part of a trial, the revised version enlarged the purpose of the paragraph to include a process analysis of "the task of bringing a murder suspect to trial and seeing that justice prevails." The process was then divided into three separate stages (arrest, trial, appeal) and explained one step at a time. For visual emphasis, each new stage was underlined when first introduced.

Exercises

1. In each of the following processes, cross out the steps that do *not* belong:

a. How to find a mate:
  (1) Spend time in popular haunts.
  (2) There is an art to catching a mate.
  (3) Wear the right clothes.
  (4) Know what to say.
  (5) Know how to behave.
  (6) A hostile attitude will not help.

Now write a well-developed paragraph explaining how a person should go about finding a mate.

b. How crime artists sketch the face of a suspect:
  (1) All available witnesses are asked for descriptions.
  (2) Unreliable witnesses are excluded.
  (3) Young witnesses are the most reliable.
  (4) The artist focuses on descriptions of these features: face, hair, eyes, ears, mouth, and distinguishing features such as scars.
  (5) Witnesses are asked to identify mug shots that resemble the suspect.
  (6) Witnesses are questioned about the suspect's nationality.
  (7) The artist produces a sketch and gets the witness's reaction.
  (8) It is always helpful if the suspect resembles someone famous.

Now write a paragraph explaining the process a crime artist uses to render the face of a suspect.

c. How to improve your reading:
   (1) Most of us can read faster than we do.
   (2) Read actively instead of passively.
   (3) Avoid regressions, that is, re-reading the same passage over and over.
   (4) You avoid regressions by forcing yourself to read faster.
   (5) Don't mouth the words with your lips as you read.
   (6) Read in word groups rather than one word at a time.
   (7) Some materials can be read faster than others.
Now write a paragraph explaining how to read faster.

2. Make a list of steps for improving some aspect of your life. Here are some possibilities:
a. neatness
b. grades in college
c. relationship with others
d. physical health
e. looks
f. personality

3. List in chronological order the steps you typically follow in reading the Sunday paper.

4. Pretend that you are dealing with a six-year-old child. Explain to this child exactly how to accomplish one of the following processes:
a. how to peel an orange
b. how to swim the breaststroke
c. how to sharpen a pencil
d. how to sweep the kitchen floor

Classifying

The classification paragraph or essay divides a subject, topic, or thing into its constituent parts or types and explains them. In both a scientific and everyday sense, classification is important to the way we think.

For example, it is nearly impossible to conceive of the biological sciences without its elaborate system of classification that pegs every living organism into a kingdom, class, order, family, genus, and species. Each of these larger categories contains many smaller types. Under the category of "class," are therefore to be found mammals, amphibians, insects, and arachnids. Under arachnids are found spiders, scorpions, mites, and ticks. This mazelike system of classification, which has struck many students as a pointless exercise designed to torment them, is a useful way of grouping living organisms by shared characteristics. It was primarily responsible for the theory of evolution, which was inferred to explain the observed similarities and differences between species.

The real aim of classification is to shield our thinking from the tyranny of uniqueness. We can imagine a time when primitive creatures must have thought every thunderstorm a singular catastrophe, every earthquake a fearfully unique event. But classification lessens our dread of these natural phenomena by enabling us to identify each individual outbreak as predictably part of a larger and known whole. Knowing the type or class to which an event belongs spares us the need to fear or futilely study every individual instance of it. If this were not so, a doctor would have to treat each case of the common cold as if it were absolutely unique. Every infection of polio would be utterly without precedent. Every thunderstorm would send us scurrying under the bed like children.

In our daily lives, informal classification similarly helps us grasp and relate to the people around us. We ask, "What type of person is he?" and the answer we give ourselves will determine whether we are trustful or suspicious, friendly or aloof. The disadvantage of this use of classification is that we sometimes hold false impressions about different types, which we unjustly use to snub or reject blameless individuals. Prejudice is classification that has gone bad. It is the wrong of unfairly smothering an individual under the blanket inaccuracies of a false type.

There are two primary ways of thinking by classification. The first places the part into the larger whole. Medical diagnosis consists essentially of this. By placing your symptoms into a certain category of disease or illness, a doctor can then treat you with the kind of medicine known to combat its effects. The second kind of thinking by classification breaks down an idea, event, or thing into its principal parts. This is the kind of classifying essayists usually do. It is intended mainly to sharpen your sense of logic and to exercise your thinking. And there are some specific injunctions that may be given for doing it well.

Base your classification on a single principle

The classifying principle or criterion is the knife that cuts the pie into wedges. If you say, "He is that kind of man," you must have some reason for saying so—whether the way he looks, the things he says, or the way he behaves. Classifying by more than one principle is a fundamental breach of logic that can lead to muddled thinking. For example, you may sort beans into two piles based on the classifying principle of whether or not they are edible by humans. If you then decided to also sort by the added principle of color, you could wind up with the right colored but poisonous bean in the edible pile and so kill some hapless diner.

Let us take a less lethal example of this basic error in classification. Your topic sentence promises to classify popular magazines by the kinds of topics they cover. First, you write, there are magazines like *People* that deal in gossip about famous people. Second, there are magazines like *Cosmopolitan* that stress high-powered lifestyles. Third, there are magazines like *Playboy* that appeal to the erotic appetites of their readers. Fourth, there are magazines like *Time* that report the news. Finally, you conclude, there are magazines like *Architectural Digest* that are subscribed to mainly by affluent suburbanites. This last entry is a poisoned bean and does not belong. Your jump from the principle of magazine topic to type of subscriber has broken the logic of the classification.

Note that the principle you use in a classification may not be as arbitrary as we may imply. Logic and common sense may sometimes suggest one principle over the other. For example, if you were asked to classify blocks identical in color, size, and weight but differing only in geometric shape, it is obvious which principle you should use. Similarly obvious principles will occur to you for various informal classifications. For example, if you were classifying the novels of a writer whose works fell into distinct periods, you would be wise to develop your essay by this obvious grouping rather than by some trivial principle.

Divide the entire topic

Completeness in a classification is a requirement of reasonableness and logic. We would wonder at anyone who wrote an essay classifying spectator sports into contact and noncontact contests but omitted football. Likewise, if you were to classify all religions into polytheism (the belief in many gods), dualism (the belief in two gods, one good and the other evil), and monotheism (the belief in one transcendent god), you would be leaving out the important category of pantheism (the belief that the whole universe is god). More obviously, you would not divide a country into north, east, and south—leaving out west.

Whether or not a reader takes your classification seriously enough to expect completeness depends on the purpose and tone of your paragraph or essay. As we have said, much of the classification of the essayist is an informal exercise in thinking to which no reasonable reader would apply the exactness of science. For example, Russell Baker, the noted columnist, once wrote an essay classifying inanimate objects into those that don't work, those that break down, and those that get lost. Given the humorous aim of that essay, it would take a singularly dense reader to quibble with Baker for omitting the category of objects that do work. Some classifications are imaginative and cannot be taken literally.

Keep your categories from overlapping

The individual categories of a subject must be kept separate one from the other or they will overlap and your classification will be flawed. Notice the overlapping segments in this attempt to classify "higher education":

    universities
    four-year colleges
    two-year colleges
    postsecondary institutions

Obviously, the last category does not belong since the other three are contained within it. To keep each category separate, use transitions that indicate when you are moving from one category to the next: "The first kind is," "The second kind is," and so forth.

Write approximately the same number of words on each entry

We would feel cheated by an essay that classifies soccer positions into backfield, midfield, and front line, and then spent five pages on the front line and a scant paragraph on the other two. Remember that a well-developed essay keeps the promise of its thesis. If you promise to classify and discuss, that is what you must do, giving equal time and ink to each individual part.

In the classification that follows, a student classifies the techniques used to combat insomnia. While the essay is informative and clearly written, it has some major weaknesses. The margins contain editorial suggestions that were heeded in the revision.

Original:

There are three techniques commonly used in the battle against insomnia, which some experts say affects more than 30 million Americans every night. The first of these, medication, may seem to be the most effective, but actually is the least and may cause the most harm. Doctors write some 20 million sleep prescriptions each

what are the three techniques? Introduce them.

year for various drugs, including dangerous barbiturates. The problem with barbiturates like <u>Seconal</u> and other drugs is that they interfere with the natural dreaming rhythm of sleep and can depress respiration. Drug therapy, agree the experts, works over the short run, but is not helpful over the long. With transcendental meditation the insomniac is taught to breathe deeply with movement of the diaphragm while slowly reciting a single syllable word known as a <u>mantra</u>. With self-hypnosis, the patient visualizes scenes of serenity. These techniques can help relax the insomniac and may even foster sleep, but they require a disciplined mind and may make the process of falling asleep into a mental struggle rather than one of relaxation. Adapting to the fact that you may be one of the people who need only four or five hours sleep a night, say scientists, will stop the worry about insomnia that sometimes aggravates or even causes it.

Transition needed to second technique, if this is it.

Where is the third technique? Develop it adequately

Revision:

There are three techniques commonly used in the battle against insomnia, which some experts say affects more than 30 million Americans every night. They are: medication, relaxation techniques, and adaptation to one's true sleep schedule. The first of these, medication, may

seem to be the most effective, but actually is
the least and may cause the most harm. Doctors
write some 20 million sleep prescriptions each
year for various drugs, including dangerous
barbiturates. The problem with barbiturates
like <u>Seconal</u> and other drugs is that they
interfere with the natural dreaming rhythm of
sleep and can depress respiration. Drug
therapy, agree the experts, works over the short
run, but is not helpful over the long haul.
Relaxation techniques comprise the second major
weapon in the fight against insomnia. With
transcendental meditation, for example, the
insomniac is taught to breathe deeply with
movement of the diaphragm while slowly reciting
a single syllable word known as a <u>mantra</u>. With
self-hypnosis, the patient visualizes scenes of
serenity. These techniques can help relax the
insomniac and may even foster sleep, but they
require a disciplined mind and may make the
process of falling asleep into a mental struggle
rather than one of relaxation. Finally, there
is what seems the least likely of all the
techniques to work: adapting to one's sleep
schedule. But this may just be the most
effective of all. Experts say that insomnia is
an illusion that is often grounded in a mistaken
idea of how much sleep one needs. Scientists
estimate that one-half the people who label

themselves insomniacs fall asleep just as fast

and stay asleep as long as normal sleepers.

Many people also do not need eight or even seven

hours sleep, but do well on only four or

five. Adapting to the fact that you may be one

of the people who need only four or five hours

sleep a night, say scientists, will stop the

worry about insomnia that sometimes aggravates

or even causes it.

Exercises

1. List the natural groups into which the following topics can be divided:
a. geological eras
b. government
c. fanaticism
d. letters
e. sins

2. Name the major category to which the following items belong. Delete any inappropriate term in each group; then write a paragraph discussing them in the groups to which they naturally belong.
a. metaphor, simile, semicolon, apostrophe, personification, allusion
b. dog, wolf, coyote, leopard, fox
c. centaur, unicorn, Medusa, dinosaur, minotaur, Cerberus
d. Elijah, Tiresias, Cassandra, Isaiah, Hannibal
e. incisors, files, canines, premolars, molars

3. Divide the contents of your local newspaper into logical major headings. Be sure that your principle of division is clear.

4. Think of some notorious criminals in history, and place them in separate categories based on a single principle of division. List at least two criminals in each category.

Writing Assignments

1. In a well-developed paragraph of at least 150 words, explain one of the following processes, or choose one of your own. Be sure to break down the process into clear, separate steps. Do not leave out any step. Introduce the process with a clear purpose statement:

a. how to study for a typical history exam
b. how to make a milkshake
c. how to lose weight and keep it off
d. how to refuse a date without being rude or hurting anyone's ego
e. how to set a formal table
f. how to cook a meal while camping in the mountains
g. how to balance a checkbook

2. Using a single principle of division, write a 500-word essay in which you classify one of the subjects listed below. Your classification should have a purpose and make a point.

Example thesis for *c:* "Regardless of whether they are fought to expand a territorial border, to recapture lost lands, or to exact revenge, all wars are barbaric."

a. professions
b. politicians
c. wars
d. house pets
e. television serials
f. computer software

3. Turn the following model into an essay developed by classification. Only the skeleton of the model is provided. If necessary, go to the library and find your own details. Some reorganization of the listed details may also be necessary:

Thesis: India's caste system divides the population into four distinct types.

The *Brahmans* are the priests and scholars.
The *Kshatrias* are the warriors and rulers.
The *Vaisyas* are the farmers and merchants.
The *Sudras* are the peasants and laborers.

Each of these castes has its own rules and traditions and is hierarchically organized. The lifestyles of the upper-class castes differ markedly from those of the lower class. The Brahmans live in luxury whereas the Sudras often suffer in terrible poverty.

4. Write a suitably organized and developed essay of between 300 and 500 words on one of the following topics:

a. Classify your life into stages through which it has passed to date.
b. Explain in detail any technical process you know well.

Chapter Eight

Comparing/Contrasting and Analyzing Cause

*H*ave ideas that are clear, and expressions that are simple.

MME. DE CHARRIERE (1740–1805)

Comparing/Contrasting

The paragraph or essay developed by comparison/contrast (often the word "comparison" is used to mean both) focuses on finding likenesses and unlikenesses between two people, ideas, objects, events, or items. For writers of expository prose, this is a routine assignment, and many essays begun with an entirely different purpose will be found to have at least one paragraph developed by comparison/contrast. For instance, let us assume that you are writing an essay for a political science class on the importance of free speech. Your thesis statement is "Argumentation is a fundamental aspect of any healthy society." But since you want to make it clear that arguing is not the same as quarreling, you decide to write a paragraph drawing a contrast between them. You begin your paragraph with the following topic sentence: "Arguing must never be confused with quarreling since the former is wholesome for society whereas the latter is pernicious." So far so good, but how to proceed from here?

Declare the bases of your comparison

Every comparison or contrast has an implicit basis. For example, if you say that so-and-so is more handsome than what's-his-name, the basis of that comparison is physical looks. If you declare that Mr. Moneybags has more money than Mr. Skinflint, your comparison is based on wealth. Before you can write a paragraph or essay comparing or contrasting any two items, you must have in mind the bases against which you intend to successively match them up. In the case of quarreling versus arguing, you might construct the following bases:

1. the reasoning involved
2. the mood created
3. the aims to be achieved

You will then show how arguing and quarreling differ in reasoning, mood, and aims.

In selecting the bases for comparing or contrasting, you should always choose those likely to reveal significant, not trivial, likenesses and differences. For example, if you are writing an essay contrasting jogging with tennis as forms of exercise, you might profitably cover their differing health benefits, risks, and expenses. But it would be trivial to focus your contrast on such secondary and inconsequential differences as which sport offers more exposure to fresh air or which is more fashionable in your hometown.

Complete the comparison by dealing with both sides

There are two sides to every comparison/contrast, and an honest essay or paragraph will cover both equally. However, a major weakness of student comparison/contrasts is the tendency to magnify on the differences of one side while ignoring those on the other. To avoid this lopsidedness, use the topics to be compared/contrasted as headings for separate columns, the bases as headings for separate rows, and then simply list the supporting facts under the appropriate row and column. Here is an example:

	Arguing	*Quarreling*
1. reasoning:	rational	emotional
	factual	embellished
	fair	biased
	consistent	contradictory
2. mood:	calm	turbulent
	reasonable	angry
	objective	subjective
	mature	childish

3. aims: discover truth   win points
             knowledge   status
             opponent's respect   opponent's defeat

This chart is a visual outline showing exactly what you must cover in the paragraph. Follow it and you are bound to give equal billing to each topic.

Use appropriate transitions to stress either likeness or difference

Transitions, as we saw on pages 122–23 of Chapter 4, are an important element in paragraph coherence. But in a paragraph that strictly compares or contrasts, they are often crucial. Here is a passage from a comparison/contrast paragraph that uses no transitions:

```
    Arguing and quarreling differ sharply in
the type of reasoning each uses.  An argument is
based on the rational presentation of ideas.
The one arguing presents the facts without
distorting or exaggerating them beyond
recognition.  Throughout the argument, he
remains fair and maintains a consistent
attitude, much the way a good sport calls fair
line shots when playing tennis.  A quarrel is an
emotional bombast in which the two sides ignore
facts and fairness.  The quarreler loads down
all statements with emotion and embellishes the
truth to the point where it cannot be
recognized.  Argument is the calm presentation
of the debater's facts.  Quarreling typically
screams out only biased or contradictory
information.
```

Without transitions, the back and forth movement of the contrast is too abrupt. Notice the difference made by the addition of transitions:

> Arguing and quarreling differ sharply in the type of reasoning each uses. <u>Whereas</u> an argument is based on rational behavior, buttressed by factual evidence, a quarrel is emotional bombast in which the two sides ignore facts and fairness. <u>In an argument</u>, the arguer presents the facts without distorting or exaggerating them beyond recognition. He remains fair and maintains a consistent attitude, much the way a good sport will fairly call line shots when playing tennis. <u>No such fairness, however, is to be found in most quarrels</u>. <u>Typically</u>, the quarreler loads down all statements with emotion and embellishes the truth to the point where it cannot be recognized. <u>While argument involves the calm presentation of the debater's facts</u>, quarreling typically screams out only biases or contradictory information.

For a listing of transitions useful for comparison/contrasts, turn to page 122.

Organize your comparisons either within or between paragraphs

A comparison may be organized either within or between paragraphs, depending mainly on the length and emphasis of the essay. If you are writing an essay based on a complex and extended comparison, you may wish to successively write about the compared items in separate paragraphs. On the other hand, for shorter and less emphatic comparisons, a single paragraph whose sentences are linked by appropriately strong transitions will do. Here is an example of self-respect and respectability compared within a single paragraph.

Self-respect and respectability are not to be confused. To have self-respect means to like yourself, to be comfortable about your values and the way you practice them in your life. It is entirely an inner judgment you make of yourself, which no one else can make of you. Respectability, on the other hand, is a judgment others make of you. The person with respectability is one who, in the eyes of others, adheres to conventional and accepted values. For example, the man with respectability will most likely be a churchgoer, a family man, someone who does not drink, does not go out at night, and is not mean to the family pet. The woman with respectability may be regarded as a good mother, a faithful wife, or a conscientious career woman. It is possible, however, to have respectability but not self-respect. For example, the man considered respectable may belittle himself for sticking to a job he does not like. The respectable woman may despise herself for staying with a husband she no longer loves. Of the two judgments, self-respect is the psychologically healthier.

Here is a similar comparison by the same student organized over three paragraphs.

Self-respect and respectability are not to be confused. To have self-respect means to like yourself, to be comfortable about your values and the way you practice them in your life. It is entirely an inner judgment you make of yourself, which no one else can make of you. The person with self-respect thinks he is basically good and worthwhile and has made this judgment of himself by his own values and not by the values of the world.

Respectability, on the other hand, is a judgment others make of you. The person with respectability is one who, in the eyes of others, adheres to conventional and accepted values. For example, the man with respectability will most likely be a churchgoer, a family man, someone who does not drink, does not go out at night, and is not mean to the family pet. The woman with respectability may be regarded as a good mother, a faithful wife, or a conscientious and ambitious worker.

However, it is possible to have respectability but not self-respect. For example, the man considered respectable may belittle himself for sticking to a job he does not like. The respectable woman may despise herself for staying with a husband she no longer loves. It is also possible to have self-respect but no respectability. For example, the conscientious objector who is sent to prison for that stand is robbed of respectability by his

opposition, but not of his self-respect. If he
had gone to fight in a war he regarded as wrong,
the world might confer "respectability" upon
him, but it would be at the cost of his self-
respect.

Which of the two organizing patterns you should use will depend on the
emphasis of your essay as will as on the complexity of the comparison. For
variety, writers frequently mix the two patterns within a single essay. Either
pattern will work if your transitions and introductory phrases are strong
enough.

In the following essay, a student compares two of the world's great
composers. The first draft of the essay violates some principles of a good
comparison/contrast, but corrections were made in the revision. Study the
first draft, along with the editorial suggestions, and notice how the revision
is a decided improvement.

Original:

    Although Beethoven's music is different

from Chopin's, both of these artists created

some of the most thrilling music ever performed.

make clear the basis of your contrast.

In fact, most people, when asked what classical

music they listen to, will include works by

Beethoven and Chopin. When the ear is tuned to

Beethoven's music, one can hear that it is

perfectly proportioned, like an Athenian temple.

In an era when people valued the classical Greek

ideals of form and rationality, Beethoven

responded by composing within the classical

rules of harmonization. [Chopin, like an untamed

stallion, broke away from all of the precise

melodies of the classical era. He was a

harbinger of the Romantic era, composing

seems out of place. make clear connection between Chopin and the basis of your contrast.

melodies that rang out with the dreams and hidden longings of the Polish people, to whom he belonged.] When analyzing Beethoven's method of composing, one sees clearly that he always adhered to the classical style, choosing traditional chords, which through variation he formed into pure, immaculate, untainted masterpieces. His "Pathetique," "Moonlight Sonata," and numerous symphonies are considered by critics to reveal perfect architectonics. ^ Chopin composed music that seemed to break all of the classical rules. He created chords that swelled into intensely dramatic, but often strangely unfamiliar, tonal combinations, bringing music to new heights through his nocturnes, scherzos, ballads, waltzes, mazurkas, and fantasies. Chopin's music was so unorthodox that many critics of his time considered it distastefully unruly and refused to call it music.

Transition needed to stress contrast

Revision:

Beethoven and Chopin, two of the world's greatest composers, differed completely as to the rules of composition they observed. When the ear is tuned to Beethoven's music, one can hear that it is perfectly proportioned, like an Athenian temple. In an era when people valued the classical Greek ideals of form and

rationality, Beethoven responded by composing
within the classical rules of harmonization.
When analyzing Beethoven's method of composing,
one sees clearly that he adhered to the
classical style, choosing traditional chords,
which through variation he formed into pure,
immaculate, untainted masterpieces. His
"Pathetique," "Moonlight Sonata," and numerous
symphonies are considered by critics to reveal
perfect architectonics. Unlike Beethoven,
Chopin seemed to abandon all of the classical
rules of composition. He created chords that
swelled into intensely dramatic, but often
strangely unfamiliar, tonal combinations.
Through his nocturnes, scherzos, ballads,
waltzes, mazurkas, and fantasies, he brought
music to unprecedented, novel heights. Chopin's
music was so unorthodox that many critics of his
time considered it distastefully unruly and
refused to call it music.

The revision improves the organization of the essay by declaring the base of the contrast before cleanly drawing it. Some initial sentences that blurred the focus of the topic sentence were eliminated. Transitions were also inserted as needed to smooth out the back and forth movement between Beethoven and Chopin.

Exercises

1. List the similarities and differences between the following pairs:
a. fast-food chains/gourmet restaurants
b. persuasion/force
c. white-collar work/blue-collar work

d. pathetic/tragic

e. love/romance

f. the attitudes of liberals and conservatives toward welfare assistance

2. Write two brief outlines for the separate development of the following subjects—within and between paragraphs (see pages 186–89).

a. the advantages of a small sports car over a large sedan (or vice versa)

b. the superiority of classroom discussion over lecturing as a pedagogic tool (or vice versa)

c. a contrast of the main street in your hometown during the day and night

d. the difference between civil disobedience and breaking the law

e. the difference between being prejudiced and being choosy

Analyzing Cause

Of all the modes of development, causal analysis is the most abstract and therefore the most difficult. The paragraph or essay developed in this mode focuses on explaining either the causes or effects of some occurrence. Exactly how that is done depends as much on the ability to think as to write (although it is arguable that the two go together). Good writing can sometimes compensate for bad thinking, but not when the subject is cause and effect.

To begin with, let us be clear about the difference between them. Consider, as our example, the awesome hurricane. Its *cause* is heat energy generated when warm ocean winds meet the cool upper air, forming a low-pressure trough behind which winds circulate in an accelerating spiral. Its *effects* may include uprooted trees, leveled houses, scuttled boats, downed power lines, flooded beachfronts, and loss of life. As you can see from the example, cause precedes an occurrence; effects succeed it. Cause always refers to some motivating event of the past, while effects always refer to some outcome in the future. The difference between the two is illustrated in this diagram:

Cause (past) ⟵—— Situation ——⟶ Effect (future)

The difficulty with writing about cause and effect is the same that accompanies any abstract subject. Mainly, you are thinking on paper—parading before a reader your capacity for reasoning. Some of the pitfalls awaiting the unwary are specious allegations about cause, shallow analysis of effects, and ideological reasoning. Many of these are blamable as much on bad thinking as on bad writing. But there are obvious traps to watch out for.

Be cautious about drawing cause-effect connections

Do you believe that divorce is caused mainly by people watching too much television? Or that the world would be automatically made right if only everyone went to church? Or that the effects of violent movies is to make future warmongers of children? We have read these and other similarly farfetched assertions of cause and effect in student papers, which seem to us to instruct against dogmatism. Do not dogmatically assert a cause unless you have solid proof to back it up. We know of no proofs that qualify any of the above assertions as more than a belief. But belief is not cause. It is only belief.

The hard fact about the world of causation is that much more is unknown than known, and what is known is always subject to revision with later evidence. Take, for example, the ongoing debate about the fate of dinosaurs. Dinosaurs were the undisputed lords of the world for eons before they mysteriously vanished during the Mesozoic era. Some scientists blame their disappearance on the draining of swamps, the dinosaurs' natural habitat; some on the onset of colder climates, to which reptiles could not adapt. Others allege that the large, clumsy dinosaur perished in competition with the hordes of small and fleet-footed mammals from which we descended. And, most recently, the theory has been proposed that a comet or an asteroid collided with the earth setting off continental wildfires whose soot killed the plant life and ultimately starved the dinosaur. All of these causes seem to make sense; yet, none can be dogmatically asserted without argument.

Our advice, then, is that you write cautiously about cause. We do not mean that you should shilly-shally or hedge your bet or give here while taking away there as tentative writers are likely to do. We mean only that you should do your homework, dig for the evidence, and set down with conviction what is truly known. You may qualify your causal speculations with such phrases as "it seems," "appearances indicate," or "the evidence points to." However, if your analysis is grounded in uncontested truth, you should say so plainly. For instance, state firmly that, "A recent study by the Palomar Corporation indicates that the amount of smoke and dust raised as a result of a nuclear war is far more extensive than anticipated by current civil defense plans." Or, "Studies have found that a major cause of obesity among Americans is overeating and lack of activity."

In particular, beware of drawing illogical cause-effect links that are circular or ideological. Here is an example of what we mean by circular reasoning:

Original: Heart infarctions are caused by a necrosis of blood

artery tissue.

By definition, an "infarction" is a "necrosis" (death) of the blood arteries; thus, all you have really said is, "An infarction is caused by an infarction."

Revision: Heart infarctions, that is, the sudden collapse of blood artery tissue, are caused when the arteries clog up and no longer allow blood to flow through.

Here is an example of an ideological pronouncement:

Original: Women slave in the house because they are trapped there and cannot get out owing to their excessive dependency on a man. That is the only reason why any woman would want to stay home and clean and cook all day.

This is entirely based on an ideological point of view, and a reader would have to share the writer's values before agreeing with this belief. It is not unreasonable to believe that some women may be trapped in the home by circumstances, but common sense also tells us that many are there by choice. Here is a more acceptable version:

Revision: Some women are trapped by circumstances into being housewives, when they would much rather be contributing in the working world. But others stay home not because of circumstances or brainwashing, but because they want to.

Nothing is ever as simple as the ideologue would have us believe. Causation is a complex force that should be written about with restraint and caution.

Use connectives to indicate a cause or effect relationship

This simply means that you should say outright whether you are talking about cause, effect, or both. Do so by using the right connectives—those phrases and words that make your meaning clear to a reader. Here are some examples along with the revisions:

Original: A corporate executive trying to close a sale in Peking should not wear white. In China, white is the symbol of mourning.

Revision: A corporate executive trying to close a sale in Peking should not wear white <u>because</u> in China white is the color of mourning.

Original: Word processors have changed the complexion of writing techniques. It is easy to make a variety of editorial changes.

Revision: One major <u>effect</u> of the computer is to make writing easy through word processing software that can quickly execute a variety of editorial changes.

In an analysis of several causes or effects, you might even number them as follows:

> The first cause is . . . .
> The second cause is . . . .
> The third cause is . . . .
> > OR
> One effect is . . . .
> Another effect is . . . .
> A third effect is . . . .

Focus on immediate rather than remote causes

In a philosophical sense, cause and effect constitute an infinite chain. Remember this rhyme?

> For want of the nail the shoe was lost.
> For want of the shoe the horse was lost.
> For want of the horse the rider was lost.
> For want of the rider the message was lost.
> For want of the message the battle was lost.
> For want of the battle the war was lost.

If we believe the premise of this jingle, we might fall into the trap of searching infinity for the cause lurking right under our noses.

But causal analysis rarely requires you to probe the philosophical mists. What is required is an analysis of proximate cause—the one nearest and most significant to the analyzed event. For example, let us say that your history instructor gave this assignment: "List two main causes leading to the adoption of the Monroe Doctrine." Among the immediate causes of the Monroe Doctrine were (1) the disagreement with Russia over the colonization of the northwest coast of the American continent, and (2) the fear that reactionary European countries would not acknowledge Latin America's newly won independence from Spain. To go beyond these to remote causes such as George Washington's policy of noninterference, or, even more remote, the notion of human freedom embodied in the Constitution, is to journey by unicycle when you might have gone by car. A sophisticated essayist can no doubt do it, but it is above and beyond the call of the assignment and, if botched, might earn you a poor grade accompanied by the comment, "Vague causal connection."

Occasionally, however, an assignment may require you to trace origins, and you will need to examine the remote. For example, if you were asked to explain the origin of the world-famous Oktoberfest, held each year in Munich, you would have to cite the celebration of the wedding between Crown Prince Ludwig of Bavaria to Princess Therese of Saxon-Hildburghausen in the nineteenth century, which evolved into the annual festival. Such special assignments aside, you should focus your analyses of cause on the immediate rather than on the remote.

The following paragraph analyzes the cause of human laughter. Although the student did an admirable job of explaining the ideas of French philosopher Henri Bergson, she needed to make some changes as indicated by the marginal editorial comments.

Original:

Your opening hints at more than definition. Begin with immediate cause. Focus on cause. Use the word "cause" in your topic sentence.

What is laughter? Dogs, birds, or lizards

don't laugh. Thus, we must assume that laughter

is the result of a higher, more developed

intelligence. Let us focus on some typical

example involving laughter. A pompous,

oversized, somber man, dressed in a spotless

pinstripe suit and vest, sits down in the lobby

of a luxury hotel to read the newspaper. But he

misjudges the distance between him and the sofa,

accidentally landing spread-eagle on the floor,
with a foolish look on his face. People run to
his aid, but it is obvious that they are more
amused than concerned. Several onlookers turn
away to keep from having their laughter
discovered. Now, if it had been obvious that
the man intended to sit on the floor, the desire
for laughing would not have surfaced. The fact
that the man's sitting down was involuntary is
what makes him the target of laughter.

Elaborate on this point with more examples.

your conclusion needs to be more definite.

Revision: *Conclude with a summary of the causal relationship you are analyzing. In other words, let your reader know exactly what causes laughter.*

What strange impulse causes human beings to
laugh? After all, dogs, birds, or lizards don't
laugh. Thus, we must assume that laughter is
the result of a higher, more developed
intelligence. But what exactly will cause in
humans this sudden reaction of a chuckle, a
giggle, a guffaw? Let us focus on some typical
example involving laughter. A pompous,
oversized, somber man, dressed in a spotless
pinstripe suit and vest, sits down in the lobby
of a luxury hotel to read the newspaper. But he
misjudges the distance between him and the sofa,
accidentally landing spread-eagle on the floor,
with a foolish look on his face. People run to
his aid, but it is obvious that they are more
amused than concerned. Several onlookers turn
away to keep from having their laughter

```
discovered.  Now, if it had been obvious that
the man intended to sit on the floor, the desire
for laughing would not have surfaced.  The fact
that the man's sitting down was involuntary is
what makes him the target of laughter.  Humans
laugh when a pie lands in some bungler's face,
when a stuck-up snob of a lady gets her skirt
caught in the door as she attempts to waltz away
in a snit, when a bucket of sewage water is
poured on an absent-minded professor daydreaming
as he passes under some putzfrau's window.  The
ridiculous element in each of these cases is a
certain mechanical inelasticity where one would
expect to find living pliability.  The cause of
laughter, in short, is clumsy obstinacy in a
situation that calls for skillful flexibility.
```

The revision more clearly spells out the causal connection, adds some specific examples as evidence, and gives a sense of purpose to the paragraph by ending on a clear topic sentence.

Exercises

1. List the causes and effects of the following situations:
a. smog in industrial cities
b. battered children (or spouses)
c. increase in drug addiction
d. growing interest in health
e. the difficulty of reaching an arms agreement with the Soviet Union
f. gravity
g. the beauty or ugliness of a certain place

2. Using the lists you created for Exercise 1, formulate a clear and concise thesis for a paragraph developed either through analysis of cause or of effect, such as: "The main causes of smog in industrial cities are factory pollution, automobile exhausts, and air inversion layers" or "The most obvious effects of smog in industrial cities are respiratory diseases, plant pollution, and an ugly environment."

Writing Assignments

1. In a 500-word essay, compare and contrast the lives and/or careers of any two significant figures of history. Use either the "within" or the "between" paragraphs method. Be sure to reveal the bases of your comparison/contrast and to deal with both sides.

2. Write a 500-word essay contrasting two societies or cultures (past or present) based on their geographical locations, their systems of government, and their general lifestyles. Be sure to state each basis of contrast and to deal with both sides. Here are a few possibilities, but many others exist: ancient Greeks and Romans, present-day Jews and Arabs, London and Paris in the eighteenth century, poor urban blacks and affluent urban blacks.

3. Focusing on a current economic, social, spiritual, or psychological problem in our society, describe the problem and write a 500-word analysis of either cause or effect. Here are a few possibilities, but many others exist: child pornography, the national deficit, lack of money for education, overcrowded prisons, excessively long and cumbersome court trials, unequal pay for women in the work force, serial marriages, apathy toward church affiliation.

4. Turn one of the following models into an essay developed either by analysis of cause or comparison/contrast. Only the skeleton of the model is provided. If necessary, go to the library and find your own details. Some reorganization of the details below may also be necessary:

a. Dag Hammerskjöld gained an international reputation when he served as secretary general of the United Nations.
> In 1955 he went on a diplomatic mission to Peking.
> In 1956 he was instrumental in establishing a United Nations emergency force to keep the peace in the Middle East.
> From 1960 to 1961 he played a strong role in gaining independence for Zaire, formerly the Belgian Congo.

USE CAUSAL ANALYSIS OF EFFECT

b. Foreign films tend to be far superior to those produced in the United States.
> Foreign films are original whereas American films are imitative.
> Foreign films usually show good taste whereas American films are often sleazy and brutal.
> Foreign films are rich in genuine slapstick comedy whereas American films rely mainly on gimmicky language and implausible situations.

There is a profound difference in the portrayal of love between men and women. For instance, in the French movie *The Last Metro*, which deals with the life of an actress and her leading man during the German occupation, one scene shows the lovers, unable to control their desires, embracing and then sinking slowly to the floor. Only their legs are shown. In an American movie, a similar scene would have been graphically sexual.

USE COMPARISON/CONTRAST

Chapter Nine

The Beginning, Middle, and Ending

*T*he point of good writing is knowing when to stop.

Lucy Montgomery (1874–1942)

Beginning the Essay

First impressions count. No doubt you've been told that by a parent urging you to wear clean clothes, wash your face, groom your hair. It happens also to be true of writing. Nothing puts off a reader more than a dull opening paragraph, one that sets the table for a banquet of warmed-over cliches and stale opinions. Become fuzzy in the middle of the essay, be boring towards the end, and an indulgent reader who has so far been entertained will forgive you. But there is no forgiving a bad first paragraph. If you inflict pain here, it is a cruelty unmixed by any earlier pleasure and therefore not forgivable.

The first paragraph is where you tell the reader what you are going to do, where you serve up your thesis statement. This is not the only place for a thesis statement, but it is the most customary. Some instructors insist that the thesis statement should always be the last sentence of the opening paragraph. In our own view, this is an insupportable orthodoxy, but if it is what your instructor wants you to do, naturally you should do it. From then on, here are some ideas about how to start off your essay on the best possible footing.

Begin at the beginning

The first law of incisive beginnings is a simple one: Begin at the beginning. This is no Oriental paradox. Many essays typically begin too soon, too distant from the point of contention and waste the first few sentences on needless fluff. Here is an example of what we mean. The assigned topic was, "Our society expects us to play many difficult and confining roles." One student began thus:

> Roles are what we all play, or so sociologists tell us. Many definitions of roles have been given, but the one that seems to fit sees the role as the equivalent of psychological clothes. Thus, an understanding of role playing is important to the individual's maturing process. We may wear the uniform of the service station attendant at work, but what we do not know is that we are also dressed in a psychological uniform. Mostly, we play at being what we are supposed to be at the moment. Roles are confining by definition, since they force a mask over one's true face. But it is my belief that this mask, and the wearing of it, is not necessarily bad. Without the comforting mask of roles, we would be thrown back on improvising on every occasion, and many of us would do badly. It is better that we have the part already written out for us by the role, and that we merely speak the lines from the script.

This is not a fatally bad beginning. The writer has some good ideas, and the analogy between role playing and the theater is cleverly put. What troubles us about this beginning, however, is that we are greeted with a needless definition and unnecessary commentary before we even know where the writer stands or what position towards roles she intends to take. Imagine your reader as an inquisitive person and your paragraph as a stranger met at a bus stop. "What are you about?" is what the reader is most likely to ask. If your personified first paragraph has any manners, it will state its business but not press on a stranger its full range of opinions too early. Here is a better opening:

```
Roles are confining by definition, since
they force a mask over one's true face.  But it
is my belief that this mask, and the wearing of
it, is not necessarily bad.  Without the
comforting mask of roles, we would be thrown
back on improvising on every occasion, which
many of us do badly.  It is better that we have
the part already written out for us by the role,
and that we speak the lines from the script.
```

We are at the beginning, the point of contention, the opening theme of the essay, and this is where we belong at the outset. To rework our beginning, we have taken a butcher knife to the fat and made the paragraph open on the meat of what the writer has to say. Later, this writer will tell us how roles have affected her life and give examples of how confining she has sometimes found them to be and, occasionally, how liberating.

As this example demonstrates, your real beginning may be buried several sentences, even paragraphs, into the essay and can be coaxed out only by the editorial blade. We have occasionally found a beginning pages into the first chapter. If you are unhappy with your beginning, try starting later in the essay. Experiment with cutting earlier paragraphs and moving a later one to the front. Sometimes this works rather well. (But sometimes it doesn't.)

Take a stand

Beginning without a firm and opinionated stand is another common fault of student essays. Here is an example of what we mean. The assigned topic was, "Why do some couples choose to live together without marrying?"

> Living together without being married is no
> longer a taboo. Millions of Americans are
> presently enjoying this state of being. Could
> this be because of the high divorce rate? Many
> people are getting divorced rather than married
> because divorces last longer. Whatever the
> reason, the fact remains that some couples
> choose to live together without getting married.

Do you see what's wrong with this? It is faltering, wimpy, droopy, and wishy-washy. The author has no position, takes no stand, commits to no cause. Students sometimes choose to deliberately perch on the fence of an argument, especially if they hold opinions contrary to the teacher's. But it is usually better to assume that your instructor is reasonable and will not punish an opposing view that is well argued, firmly backed, and coherently stated. (Our experience tells us that most instructors welcome student opinion that differs from their own.)

Contrast that beginning with this one, which thumps out its writer's unflinching opposition to the topic:

> Living out of wedlock is a fashionable and
> trendy arrangement today practiced by couples of
> nearly every age group. It is said to be a less
> complicated alliance than marriage, to ease the
> complications when the day of separation finally
> comes, and to more fairly split the expenses and
> chores of housekeeping. But it is still an
> arrangement that makes a virtue out of
> convenience and temporariness in relationships,
> and that is exactly why it is morally and
> socially bankrupt.

Do you feel your hackles rising? Or conversely, do you find yourself nodding vigorously? If you have either reaction, good! The opening paragraph has done its job—it's gotten your interest, and whether it has done that by riling you to a fury or sending you into a thunder of applause is beside the point. The point is that you want to read on, and that is exactly what a first paragraph should make you want to do. But nobody ever wants to go on reading wishy-washy writing, especially not instructors who are every semester splattered with a barrage of tentative opinions.

Do you have no opinion on the topic? Then change your topic (and reread the chapter on finding the thesis). Find an opinion! There is no magic formula for doing this, but reading decidedly helps. Read magazine articles, newspaper stories, books, and even cartoons, and soon you will find yourself reacting with agreement or opposition to an author's point of view. That reaction is the beginning of opinion.

Use various kinds of openings

Your essay does not have to lurch off with an introductory preamble patently intended as an usher for its thesis. And even if you intend to seat your thesis in the same pew every time—as the final sentence of the opening paragraph—you can at least lead it there by a different aisle.

You can, for example, begin with an **anecdote**. This example comes from a student paper in psychology that attempts to define *normal*:

```
One cold winter afternoon Fumiko Kimura

calmly walked into the turbulent Pacific Ocean

holding her four-year-old son and six-month-old

daughter by the hand. She meant to take her

life and the lives of her two children after

discovering that for the last three years her

husband had secretly kept a mistress. The

children drowned, but Fumiko herself was rescued

and tried for murder. To the general American

public her actions appeared bizarrely abnormal,

but in the Japanese community, where seppuku

(ritual suicide) has been traditional in cases

of tarnished honor, the action appeared normal.

What, then, is normal? The term normal . . . .
```

You can open with what journalists call a **bullet lead**—a short, punchy sentence that clouts the reader on the side of the head and says, "pay attention." Admittedly, bullet leads are not easy to think up, but they reward the effort in effectiveness. Here is an example:

> Your spouse can give you lung cancer. And
> so can your boyfriend, your girlfriend, your
> grandmother. Anyone who smokes regularly and
> heavily around you can give you lung cancer.
> Scientists are discovering that passive smoking
> is deadlier than they had imagined.

This opening grabs your attention right away by being direct, blunt, and unequivocal.

Also effective is the **spotlight opening**, which begins in the middle of things with an image, a scene, or description that dramatizes the topic. You get the chance to insert catchy details and create an impression of reportorial immediacy before launching your thesis. Here is an example:

> The victim, a woman in her mid-twenties,
> was found slumped on the living room floor, the
> side of her head partly bashed in by the blow
> from an ashtray. The house had been ransacked,
> the furniture overturned, clothes strewn over
> the bed. For all his cruelty, the thief earned
> blood wages of $20, which the victim had hidden
> in a vanity drawer. Ten years later, as the
> recovered victim was shopping in downtown
> Chicago, she came face to face with her
> attacker, screamed for the police, and had him
> arrested. But the charges were dropped because
> the statute of limitations on the crime had
> expired. This unexpected outcome seemed to the

```
victim a grave injustice. But although it

allows an occasional criminal to get away with a

crime, the statute of limitations is a

worthwhile curb that does more good than harm.
```

Of course, one should not invent such details, but should uncover them by honest research. Do your homework, find the details you need, and you are ready to create a spotlight opening that will add drama to your thesis.

Finally, you may open with a **quotation**. If the quotation is apt and neatly sums up some essential element of your thesis, it can be an effective beginning. On the other hand, if the quotation is blurry or irrelevant, you could be off to a bad start. Here is an example of a good start from a student essay arguing against admitting children with AIDS to public schools.

```
Lord Salisbury once wrote in a letter, "No

lesson seems to be so deeply inculcated by the

experience of life as that you should never

trust experts."  That is the crux of the debate

about whether children who are stricken with

AIDS (acquired immunity deficiency syndrome)

should be allowed to go to public schools.

History tells us that the medical experts have

been wrong enough in the past about the spread

of disease to justify withholding the sick

children from public schools.
```

It is possible to write an essay with a bad beginning but a good middle. Many have done so, claiming that they were cold at the start but progressively warmed to the topic as they went on. One answer to this complaint is to wait until you are loose and thoroughly warmed up before rewriting your beginning.

Exercises

1. From the following paired openings, choose the one with greater reader appeal. Be prepared to give reasons for your choice.

a.(1)   Shakespeare's *King Lear* has often been hailed by critics as Shakespeare's greatest play because the main character vividly dramatizes important truths about life. The play is filled with plots and counterplots that underscore the complexities of life and its sorrows. It is a play that reaches magnificent tragic heights. All of the main characters are three-dimensional and therefore believable. No wonder the popularity of this play has lasted for over three centuries.

(2)   He disowned the only daughter who truly loved him. He spoiled the two daughters who flattered him to get his money and power. He was a vain old man with a mammoth craving for monopolized attention. But in the end he is more sinned against than sinning when, bereft of his kingdom and his sanity, he is pushed out into a raging storm and left to rant and rage on the weather-beaten heath. Few other plays in any language portray more vividly the wretchedness of human life than does *King Lear*.

b.(1)   Ulysses S. Grant, the man who won the Civil War, represents one of history's typical paradoxes—the mediocre person who, through some mysterious combination of circumstance, achieves momentary splendor. Despite the many sleazy facts associated with his life (his drinking, his swindles, and his lower-class tastes), he stumbled onto history's center stage to thrill the audience for a scene or two. He made the American dream come true by becoming a successful military commander and gaining two terms in the White House. Grant has become the symbol of the extraordinary possibilities contained within the ordinary.

(2)   Ulysses Simpson Grant, who lived from 1822 to 1885, became commander in chief of the Union Army during the Civil War and eighteenth president of the United States. Grant was in many ways not a spectacular man. For instance, before joining the army, he was a simple clerk selling cordwood in St. Louis and Galena. He was even forced to resign from the army in 1854 because of excessive drinking. He failed in his attempts to become a farmer and a businessman. His presidency was a national disgrace because of considerable corruption. Yet, Grant made a lasting name for himself.

2. Identify the kinds of leads used in the following opening paragraphs:

a.   It began just the way a good spy story should. Early in 1981 an unnamed Frenchman walked into the Paris headquarters of the Direction de la Surveillance du Territoire, the French counterintelligence agency, carrying a letter that he said he had been asked to smuggle out of Moscow. . . .
—"Secret Admirer," *Time*, January 20, 1986.

b.   For some, it was like being told chocolate cures cancer. A study recently released by a Johns Hopkins researcher showed that moderate beer drinkers were sick 25 percent less often than teetotalers or those who drink stronger spirits.
—"Beer Drinkers Grab onto Study Results with Gusto," *Atlanta Constitution*, January 14, 1986.

c.   I once had a gutsy English teacher who used a drugstore paperback called *Word Power Made Easy* instead of the insipid fare officially available. It contained some nifty words and she would call upon us in turn for definitions. . . .
—Stephen Jay Gould, "Agassiz in the Galapagos."

3. Choose one of the following controlling ideas and find a quotation that could be used as a suitable opening:
a. Total dependency on someone of the opposite sex is destructive.
b. People exaggerate when they apply for a job.
c. Chicago (or New York, or Los Angeles, or any other major city) is a fascinating city.
d. Punctuality is a good habit to cultivate.

The Middle

Problems of careless, frail, or nonexistent transitions between paragraphs are typical middle essay weaknesses. It is a mistake to think that because paragraphs are sequential their ideas must follow logically. Logical continuity between the ideas of different paragraphs is the result of some deliberate bridging by the writer—mainly through the use of transitions. Your aim in the middle of the essay should therefore be to caulk the seams between your paragraphs until their separate topics and ideas dovetail with the continuity and smoothness of watertight planking.

How do you accomplish this? First, you master some common techniques for making paragraph transitions. Second, you put them to use in your essay. Transitions between paragraphs have two functions: they signal an end to the present discussion; they announce a new beginning. Indirectly, they say to a reader, "We've done with this now; we're about to take up that."

In a few instances, when paragraphs succeed one another with a clear and obvious sameness of purpose, no formal transitions between them is necessary. Here is an example:

Next to Hitler, Goring was the most popular Nazi leader in the country and the most powerful. As prime minister and minister of the interior of Prussia, he had a great deal of power in the most important and largest part of Germany. He had control of the Prussian police and of most of the rest of the government apparatus. He set up the Gestapo, the secret police, to terrorize any lurking opposition and founded the concentration camps in which to incarcerate any who defied the Nazi authority or who were Communists, Socialists, liberals, pacifists, and/or Jews. He was president of the Reichstag. He was boss of German aviation, both civil and now military. He would soon be given more titles by Hitler that would make him pretty much the czar of the economy.

He got things done. He also loved luxury and opulence and already had begun to acquire several castles and to build a fantastic showplace outside Berlin which he called Karin Hall, after his deceased Swedish wife. He was also said to be a morphine addict, though he would kick the habit for fairly long periods only to fall back into it when the strain of life got him down. Goring was an authentic war hero, the last commander of the famed Richthofen Fighter Squadron, one of the rare holders of Germany's highest war decoration, *Pour le Merite*, though he was only an army captain when he was mustered out.
—William L. Shirer, *The Nightmare Years: 1930–1940.*

The writer uses no formal transition between the paragraphs because they are both focused on the common purpose of describing the Nazi war criminal Hermann Goring.

Instances like this aside, it is usually necessary to join paragraphs by some formal transitions of varying strength, depending on the degree of difference between the linked paragraphs' contents. Where there is an obvious similarity in the ideas of two paragraphs, or even in their purpose, little or no transition is needed. But where there is a gaping difference in idea and purpose, some obvious bonding between the paragraphs will be necessary or your essay will seem disjointed. Here are some ideas for linking paragraphs together with smooth transitions.

Repeat key words at the beginning of each new paragraph

Repeating key words from the thesis statement at the beginning of each new paragraph is a good transitional technique for short essays. The repetition holds the reader's attention on the subject while cementing the paragraphs together with a common theme. Here is an example from a student essay:

Social pressure is an ever present force.
Whether it is experienced in small or large
degrees, social pressure affects all of us. We
get it from the people at work, from friends,
and even from our parents.

At my own job I am under constant <u>social</u>
<u>pressure</u> to do well. Being a bank teller, I am
graded each week by a merit system which reviews

overages and shortages in my money drawer and my

relationship with my customers. I have also

found that fellow workers can exert a great deal

of pressure. For example, every year the bank

has a number of parties. Being a nondrinker and

a nonsmoker I prefer not to go to the parties.

Even though I have explained my reasons for not

attending, there is still the ever present

<u>pressure</u> from co-workers for me to attend the

parties, usually with a few added "goody-two-

shoes" remarks.

    Friends also have a way of exerting <u>social</u>

<u>pressure</u>, though it is usually very subtle.

During my last year in high school my best

friend's personality began to change, and our

friendship slowly dwindled. A few months ago

she told me that she had gotten involved with

the wrong crowd during our senior year, and

before she realized what was happening she had

let herself be persuaded into all sorts of

trouble.

The underlined key words serve as a kind of thematic glue between the paragraphs, enabling a reader to follow the writer's reasoning easily.

Begin the new paragraph by restating the idea that ended the old

Restating an idea is a subtler and more complicated transition used mainly in long essays. Here is an example:

    A revolution within our society has been

raging for over a decade, causing radical

changes to occur in the roles of the female. A

concept of individualism without regard to sex
has evolved into the American ethic with
dramatic results. Women have gained a greater
sense of worth that has led to increased sexual
freedom and career potential. Women have also
gained a greater equality in the home, becoming
breadwinners with a more mutual sharing of the
housework. They have been released both in the
job market and in styles from the traditional
female roles of the past. But what of the
male's freedom? If the female has the right to
break with the old norms, why does the male
still have to perform within strict masculine
guidelines? While the female has been able to
assume new roles, the male has been only further
imprisoned in his old ones.

The imprisonment of the male is partly
social and partly self-imposed. Society has
long dictated the roles of the sexes and even
with the advent of women's liberation, not much
has dramatically changed for the male . . . .

Notice that the idea that ended the first paragraph is restated at the beginning of the second, resulting in a smooth transition.

Ask a rhetorical question

A question that sums up and extends the note on which the previous paragraph ended can also serve as a strong transition. Here is an example taken from a student essay on sailboats:

There are three main types of rigs among small
pleasure sailing craft with keels. The first is the

```
sloop.  This rig consists of a single mast and
two sails, a main and a jib.  The second is the
cutter.  This rig uses a main and usually two
small jibs.  Cutters have the advantage of
having two smaller and more manageable jibs in
place of a large and unwieldy one.  The third is
the ketch, and its variation, the yawl.  This
rig uses two masts and usually three sails:  the
mizzen, the main, and a jib.

    What prevents the keel sailboat from
capsizing?  The answer is grounded in the laws
of physics and in the design of keel boats.
When the boat heels, its rudder . . . .
```

Naturally, the question must not only be to the point, it must nudge the discussion into the topic of the new paragraph.

Use transition phrases

Many writers have and use a stock of favorite transition words and phrases to lash together paragraphs. These include such faithful standbys as "besides," "however," "in that case," "also," "needless to say," and "on the other hand." These phrases help the reader by pointing out the new path that the writing intends to take; they also help the writer to alter course. Here is an example from a student essay contrasting love and lust:

```
    One of the main differences between love
and lust is the length of time that the feeling
lasts.  Lust is an immediate reaction towards a
person, and it can fade rather quickly with the
prospect of another relationship.  A common
example of a feeling of lust is when a young
student develops an interest in a teacher, often
referred to as a "crush."
```

<u>On the other hand</u>, love is not nearly as
easy to get over as lust and lasts a great deal
longer.   When two people are really in love, the
relationship between them could easily last a
lifetime.   Love is also not affected by
newcomers or new prospects, but seems to feed on
and grow with the intimacy between the lovers.

"On the other hand," warns the reader that a contrast is upcoming in the
new paragraph while setting the stage for the new business at hand. The
suitability of a transition phrase or word depends on what your new paragraph will do and the direction it will take. See Chapter 4 for a listing of
some common transition terms and their meanings.

Use an initial summarizing sentence

Magazine writers love this one, which students seldom use: You
simply open your new paragraph with a sentence that refers to and sums
up the meat of the discussion in the old. This gentle reminder of what has
already been said becomes a lead-in for your new material. Here is an example from an essay on local governments:

The basic idea of local government is that
it will solve local problems and be responsive
to local citizens.   Some of the pressing day-to-
day requirements of a community can only be met
by immediate and local response.   So local
governments run the schools, pick up the
garbage, and provide police protection for the
community.

<u>But making the life of its citizens run</u>
<u>smoother is not all local governments do.</u>   What
they are mainly supposed to do is give each
citizen the feeling of participation in his own
destiny.   This feeling . . . .

When we come to this opening sentence, we immediately think, "Aha! More on what local governments do will follow" and so the two paragraphs are neatly joined by a single suture.

Use a transition paragraph

Finally, there is the transition paragraph, which is a small, specialized paragraph used to shift the focus of writing between major themes. Because they are usually short and centered on a single topic, student essays seldom use transition paragraphs. But if you should need to lever your writing from one major topic to another, the transition paragraph is a handy fulcrum for doing it. Here is an excerpted example from a student paper on the unhappy lives of some European monarchs. The writer wraps up her discussion of Richard II in the first paragraph, then uses a transition paragraph (underlined) to shift her focus to the fate of Marie Antoinette.

```
    . . . And so Richard, only 33 years old, ended

his days a prisoner in Pontecraft Castle, where

Shakespeare tells us he was murdered by noblemen

loyal to Henry IV.  But even this is uncertain,

and some historians argue that he starved

himself to death.

    But sad as his last years were, Richard was

at least spared the humiliating fate reserved

for Marie Antoinette.

    Marie Antoinette was born in 1755,

the daughter of Austrian Archduchess Maria

Theresa and Holy Roman Emperor Francis I.  Her

marriage to the dauphin, later King Louis XVI of

France, took place when she was 15 and was

intended . . . .
```

Since they perform a specialized function, transition paragraphs are typically skimpy, have no topic sentence, no specific details, and no organizing pattern. They are useful only for making major transitions.

A final word on transitions. Should you find yourself stumbling badly between topics and fumbling for ways to stitch your paragraphs together, the best answer may be to rethink what you are trying to do. A well-thought-out essay shows few of its seams, and with a definite mastery of the material and a sound overall plan, a writer should not have to grope desperately for ways to tie together paragraphs. If that is what you find yourself doing, your inability to find the right transitions may be a symptom of something else wrong with your essay. Perhaps you have not yet decided exactly how to break down your subject. Or you may have taken on more than you can handle. Rather than struggling for the right word or phrase, give some thought to what you really are aiming to do and whether or not you have the order of topics properly worked out.

Exercises

1. Explain the transitions used between the following pairs of paragraphs:

a.   Most tarantulas live in the tropics, but several species occur in the temperate zone and a few are common in the southern U.S. Some varieties are large and have powerful fangs with which they can inflict a deep wound. These formidable looking spiders do not, however, attack man; you can hold one in your hand, if you are gentle, without being bitten. Their bite is dangerous only to insects and small mammals such as mice; for a man it is not worse than a hornet's sting.

Tarantulas customarily live in deep cylindrical burrows, from which they emerge at dusk and into which they retire at dawn. Mature males wander about after dark in search of females and occasionally stray into houses. After mating, the male dies in a few weeks, but a female lives much longer and can mate several years in succession. In a Paris museum is a tropical specimen which is said to have been living in captivity for 25 years.

—Alexander Petrunkevitch, "The Spider and the Wasp," *Scientific American.*

b.   Not that people think that love is not important. They are starved for it; they watch endless numbers of films about happy and unhappy love stories, they listen to hundreds of trashy songs about love—yet hardly anyone thinks that there is anything that needs to be learned about love.

This particular attitude is based on several premises which either singly or combined tend to uphold it. Most people see the problem of love primarily as that of *being loved*, rather than that of *loving*, of one's capacity to love. Hence the problem to them is how to be loved, how to be lovable . . . .

—Erich Fromm, *The Art of Love.*

c.   Let us take, first, the plastic arts, sculpture and painting; and to bring into clear relief the Greek point of view let us contrast with it that of the modern "impressionist." To the impressionist a picture is simply an arrangement of colour and line; the subject represented is nothing, the treatment is everything. It would be better, on the whole, not even to know what objects are depicted; and, to judge the picture by a comparison with the objects, or to consider what is the worth of the objects in themselves, or what we might think of them if we came across them in the connections of ordinary life, is simply to misconceive the whole meaning of a picture. For the artist and for the man who understands arts, all scales and standards disappear except that of the purely aesthetic beauty which consists in harmony of line and tone; the most perfect human form has no more value than a splash of mud; or rather both mud and human form disappear as irrelevant, and all that is left for judgment is the arrangement of colour and form originally suggested by those accidental and indifferent phenomena.

In the Greek view, on the other hand, though we certainly cannot say that the subject was everything and the treatment nothing (for that would be merely the annihilation of art) yet we may assert that, granted the treatment, granted that the work was beautiful (the first and indispensable requirement), its worth was determined by the character of the subject . . . .

—G. Lowes Dickenson, *The Greek View of Life.*

d.   The word *stress*, like *success, failure,* or *happiness,* means different things to different people, so that defining it is extremely difficult although it has become part of our daily vocabulary. Is stress merely a synonym for distress? Is it effort, fatigue, pain, fear, the need for concentration, the humiliation of censure, the loss of blood, or even an unexpected great success which requires complete reformulation of one's life? The answer is yes and no. That is what makes the definition of stress so difficult. Every one of these conditions produces stress, but none of them can be singled out as being "it," since the word applies equally to all the others.

Yet, how are we to cope with the stress of life if we cannot even define it? The businessman who is under constant pressure from his clients and employees alike, the air-traffic controller who knows that a moment of distraction may mean death to hundreds of people, the athlete who desperately wants to win a race, and the husband who helplessly watches his wife slowly and painfully dying of cancer, all suffer from stress. The problems they face are totally different, but medical research has shown that in many respects the body responds in a stereotyped manner, with identical biochemical changes, essentially meant to cope with any type of increased demand upon the human machinery . . . .

—Hans Selye, *Stress Without Distress.*

Ending the Essay

There are many ingeniously bad ways to end an essay, with new ones being invented every semester. But there is one astoundingly bad ending that enjoys nearly universal favor among student writers, and we intend to do our best to persuade you against using it. To demonstrate, we will use it as a hypothetical ending to this chapter:

```
        And so as you can see from our examples and

from what we have said before, you should try to

give your essay an inviting beginning, a solid

middle, and a crisp ending.  These are the

reasons why we think students who pay attention

to their beginnings, middles, endings, and

writing voice will write better essays.
```

The "as-you-can-see-these-are-the-reasons" ending is the weakest imaginable and is the one note you should never, never strike in your ending. This
is a bad ending because it insultingly implies that your reader cannot understand your reasons nor infer what you mean without being pointedly told.
Bad writers often feel compelled to point out the obvious; good writers assume that their readers are clever enough to fathom the moral of an essay
or tale for themselves. Your reader can obviously grasp your reasons and
already knows that they are your own and why you think them important.
It is therefore unnecessary to rehash the point further. End abruptly, capri-
ciously, even prematurely if you must; but never end with the "as-you-can-
see-these-are-the-reasons" refrain.

Aside from this single principle, our message on endings is necessarily abstract. We cannot tell you how to end your essay without looking over
your shoulder as you write it. What we can say is that endings, like beginnings and middles, are frequently improved by editing. Here, as an example,
is the unedited ending of the essay on male and female roles:

```
        Altogether, the pressure of peers and

reverse reaction to women's liberation have

brought man even closer to the traditional male

role.  He still must represent the strong,

dominant type on the outside while keeping

sensitivity and weakness buried deep inside.

Man must remain a contradiction to his real

needs as long as society keeps the keys.  For

that reason, I believe that men will not be free

for a long time.  Men need to have their own
```

```
male revolution before they can break out of the

macho shell.  From what I have already said, I

don't know if this will ever happen.
```

Look at what happens to this ending when we pare away the last three sentences:

```
Altogether, the pressure of peers and

reverse reaction to women's liberation have

brought man even closer to the traditional male

role.  He still must represent the strong,

dominant type on the outside while keeping

sensitivity and weakness buried deep inside.

Man must remain a contradiction to his real

needs as long as society keeps the keys.
```

Can you tell the difference between them? The first ending seems to peter out on the halfhearted expression of an opinion; the second comes to a clean and emphatic end. Because you cannot give it the documentation, support, or elaboration it would enjoy in the middle of an essay, the opinion expressed in an ending paragraph is strictly an orphan. Put your opinions in earlier, where you can defend them. Save the last paragraph for conclusions.

Like the example, many student endings tend to be two or three sentences too long, mainly because of the composing momentum. By the time you are at the end, you've developed a head of steam and hate to stop. But stop you must, when it is time. Here, for example, is the ending paragraph of a research paper on poetry therapy:

```
If poetry therapy continues to be accepted

and practiced at the rate it is now, it could

end up becoming one of the most widely practiced

methods of therapy around.  Then perhaps poets

will finally be recognized for the major role

they played and still play in helping to keep

people who live in an insane society at least
```

partly sane. According to the author of The
Poetry Cure,

> When the day comes that poetry is an
> acceptable means of treatment we will
> understand Ludwig Van Beethoven and
> his statement, "How can we ever
> sufficiently thank that most precious
> treasure of a nation--a great poet?"

The author goes on to express the importance of
the continued practice of poetry therapy when he
exclaims, "Not until mankind learns the
importance of creative expression to his health,
shall we have a better moral world."

Gauging the best stopping point requires an experienced ear, and ours tells us that the writer goes one quotation too far. After editing, this is what her ending sounded like:

> If poetry therapy continues to be accepted
> and practiced at the rate it is now, it could
> end up becoming one of the most widely practiced
> methods of therapy around. Then perhaps poets
> will finally be recognized for the major role
> they played and still play in helping to keep
> people who live in an insane society at least
> partly sane. According to the author of The
> Poetry Cure,
>
> > When the day comes that poetry is an
> > acceptable means of treatment we will

> understand Ludwig Van Beethoven and
>
> his statement, "How can we ever
>
> sufficiently thank that most precious
>
> treasure of a nation—a great poet?"

With removal of the final quotation, which seemed an afterthought, the ending now has more authority. Note also that the improvement is not the result of additional writing, but of editing. Endings, like beginnings, can often be improved by paring down.

Some other obvious observations may be made about endings. First, good endings always touch on their beginnings, but not too blatantly. You do not have to tie an obvious knot between them, merely hint at the existence of a common thread. Here, for example, is the beginning of an essay by Pearl Buck:

> I have long looked for an opportunity to pay a certain debt which I have owed since I was seven years old. Debts are usually burdens, but this is no ordinary debt, and it is no burden, except as the feeling of warm gratitude may ache in one until it is expressed. My debt is to an Englishman, who long ago in China rendered an inestimable service to a small American child. That child was myself and that Englishman was Charles Dickens. I know no better way to meet my obligation than to write down what Charles Dickens did in China for an American child.

It is clear what the author is starting out to do in this essay: pay homage to Dickens. Here is her ending:

> This is what Dickens did for me. His influence I cannot lose. He has made himself a part of me forever.
> —Pearl Buck, "A Debt to Dickens," *Saturday Review*, April 14, 1936.

In this ending paragraph is contained a glimpse of the beginning. But it is only a glimpse. Some business has been transacted in the essay, and the final paragraph concludes it with that quick backward glance to the beginning which is so characteristic of good endings.

Here is another beginning taken from an essay by H. L. Mencken:

> On a winter day some years ago, coming out of Pittsburgh on one of the expresses of the Pennsylvania Railroad, I rolled east-

ward for an hour through the coal and steel towns of Westmoreland county. It was familiar ground: boy and man, I had been through it often before. But somehow I had never quite sensed its appalling desolation. Here was the very heart of industrial America, the center of its most lucrative and characteristic activity, the boast and pride of the richest and grandest nation on earth—and here was a scene so dreadfully hideous, so intolerably bleak and forlorn that it reduced the whole aspiration of man to a macabre and depressing joke. Here was wealth beyond computation, almost beyond imagination—and here were human habitations so abominable that they would have disgraced a race of alley cats.

And here in this essay's ending:

> Here is something that the psychologists have so far neglected: the love of ugliness for its own sake, the lust to make the world intolerable. Its habitat is the United States. Out of the melting pot emerges a race which hates beauty as it hates truth. The etiology of this madness deserves a great deal more study than it has got. There must be causes behind it; it arises and flourishes in obedience to biological laws, and not as a mere act of God. What, precisely, are the terms of those laws? And why do they run stronger in America than elsewhere? Let some honest *Privat Dozent* in pathological sociology apply himself to the problem.
> —H. L. Mencken, *A Mencken Chrestomathy.*

Ugliness is thematically present at the beginning of this essay and, with a slight variation, also at the ending. The lesson here is that if your ending is utterly and untraceably distant from your beginning, you may have ventured a paragraph too far.

Second, an ending should not introduce a topic not already thoroughly covered in the essay. The ending is not the place for asides, for additions, for overlooked ideas, for last minute chest-thumping. It should take you to the limit of your thesis and no further. Here, for example, is the beginning of a student essay on social pressure.

> Social pressure is an ever present force. Whether it is suffered in small or large degrees, each one of us experiences social pressure from the people we work with, from friends, and even from parents.

Having described the social pressure often exerted by co-workers, friends, and parents, the writer should have been content to stop. Instead, she blundered into a secondary topic in her ending:

> Social pressure can be bad and it can also work some good. The key is learning which pressures are meant for your benefit and which ones are not. How can you do this? First, you should ask yourself whether you are being pressured into something that goes against your conscience. If you are, then the pressure is bad and shouldn't be tolerated. Second, you should ask yourself what your own inclinations are in this matter. If you find that what you truly want is not what the pressure dictates, you should follow your own mind so long as your desires are not immoral or illegal. Live your own life, not the life of your parents or friends. There are also other things you can do to resist social pressure.

How to resist social pressure is not part of the essay's thesis. We suggested the student edit it out. Here is what her revised ending looked like:

> Social pressure can be bad and it can also work some good. The key is learning which pressures are meant for your benefit and which ones are not.

This rounds out things nicely, with little fuss and bother.

Primarily, a good ending should bring the essay to a close that is both logical and necessary. It is logical because having done what you said you would do in the thesis statement, the only reasonable course left is to stop. And it is necessary because anything else you write will stray beyond your thesis and make you seem long-winded. Here are some models of good endings that demonstrate what we mean:

From an essay by Will and Ariel Durant, discussing the contributions of Boris Pasternak, Aleksandr Solzhenitsyn, and Yevgeni Yevtushenko to Russian literature:

> But it may be wise for us of the West to assume that the spirit of Russia today is voiced not by the tender longings of Pasternak, nor by the bitter memories of Solzhenitsyn, but by the ardor and courage of Yevtushenko. "I want to believe," he writes, "that everything is still ahead of me, as it is for my people." Let us heartily wish them well in their internal affairs despite their sins and ours. Perhaps their experiments and their sufferings will bring some costly but precious increment to the frail intelligence of mankind.
> —Will and Ariel Durant, *Interpretations of Life.*

From an article, written by Jack Smith for *Los Angeles Magazine,* gently satirizing modern hostesses who rarely start and end their parties on time:

> Years after the war, when Gen. Smith had retired and was living in a rose-covered cottage at La Jolla, I was sent down with photographer Bruce Cox to interview him. We had an appointment for 1000 hours. I warned Cox that when Gen. Smith said 1000 hours, he didn't mean 1001. We got to the cottage on time, but Cox used up a minute or two getting his gear out of the trunk, and I told him, "I'm going on. I don't want to be late."
> I rang the doorbell. Gen. Smith himself opened the door.
> "Good morning, General," I said. "I hope I'm not late."
> The general looked at his watch and then gave me a remonstrative look.
> "Well," he said, "only a minute."
> Why can't hostesses be like that?
> —Jack Smith, *Los Angeles Magazine,* January 16, 1986.

From a student essay written on the thesis: "My idea of a beautiful woman is a big buxom German opera singer":

> Daily I pray to the great god Odin to send me a
> woman such as this.

From an article, written by Richard Leakey and Alan Walker for *National Geographic*, describing the unearthing, near Lake Turkana in Kenya, of a fossil skeleton belonging to *homo erectus*:

> Only luck, the presence of a supply of underground water, and the scanty shade of a few parched thorn trees first drew us to the Nariokotome River and the skeleton of the boy from Lake Turkana. During the 1985 excavation, we began to uncover the last of the missing bones, adding another page to his biography—and to mankind's.
> —Richard Leakey and Alan Walker, *National Geographic,*
> November 1985.

Finally, here is the closing paragraph of Eudora Welty's literary biography:

> . . . I am a writer who came of a sheltered life. A sheltered life can be a daring life as well. For all serious daring starts from within.
> —Eudora Welty, *One Writer's Beginnings.*

While there are no pat formulas for writing such good endings, there is a little exercise that often works for us. Write and rewrite the essay to your heart's content: do the preliminary reading and editing, make several passes at the beginning and middle, and then turn your attention to the ending. If you are unhappy with the ending because it seems weak or somehow a let-down, lop off the final sentence. If it is still unimproved, take out another sentence. Continue doing that until you suddenly find yourself at a paragraph or sentence that recaps the promise of your thesis and rounds out what you have already said with a note of finality. That is your true ending.

Exercises

1. Explain which of the following pairs of endings is more effective for each thesis statement and why.

a. Thesis: Grave differences distinguish the working days of a blue-collar worker from that of a white-collar worker.

(*1*)   The workers leave their jobs in different ways. The blue-collar worker attempts to wash the grit of the day's work from his hands, hands which will never be clean, for dirt has found a permanent hiding place in their tiny creases. He says goodbye to his former enemy, but now his friend, the clock. His only worries are where to go drinking when his work is done. The white-collar worker leaves when his work is done. He may have to turn out the lights. He heads home with his job on his mind, wondering whether he will make his forecasts, whether he is maximizing his investments.

(2)   The workers leave their jobs in different ways. The blue-collar worker attempts to wash the grit of the day's work from his hands, hands which will never be clean, for dirt has found a permanent hiding place in their tiny creases. He says goodbye to his former enemy, but now his friend, the clock. His only worries are where to go drinking when his work is done. The white-collar worker leaves when his work is done. He may have to turn out the lights. He heads home with his job on his mind, wondering whether he will make his forecasts, whether he is maximizing his investments. But he can find peace of mind in an exercise program or some regimen of meditation. These remedies have proven to be effective in many cases for easing the transition from work to home, and are even thought by some authorities to forestall heart attacks.

b. Thesis: Today's American women are discovering that through prepared natural childbirth, they may deliver their babies more safely and easily than with the aid of drugs or surgery and have a beautiful, memorable experience in the process.

(1)   Because of these reasons and other factors already discussed in the essay, it is clear that natural childbirth is superior to the drug-assisted version preferred by many hospitals and sponsored by numerous gynecologists. The couple who follows nature's way, as the examples show, will have by far an easier time of delivery than those who allow hospitals to bully them into artificial delivery.

(2)   A relaxed, fearless woman can nearly be assured of delivering an alert baby whose head is not banana-shaped from a long second stage or bruised from the use of forceps. She will be proud of her own strength and perseverance, and her husband will have shared the experience with her. A couple who completes childbirth as Mother Nature dictates, but with a confidence stemming from practice and discipline, will have memories to cherish forever.

Writing Assignments

1. Write a 500-word essay arguing against one of the social nuisances listed below. Begin your essay at the *point of contention.* In other words, let your reader know immediately where you stand on the issue.
a. dealing with people who are habitually late
b. paying the exorbitant interest rates charged by today's credit card companies
c. having to make small talk at social functions
d. buying mechanical devices that immediately break down
e. living with a sloppy roommate

2. Write a 500-word essay describing a social injustice. Begin either with an *anecdote* or with a *spotlight* opening that dramatizes the injustice.

Here are some possible subjects:
a. bag ladies forced to sleep out in the open
b. the high cost of funerals
c. cruelty to animals
d. the hard life of migrant farm workers
e. hungry children in third world countries

3. Write a 500-word essay on some aspect of modern life that endangers everyone. Begin with a *bullet lead*. Here are some possible subjects:
a. lack of exercise
b. drugs
c. cigarette smoke (or some other dangerous air pollutant)
d. too much technology
e. lack of respect for the elderly

4. Write a 500-word essay for which one of the following quotations would serve as an excellent opening. Be sure to introduce the quotation:
a. "At 20 years of age, the will reigns; at 30, the wit; and at 40, the judgment."—Benjamin Franklin
b. "Two roads diverged in a wood, and I—
   I took the one less traveled by,
   And that has made all the difference."—Robert Frost
c. "For it is your business, when the wall next door catches fire."—Horace
d. "I think that I shall never see
   A billboard lovely as a tree
   Indeed, unless the billboards fall
   I'll never see a tree at all."—Ogden Nash
e. "Of all the needs (there are none imaginary) a lonely child has, the one that must be satisfied, if there is going to be hope and a hope of wholeness, is the unshaking need for an unshakable God."—Maya Angelou
f. "So, if we must have a draft registration, I would include young women as well as young men. I would include them because they can do the job. I would include them because all women must gain the status to stop as well as to start wars. I would include them because it has been too easy to send men alone.
   "I would include them because I simply cannot believe that I would feel differently if my daughter were my son."—Ellen Goodman

5. Write a 300-word essay with two alternative endings on a subject of your choice. Write a paragraph analyzing which is the better ending and why.

6. Using the techniques you have learned in this chapter, rewrite and improve the ending of one of your other essays.

PART THREE

Writing and Rewriting
Sentences

Chapter Ten

Rewriting Sentences for Clarity and Conciseness

Of every four words I write, I strike out three.

NICOLAS BOILEAU (1636–1711)

Joseph Grand, a municipal clerk, has an unusual ambition: It is to write the perfect sentence. But he finds the task to be enormously difficult. Once he has perfected this sentence, which is to be the start of a great work, he expects all other words and sentences to automatically follow. "Gentlemen, hats off!" the astonished publisher will cry after reading the manuscript—or so Grand fantasizes.

This odd clerk was never one of our students. He is a character from the novel *The Plague* by the French writer Albert Camus. His perfect sentence?

> One fine morning in the month of May an elegant young horsewoman might have been seen riding a handsome sorrel mare along the flowery avenues of the Bois de Boulogne.

"That's only a rough draft," admits Grand. "Once I've succeeded in rendering perfectly the picture in my mind's eye, once my words have the exact tempo of this ride—the horse is trotting, one-two-three, one-two-three, see what I mean?—the rest will come more easily and, what's even more important, the illusion will be such that from the very first words it will be possible to say: 'Hats off!' "

Perfect sentences are not written; they are rewritten, and Monsieur Grand was right in grasping this fact. That the perfect sentence must not only be grammatically exact, but should also use rhythm to underscore meaning was also another truth he correctly understood.

But perfect or imperfect, the sentence by itself is of little practical use to the working writer, and Monsieur Grand was wrong to overweigh its importance in isolation. The sentence is merely one small boxcar in the train of meaning and can bear only so much freight. To be useful, it must be linked to other sentences in a common purpose. For purpose is the locomotive that drives expository prose and shapes its individual sentences. Find your purpose and your controlling idea, and you will at least know what kinds of sentences you must write.

What is a perfect sentence? We confess that we cannot say because we do not know. Perfection is an ideal of art, and the writing we are trying to teach in this book is intended for the practical world, not the artistic. "Don't let it end this way. Tell them I said something," muttered the Mexican revolutionary Pancho Villa on his deathbed. He was trying to think of something perfect to say on this grim occasion, but nothing came to him. The reach for perfection often has this cruel effect of making the writer or speaker mute and tongue-tied.

What, then, is a good sentence? It is a sentence that is clear, concise, and emphatic. If it is also memorable, then it is nearly perfect.

Rewriting the Sentence for Clarity

There are three basic principles for writing clear sentences: avoid mixed constructions, use parallel constructions, and make reasoned constructions.

Avoid mixed constructions

Implicit in every sentence is a certain grammatical pattern. Native speakers unconsciously use these patterns to anticipate the endings and meanings of sentences. For example, if I start off a sentence this way, "When I was a young boy growing up on an island," you automatically expect the second half to begin something like this, "I used to think it would be fun to live on a continent." When I was this, then I thought or did that is the pattern implicit in this sentence. If a sentence begins with the words, "Looking around the room, . . . " you expect a subject to immediately follow, as in, "Looking around the room, I saw a well-dressed, matronly lady standing in the corner." You do not expect this kind of pattern: "Looking around the room, a well-dressed, matronly lady I saw standing in the corner," or "Looking around the room, the corner showed a well-dressed, matronly lady." These examples make no sense.

A sentence that begins with one pattern then lurches off into another, is said to have a mixed construction. Its beginning leads us to expect a certain pattern; its ending serves up another. And since it is an ending we did not expect, we have to puzzle over its syntax to understand what the sentence says. Here are some examples of mixed constructions, along with their corrections.

Mixed: In this description of World War I focuses on the assassination of Archduke Francis Ferdinand of Austria–Hungary by a Serbian nationalist.

Rewritten: This description of World War I focuses on the assassination of Archduke Francis Ferdinand of Austria–Hungary by a Serbian nationalist.

Mixed: Many adolescents show hostility to authority figures, but who want to be authorities themselves.

Rewritten: Although they show hostility to authority figures, many adolescents want to be authorities themselves.

Mixed: When countries try to negotiate nuclear missiles engenders fear in the public.

Rewritten: When countries try to negotiate nuclear missiles, they engender fear in the public.

Mixed: The art critics noticed the impressionists who ridiculed Monet used his techniques.

Rewritten: The art critics noticed that those impressionists who ridiculed Monet used his techniques.

Mixed constructions rarely occur in a manuscript that has been reread. Such twisted sentences can nearly always be caught on a second reading.

Use parallel constructions

A parallel construction creates a smooth and expected rhythm by balancing word for word, phrase for phrase, and clause for clause in a sentence. Consider the following example:

Not parallel: What can society do about youngsters who go to

school hungry, child abuse, and cruel neglect?

The sentence reads smoothly until we reach "child abuse," when a disruptive break in its rhythm occurs. It begins with a relative clause—"who go to school hungry"—which is then immediately (and unexpectedly) followed by two intrusive noun phrases, "child abuse," and "cruel neglect." Such an unparallel sentence, because of its departure from the normal grammatical rhythm, is harder to understand than a parallel one. Here are possible rewritten versions:

Parallel: What can society do about youngsters who go to school

hungry, who are abused, and who are cruelly

neglected?

OR

What can society do about hungry, abused, and

neglected children?

OR

What can society do about children who suffer hunger,

abuse, and neglect?

These sentences are parallel: they use the natural and expected grammatical rhythms and are therefore easier to understand than unparallel equivalents.

Here are some additional examples of unparallel sentences and their improved revisions. The unparallel element is underlined in each example.

Not parallel: Pope Paul gained popularity because of his

outgoing personality and being tough on

Communism.

Parallel: Pope Paul gained popularity because of his

outgoing personality and his tough stand on

Communism.

Not parallel: For most people—their bodies flabby, their muscles weak, and <u>having bad posture</u>—aerobics is an excellent exercise.

Parallel: For most people—their bodies flabby, their muscles weak, and their posture bad—aerobics is an excellent exercise.

Not parallel: An intimate relationship, <u>a job that poses some challenges</u>, and a purposeful life are ingredients everyone needs.

Parallel: An intimate relationship, a challenging job, and a purposeful life are ingredients everyone needs.

Not parallel: Ivan the Terrible was autocratic, stern, and <u>he had no mercy toward his foes</u>.

Parallel: Ivan the Terrible was autocratic, stern, and merciless.

Make logical constructions

A good sentence has not only a normal grammatical pattern and rhythm, but also an inherent sense of logic. Consider the following sentence:

Unclear: The prime minister delivered a brilliant parliamentary speech on the limits of world trade, and the American tourists watched the tennis matches at Wimbledon.

Because no plain connection is made between the two events--the prime minister's speech and the tourists who watched the tennis matches--the sentence seems odd or even illogical. Notice the difference when the connection is made clearer:

Rewritten: Although the prime minister delivered a brilliant parliamentary speech on the limits of world trade,

```
        the American tourists did not attend the speech,

        preferring to watch tennis at Wimbledon.
```

To the grammarian, the sentence may be defined as words arranged according to accepted rules of syntax. But to the writer, the sentence consists not merely of words but of ideas; the good sentence, of ideas expressed in clearly logical relationships. How can such clarity be achieved? "Mainly," wrote the noted stylist F. L. Lucas, "by taking trouble."

Below are some examples of sentences whose ideas and relationships were initially unclear. By taking trouble, the students improved them in revision.

Unclear: Many elderly people need medical care, and what is

```
        the government doing with all of our taxes?
```

The connection between the medical needs of the elderly and the query about what is happening to the U.S. tax dollars is not clear:

Rewritten: One cannot help but wish that the government would

```
        give some of its tax dollars to the elderly so

        that they can receive needed medical care.
```

Unclear: A skirmish is when small bodies of troops clash in

```
        a minor encounter during a war.
```

In defining a word or a concept, it is clearer to state *what* it is rather than *when* or *where* it is. Here is a better definition of a skirmish:

Rewritten: A skirmish is a minor clash between small bodies

```
        of troops during a war.
```

Here is another example of this same flaw:

Unclear: To politicize an issue is where it is discussed

```
        only in terms of its political framework.
```

Rewritten: To politicize an issue is to discuss it within a

```
        political framework.
```

Sometimes the ideas of a sentence may be muddled by the use of a **dangling modifier**—a group of words that are either unconnected to any element in the sentence or that are mistakenly attached to the wrong word. Here is an example:

Dangling: `At the age of six, Henry Adams's grandfather took`

   `him to school.`

"At the age of six" is a dangling phrase. Where it is positioned, it makes "grandfather" six years old when he took his grandson to school—clearly impossible. Here is a revision:

Rewritten: `When Henry Adams was six, his grandfather took him`

   `to school.`

OR

   `Henry Adams was six when his grandfather took him`

   `to school.`

Here are further examples of danglers, followed by corrections:

Dangling: `Looking down in horror, a huge green lizard`

   `slithered away.`

The dangling participial phrase makes it seem as if the lizard were looking down—"in horror." Here is the rewritten version:

Rewritten: `Looking down in horror, I watched a huge green`

   `lizard slither away.`

Dangling: `Desperate from hunger, the government finally gave`

   `the starving families barrels of rice.`

This dangling phrase "desperate from hunger," makes the government, not the people, hungry.

Rewritten: `Desperate from hunger, the starving families were`

   `finally given barrels of rice by the government.`

Another kind of unreasoned absurdity is caused by the **misplaced modifier**—a word or phrase whose position in the sentence is too far removed from the word it modifies:

Misplaced: `Many psychiatrists deny that a young boy develops`
`unconscious sexual feelings for his mother in`
`Germany.`

Obviously it is the psychiatrists who are in Germany, not the young boy:

Rewritten: `Many psychiatrists in Germany deny that a young`
`boy develops unconscious sexual feelings for his`
`mother.`

Misplaced: `In Tolstoy's famous novel, Anna Karenina flings`
`herself under an oncoming train which she had`
`decided to take.`

It is her life, not the train, that Anna decides to take:

Rewritten: `In Tolstoy's famous novel, Anna Karenina decides`
`to take her life by flinging herself under an`
`oncoming train.`

Similar to the dangling or misplaced modifier, the **squinting modifier** is awkwardly placed between two words and could modify either one:

Squinting: `He said long ago he lost his honor.`

"Long ago" is the problem. Did he lose his honor long ago, or did he say it long ago?

Rewritten: `Long ago he said he lost his honor.`

OR

`He said he lost his honor long ago.`

Awkward shifts (in person, number, voice, tense, or mood) can often muddy the logical relationships a writer means to express between the ideas of a sentence. Some typical examples follow:

Person shift: `When one is jealous, you tend to act like a`
`child.`

The sentence starts out with "one" as the subject, but then suddenly shifts to "you." Usually, the best way to correct a shift in person is to rewrite the entire sentence:

Rewritten: A jealous person tends to act like a child.

Number shift: After a cat wakes up from his nap, they lick
themselves all over.

The sentence begins with one cat, then shifts to many.

Rewritten: When cats wake up from their naps, they lick
themselves all over.

OR

When a cat wakes up from his nap, he licks himself
all over. (Also: When a cat wakes up from her nap,
she licks herself all over.)

Voice shift: The farmers were angry about facing the same old
pollution problems, so their meetings were used to
plan new strategies.

The shift here is from the active to the passive voice. If you start with the
active voice, you should also finish with it. (It is also more forceful than the
passive voice.)

Rewritten: The farmers were angry about facing the same old
pollution problems, so they used their meetings
to plan new strategies.

Tense shift: Tom Sawyer recounts the adventures of a boy who
has been dominated by an aunt and hated
repression; consequently, he escapes with his
friend to find freedom from authority.

Here the writer has giddily shifted tenses from the present ("recounts"), to
the present perfect ("has been dominated"), to the imperfect past ("hated"),
and then back to the present ("escapes").

Rewritten: Tom Sawyer recounts the adventures of a boy who
was dominated by an aunt and who hated repression;

```
consequently, he escaped with his friend to find

freedom from authority.
```

The only verb used in the present tense is "recounts" because the story of Tom Sawyer is still the same today as it was yesterday.

Mood shift:
```
            When you write, make your subjects and verbs

            agree in number, and also you should not shift

            tenses unnecessarily.
```

Even if you do not know the formal definition of mood, your ear should still tell you that something is wrong with this sentence. English verbs are said to have three moods: the indicative, imperative, and subjunctive. By mood is meant the manner in which a statement is intended. The indicative mood is used to make a statement or ask a question: the imperative, to give a command; the subjunctive, to express a wish or a condition contrary to fact ("If I were you . . ."). The shift here is from the imperative mood to the indicative.

Rewritten (in the imperative):
```
                        When you write, make your

                        subjects and verbs agree in

                        number, and do not make

                        unnecessary shifts in tenses.
```

Rewritten (in the indicative):
```
                        When you write, you must make

                        your subjects and verbs agree in

                        number, and you must also not

                        make unnecessary shifts in tense.
```

Most of the errors described in this section are commonly caused by hasty writing and no rewriting. Remember that your reader owes you only one reading; but you owe your reader several rereadings and rewritings of your own work.

Exercises

1. Identify the construction error (mixed, not parallel, illogical) of each sentence below. Then rewrite the sentence to correct it.

a. In this incident affecting the hero of the story focuses on all of his selfishness and immaturity.

b. He was beaten and robbed, and then they left him in the gutter to die.
c. Their grandfather paid all of their bills even though he is living on a small pension.
d. When the leaves turn gold, when the days get longer, and as soon as the sky is blustery, we know that fall is here.
e. When people are insecure results in the worship of a supreme being.
f. Burned and collapsed, the people of Columbia must rebuild their houses.
g. Bertrand Russell argued for world peace in the fall of 1918.
h. Tourists visiting Venice can see Harry's Bar floating down the Grand Canal.
i. The jury deliberated for several weeks; then suddenly the case is dismissed.
j. An "interdiction" is when something is placed under religious or legal sanction.

Writing Assignments

1. Use one of the following ideas as a springboard for a 500-word essay in which you pay particular attention to clarity. Check every sentence to assure that you have avoided mixed, unparallel, and illogical constructions:
a. Junk food has its merits.
b. Teachers should (or should not) try to be intimate with their students.
c. The movie "_____" should be censored.
d. It is cruel to produce malignant tumors in dogs to find a cure for human cancer.

Rewriting the Sentence for Conciseness

Three essential principles of concise writing are: Don't repeat yourself. Don't use unnecessary words. Don't use big words.

Don't repeat yourself

Needless repetition, also called "redundancy," is often caused by a writer unnecessarily saying the same thing more than once. If you say something once, you do not need to say it again in the same sentence unless you are deliberately trying to be emphatic. Here are some examples taken from student papers along with their more concise, rewritten versions:

Repetitious: Van Gogh was assiduous in making revised changes

on his canvases.

"Revised" and "changes" mean the same; one or the other can therefore be cut.

Rewritten: Van Gogh was assiduous in making changes on his canvases.

Repetitious: The artists of the Renaissance period delighted in and were pleased by fleshy women.

To delight in fleshy women is the same as to be pleased by them.

Rewritten: The artists of the Renaissance period delighted in fleshy women.

Repetitious: The new city hall was blue in color and square in shape.

Obviously, *blue* is a color and *square* a shape.

Rewritten: The new city hall was blue and square.

Repetitious: After the Civil War had come to an end and was terminated, reconstruction was slow.

In this sentence "end" and "terminated" are synonymous. Moreover, the phrase "after the Civil War" already signals that the war had ended.

Rewritten: After the Civil War, reconstruction was slow.

Repetitious: For a long period of time, the sky was cloudy in appearance.

"Time" is already implied in "long period," and "appearance" in "the sky was cloudy."

Rewritten: For a long time the sky was cloudy.

Don't use unnecessary words

"Let thy words be few," admonishes the Bible. It is advice as applicable today as it was in the time of the prophets. Less is often more in the well-written work. But learning to prune your sentences of unnecessary words is a skill acquired mainly by doing. Eventually, you get a "feel" for how cutting a word here and there can actually sharpen your meaning. Nevertheless, there are some known kinds of wordiness that writers look for and, when they find, mercilessly cut.

The first is the **prefabricated phrase**—words that are packaged in a convenient clump. Some common examples are "a full and complete report"; "a dyed-in-the-wool Republican" (or anything else believed to be genuine); "first and foremost among them"; "based on various and sundry experiences"; "the consensus of their opinions"; "for all intents and purposes"; "It is incumbent upon us all"; "last but by no means least"; and "deserving of your most serious consideration."

Usually such phrases can economically be replaced by a shorter expression or even by a single word. A "dyed-in-the-wool Republican" is nothing more than a "true" or "authentic" Republican. "It is incumbent upon us all" can usually be replaced by a single "must." Instead of writing, "It is incumbent upon us all to try to be good citizens," you can write, "We must all try to be good citizens." Prefabricated phrases are ineffective blobs of words, and "it is incumbent on you" to avoid them "as if your life depended on doing so" lest your sentences become as serpentine and wordy as this one and others like it that are commonly found in corporate shareholder reports.

A second major source of wordiness is caused by a **phrase taking the place of a word.** Why any working writer would prefer a phrase to a word is beyond imagining. Phrases take longer to type, use more space, yet often say less than the aptly chosen word. But the lamentable truth is that dozens of phrases are nowadays used by some writers when a single word would be just as effective. Here are some examples:

> the reason being that
> due to the fact that } because, since
> considering the fact that

Wordy: `The Red Cross sent supplies to Columbia due to the`

> `fact that a volcano had erupted.`

Rewritten: `The Red Cross sent supplies to Columbia because a`

> `volcano had erupted.`

> despite the fact that
> regardless of the fact that } although, even though

Wordy: `Despite the fact that the patient was well, she`

> `needed constant reassurance.`

Rewritten: `Although the patient was well, she needed constant`

`reassurance.`

in the event that
if it should happen that
$\Big\}$ if

Wordy: `In the event that the painting is sold, the museum`

`will purchase another masterpiece.`

Rewritten: `If the painting is sold, the museum will purchase`

`another masterpiece.`

has the opportunity to
is capable of
has the capacity to
is in a position to
$\Big\}$ can

Wordy: `A nuclear war has the capacity to extinguish all`

`life.`

Rewritten: `A nuclear war can extinguish all life.`

there is a chance that
the possibility is that
it could happen that
$\Big\}$ may, might, could

Wordy: `There is a chance that punk rock will go down in`

`musical history as an art form.`

Rewritten: `Punk rock may go down in musical history as an art`

`form.`

The lesson of this entire section can be nicely summed up in the words of the German writer Goethe: "The master reveals himself in his restraint." Say what you have to say. And when you have said it, stop.

Don't use big words

For the writer of expository prose, exactness should govern the choice of words, not size. If the bigger word is the more exact, then use it. But often it is not. English is rich in synonyms, and its vocabulary is peculiarly layered. The bigger word is layered over the smaller one under which lies the image, idea, or object that is its meaning. Consider, for example, a big word like "senectuous," as it is used in the following sentence:

> She [*The Goliath*] was a small, senectuous battleship which had been launched when Victoria was still Queen.
> —William Manchester, *The Last Lion: Winston Spencer Churchill, 1874–1932.*

"Senectuous" will evoke no image in most minds. It means, quite simply, "old," but even those readers who know this must first translate "senectuous" into "old" before visualizing the sort of battleship the author intends. Here is the same sentence without the big word:

> She was a small, old battleship which had been launched when Victoria was still Queen.

Now it is instantly clearer what kind of battleship *The Goliath* was.

Why smaller words should have this evocative power over our minds while bigger words do not is in part explainable by the way we learn language. We learn the smaller, commoner words first and always in association with specific sights or images. It is an odd parent, indeed, who would answer a child's question about why a certain man is wrinkled and bent with the explanation that he is "senectuous." Most likely, the parent would say that the man is "old," and this image would become associated with the word in the mind of the child. Similarly, we are urged from childhood to blow our "noses," never our "proboscises." It is only much later, after "old" and "nose" have become firmly associated with specific images in our minds, that we learn their synonyms of "senectuous" and "proboscis" from a dictionary. But words gotten from a dictionary cannot have the power of those whose meanings were impressed upon us by the images and scenes of life.

Edward Thompson, editor in chief of *The Reader's Digest,* defines a word that immediately brings an image to mind as a "first degree word," and all others as "second" or "third" degree words. First degree words are usually the simpler and better known. They are also the words most useful to expository writers. Here is a list of some big words, followed by their first degree, and shorter, synonyms:

initiate	start
terminate	end
inundate	flood
lugubrious	sad
habitation	home
impecunious	poor
utilization	use

visage   face
subsequent   after

Use the exact word you need. Never use a word merely because it is big and sounds impressive. That will only make your writing seem pompous. Here are some examples:

Pompous: To achieve economic independence, it is essential

that students be cognizant of the fact that

computing the number of dollars utilized each month

is an essential aspect of budgeting.

Concise: To achieve economic independence, a student must

budget by counting the number of dollars spent each

month.

The second version is clearly the easier of the two to grasp. Here is another example—this one from the preface of a history book:

Pompous: Because certain historians were desirous of

maintaining the pursuit of historical accuracy,

they treated the Pilgrims and the Plymouth Colony

in a nonidealized manner, not taking into account

the role and impact of the idealized Thanksgiving

story as it was contingent upon the formation and

preservation of the American character or its

values and goals.

Cleared of its bloated phrases and heavy nouns, the sentence has a rather straightforward meaning:

Concise: For the sake of historical accuracy, certain

historians emphasized the faults of the Pilgrims and

the Plymouth Colony, while discounting the impact

their idealized Thanksgiving story had on the

formation and preservation of the values and goals

in the American character.

The rewritten version is clearer because it uses fewer words.

Conciseness is rarely present in any first draft and is almost never the result of writing. But it is one of the happier effects of repeated rewriting.

Exercises

1. Identify the cause of wordiness (repetition, unnecessary words, big words) in each of the following sentences. Then rewrite the sentence to make it more concise.

a. Today it is almost virtually impossible to find a student who has memorized by heart even the first two paragraphs of the Declaration of Independence.

b. In a recent *Scientific American* article, written in a highly critical manner of expressing oneself, the question was asked, "How much intense heat would be caused by a breach in the reactor vessel?"

c. It is a fact that novelists are probably more sensitive to the atrocities of our age than are most of the rest of us.

d. Psychologists have become cognizant of the fact that nowadays the word *stress* is enjoying a peak of popularity.

e. It would appear that every avenue should be explored to make a conscious effort to reduce smog in all major cities.

f. Many bureaucrats avoid and shy clear of the decision-making process by submitting a problem to their superiors without recommendation, knowing beyond the shadow of a doubt that the matter will be sent back for further study.

g. Bertrand Russell was an atheist who did not believe in God.

h. Since the time of the fifteenth century, medicine has advanced considerably in its ability to treat and manage the disease of syphilis.

i. Every well-read botanist is cognizant of the fact that George Bentham was a pioneer in the field of systematic botany.

j. In its most genuinely pure form, *fresco* is the art of painting upon the material of damp, fresh lime plaster.

Writing Assignments

1. Make up a topic sentence for each of the following subjects, then write six sentences that support it. Rewrite each sentence for wordiness.

a. when no answer is an answer
b. a note asking your teacher permission to be absent during a test
c. smoking in restaurants
d. how eating crabs is a nuisance

2. Write a one-page paragraph about the dangers of peer pressure. Bring the paragraph to class and exchange it for a paragraph written by a classmate. Edit each other's paragraphs for wordiness.

Chapter Eleven

Rewriting Sentences for Emphasis

*T*hen rising with Aurora's light,
The Muse invoked, sit down to write;
Blot out, correct, insert, refine,
Enlarge, diminish, interline.

JONATHAN SWIFT (1667–1745)

An emphatic sentence is one whose words are arranged in the strongest possible sequence so as to deliver meaning with the greatest possible impact. The emphasis of any sentence will vary greatly with its context. A sentence may be unemphatic because it is too similar in construction to the sentences before or after it. Or it may be unemphatic because its words are arranged in a weak sequence. In sum, emphasis is largely a relative judgment of style and not an absolute judgment of grammar.

Nevertheless, there are some known characteristics associated with emphatic sentences. Among them are appropriate balance, structure, sound, variety, and diction. We will consider each one in turn.

Write Balanced Sentences

A balanced sentence is one whose grammatical parts are parallel. We have already discussed parallelism as an aid to clarity in Chapter 10. But the parallel sentence is not only easier to understand, it is also more emphatic. Compare the following two passages:

```
We have plenty of statutes that forbid people to
kill each other and also make it wrong to maim
or even just to be threatening with weapons.
```

```
We have plenty of statutes that forbid people to
kill, maim, or threaten each other with weapons.
```

Part of the greater emphasis in the second sentence comes from the parallelism of its three infinities: "kill," "maim," and "threaten." Here is another example of a nonparallel sentence, followed by a parallel version:

Not balanced:
```
                Simple signing can be observed in nature: dogs
                bark at the door to be let in; rabbits thump to
                call each other; the cooing of doves is an
                expression of feelings; and when a wolf defends
                his kill, he growls.
```

Balanced:
```
                Simple signing can be observed in nature: dogs
                bark at the door to be let in; rabbits thump to
                call each other; doves coo to express feelings;
                and wolves growl to defend their kills.
```

The parallel version establishes a simple subject-verb structure ("dogs bark"), which is then balanced against others in the sentence ("rabbits thump," "doves coo," "wolves growl"). In the nonparallel version, the third example ("the cooing of doves is") and the last ("when a wolf growls") take the reader by surprise, upset the expected harmony, and dilute the emphasis.

Balancing the parts of a sentence can create a pleasing rhythm while underscoring emphasis. One useful principle to remember is that a sentence is better balanced, as well as more emphatic, if its coordinate parts are arranged in order of increasing length. Here is an example:

Balanced:
```
                Finally, it is important to remember that gun
                laws are confusing, that statistics can be
                juggled to distort the truth, and that passing
```

```
the wrong kind of legislation could be

expensive as well as counterproductive or

useless.
```

The three parallel *that* clauses are arranged in climactic order of increasing length, adding to the balance and emphasis of the sentence. Moving from long to short would seem anticlimactic:

Not balanced:
```
                 Finally, it is important to remember that

                 passing the wrong kind of legislation could be

                 expensive as well as counterproductive or

                 useless, that statistics can be juggled to

                 distort the truth, and that gun laws are

                 confusing.
```

Some uses of parallelism are admittedly complex, requiring that balance be established between several elements of a single sentence. Here is an example:

Balanced:
```
             These educated young women prefer to seek

             independence through a satisfying career rather

             than to settle for dependence through a

             stultifying marriage.
```

In this sentence, the noun "independence" is balanced against the noun "dependence"; "through a satisfying career" is balanced against a prepositional phrase, "through a stultifying marriage." Here is the same idea unemphatically expressed without balance:

Not balanced:
```
                 These educated young women prefer to seek

                 independence through a satisfying career, but

                 being dependent on a marriage that stultifies

                 is not such a good idea in their view.
```

The use of correlative conjunctions ("either . . . or," "neither . . . nor," "not only . . . but also," "both . . . and," "whether . . . or") automatically encourages parallel phrasing in a sentence:

Balanced: The ideal among American writers today is not

only picturesque and exhilarating expression,

but also correct and reassuring utterance.

Here the correlative conjunction "not only . . . but also" is the pivot on which "picturesque and exhilarating expression" is balanced with "correct and reassuring utterance." Here is another example:

Balanced: The alternatives presented by modern technology

are either that we shall all be killed

instantly or that we shall all be bored to

death slowly.

In this sentence, grammatical balance is partly due to the use of a correlative conjunction ("either . . . or"). The "either" side of the sentence stands in opposition to the "or" side; but both halves are phrased identically in clauses introduced by "that." (For more on parallelism, refer back to pages 234–35.)

Structure Your Sentences to Be Emphatic

The most important idea of an emphatic sentence is usually saved for its ending. There, it is more conspicuous and climactic than when buried in the middle. Save your best for last, then, and your sentences will seem more emphatic. Study the following examples:

Weak ending: People who eat a high-salt diet over many years

are predisposing themselves to hypertension the

same way cigarette smokers predispose

themselves to lung cancer, according to recent

population studies.

The most important idea of this sentence is not that recent studies have been performed, but what they reveal. It is this idea that should come last:

Strong ending: According to recent studies, people who eat a

high-salt diet are predisposing themselves to

```
hypertension the same way cigarette smokers

predispose themselves to lung cancer.
```

The grim warning words "lung cancer" are now in a highlighted position—at the end of the sentence. Here is another example:

Weak ending:
```
                  Lin Yutang understood the enigmatic quality of

                  artistic creation when he wrote that an

                  oversupply of glandular secretions is what

                  genius is due to.
```

Prepositions are among the weakest words and usually do not belong at the end of a sentence. Note that there is no grammatical rule against ending a sentence with a preposition, although there is widespread superstition to that effect. But to end a sentence on a preposition is to end it weakly. Here is the sentence revised:

Strong ending:
```
                  Lin Yutang understood the enigmatic quality of

                  artistic creation when he wrote that genius is

                  due to an oversupply of glandular secretions.
```

Preferring the active over the passive voice is another good rule for ensuring an emphatic sentence structure. Here is a sentence, taken from a student essay, whose vigor has been sapped by overuse of the passive:

Passive:
```
          Special commissions, encounter groups, task forces,

          and think tanks have been appointed by the government

          in an attempt to achieve a better grade of collective

          thought.
```

Notice how the active voice quickens the pace of the sentence while instilling it with vigor:

Active:
```
        In an attempt to achieve a better grade of collective

        thought, the government has appointed special

        commissions, encounter groups, task forces, and think

        tanks.
```

In the passive voice, the subject does not act; it is acted upon, with a resulting tendency toward wordiness. Here is an example:

Passive: `The museum will be owned by the city; the major art`

`works will be donated by wealthy patrons, and the`

`upkeep of the building will be supported by grants`

`from huge corporations.`

Here is a a leaner version in the active voice:

Active: `The city will own the museum; wealthy patrons will`

`donate the major art works, and grants from huge`

`corporations will support the upkeep of the`

`buildings.`

We do not mean that you should never write in the passive voice, only that you should do so rarely. In special circumstances when you wish to emphasize an action rather than an actor, when you wish to highlight the one acted upon rather than the act itself, the passive voice is indeed appropriate. But as a general rule, the active is the stylistically stronger. Here are three examples of the appropriate use of the passive:

> Jesus was burdened by the sins of the world.
> The whole town was neglected by the rich, who did not care.
> The school was destroyed by an enormous billow of flame.

In the first two examples the one acted upon is more important than the actor; in the third, the action—the school was destroyed—is more important than what destroyed it. In all three cases the use of the passive voice is justified. These scant exceptions aside, the active voice is nearly always a stylistic better choice than the passive.

Eliminating slow sentence openers is another way to achieve an emphatic structure. Such slow openers include "There is . . . ," "There are . . . ," "It is interesting to note that . . . ." Cut them out and open directly on your main idea:

Slow start: `There are many youngsters in America who are`

`completely misunderstood because they do not act`

`like their peers.`

Direct start: `Many youngsters in America are completely`

> misunderstood because they do not act like their
> peers.

Slow start: It is essential to understand that gifted
children are more prone to feelings of loneliness
and depression than are normal children.

Direct start: Gifted children are more prone to feelings of
loneliness and depression than are normal
children.

Your own sentences will be more emphatic if you begin by getting straight to the point.

A string of prepositional phrases can also weaken the structure of a sentence and lessen its emphasis. Multiple *of's* are among the chief offenders. Here is an example, taken from a student paper on the great pyramid of Giza:

> The pyramid of Giza, the only remaining one of
> the seven wonders of the ancient world, proves
> to be the greatest and most enduring of all
> monuments of all times.

With a few simple deletions, we can eliminate two *of's:*

> The pyramid of Giza, the only remaining one of
> the seven wonders of the ancient world, proves
> to be among the greatest and most enduring
> archaeological discoveries.

An *of* or *by* phrase that indicates possession or authorship can often be eliminated by the possessive form of the noun: "The people of the country" becomes "the country's people." "The poem by Shakespeare" becomes "Shakespeare's poem." But be careful here, for sometimes *of* phrases do not indicate possession. For instance, if you change "the murder of Julius Caesar" into "Julius Caesar's murder," you ambiguously imply that Caesar committed murder. Here is another passage laden with *of* phrases:

Original: The decision of the Cabinet and the general
consensus of the Senate of the United States of
America are of intense interest to scholars of the
diplomatic stance of our country of that time.

Rewriting this passage to rid it of its excess *of's* meant recasting it into the active voice.

Revision: Scholars studying the diplomatic stance of America
then are intensely interested in the Cabinet's
decision and the Senate's general consensus.

The revision has reduced the sentence to one *of* phrase.

Although the rules of grammar are not properly the focus of this chapter, we cannot resist mentioning two primary flaws that often spoil the structure of student sentences: namely, the **comma splice** and the **fragment.** A comma splice is the incorrect use of a comma between two complete sentences not joined by a conjunction such as *and, or, for, nor, so,* or *yet.* Here is an example:

Comma splice: Americans are dreamers, they marry out
of hope that their dreams will come
true.

A comma splice may be corrected by changing the comma to a period or, if the sentences are closely related in thought, to a semicolon:

Comma splice corrected: Americans are dreamers. They marry
out of hope that their dreams will
come true.

Unlike the comma splice, which fuses two complete sentences into one and separates them by a comma, the fragment is a phrase or clause mistakenly punctuated as if it were a complete sentence:

Fragment: Some third world nations in their despair
have come to think that the answer to
reason is unreason. The answer to
violence, more violence.

This fragment may be corrected by joining it to the preceding sentence by a comma:

Fragment corrected: Some third world nations in their despair
have come to think that the answer to
reason is unreason, the answer to
violence, more violence.

A fragment may also be corrected by turning it into a complete sentence with a full subject and predicate. Here is an example:

Fragment: American Indians are unlike other minority
groups in this country. Because they do
not want to be integrated or assimilated
into the dominant white culture.

Fragment corrected: American Indians are unlike other minority
groups in this country. They do not want
to be integrated or assimilated into the
dominant white culture.

Write Sentences That Sound Emphatic

Words have sounds, and sophisticated readers who do not read aloud can still hear them. Poets deliberately use the sounds of words to emphasize meaning. Writers of expository prose, too, should develop an ear for how sentences sound. It is relatively common to find the emphasis of expository writing ruined by a clumsy combination of syllables. Here, for example, is a sentence overburdened with internal rhymes.

Rhyming: Twain's preoccupation and obsession with the
indication that human beings were a corruption of
their original nature added a cold and pessimistic
tone to his later writings.

The repetition of the -*tion* sound in the first two lines detracts from the text's meaning. A slight rewording improves the passage:

Revision: `Twain's obsessive preoccupation with the idea that`

`human beings had corrupted their original natures`

`added a cold and pessimistic tone to his later`

`writings.`

In the following sentence, the student was unaware of overusing the *-ought* sound:

Rhyming: `Without further thought, they bought another parcel`

`of arid land, which taught them many hard lessons`

`about the so-called simple romantic life.`

But in a line-by-line editing of the work, the student noticed the grating sound and corrected it:

Revision: `Without further thought, they purchased another`

`parcel of arid land, from which they learned many`

`hard lessons about the so-called simple romantic`

`life.`

Sometimes the problem is not with rhyme, but with alliteration— the repeated use of words that have similar initial sounds. Here is an example:

Alliteration: `In past periods, parents paid attention to the`

`plow and the pasture, being pushed to pursue hard`

`work because of their fear of poverty and of`

`possible health problems.`

The popping of these initial *p's* gives the passage an unintentionally comic overtone. Here is an improved version:

Revision: `In ages past our forebears devoted their energies to`

`the back-breaking labor of farming, being pushed to`

`this hard work by constant fear of poverty and`

`disease.`

You can avoid unpleasant combinations such as these if, in one of your rewriting passes, you read your manuscript aloud.

Vary Your Sentences

Judged alone, a sentence may seem flawless, but set in a paragraph beside others of an identical length and construction, it will invariably appear colorless and unemphatic. To avoid writing monotonous paragraphs, a writer must therefore pay attention to the length and grammatical construction of sentences. A paragraph crammed with nothing but short sentences will strike any reader as boring. The same effect is likely to occur if all the sentences of a paragraph are of an identical construction, even if their length is varied. Here is an example of both flaws, sameness in sentence length and construction, in a single passage:

Original: After years of trial and error, Disney finally found the character he was looking for. This character was called "Mickey Mouse." Mickey Mouse was first introduced in the cartoon Plane Crazy. The most famous of the Mickey cartoons was Steamboat Willie. It was the first sound cartoon made. It was a great achievement for Disney. Mickey's fame spread all over the world. By 1930, Mickey was established as the cinema's most popular cartoon character. Mickey was a moralist with a sense of fun. He was a character loved by all ages. Walt Disney reached his peak of success with Mickey Mouse.

This is cookie-cutter writing, with each sentence being pressed out of the same pattern. Here is the passage after the student reworked it for sentence variety:

Revision: After years of trial and error, Disney finally found the character he was looking for. This character,

called "Mickey Mouse," was first introduced in the
cartoon <u>Plane Crazy</u> and later found ultimate fame in
<u>Steamboat Willie</u>, the first sound cartoon ever made
and thus a great achievement for Disney. By 1930,
after his fame had spread all over the world, Mickey
was established as the cinema's most popular cartoon
character. Because Mickey was a moralist with a
sense of fun, he became a character loved by people
of all ages. In him, Walt Disney reached his peak
of success.

Four sentences were condensed into four participial phrases ("called 'Mickey Mouse' . . . first introduced . . . found ultimate fame . . . the first sound cartoon ever made"), and two were turned into adverbial clauses ("after his fame had spread . . . ." and "Because Mickey was a moralist . . . ."). These simple changes infuse variety into the syntax and rid the passage of its plodding gait.

Suddenly reversing the order of a sentence is another way to achieve syntactic variety in a passage. Here is an example:

Original: Churchill's unique personality made him highly
respected among the allies. It also brought him
considerable criticism. Churchill was often seen on
German and Italian propaganda posters as a large
pig, a fat cow, or an assortment of other animal
shapes because of his rotund body.

Revision: Churchill's unique personality made him highly
respected among the allies. It also brought him
considerable criticism. Because of his rotund body,
Churchill was often seen on German and Italian
propaganda posters as a large pig, a fat cow, or an
assortment of other animal shapes.

While the first two sentences share an identical subject-verb construction, the last reverses this order by opening with the subordinate clause, *"because of his rotund body."*

Much of the labor a writer must spend in varying a paragraph's sentences is based on common sense. Don't use several sentences in a row that have the same subject-verb construction. That's boring. At the same time, don't write a series of sentences that are uniformly short (they're tedious) or uniformly long (they're hard to read). As a general rule, a short snappy sentence used after a series of long ones tends to add an emphatic punch. Here is an example:

A civilized classroom atmosphere is one in which both the teacher and the students have a profound respect for each other. The teacher, on one hand, greets the students politely at the start of the lecture hour, does not interrupt a student's question or commentary, and listens attentively to all student reports—without slouching in a chair, planting both feet on a desk, or chewing gum at the lectern. On their side, the students respond by paying full attention to the content of the lesson, without whispering to each other, fidgeting restlessly, or looking bored to death. In a civilized classroom, both teacher and students pay attention to the ideas being discussed because they want to further in each other what William James called the "theoretic instinct"; that is, our basic need to know reasons, causes, and abstract concepts about life on our planet.

This classroom, in short, is a special place.

Notice that the final sentence ends the paragraph with an emphatic ring merely by being strikingly short and therefore different. If you will look back to the student paragraph on page 124, you will see that in the revised version the final sentence was drastically cut to pack just such a punch.

Use Inventive Diction

A diction marked by clarity, accuracy, and conciseness should be the first concern of the expository writer. Beyond these basics, if you can also use words that are memorable and imaginative, your writing will be superior. But it is only the rare writer to whom freshness and originality in diction come as natural gifts. For most of us, the imaginative image, the enlightening phrase or metaphor, do not spring readily to mind, but are found—if at all—only through the labors of rethinking and rewriting.

We have already discussed imaginative language in Chapter 5 under the techniques of narration (see pages 136–41), and everything we said there applies here as well. For the expository writer, a fresh diction can make the difference between a drab and a colorful passage. Compare the following two passages taken from a student paper:

Original:

        Volcanoes constantly attack the edge of the

North American plate, from Chile to Alaska.

Mount St. Helens, the most active of the Cascade

volcanoes, rises 8,000 feet above sea level and

sits dangerously close to the fault line that

lies between two immense plates of the earth's

disconnected crust. On May 18, 1980, an

earthquake caused Mount St. Helens to erupt with

great violence. The most severe in a series of

quakes had forced the growing bulge on the north

side of the mountain to become loose, throwing

tons of volcanic debris over the Toutle River

Valley. Suddenly the shining blue sky above the

serene Toutle River turned into a dark gray

sight. Covered by tons of ash, the once lush
green forest was transformed into a bare place.
The top of Mount St. Helens had gone, leaving
behind nothing but death and destruction.

Revision:

      Volcanoes constantly pepper the edge of the
North American plate, from Chile to Alaska.
Mount St. Helens, the most active of the Cascade
volcanoes, looms 8,000 feet above sea level and
sits dangerously close to the fault line that
makes a jagged subterranean crack between two
immense plates of the earth's fractured crust.
On May 18, 1980, an earthquake caused Mount St.
Helens to erupt with a stupendous and violent
bang. The most severe in a series of quakes had
punched a hole in the swollen north face of the
mountain, hurling tons of volcanic debris over
the Toutle River Valley. Suddenly the shining
blue sky above the serene Toutle River became a
suffocating gray nightmare. Choked to death by
tons of ash and lava mud, the once lush green
forest was transformed into a lunar landscape.
The peak of Mount St. Helens had been sheared
off completely, and out of the decapitated
mountain an irresistible onrush of lava, fire,
death, and destruction erupted.

The second version uses a decisively more colorful diction than the first. In
the first sentence, the verb *attacks* is replaced with the more colorful verb

peppers. The fault line is described as "a jagged subterranean crack" in the earth's "fractured crust." A "growing bulge" that had come loose on the north side of the mountain is changed to "the swollen north face of the mountain" through which a hole had been punched. Instead of erupting "with great violence," as it does in the first version, the volcano erupts with "a stupendous and violent bang" in the second. Other changes in diction are made here and there, all with the effect of making the revision more vivid and dramatic.

No one can be taught how to write vividly and colorfully. Knowing what a metaphor or a simile is might enable you to write one, but it will not necessarily be one that is unforgettable or even apt. But you can be taught the method by which it is possible, through sheer persistence, to write more vividly. That method is rewriting. Rework your text constantly, pore over your every verb and image, and eventually your diction will become livelier and sharper. What you are looking for is the striking word, the sharp image, the fresh figure of speech.

In trying to find the striking word, the hardest lesson for writers to learn is not to overdo. You can easily be too singular in your diction, with the result that the writing sounds bizarre and overworked. Never choose a word merely to impress. For instance, the underlined word in this sentence just does not fit:

```
Anorexia nervosa is a serious, sometimes

jeopardous disorder that typically occurs in

adolescent women.
```

In the context of this sentence, *jeopardous* is fancy-pants writing; an expression such as *life-threatening* or *fatal* would better suit the tone of this sentence. Here is another misfit:

```
A knowledge of three aspects of semantics can

beef up one's writing.
```

Here the opposite error has occurred: *beef up* is too slangy for this sentence. *Improve,* though not novel or exotic, is a better choice.

Unfortunately, no specific rule, if applied, will always lead you to choose the ideal word. Repeated rewriting with an ear to your context is our only suggestion. It is an unmagical formula, but it works.

Here are several examples of how students improved their word choice as a result of careful revising. The problem word is underlined, and the replacement used in the revision is, in every case, a better choice.

Original: Geologists <u>perceived</u> the lateral bulge from strategic locations as it reached an extension of 320 feet.

Revision: Geologists <u>observed</u> the lateral bulge from strategic locations as it reached an extension of 320 feet.

Perceived implies casual awareness rather than careful geological study.

Original: We cannot call any proposition "certain" as long as valid arguments exist <u>contra</u> it.

Revision: We cannot call any proposition "certain" as long as valid arguments exist to <u>refute</u> it.

The Latin word used in the original is pretentious.

Original: It is difficult to explain why in the United States 50 million cigarette smokers have not been scared enough to give up a habit that <u>massacres</u> 250,000 lives each year.

Revision: It is difficult to explain why in the United States 50 million cigarette smokers have not been scared enough to give up a habit that <u>snuffs out</u> 250,000 lives each year.

Massacre is an overstatement, implying violent bloodshed, which smoking does not cause.

Original: All prisoners were made to eat garbage until most of them started to <u>regurgitate</u>.

Revision: All prisoners were made to eat garbage until most of them started to <u>vomit</u>.

Regurgitate is a euphemism.

Original: American education is in very big trouble.

Revision: American education is in trouble.

Very and *really* are intensifiers, but their overuse in speech and writing has robbed them of their capacity to make any adjective more intense. Better to find a synonym that means exactly what you have in mind. For instance, instead of "very cold," you might write "freezing," "ice cold," or "bitter cold." Instead of "really stupid," use "inane," "doltish," or "brainless."

Original: We must keep in mind that every gifted child not allowed to enhance his or her possibility is a lost opportunity and a reckless waste of society's potential.

Revision: We must keep in mind that every gifted child not allowed to enhance his or her natural talents is a lost opportunity and a reckless waste of society's potential.

Possibility is a meaningless catch-all word. Others like it are *thing(s), aspect(s),* and *factor(s).* These words are not wrong, just mushy. Whenever possible, use a more specific word.

Sometimes a good thesaurus will suggest a better, sharper word over the one that comes readily to mind. Beware, however, of choosing an unknown synonym merely because it seems impressive. Words have subtle connotations that can only be grasped from repeated encounters with them in a written or spoken context.

Memorable writing also consists of detailed observations made in sharp, apt images. Through the use of representative and unforgettable details, the writer conjures up a scene in the reader's imagination. Here are some examples, taken from famous works and writers:

> The louder he talked of his honor, the faster we counted our spoons.
> —Ralph Waldo Emerson

> People by the hundreds were flailing in the river. I couldn't tell if they were men or women; they were all in the same state: their faces were puffy and ashen, their hair tangled, they held their hands raised and, groaning with pain, threw themselves into the water. I had a violent impulse to do so myself, because of the pain burning through my whole body. But I can't swim and I held back.
> —Futaba Kitayama, giving an eyewitness
> account of the atom bomb exploding over
> Hiroshima

The foxes barked in the hills and deer silently crossed the fields, half hidden in the mists of the fall mornings.
—Rachel Carson

I find some difficulty in describing what a "meatball' was. Meatballs were usually day students or scholarship students. We were at Harvard not to enjoy the games, the girls, the burlesque shows of the Old Howard, the companionship, the elms, the turning leaves of fall, the grassy banks of the Charles. We had come to get the Harvard badge, which says "veritas," but really means a job somewhere in the future, in some bureaucracy, in some institution, in some school, laboratory, university or law firm.
—Theodore H. White

The untouched savage in the middle of New Guinea isn't anxious; he is seriously and continually *frightened*—of black magic, of enemies with spears who may kill him or his wives and children at any moment, while they stoop to drink from a spring, or climb a palm tree for a coconut. He goes warily, day and night, taut and fearful.
—Margaret Mead

The actual headache, when it comes, brings with it chills, sweating, nausea, a debility that seem to stretch the very limits of endurance. That no one dies of migraine seems, to someone deep into an attrack, an ambiguous blessing.
—Joan Didion

What all of these examples have in common is a picturesque sharpness. Each passage unforgettably captures, with a grace and elegance that is never effortless, an exact idea. The best way to create sharp images is to be meticulous in your observations and faithful in your transcriptions of them on paper.

Finally, emphatic writing is frequently characterized by the use of fresh figures of speech. A **figure of speech** is the opposite of **literal language.** Literal language renders meaning factually: "He left quietly, without being seen or heard." A figure of speech renders meaning imaginatively: "He stole away like a thief in the night." The metaphor and the simile are the most common figures of speech (see pages 143–46 for a definition), and appropriately used, add emotional intensity to writing. Here are some examples of apt metaphors, taken from the works of well-known writers:

Man was born free, and everywhere he is in chains.
—Jean-Jacques Rousseau

Wide is the gate, and broad is the way, that leadeth to destruction, and many there be that go in threat.
—St. Matthew

Old religious factions are volcanoes burnt out.
—Edmund Burke

For frequent tears have run the colours of my life.
—Elizabeth Barrett Browning

Gossip is a sort of smoke that comes from the dirty tobacco pipes of those who diffuse it; it proves nothing but the bad taste of the smoker.
—George Eliot

[Robert E.] Lee was tidewater Virginia, and in his background were family, culture, and tradition—the age of chivalry transplanted to a New World which was making its own legends and its own myths.
—Bruce Catton

I wanted to live deep and suck out all the marrow of life, to live so sturdily and Spartan-like as to put to rout all that was not life, to cut a broad swath and shave close, to drive life into a corner, and reduce it to its lowest terms. . . .
—David Thoreau

From a mechanistic viewpoint, companies with many outlying plants and offices can be more efficient if their people "resources" become interchangeable cogs.
—Vance Packard

But even if we choose wisely in the light of an apparent alignment of mutual needs, the crack in the marriage foundation that splits wide open is, simply, ignorance—the appalling ignorance of the realistic obligations of marriage itself.
—Norman Sheresky and Marya Mannes

This is the way it is with the white man in America: He's a wolf—and you're a sheep.
—Malcolm X

And here are some similes—like metaphors except that the comparison is explicitly drawn through the use of *like* or *as:*

His words, like so many nimble and airy servitors, trip about him at command.
—John Milton

And then one or other dies. And we think of this as love cut short, like a dance stopped in mid-career or a flower with its head unluckily snapped off—something truncated and therefore lacking its due shape.
—C. S. Lewis

He had an upper-class Hoosier accent, which sounds like a bandsaw cutting galvanized tin.
—Kurt Vonnegut

The great enemy of clear language is insincerity. When there is a gap between one's real and one's declared aims, one turns as it were instinctively to long words and exhausted idioms, like a cuttlefish squirting out ink.
—George Orwell

Good metaphors and similes that sound effortless are usually composed only with the most strenuous effort. They bring an element of surprise into writing that catches us off guard and makes us think.

Exercises

1. An excellent exercise to help you master a variety of sentence types is **sentence combining.** It will give you practice in combining simple sentences into larger, varied, and more complex ones. Each of the following clusters of short sentences, when properly combined, can make a single sentence. Study the model.

Short sentences:	(1) Benjamin Franklin was an American statesman.
	(2) He was a printer.
	(3) He was a scientist.
	(4) He was a writer.
	(5) He was born the son of a tallow chandler and soapmaker.

Combined sentence: Benjamin Franklin, born the son of a tallow chandler and soapmaker, became a printer, scientist, writer, and American statesman.

Combine the following short sentences into a single long one.

a. (1) A hat provides considerable psychological security.
    (2) It protects the face.
    (3) A hat hides one's face.
    (4) The hiding is from curious onlookers.
    (5) These onlookers threaten one's identity.

b. (1) Buddhism arose in India in the sixth century B.C.
    (2) It was a protest.
    (3) The protest was against the overdeveloped ritualism of the Hindus.
    (4) Sometimes these sacrificial cults even involved sacrificing human beings.

c. (1) The passage of liquor laws has always been prompted by a public desire.
    (2) The desire was to prevent immoderate use of intoxicants.
    (3) The passage was also prompted by the need to raise revenue.
    (4) Liquor laws are legislation designed to restrict, regulate, or totally abolish the manufacture, sale, and use of alcoholic beverages.

d. (1) Changes in table manners reflect changes in human relationships.
    (2) Such changes have been documented for Western Europe.
    (3) Medieval courtiers saw their table manners as distinguishing them from crude peasants.
    (4) By modern standards the manners of medieval courtiers were unrefined.

e. (1) Today, efforts to improve the drab conditions of army life are always thwarted.
    (2) Recruits could be permitted to personalize their sleeping quarters.
    (3) Recruits could be allowed to choose their own hairstyles.
    (4) But conditions of army life are not improved.
    (5) Efforts to do so are regarded by many senior officers as responsible for breakdowns in order and discipline.

f. (1) Mr. Simmons will be an excellent addition to top management.
    (2) He has been employed by Home Federal Saving for 20 years.
    (3) He is knowledgeable about all areas of banking.
    (4) There areas include foreign deposits.

g. (1) Television newscasters are victims of the rating game.
    (2) They are hired and fired on the basis of how entertaining they make the news.
    (3) The rating game is controlled by anti-intellectual viewers.

h. (1) The early Incas did not have the wheel.
    (2) They did not have paper either.

(3) Nevertheless, their architectural and engineering achievements were spectacular.
(4) They established an elevated network of roads.
(5) They built beautiful palaces.

i. (1) Martin Luther was the German leader of the Protestant Reformation.
(2) He was born in Eisleben, Saxony.
(3) His family were small, but free, landholders.
(4) His family encouraged him to attend the cathedral school at Eisenach and later the University of Erfurt. At the University of Erfurt he studied law.

j. (1) Toward the end of the nineteenth century, the Belgian sheepdog began to decline in population.
(2) This gradual decline was the result of several new factors.
(3) First of all, the widespread use of fencing became popular.
(4) Also, rail transportation became available.
(5) The threat of marauding animals no longer existed.

   2. **Classical imitation** is one of the best exercises to help you write sentences that have balance and rhythm. In this exercise, you are allowed to change the content, but not the grammatical structure, of the sentence or passage you are imitating. If the original begins with a subordinate clause followed by a main clause, so must your imitation. If parallelism is used in the original, it must also be used in your imitation. Even figures of speech must be imitated.
a. Imitate the following sentence structures:

Model: "Speak of the moderns without contempt and of the ancients without idolatry."—Earl of Chesterfield

Imitation: Think of the poor without scorn and of the rich without envy.

(1) "The humorous story is strictly a work of art—high and delicate art—and only an artist can tell it; but no art is necessary in telling the comic and witty story; anybody can do it."—Mark Twain
(2) "The earth is filled with a vague, a dizzy, a tumultuous joy."—Anonymous
(3) "No one can be perfectly free till all are free; no one can be perfectly moral till all are moral; no one can be perfectly happy till all are happy."—Herbert Spencer

(4) "Let us therefore brace ourselves to our duties and so bear ourselves that if the British Empire and its Commonwealth last for
a thousand years, men will still say, 'This was their finest
hour.' "—Winston Churchill

(5) "As he was valiant, I honour him; but, as he was ambitious, I
slew him."—Shakespeare

b. Imitate the following figures of speech.

Model: "The moonlight spread a wash of gauzy silver over the clear
spaces of the garden, and the shadows were cobalt blue."—
Katherine Anne Porter

Imitation: The fog wrapped a mysterious cloak of gray over the
city, and the lights became blurred halos.

(1) "She was created to be the toy of man, his rattle, and it must
jingle in his ears whenever, dismissing reason, he chooses to be
amused."—Mary Wollstonecraft

(2) "Russian winter in this new guise attacked them on all sides; it
cut through their thin uniforms and worn shoes, their wet clothing froze on them, and this icy shroud molded their bodies and
stiffened their limbs."—Count Philippe-Paul de Segur

(3) "She is the crown of creation, the masterpiece."—Germaine
Greer

(4) "When he hung up his shirt to dry, it would grow brittle and
break, like glass."—Isaac Bashevis Singer

(5) "The lake was quite black, like a great pit."—D. H. Lawrence

c. Imitate the following entire passages. You do not need to imitate slav-
ishly. If a slightly different idea from the one in the original occurs to
you, do not hesitate to write it down.

Model: Piccadilly before dawn. After the stir and ceaseless traffic of the day,
the silence of Piccadilly early in the morning, in the small hours, seems
barely credible. It is unnatural and rather ghostly. The great street in its
emptiness has a sort of solemn broadness, descending in a majestic
sweep with the assured and stately ease of a placid river. The air is
pure and limpid, but resonant, so that a solitary cab suddenly sends the
whole street ringing, and the emphatic trot of the horse resounds with
long reverberations.
—W. Somerset Maugham

Imitation: Laguna Beach at sunrise. Before the whirring

noises of traffic or the youthful shouts of surfing

fanatics rend the air, a delicious soft breeze
wafting down Pacific Coast Highway past the old
Victor Hugo Inn, seems especially enjoyable. The
world is quiet and peaceful. The Pacific Ocean,
seemingly stretching clear to the end of the world,
curls over the sand like the soft hair of a
flirtatious girl. The sky is a velvety aqua blue,
but damp, so that three or four big marshmallow
clouds floating in the West prophesy that the
afternoon may witness a few unusual raindrops,
and the mournful sound of a screeching sea gull
fades away into the mysterious air.

Imitate the following passages.

(1) But that night after dinner and a whisky and soda by the fire before
going to bed, as Francis Macomber lay on his cot with the mosquito
bar over him and listened to the night noises, it was not all over. It was
neither all over nor was it beginning. It was there exactly as it happened with some parts of it indelibly emphasized and he was miserably ashamed at it. But more than shame he felt cold, hollow fear in
him. The fear was still there like a cold slimy hollow in all the emptiness where once his confidence had been and it made him feel sick. It
was still there with him now.
—Ernest Hemingway

(2) But if a man would be alone, let him look at the stars. The rays that
come from those heavenly worlds will separate between him and what
he touches. One might think the atmosphere was made transparent
with the design, to give man, in the heavenly bodies, the perpetual
presence of the sublime. Seen in the streets of cities, how great they
are! If the stars should appear one night in a thousand years, how
would men believe and adore; and preserve for many generations the
remembrance of the city of God which had been shown! But every
night come out these envoys of beauty, and light the universe with
their admonishing smile.
—Ralph Waldo Emerson

(3) He did not feel weak, he was merely luxuriating in that supremely
gutful lassitude of convalescence in which time, hurry, doing, did not
exist, the accumulating seconds and minutes and hours to which in its

well state the body is slave both waking and sleeping, now reversed and time now the lip-server and mendicant to the body's pleasure instead of the body thrall to time's headlong course.
—William Faulkner

Note: In imitating the passage above, try simply to imitate the stream of consciousness creating a feeling (in this case, languor); your imitation need not be exact.

(4) I believe a leaf of grass is no less than the journeywork of the stars,
    And the pismire is equally perfect, and a grain of sand, and the egg of the wren,
    And the tree-toad is a chef-d'oeuvre for the highest,
    And the running blackberry would adorn the parlors of heaven,
    And the narrowest hinge in my hand puts to scorn all machinery,
    And the cow crunching with depressed head surpasses any statue,
    And a mouse is miracle enough to stagger sextillions of infidels,
    And I could come every afternoon of my life to look at the farmer's girl boiling her
    iron kettle and baking shortcake.
    —Walt Whitman

Note: Following Walt Whitman's form, make up your own list of nature's miracles.

3. The purpose of this writing assignment is to give you practice at **editing** sentences. Choose a topic from the list below and write a 500-word essay on it. Make sure that the first draft of your essay is controlled by a thesis, written in unified and logical paragraphs, and uses correct spelling and punctuation. Next, rewrite each sentence to improve clarity and emphasis, and to eliminate wordiness. Finally, rewrite your sentences for liveliness and color. Bear the following questions in mind as you rewrite:

a. Is the sentence unmistakably clear?
b. Have I avoided repetitions, deadwood, prefabricated phrases, and pompous words?
c. Are all of my sentences balanced? Do they read well aloud?
d. Would an apt figure of speech add sparkle?

Topics to choose from:
(1) Describe the most painful change ever experienced in your life. State what brought about the change and how you handled it.
(2) Write an analysis of what spring (summer, fall, or winter) means to you. Describe emotions as well as landscapes.
(3) Choose a high school or college course that taught you some-

thing valuable or fascinating. Explain as clearly as possible, what the course taught you and why you consider this information exceptional.

(4) Write an essay on the major personality traits you would expect to find in a U.S. president. Explain why each trait is important and what could happen if it was missing.

(5) Describe the person who so far has had the most profound influence on your life. Use concrete details to create a lively portrait. Be specific about the exact nature of the person's influence.

Appendix: Proofreading and Marking Your Drafts

After revising your sentences and making appropriate corrections, you should also check your text for errors of misspelling, bad spacing, omitted letters or words, and so on. A knowledge of standard proofreaders' symbols will save you time and effort as you work to clean up your final copy. For your own use, then, here is a list of the most commonly used proofreading symbols:

Symbol	Meaning
factry	insert a letter
antecedant	replace a letter
One make choices	insert a word
In Peking	replace a word
in the west	capitalize
He is a bank President	use lowercase
recieve	transpose letters
to quickly move	transpose words
a display of dazzling light	move word(s)
the future ofthe world	insert a space
a birth mark	close up the space
disappear	delete a letter and close up

Symbol	Meaning
every ~~last taxable~~ dollar	delete word(s)
a ~~treacherous~~ enemy	stet (restore what was deleted)
her own self—esteem. ⌐Her physical stress	run the line on (no paragraph)

What follows is a page from a student essay with proper proof marks:

When I was ten and living in florida, I
learned that dogs may *always* not be man's best friend.

I liked to d*i*scover new places, and one
afternoon, while riding a *bicycle* ~~bycicle~~ on the out‑
skirts of my neighborhood, I discovered a train
station. As I was leisurely rolling by the
warehouses ~~wherehouses~~, I noticed three large dogs about
fifty yards in#front of me. Since I had a dog of
my own, and he wouldn't (without a reason) bother
anyone, I pa*i*ed no*t* attention to these *C*anines.
But, as I got closer, the dogs started to
appro*a*ch me with menac*ing* growls and barks. At
this point I began to feel uneasy, so I turned
around to ride in the other direction. As soon
as I turned, all three dogs started to chase me
and nip at my he*e*ls. I tried to pick up speed
in order to create some distance between me and
these malign creatures, but to no av*ail*. One of
the dogs s*u*nk his teeth *a* into my leg (deeply) and
not would let go, no matter how hard I pulled. Only

when I gave a violent yank he did finally let
go. At this point, I did'nt think about pain; I
only though about riding for my life.

PART FOUR

Special Purpose Essays

Chapter Twelve

The Argumentative Essay

W*ords can be more powerful, and more treacherous, than we sometimes suspect; communication more difficult than we may think. We are all serving life sentences of solitary confinement within our bodies; like prisoners, we have, as it were, to tap in awkward code to our fellow men in their neighboring cells.*

F. L. Lucas (1894–1967)

The purpose of an argumentative paper, pure and simple, is to persuade a reader to the writer's point of view. As the writer, your starting assumption is that your reader holds either a neutral or opposing belief from your own and must be rid of that mistaken conviction. To do so, it is useful to think of your argument as having three principal parts: its proposition, its sources of proof, and its logical links.

The Proposition of an Argument

The proposition of an argument is the stand it takes on an issue, the position it tries to prove or defend. This is its thesis, which is therefore governed by all the advice we have already given in Chapter 3 on how to write one effectively. But propositions are also different enough from ordinary theses to merit special attention.

First and most obvious, a proposition must be for or against some topic or issue. It should not straddle the fence, should not hem and haw (nor should any good thesis), but should boldly proclaim the writer's stand. Here is an example of a weak proposition:

Original: `Nuclear power should be banned from our midst.`

Readers of Chapter 3 will immediately recognize this sentence as too broad to be a good thesis. But it is also a wishy-washy proposition. The reader knows that the writer is against nuclear power, but not why. For the writer's part, if this opposition is not grounded in well-rehearsed reasons, some will have to be immediately found or the argument must come to a dead stop. We think it smarter to decide on the supporting evidence and reasons and include them in the wording of the thesis. Here is a rewritten version:

Revision: `Because nuclear power plants have become too`

`expensive to build and have lost public acceptance,`

`they should be banned.`

Now the writer knows where the argument is going. And readers know where they are being taken.

Second, a proposition should not be unprovable. Unprovable propositions are those based mainly on personal values or beliefs. Here is an example:

Original: `Casual sex is wrong because it is against the moral`

`code given by God.`

On the other hand, here is a nearly equivalent, but more arguable, proposition:

Revision: `Casual sex involves one in an empty, risky, and`

`unfulfilling commitment usually based only on`

`physical attraction.`

You now have at your fingertips varied sources of evidence. You could back up your allegation of emptiness with testimony and anecdote. You can prove risk by citing pregnancy statistics and rate of venereal infection. Where formerly it had only scripture on its side, the reworded thesis now enlists the support of psychology, statistics, and common sense. Arguing in favor of some cause or cherished belief is not wrong, it is simply harder to do than to defend a provable issue.

Below are two more examples of unarguable propositions:

Original: `Fauvism was a clumsy, meaningless period of art.`

This proposition is based on personal taste and would be discounted by serious art critics.

Original: The purpose of all life is to evolve from plant

existence to spiritual existence.

Again, this is an unprovable proposition that cannot be backed by any objective certainty.

Third, a proposition should not rest on a shaky premise. The premise of a proposition is any major assumption it makes or takes for granted. Here are some examples of what we mean:

Thesis: Abortion should be outlawed because it denies the

constitutional guarantee of life to the unborn.

Premise: The fetus is a human being entitled to

constitutional guarantees.

Thesis: The reinstatement of capital punishment throughout

the nation will be an effective deterrent against

major crimes.

Premise: Capital punishment deters crime.

Both theses take for granted the truth of a suspect premise. Yet, if the fetus is not a human being, it is not entitled to constitutional guarantees; and if capital punishment does not deter crime, deterrence cannot be an argument for its reinstatement.

Finally, if you have the choice, we advise you to choose an argumentative proposition that takes advantage of your own personal strengths and expertise. For example, let us say that you have had extensive experience working at a family planning clinic. This background gives you a rich source of testimonial evidence about the value of family planning that would be useless in an argument on the topic of air pollution. In that case, you'd be clearly better off writing your argument on some issue of family planning since it is always more prudent to argue about what you know firsthand than what you don't.

Sources of Proof

The usual sources of proof are testimonials, experience, anecdotes, facts, statistics, and reasoning. Taken together, these make up the backing or evidence for an argument.

Testimonials

A testimonial is the account of either an expert or eyewitness that supports your case and is usually given in the form of a direct quotation. The formula for citing testimonial evidence is quite straightforward: Give the credentials of the expert or eyewitness, cite the source of the quotation if you have one, and add whatever interpretative comment you think necessary. Here is an example of expert testimony:

> Proponents of nuclear power say nuclear
> power is safe. According to Lynn Weaver, Dean of
> the School of Engineering, Auburn University,
> "There is broad agreement that our current plans
> for storing radioactive waste are prudent and
> safe."

The speaker, as dean of engineering in a major university, we take to be a believable expert on this issue.

Note that being believable is not the same as being right. Naturally, you hope the opinions of your experts are right, especially when you quote them to back up your own argument. But the burden of choosing right experts is entirely on you. Some self-proclaimed experts turn out to be plainly wrong, while others are badly at odds with their own peers. Consult volumes of *Who's Who,* read magazines, journals, and books in the field, and you will soon find a core of recurring names favorably mentioned in different publications. This is the group from which a sterling testimonial can be gotten.

In citing an expert's credentials, use common sense. Cite the credentials in all their naked glory if the expert is not internationally known; leave them out if the expert enjoys global or historical fame. For example, Jesus needs no introduction as an expert on theology, neither does Aristotle on philosophy, nor Queen Elizabeth I on royalty. But other experts who are less recognizable should be touted. Here is an example from a paper on the proposed Star Wars missile defense system in which the writer should have touted his expert but didn't:

Original: The tiered strategy will make the total defense more
effective. Robert Jastrow explains this strategy in
simple terms in his article "The War against Star
Wars," which appeared in Commentary.

Since Jastrow's name is not likely to bring a light of recognition to every face on a bus, his credentials, briefly listed, would have made this quotation more impressive:

Revision: The tiered strategy will make the total defense more

effective. Robert Jastrow, noted astronomer and

author of many books, explains this strategy in

simple terms in his article "The War against Star

Wars," which appeared in <u>Commentary</u>.

On the other hand, it is perfectly acceptable to gloss over the credentials of an expert being quoted not for what he or she is presumed to know, but for what he or she has seen or done. Here is an example from a student paper arguing for gun control:

Gun control enforcement is needed because

handguns in the United States are too easily

obtained. In an article "Wretchedness Is a Warm

Gun," author Bill Lueders describes his going on

a gun-buying spree. He purposely dressed the

part of a fanatic with buttons that read "Smash

the State" and "Kill 'em All and Let God Sort

'em Out!" He then took five or six Vivarin, a

legal stimulant, downed a six-pack of beer, and

proceeded to see if anyone would refuse to sell

him a gun. No one did.

Leuder's credentials are unmentioned because who he is and what he knows are less important to his testimony than what he did—and that is told.

Properly used, testimonial opinion can give a persuasive boost to your argument. In effect, it says to your reader, "I'm not alone in this opinion. These experts agree with me." But you should also be certain that you quote only authentic experts, and then only on the subject of their acknowledged expertise.

Experience

In some arguments the evidence of experience has a definite place, if only to illustrate or dramatize a point. Here is an example, from a student paper advocating breast-feeding. The writer has already covered the physiological and biological benefits of breast-feeding. Now she dramatizes her case with her own experience.

> But these facts and statistics tell only
> part of the story. What no one can ever really
> tell is how personally fulfilling breast–feeding
> is to the infant and the new mother. When I put
> my baby to my breast, a feeling comes between us
> that it indescribable. Writers such as Diony
> Young and Mary K. White call it "bonding,"
> meaning that between me and my baby an
> attachment is being formed that will last a
> lifetime. But it is more than that. It is a
> feeling of closeness and satisfaction that is
> impossible to put into words.

Sometimes the experience of someone else may be useful, as in the following argument against dial-porn telephone recording services:

> Last summer, a neighbor admitted that his
> teenage son had wasted a whole week's paycheck
> on dial–porn messages, introducing his less
> sophisticated friends to them.

Granted, this is not a hardheaded fact such as one might use to crack open a closed mind. But it is just this sort of personal and enlivening touch that makes an argument persuasive.

Anecdotes

An anecdote is a brief story that drives home a point. Like experiences, anecdotes by themselves do not make a defensible argument, but they can and do add dramatic impact. Here is an example from a student paper:

```
He is 5'7" tall, and he weighs 96 pounds.

He has a poor appetite, has trouble sleeping, is

withdrawn--all the classic symptoms of

depression.  When I visit him, he rarely smiles,

sometimes cries, and answers my questions in a

flat monotone voice.  He is 13, and he is my

son.  He has been diagnosed as having a Major

Depressive Episode.  I have watched Ronnie go

steadily downhill since his father and I

divorced seven years ago.  Ronnie never adjusted

to the breakup of his family, to having a father

he rarely saw or heard from.  Ronnie doesn't

like living in a hospital, but he wasn't happy

at home, and doctors warned that he was

suicidal.
```

The thesis of this paper is that adolescent suicide is directly related to the high rate of divorce, and the writer uses the anecdotal example of her own son's depression to underscore that point. Anecdotes of this kind do not prove anything; but they do make an argument compelling.

Facts

A fact is a relationship, force, or law of reality whose effect is independent of human belief. Lack of vitamin C in the human diet causes scurvy, and whether or not you believe that will not prevent you from getting scurvy if you fail to take vitamin C. People do not always universally agree on what is a fact and what isn't, but a fact will have its own way regardless of its doubters.

A fact may strike you as the same as a truth, but the two are substantially different. A truth is some idea in which a large number of people, perhaps even a majority, believe. When most of its believers give it up, the truth is demoted to a myth. For example, there was a time when people believed that the world was flat. Now we know that the world is round, and that belief in the former "truth" of its flatness was mistaken. But the fact of the world's roundness remained unaltered during the rise and fall of this former "truth."

Facts and truths are the staples of argumentative papers, and all writers use them. For all your cited facts and truths, you should provide the reader with a context, an interpretation, and a traceable source. Resist the temptation to weigh down the page with every fact you uncover in your research. Quote and cite as necessary to prove your case, but never for mere show. Here are some ways students have properly used facts. From a paper arguing that gifted students are tragically neglected:

> Writing for <u>Science</u> magazine, psychologist
> Constance Holden states that gifted children are
> often labeled "obnoxious," "unruly,"
> "hyperactive," or "rebellious," because they are
> inquisitive, active, often need little sleep,
> and get into things.

From a paper arguing that the present high school diploma does not adequately prepare students for earning a living:

> According to a 1985 U.S. Census Bureau report,
> the high school dropout rate is steadily
> increasing despite the job problems encountered
> by those who lack a high school education.

From a paper arguing against drinking alcoholic beverages:

> One of the worst results of heavy drinking is
> cancer of the pancreas. In his book <u>Alcohol</u>
> <u>Addiction, Who Is in Control?</u> Dr. Joseph P.
> Frawley explains clearly how the high level of
> sugar in alcohol causes the pancreas to take a
> severe beating as it attempts to create enough
> insulin to maintain a healthy chemical balance
> within the body. Eventually, however, the
> pancreas loses the battle and becomes cancerous.

Each of these examples consists of a fact along with a traceable source.

Statistics

A statistic is a mathematical expression of some trend or relationship. The spread sheets of bookkeepers, the research of scientists, and the forecasts of economists are typically based on statistics. Statistics do not occur in nature but are strictly man-made, which means that they must always be cited with an accompanying source. Here are two examples of how students have used statistics:

> Opponents of gun control argue that their right
> to self-protection would be taken away if a gun
> control law were passed. However, guns in the
> home increase the danger of accidents and crimes
> of passion. According to the FBI, 47 percent of
> all murders in 1983 were committed by relatives
> or persons acquainted with the victim.

> Perhaps the most important argument supporting
> the continuation of nuclear power is that if the
> United States pulls back from the nuclear
> industry and does not develop other energy
> possibilities such as fusion power, the country
> may find itself fighting over what little fuel
> remains in 100 years. Alvin Weinberg reveals
> that in a year's time a 1,000 megawatt nuclear
> plant produces as much electricity as 8 million
> barrels of oil or 2.5 million tons of coal. He
> also states that if by the year 2000 the nation
> replaced the originally planned 300 nuclear
> plants with coal burning plants, it would need
> an additional 750 million tons of coal per year.

These two examples of the use of a statistic we may take as models. They give the statistic both a source and a context, using it to make a point. The point of the first passage is that guns in the home increase the likelihood of accident and crimes of passion. The point of the second passage is that nuclear energy plants are a necessity for the future.

Reasoning

Reasoning refers not only to the claims of evidence you make on behalf of your thesis, but to the logical strategies you use to present your case. A typical argument will state a thesis and then marshal evidence behind it. But the alert writer will also look for chinks in the armor plating of the opposition's case, and when one is found, pierce it with a counterclaim. In the example above, for instance, the writer quotes the argument used by pro-gun advocates that guns are needed for self-protection, and then refutes it with a statistic.

Another useful strategy is to expose inconsistencies you uncover in the argument of the opposition. In the minds of reasonable men and women everywhere, there is an expectation that legitimate arguments will be consistent. If you can find an inconsistency in the views of the opposition, you should therefore blare it out for all the world to hear. Here is an example, from a student paper against abortion:

> Now we have laws. We do not have any laws
> which govern the lives of plants. We have but
> one law which governs the life of an animal.
> That animal is man. The law has been written
> and rewritten down through the course of the
> centuries—in stone, on leather, on parchment,
> on paper, in languages that have been lost and
> long forgotten. But the law has remained the
> same. No man, it states, may take the life of
> another man. Perhaps you would recognize it
> this way: "We hold these truths to be self-
> evident—that all men are created equal and are
> endowed by their Creator with certain
> inalienable rights—that among these rights are
> life . . . ." Or this way, quite simply stated
> in another book: "Thou shalt not kill." But

whatever their form, the laws are there. And
there were no qualifications written into these
laws on the basis of age. What the matter boils
down to it this: A human life has been
determined by us, for centuries, millennia, to
be sacred, and we have determined that it cannot
be taken away. And a fertilized egg is human
life.

For any violations of these laws to occur,
especially on a grand scale as is happening
today, a mentality has to have been developed
through which those who are going to commit a
wrong can justify their actions and can appease
the guilt that they might feel—the guilt that
they might feel if they had to admit that they
were killing a living human entity. And this is
what we have done.   This is what we are doing.
We have learned to call a flower a stone. . . .

The writer thinks he has found an inconsistency in the views of pro-abor-
tionists—namely, that they exempt the living fetus from the ancient law
against murder—and he is quick to expose it. Note that exposing an inconsistency in an argument is not the same as making an *ad hominem* attack.
The first is directed against a weakness seen in the argument itself; the second, against its advocate's character.

A third strategy writers can use to make their arguments compelling
is an ethos appeal—"ethos" being the Greek word for "character." In one
study a recorded speech was played back to three groups of students, who
were respectively told that it had been given by the surgeon general of the
United States, the secretary general of the Communist party in America, and
a college sophomore. The results showed that the group most impressed by
the speech was the one who thought it had been made by the surgeon
general. Since the speech was the same one given to the less persuaded
groups, something other than literary merit was responsible for its superior
effect. This factor has been labeled "ethos" and defined as the perception by
an audience of a writer's or speaker's character.

Studies have isolated three characteristics linked with perceived character in a speaker: trustworthiness, competence, and dynamism. Trustworthiness and dynamism are plainly easier for a speaker to demonstrate than for a writer, but writers can put ethos to work in their essays by a display of competence. If you have some special experience or association with your topic, you should therefore tell it. Here is an example. The writer's thesis is that animal experiments should be banned because they are often unnecessarily cruel. In the paragraph below, he makes an "ethos" argument:

> As a medical technician, I have worked for the experimental lab of a major university and seen for myself the treatment that animals suffer. When we receive a shipment of dogs, the first thing we do is schedule them for ventriculocordectomy. We anesthetize the animals and then surgically sever their vocal cords so that they can make no sounds during the experiments and bother the researchers. I myself have performed scores of ventriculocordectomies and know that the experience, which the university insists is painless, is deeply traumatic to dogs. Once the animal revives and finds that it can make no sound, its look of anguish and grief is unbelievable.

We tend to believe this piece of writing not only because of its specific detail, but because of its ethos appeal—the competence we attribute to the writer because of his experience. This same opinion from the pen of one who has never set foot into a laboratory would simply not be as believable.

Finally, your choice of evidence to support your case can in itself be an important strategy of reasoning. Bear in mind that the battering ram of facts and statistics is not always the best proof of a point. Sometimes the brute force of facts will not persuade as effectively as the soft touch of an anecdote or the breath of an ethos appeal. Admittedly, some arguments can be proven only by the sheer weight of facts. For example, geological data are the only possible sources of proof for any theory explaining the extinction of dinosaurs. But other propositions are provable by anecdote, experience, and ethos just as readily as by facts. For example, if you were arguing that a long delay in bringing an accused person to trial is a harsh injustice, and if you yourself have suffered at the hands of a slothful court, your account could be more moving than a pure recital of facts.

Logical Links

In Chapter 3, we discussed possible inconsistencies in an argument, and we would urge you to review that material before writing your own argumentative essay. Here we wish to stress the importance of the logical links that tie your statements of belief, theory, and conclusion into a chain of reasoning.

All arguments consist of statements linked in logical relationships. A common example is the assertion that if this is so, then that is so. By this we mean that if the first half of the statement is true, then so must be the second. When the link is one of compelling necessity, an assertion of this kind is logical. For example, it is entirely logical to assert that if you fall from a 20-story building onto the street below, you will likely be killed, since experience teaches us that death is the most probable outcome of such a plunge. But it is more prejudicial than logical to say that if a person is a woman, she will automatically not understand debates about missile defense systems. That conclusion does not necessarily follow.

So heavily dependent is a logical argument on these links between its parts that it is possible to chart the exact steps in reasoning from proposition to conclusion. Here is an example of an argument whose statements are poorly linked:

Original: The evidence linking rock music at concerts

with hearing loss in the audience is clearly

established; therefore, rock music should be

abolished. Medical doctors say that once hearing in

the high frequencies is lost, it never returns

during the lifetime of the individual. Hence, since

rock concerts cause permanent damage to the

listener's hearing, they should be banned. It has

also been demonstrated that some rock music contains

what is known as "backward masking," which is where
a hidden message is present in the song and designed
to influence listeners. Some authorities have shown
that backward masking has been used to promote
Satanism, unbeknownst to the innocent listener.
Therefore, since backward masking can be used to
exert influence over a listener, rock concerts
should not be allowed.

And here is a sketch of the major parts of the author's argument, showing the logical links between them:

1. Evidence exists that links exposure to rock music at concerts to hearing loss in listeners;

   therefore,

   rock music should be abolished.

2. The damage done to the hearing of listeners is permanent;

   hence,

   rock music should be banned.

3. Rock music uses "backward masking" to influence listeners;

   therefore,

   rock concerts should be abolished.

The weaknesses in this argument are readily apparent from this sketch. For example, common sense tells that it is not only rock music played at concerts that can cause hearing loss in an audience, but excessively loud music of whatever type. Classical overtures played loudly enough will just as surely lead to hearing loss in concert-goers. The second reason is no more logically linked to its conclusion than the first. Granted that high-frequency hearing loss is genuine among people who frequent rock concerts, but that is a better argument for turning down the volume of the amplifiers than for banning the concerts. Finally, the "backward masking" the writer refers to is allegedly present only in recorded rock music, but technically impossible in live performances. It cannon therefore be cited as a logical reason for banning rock concerts.

The argument is weak mainly because it implies a relationship of logical necessity between assertions and conclusions where none exists. Here is a revision that remedies this flaw:

Revision: The evidence linking rock music at concerts with hearing loss in the audience is clearly established and is a solid argument for turning down the volume of the amplifiers. According to some writers, there are 13 million Americans who have suffered permanent hearing loss, usually from nerve impairment. The number one cause of this loss, writes an expert in the April 1984 issue of <u>Glamour</u> magazine, is prolonged exposure to loud noise. But rock concerts are not the only damaging source of loud music. Studies done in Sweden and summarized in the June 12, 1982, issue of <u>Science News</u>, have found that classical musicians also suffer hearing impairment from pursuing their careers. Trombone and French horn players were found to have suffered the greatest hearing loss. Some classical concerts monitored in Swedish opera houses have exceeded 85 decibels, which is a higher noise level than Swedish national standards allow in the workplace. Rock concerts can cause hearing loss in an audience, but so can Beethoven concerts. What's at issue is not the music itself, but how loudly it is played.

This argument is stronger not only because it cites evidence that is specific, but also because the links between its assertions are reasonable and logical.

The links between the assertions and conclusions of an argumentative essay should be forged with iron-clad logic. Yet it is easy to confuse or misstate them during the actual writing. One way to avoid this error is to sketch out the major points of your argument before you write it. For example, if you are writing an argument against capital punishment, a diagram of your major ideas and the links between them might look like this:

Capital punishment is wrong

because

it does not deter crime

because

it puts society on equal moral footing with the murderer

because

it debases the value of human life

because

it is arbitrarily practiced

because

it can lead to a catastrophic mistake.

From this brief chart, you know the major parts of your argument as well as the logical links that must connect them.

What follows is a student paper arguing for the abolishment or reformation of Halloween as a traditional festival. The original draft used an impressive satirical touch and an exaggerated sense of horror to expose the dangers of Halloween. However, it did not include enough evidence to support its contention that sugar was unhealthy, nor did it take sufficiently into account the opposition's viewpoint. Its ending was also notably weak. Study the original draft, with the instructor's suggestions; then, notice how the student incorporated these suggestions into the revised copy. The second version features a clear proposition supported by facts, expert testimony, witness, and experience. It also acknowledges and then promptly destroys the opposition's point of view:

Original:

Your opening is too abrupt. Why not begin with a negative description of a Halloween scene?

A Night to Forget

Halloween, as a traditional American festival, should be eliminated from our calendars because it spawns crime and poor health.

Halloween today represents a conglomeration of ancient customs and religious beliefs. According to the <u>Encyclopaedia Britannica</u>, the

celebration of Halloween can be traced back to
the Celtic Winter Festival. On this occasion
the Celts would celebrate the autumn harvest and
the coming of winter. At this time, it was *wordy*
believed that ancestors who had died during the
year passed into the spirit world, and it was
customary to masquerade in order to frighten
away evil spirits who might try to stop them on *Use a more striking expression.*
their way. In the eighth century, Pope Gregory
III decided to give the event a more religious
thrust and declared it All Saints' Day, or All
Hallows' Day, to be celebrated on November 1.
On the eve of this day adults and children
would go from house to house offering to fast
for the saints in return for money or some other
gift. The Irish later added the superstition
that "little people" roamed the roads and played
pranks on All Hallows' Night, thus providing
practical jokers with a perfect opportunity to
be mischievous without consequences. In the
nineteenth century, the Irish brought this
wretched mess of customs to this country, where *Here you do take into account the opposition, but some parents would be upset at the idea of arguing against Halloween. You should mention their views somewhere in this argument.*
it has been deteriorating ever since.

Halloween has been a great commercial
success, and no doubt candy makers and costume
companies would hate to see it go. Confection
manufacturers sell huge quantities of their
packaged junk food during the month of October.
Costume designers of today create increasingly

elaborate disguises for the occasion.
Sophisticated kids of today reject the
traditional, but far less expensive, ghosts and
goblins of yesteryear. If the little darlings
don't demand a Darth Vader cape and helmet for
$49.95, they need other elaborate components in
order to make a social statement. Last year I
had at my door a playboy bunny, a Rubic's cube,
a medfly, and a formal dinner table, complete
with silver candelabra and white wine.

And the reward for this creative effort?
Usually a 20-pound bag of assorted candy and gum
that a parent wouldn't allow a child to touch
during the rest of the year. Sugar is bad for
the health and yet children are allowed nearly
unlimited quantities of it during Halloween.
Even more ludicrous is the tolerance of mass
vandalism. Trick-or-treaters today leave home
armed with toilet paper, spray paint, raw eggs
and shaving cream—ready to do battle with the
first helpless old lady to run out of candy, or
the first kid they see dressed as a fairy
princess or Mickey Mouse. No longer do homeowners
dare to darken their houses, leave the car on
the street, place pumpkins on the doorstep, or
hand out apples, for fear of reprisals.

The many incidents of property damage that
occur during Halloween keep the police busy.
It's time we took Halloween out of the hands of

[handwritten margin note: needs supporting evidence]

[handwritten margin note: support this assertion with some evidence]

adults or juvenile delinquents and returned it *weak ending, needs more punch.*
to a harmless custom, or forgot it completely.

Revision:

A Night to Forget

Picture streets mobbed with wildly excited
children. Imagine these untamed urchins banging
on door after door in hideous disguises,
greedily demanding sweets. Consider what might
happen if the little beasts were armed with raw
eggs or shaving cream. It happens. Otherwise
conscientious parents encourage their offspring
to beg shamelessly in the streets and condone
mass consumption of useless sugar. Is it a
country gone mad? No, it's Halloween. Halloween
has become a night of terror for those unarmed
with goodies and a night of anxiety and torment
for police and many parents. It's time we
examine this festival of horror and either
revamp or eliminate it completely.

Traditionalists will no doubt gasp with
horror at the thought of abandoning such a
quaint celebration. They may contend that in
our rapidly changing world young people need to
cling to some form of tradition now more than
ever before. But what tradition is it? Most
adults agree that Halloween includes ghosts,
goblins, and goodies, but beyond that, just what
exactly are we celebrating?

Halloween today represents a conglomeration of ancient customs and religious beliefs. According to the Encyclopaedia Britannica, the celebration of Halloween can be traced back to the Celtic Winter Festival. On this occasion the Celts would celebrate the autumn harvest and the coming of winter. It was believed that ancestors who had died during the year passed into the spirit world, and it was customary to masquerade in order to frighten away evil spirits who might hinder them on their journey. In the eighth century, Pope Gregory III decided to give the event a more religious thrust and declared it All Saints' Day, or All Hallows' Day, to be celebrated on November 1. On the eve of this day adults and children would go from house to house offering to fast for the saints in return for money or some other gift. The Irish later added the superstition that "little people" roamed the roads and played pranks on All Hallows' Night, thus providing practical jokers with a perfect opportunity to be mischievous without consequences. In the nineteenth century, the Irish brought this wretched mess of customs to this country, where it has been deteriorating ever since.

Halloween has been a great commercial success, and no doubt candy makers and costume companies would hate to see it go. Confection

manufacturers sell huge quantities of their
packaged junk food during the month of October.
Costume designers of today create increasingly
elaborate disguises for the occasion.
Sophisticated kids of today reject the
traditional, but far less expensive, ghosts and
goblins of yesteryear. If the little darlings
don't demand a Darth Vader cape and helmet for
$49.95, they need other elaborate components in
order to make a social statement. Last year I
had at my door a playboy bunny, a Rubic's cube,
a medfly, and a formal dinner table, complete
with silver candelabra and white wine.

   And the reward for this creative effort?
Usually a 20—pound bag of assorted candy and gum
that a parent wouldn't allow a child to touch
during the rest of the year. For years,
dentists and doctors have warned parents and
children against the evils of sugar. Dr. John
Yudkin, a distinguished British physician,
biochemist, and researcher, has devoted his
career to exposing the ill effects of sugar in
the diet. In his book Sweet and Dangerous, Dr.
Yudkin contends that a high intake of sugar
contributes to tooth decay, diabetes, heart
disease, and obesity. In addition, recent
studies done at Stanford University suggest that
a correlation exists between sugar intake and
behavioral problems in children and adults.

Yet, on Halloween everyone overdoses on sugar.

Even more ludicrous than setting aside a night for children to gather killer candy is the tolerance of mass vandalism. Trick-or-treaters today leave home armed with toilet paper, spray paint, raw eggs and shaving cream—ready to do battle with the first helpless old lady to run out of candy, or the first kid they see dressed as a fairy princess or Mickey Mouse. For fear of reprisals, no longer do homeowners dare to darken their houses, leave a car on the street, place pumpkins on the doorstep, or hand out apples.

Sergeant Moreno of the Glendale, California, Police Department stated that the police department switchboard is heavily engaged on Halloween night. In recent years, each November first issue of the Los Angeles Times has reported at least one incident of acid-laced cookies or razor-blade-embedded apples passed out to an unsuspecting trick-or-treater. These incidents don't begin to cover the property damage that goes unreported. Last year I shoveled my way out of my driveway strewn with pumpkin carcasses, got into my car splattered with eggs, drove to pick up my daughter covered with shaving crean, and returned to my garage plastered with spray-painted obscenities.

Enough is enough! Of course, who doesn't love to see the little tykes with their cute little faces peeking out of an adorable Snoopy

costume? And certainly, everyone gets a kick out

of peculiar expressions carved into pumpkins,

but the rest of this crazy celebration is out of

control! How about having a mandatory

retirement for trick—or—treaters? Twelve years,

puberty, facial hair, voice change, or the onset

of acne——whichever comes first. What if we were

to unite in refusing to give away useless,

harmful sugar products and passed out notepads,

pencils, or balloons instead? Since we are

celebrating an occasion with questionable merit,

what's to keep us from making up some new rules?

It's time we took Halloween out of the hands of

hedonistic adults or juvenile delinquents and

returned it to a harmless custom, or forgot it

completely.

Exercises

1. Give the following argument a careful reading. In view of every-thing you have read in this chapter, how does the argument measure up? Write a brief critical review.

THE LIBERTINE EQUATION

The programs and actions growing out of libertine thought and its ideologies, have put society in bondage to the indifferent with disturbing consequences. It strikes me in this manner.

Ultra liberal thought in its libertarian way, racing on its erratic course deep within the sanctuary of man and woman, soon bursts forth upon society. Confused, discontented, immoral, demanding, abusive, with no restraints and in their frenzy call it freedom.

This is not freedom, this is an abuse of freedom in which society becomes a slave to turbulent thought, shiftlessness and wanton desires.

It is a delusion, the leading of individuals the wrong way down a one-way street. It is an intellectually organized view and principle presented in such a way, even though it is misleading, to meet the permissive demands of the time. This sort of libertine equation has just about bankrupted society morally and financially.

Society and religion must find a way to unwind from this dangerous thought that knows no evil, sees no evil, hears no evil; that has no moral or financial balance; that plays upon the weaknesses of human nature to gain its popularity. This kind of speculative philosophy has been the scourge of nations down through the ages.

Every so often history repeats itself and moral society has had to deal with this type of thinking and behavior. If in this present day and time it is allowed to continue, everyone will be engulfed in this delusion. For when the bell tolls, it tolls for all.

May I say in all fairness, while we cannot condone disoriented, undisciplined runaway thoughts and actions, we also cannot allow narrowness and cynicism to govern our lives. Both can be ruinous and so cloud the mind to reality and sane thought.

—Robert J. Carley, letter reprinted from *Mobile Press-Register*, October 3, 1981.

2. Quote two expert testimonies and cite three facts for each of the following arguments:
a. pro or con gun control
b. pro or con nuclear energy plants
c. pro or con censorship
d. pro or con animal experimentation

3. Narrate an experience (yours or someone else's) that would support one of the following arguments:
a. A college education is not for everyone.
b. Much of contemporary poetry cannot be explained.
c. Most T.V. advertising is socially and culturally biased.
d. The typical white wedding dress is a shameful waste of money.
e. Certain customs followed by "gentlemen" relating to "ladies" should be maintained (or abolished).

Writing Assignments

1. Choose a social custom or tradition which you do not particularly like. Propose a change and defend it in an argumentative essay.

2. Write an argument for or against one of the following subjects:
a. legalized pornography
b. U.S. intervention in the affairs of third world countries
c. restructuring of the income tax system
d. censorship of song lyrics
e. abstract art
f. a national welfare system (as opposed to a statewide one)
g. mandatory registration of known AIDS carriers

3. "Dictionary definitions should prescribe ideal usage rather than reflect the way words are actually used." Write an argument for or against this idea.

Chapter Thirteen

Literary Papers and Essay Exams

*K*nowledge is the foundation and source of good writing.

Horace (65–8 B.C.)

Literary Papers

In writing a paper about literature, it is useful to imagine yourself as a lawyer and the analyzed work as your client. If you say that this is what your client meant, your client should be allowed to testify freely to that effect. We suggest this pretense because experience teaches that student papers on literature seldom support their interpretations with adequate references to the work. Yet the emphasis of a literary paper should always be on the work itself, and not on any other unrelated event or memory it may call to mind.

For example, we had one student who interpreted a certain poem as being about alligators although no mention of that reptile was to be found anywhere in the text. Pressed to expose the beast, he rambled on about some remembered episode with an alligator in his childhood. That literature can and does arouse such unique associations in each of us is part of its charm. But sober analysis calls for proof, and if your paper cannot support your interpretation with material from the text itself, you may be guilty of a misreading.

But can a work not have a valid but different meaning for everyone? This objection to the idea that an interpretation of literature can be right or wrong is often raised by students. And it is an undeniable truth that literature can and does evoke different meanings in different minds. But so can the Grand Canyon. Yet no self-respecting student would write a geology paper about how the Grand Canyon brought to mind an alligator, even if it did. To do so is to focus not on the canyon itself, but on the associations it evokes in the student's mind. It makes the analyzer, rather than the analyzed, the central theme of the paper, which is not what either a geological or a literary paper requires. The first wants you to focus on the rocks in the canyon; the second, on the words on the page.

What a literary paper requires is analysis of the work itself. You state your interpretation of the work and you prove it. You show the thinking and evidence that led to your conclusions. You make a point about an author and you back it up with quotations from the author's work. Along the way, you may also find yourself doing one or all of the following tasks:

Finding the theme

The main idea of the literary work is called its theme, and understanding and expressing it is a basic function of any literary paper. Characteristically, bad literature will trumpet theme as crassly as a television deodorant commercial, while good literature will express it in the subtleties of real life.

So how do you find the theme of a literary work? You might begin by examining its title. In a longer work, title may give no hint about theme. For example, *A Passage to India* gives little inkling about the theme of culture conflict in that famous novel. But the titles of other novels such as *The Good Earth,* or *For Whom the Bell Tolls,* do hint of their themes—that owning land is important, and that war is a call to death.

In shorter works, a title can be as illuminating as a lightning bolt. Here is an example of a poem that is nearly meaningless without its title:

> Last night
> a snail
> crawled out
> my ear.
> I feel
> some bad
> times
> coming.

What does this mean? The title tells us:

Omen

Last night
a snail
crawled out
my ear.
I feel
some bad
times
coming.

Sometimes, especially in a play, the theme of a work will be expressed by one of its characters. We do not mean that the character will suddenly abandon his or her role and mount a pulpit. But he or she will nevertheless have the last word—in emphasis if not actual sequence—and it will be given with the finality of a summation. Here is such a speech from *Death of a Salesman*. It is delivered by Willy Loman's wife, Linda, and crisply sums up the compassionate theme of the play—that obscure or unimportant people may suffer immensely.

> . . . I don't say he's a great man. Will Loman never made a lot of money. His name was never in the paper. He's not the finest character that ever lived. But he's a human being, and a terrible thing is happening to him. So attention must be paid. He's not to be allowed to fall into his grave like a old dog. Attention, attention must finally be paid to such a person.

However, you should not approach the business of finding and expressing a work's theme as if you were coring an apple. Novels, plays, or poems are likely to have several themes, and the one you uncover must not only be expressed, but also documented by references to the work itself.

Summarizing

To summarize does not mean to give a blow-by-blow recounting of what any reader of the work already knows. Rather, it means to condense in your own words the content and theme of the work and to add, as you do, your own comments and perspective on it. Here is an example of what we mean. Students were asked to summarize the theme of this verse:

> "Yes," I answered you last night;
> "No," this morning, sir, I say:
> Colors seen by candlelight
> Will not look the same by day.
> —E. B. Browning

One student wrote this:

> The poem tells us that candlelight has the
> ability to hide all kinds of cracks and flaws in
> a room. Because the candles cast such a soft
> light, much of the room remains hidden in
> shadows. Perhaps a woman is speaking to a real
> estate salesman. She had dined in a certain
> house by candlelight and loved the place so much
> that when it went up for sale, she wanted to buy
> it. But when she sees the place in the harsh
> light of day, the color of the wallpaper looks
> hideous and she does not want the house at all.

This summary is based on a much too literal-minded reading of the verse and therefore leads nowhere. Here is a better summary:

> The poem warns us that romance must not be
> confused with true love. It tells us that a
> romantic setting, such as a candlelit dinner in
> a cozy little bistro, can cause infatuation and
> may even elicit promises of undying love from a
> lover. But such a feeling rarely passes the
> test of reality involving a daily routine of
> work and paying bills. This lighthearted verse
> is in the ancient tradition of poems that
> puncture the myth of romantic love by pointing
> out how it promises everything but delivers
> nothing.

The author of this second summary does not merely serve up the meaning of the poem on the platter of a prose summary—giving us her words instead

of the poet's. Instead, she clarifies the theme by commenting on it; she identifies the tone of the poem; and she mentions the ancient tradition to which
it belongs.

Paraphrasing

To paraphrase means to restate in your own words some event or
happening in a literary work. The paraphrase has two aims in a literary
paper. One is to firmly anchor the literary paper onto the analyzed work
itself and so curb any inclination a writer might have to drift. Another aim
is to prove that you have actually assimilated the work and know what you
are talking about.

Primarily, accurate paraphrasing is part of the evidence necessary to
prove any point you wish to make about the literary work. Here is an example. The student is making a point about foreshadowing in the short
story "The Lottery":

> In the short story "The Lottery," by
> Shirley Jackson, there are definite hints and
> clues that someone will die. Black is the
> symbolic color for death in our society, and
> throughout Jackson's story it occurs numerous
> times. The little black box which the people
> draw their lots from is referred to over and
> over again. Jackson also portrays Mrs.
> Hutchinson as a very frightened woman. For
> example, when she realizes that someone in her
> family is going to be picked, she begins
> screaming that the drawing was unfair and should
> be done over again. Before we even find out
> that she is going to be the one to die, we have
> several inklings of that outcome.

What is the difference between a paraphrase and a summary?
Mainly a technical one. The paraphrase restates incidents and events in the
work more or less as they happened. A summary expresses broad themes

or ideas of the work without necessarily recounting any of its actual details. Here is an example of a summary about "The Lottery":

"The Lottery" is about scapegoating and the symbolic function it can serve in a community. It recounts the annual tradition in a certain community of stoning a member by drawing lots. Implied in the story is the idea that even if not deliberately elected, the scapegoat eases the fears of a community by making one of its members bear the brunt of misfortune and evil that all dread.

The paraphrase can be convincing evidence of your grasp of plot and outcome in a work. There is, however, a tradition of misuse of the paraphrase evident in many student papers: namely, as a padding device. Any one can stretch one page into two through a picky paraphrase. Here is an example. The student was asked to write a paragraph or two on a favorite book and to say what was appealing about it:

Of the many books I have read, The Stand by Stephen King is my favorite. The story takes place in the United States in the present time. There had been an accident in a germ warfare plant. Some people escaped with the deadly virus and they accidentally infected men at a nearby gas station.

Eventually, the virus spread, killing millions of people. Soon survivors split up into two groups. One group is led by a man who is the devil. The second group is led by an old woman who is very religious.

```
The two sides organize, with the bad group

wanting to destroy the other.  The good group

sends people to make peace but they are captured

and held prisoner.  When these people are about

to be executed, one of the bad brings in a

nuclear bomb.  The bomb explodes with help from

the good group destroying all the bad.

      This is my favorite book.  It is long but

quite enjoyable.
```

Using a paraphrase this way makes your paper trivial and waters down its impact. Moreover, it is a blatant case of padding. Paraphrase when you have to and only as necessary to prove your point.

Quoting

Quoting means copying exactly a passage from a written work. Every essay interpreting literature should include quotations from the analyzed work. Set a context for the quotation, cite it accurately, and relate it to the point you are making. The conventions on the use of quotations are easy to remember and practice: If the quotation is shorter than four lines, integrate it grammatically into your text and set it off within quotation marks. Here is an example of a quotation that is badly integrated within the text of the paper:

```
Hawthorne uses symbolic objects to convey his

theme that mankind is basically evil.  He uses

the forest to show "no church had ever been

gathered nor solitary Christian prayer," as a

symbol for the essence of evil and places the

most goodly and respectable persons within the

confines of this dark and dreary world.
```

Although accurate, the quotation is not grammatically integrated within the sentence. Here is an improvement:

Hawthorne uses symbolic objects to convey his
theme that mankind is basically evil. He uses
one of nature's objects, the forest, "where no
church had ever been gathered nor solitary
Christian prayed," as a symbol for the essence
of evil and places the most goodly and
respectable persons within the confines of this
dark and dreary world.

A quotation longer than four lines is reproduced exactly without quotation marks and indented ten spaces from your left margin (assuming a typewritten page). If the quotation is of a single paragraph, its initial line need not be indented. But if it consists of two or more paragraphs, the initial line of each quoted paragraph is indented three spaces. Here is a example:

The following lines from "The Short Happy Life
of Francis Macomber" describe Hemingway's
typical female—a combination of cruelty and
good looks:

How should a woman act when she
discovers her husband is a bloody
coward? She's damn cruel but they're
all cruel. They govern, of course, and
to govern one has to be cruel
sometimes. Still I've seen enough of
their damn terrorism.

"Have some more eland," he said to
her politely.

That afternoon, late, Wilson and
Macomber went out in the motor car with
the native driver and the two gun—

bearers. Mrs. Macomber stayed in the
camp. It was too hot to go out, she
said, and she was going with them in
the early morning. As they drove off
Wilson saw her standing under the big
tree, looking pretty rather than
beautiful in her faintly rosy khaki,
her dark hair drawn back off her
forehead and gathered in a knot low on
her neck, her face as fresh, he
thought, as though she were in England.

In longer papers on literature, quotations from both primary and secondary sources may be used. The distinction between the two is a simple one: The work you are analyzing is the primary source; any other writing or opinion about it is a secondary source. In support of your interpretation, you may wish to cite such secondary sources as the views of other critics. And for such quotations, you should use exactly the same format as for a primary source.

Analyzing form

The form of a literary work is the sum of its physical characteristics—its language, imagery, diction, syntax, and grammar. When we speak of form we mean the way an idea is expressed, whether with rhyme, in prose, with repetition, in images, or plainly; when we speak of content, we mean the idea itself, its proposition, merit, consequences, or tradition. Form and content are not divisible in any practical sense, but literary criticism often treats each as if it were capable of standing alone. A critic may therefore write at length about the form of the poem, or more usually, its content, as if the one could exist without the other.

It is not always appropriate or necessary to analyze the form of a work in a literary paper. The work may have no distinctly recognizable form, or its uninspired use of form may be unworthy of comment. But occasionally, if you spot something significant in the form of a work, you should mention it in your paper. For example, the poem on page 309, "Omen," is a variation on the haiku, a Japanese poem of 15 syllables, and the student who knows and mentions this fact in a paper will likely make a stronger impression than the one on whom it is lost.

What follows is the first draft of a student paper analyzing a short story by William Carlos Williams. As the result of one tutorial session with her instructor, the student made the editorial changes indicated. They consist mainly of some additional summarizing and explicating. The final version is a considerable improvement over the original.

Original:

Critical Analysis of

"The Use of Force"

by

William Carlos ~~W. C.~~ Williams

"The Use of Force," written by *William Carlos* ~~W. C.~~ Williams, is the story of a frightened child who attempts to hide a sore throat so as to avoid being treated by the doctor. The story vividly illustrates *the Universal truth* that fear—an unpleasant and often strong emotion—can lead to violence and irrational behavior. The narrator, *an old-fashioned country doctor making his rounds during a diphtheria epidemic,* ~~who is the doctor himself~~ is the spokesman for the theme. It is through him that we feel the *anger, the rebellion, and the intense* ~~intensity of the~~ fear that the girl is experiencing; *through him we also experience* the apprehension of the *the narrator's* parents and ~~his~~ own inner fear of not being able to help her as a doctor. "The child was fairly eating me up with her cold, steady eyes" he tells us, as he notices for the first time the terror reigning within her. He also doesn't fail to notice the nervousness and apprehension of the parents, who were "eyeing [him] up and down distrustfully" upon his arrival.

Furthermore, we ~~are informed~~ *realize, from the information the narrator gives us,* that the parents of the child are uneducated, ~~when~~ *for* they ~~apply~~ *use* such ~~sentences~~ *language* as "it don't do no good" and "her throat don't hurt her." From this we can conclude that one of the reasons for the parents and the child being apprehensive is their ignorance, ~~that has~~ *which in time has* developed into a *deep* fear—~~caused~~ *fear of* ~~by the anticipation of~~ an unknown, *unanticipated* danger.

As the story builds ~~up~~ towards its climactic ~~point~~ *x*, the narrator ~~illustrates how~~ *,s fear grows and* ~~that fear is~~ *becomes* intensified ~~and~~ *until it's* eventually released through violent and irrational behavior. The doctor is at first *controlled and* reasonable when "speaking quietly and slowly" he approaches the child for a throat examination. But the ~~hesitant~~ child, filled with fear and fury, "clawe~~s~~*d* instinctively" ~~for~~ *at* {his} eyes" in a sudden outbreak of violent behavior. "Then the battle began" the narrator tells us. Enraged with the parents of the child for not allowing him to handle the case himself, and frightened that the child ~~may~~ *might* have diphtheria, ~~he~~ *the doctor* now ~~had to~~ *must* examine her no matter how ~~violent he himself became.~~ *much she resists.* *The confrontation between doctor and patient turns into a fierce jungle combat as each side loses control. Ironically, the doctor, whom we normally think of as a detached and reasonable person, is filled with a violence similar to that of the child. He says:*

"In a final unreasoning assault I overpowered the child's neck . . . forced the heavy silver spoon . . . down her throat till she gagged . . . now truly she was furious . . . now she attacked."

In essence both the doctor and the child
were frightened, but for different reasons: One
feared the death of a small human being, and the
other feared the thought of being hurt by a
stranger. ~~But~~ ironically both feared each
other, and both turned ~~against each~~ *on the* other in
violent behavior to protect themselves from what
they thought was the danger. *The lesson is clear: Even the most rational among us may act irrationally when enough stress is present.*

Revision:

Critical Analysis of

"The Use of Force"

by

William Carlos Williams

"The Use of Force," written by William
Carlos Williams, is the story of a frightened
child who attempts to hide a sore throat so as
to avoid being treated by her doctor. The story
vividly illustrates the universal truth that
fear——an unpleasant and often strong emotion——
can lead to violence and irrational behavior.

The narrator, an old-fashioned country
doctor making his rounds during a diphtheria
epidemic, is the spokesman for the theme. It is
through him that we feel the anger, the
rebellion, and the intense fear that the girl is
experiencing; through him we also experience the
apprehension of the parents and the narrator's

own inner fear of not being able to help her as
a doctor. "The child was fairly eating me up
with her cold, steady eyes" he tells us, as he
notices for the first time the terror reigning
within her. He also doesn't fail to notice the
nervousness and apprehension of the parents, who
were "eyeing [him] up and down distrustfully"
upon his arrival. Furthermore, we realize, from
the information the narrator gives us, that the
parents of the child are uneducated, for they
use such language as "it don't do no good" and
"her throat don't hurt her." We can conclude
that one of the reasons for the parents and the
child being apprehensive is their ignorance,
which in time has developed into a deep fear--
fear of an unknown, unanticipated danger.

As the story builds towards its climax, the
narrator's fear grows and becomes intensified
until it is eventually released through violent
and irrational behavior. The doctor is at first
controlled and reasonable when "speaking quietly
and slowly" he approaches the child for a throat
examination. But the child, filled with fear and
fury, "clawed instinctively" at his eyes in a
sudden outbreak of violent behavior. "Then the
battle began," the narrator tells us. Enraged
with the parents of the child for not allowing
him to handle the case himself, and frightened
that the child might have diphtheria, the doctor

now must examine her, no matter how much she resists. The confrontation between doctor and patient turns into a fierce jungle combat as each side loses control. Ironically, the doctor, whom we normally think of as a detached and reasonable person, is filled with a violence similar to that of the child. He says: "In a final unreasoning assault I overpowered the child's neck . . . forced the heavy silver spoon . . . down her throat till she gagged . . . now truly she was furious . . . now she attacked."

In essence, both doctor and the child were frightened, but for different reasons: One feared the death of a small human being, and the other feared the thought of being hurt by a stranger. Ironically, both feared each other, and both turned on the other in violent behavior to protect themselves from what they thought was eminent danger. The lesson is clear: Even the most rational among us may act irrationally when enough stress is present.

Exercises

1. In one sentence, summarize the following poem:

Not Marching Away to Be Killed

Peace is the men not marching away to be killed.
I never saw my father marching away to be killed.
He was killed before I was born. But my mother
Always spoke of the men marching away to be killed.
Not "marching to the war" or "into action"

Or even "marching to fight for this country."
Although she was a soldier's daughter and a soldier's
Widow, "Marching away to be killed"
Was the fundamental reality for her.

For me

Peace is the man I love not
Marching away to be killed.
—Jean Overton Fuller (b. 1915)

2. Choose three quotations from the story "Young Goodman Brown" by Nathaniel Hawthorne that illustrate the main character's original innocence. Then choose three quotations that illustrate his guilt. (A copy of this short story will be found in your college library.)

3. State the theme of Shirley Jackson's "The Lottery." Whom do the characters represent? What is the tone of the story? Who is the narrator? Interpret the symbolic meaning of the lottery itself. (A copy of this short story will be found in your college library.)

The Essay Exam

What is an instructor looking for in the answer to an essay examination? First, **understanding** of the material. You are expected to demonstrate a grasp of the subject matter, not merely to plunk down the facts. An answer consisting of lumps of facts bobbing among watery sentences is only an answer, not an essay. The essay exam is forgiving of the student who knows the material, but does not know it exactly, and positively generous to the one who knows how to express ideas in coherent paragraphs. It requires an essay as its answer, which means that you must frame your topic in a thesis behind which you marshal your facts as support or proof.

Second, the **organization** of the essay is important. If you know your facts but present them in a jumble, your essay's disorganization might even be taken to mean that you have not mastered the subject. That is like being ticketed for speeding when you are only badly parked. Organization counts, whether you are writing for psychology or English.

Third, the **selection** of material you include in your essay counts. It is as important to leave out irrelevant material as it is to include the relevant. If you spent a Sunday cramming on a topic that doesn't appear on the exam, don't just throw it in anyway for good measure. Give only the answer that the question wants, not the one you have carefully prepared.

Finally, if your essay is between a middle and high grade, the inclusion of **factual knowledge** will swing the decision in your favor. You must be correct in your facts, cite authorities accurately, be precise in your recall of events, dates, and names.

That, more or less, is what instructors look for in an essay examination. So how do you go about giving them what they want? We have some suggestions for doing exactly that:

Read the question carefully

This advice may strike you as fresh as Mother's admonition to wear a coat in chilly weather. But it is a fact that many students answer essay exam questions badly because they have misread the question. For instance, here is a question from a class in European history:

```
Define the Yalta Conference of 1945, explaining

who the participants were and what role they

played, and analyzing the major effects of the

conference.
```

If you study this question carefully, you will realize that it asks you to accomplish three tasks: (1) to *define* the conference, (2) to *explain* the participants and their roles, and (3) to *do an analysis of the effects* of the conference. To answer it correctly, you must follow this exact order of topics in your essay. Most instructors can judge whether or not you have adequately answered the question by quickly scanning your answer. If any part has not been answered, your grade will be lowered. Before attempting to answer an essay exam, then, always ask yourself what the instructor is after, and if you can't tell, don't write a word until you can.

Think before you write

In other words, don't simply jump in and start writing. Think. Prewrite your answer. Jot down important subtopics and ideas you should cover. Put them side by side with the question and ask yourself if they really answer it. If the exam allows a choice of questions, use part of this pause to decide which question you can best answer in the allowed time.

Organize your essay

We grant that all writers do not equally benefit from advanced organization and that this particular wisdom may therefore not be for you. But many writers will write a better essay if they systematically choose an organizing pattern for it. The pattern you use will naturally depend on how the question you answer is worded. Here are some examples of actual essay questions, along with the organizing mode or pattern a writer might use to answer them:

From Humanities

To demonstrate your understanding of the Aristotelian concept of "hamartia," discuss an incident in which you or someone you know was guilty of this error.

Suggested mode: *narration*

"Discuss" is one of those catch-all terms with multiple meanings depending on the context of the question. The error in judgment committed by the central character of a tragedy and resulting in his or her downfall is called "hamartia." And what this question wants is a narrative instance of this frailty. Narration is therefore the mode you should use to write on this topic.

From Geography

You have been transported to a tropical forest area of the world. Discuss the kind of flora and fauna you see about you.

Suggested mode: *description*

In this case "discuss" really means describe. The clue is in the wording of the question, which is asking you to tell what you see. If we were answering this question, we would also explain why we should see what we say we do. Doing so tells the instructor that we understand the natural forces behind the formation of a tropical rain forest.

From Western Civilization

Your author writes, "If there was one primary factor which operated more than others to accomplish the downfall of Roman civilization, it was probably *imperialism*." What does he mean by *imperialism?*

Suggested mode: *definition*

As a general rule, any question that probes for "meaning" is fishing for a definition. But there's a catch here: The term we are asked to define is cemented to the context of Rome's downfall. All the examples and details we use to back up our definition of this word we would therefore draw from the Roman experience.

From Art History

Write an essay that discusses Picasso's "Blue Period."

Suggested mode: *example*

In fact, this question calls for a mixed mode response. You must first define Picasso's "Blue Period," but thereafter the essay should focus primarily on examples of paintings typical of it. Note that examples are usable in essays of all modes. However, once you have defined "Blue Period," this particular essay should concentrate on the discussion of successive examples.

From History

Write an essay describing the stages of the Hegelian dialectic.

Suggested mode: *classification*

A classification essay, as we learned in Chapter 7, focuses primarily on dividing a whole into its constituent parts. On the surface, this question seems to ask for a description. But what it is really after is a listing and discussion of the parts of a whole, which is the typical subject of the classification essay.

From Government

Write an essay detailing the steps a candidate must take to qualify for a congressional election.

Suggested mode: *process*

We have said elsewhere that the process mode is relatively easy to write. You simply recount how a thing is done, usually detailing sequential steps in time. Most "how to" questions implicitly call for a process answer.

From English Literature

Write an essay in which you state the major differences in subject matter and style between the English poets of the 18th century and those of the Romantic era.

Suggested mode: *comparison/contrast*

Not all comparison/contrast essays will be so conveniently worded. This one not only tells us what it wants, it also provides the bases for our comparison/contrast. To organize the essay into its major topics, you need merely to list how poetry of the 18th century and Romantic period differ in subject matter and style.

From Sociology

What are some of the major reasons for the so-called "unresponsive bystander syndrome" in densely populated urban areas?

Suggested mode: *causal analysis*

Although you will mainly be analyzing cause in answering this question, you should begin by defining the syndrome and giving an example of it. Doing so sets a context for the discussion of reasons that will follow.

From Political Science

Argue for or against this statement: "There is absolutely no question that 110,000 Japanese Americans living on the west coast of the United States should have been interned in concentration camps during World War II."

Suggested mode: *argumentation*

This is an unambiguous assignment: You merely need to put on your argumentative cap, choose a side, and begin by prewriting the principal points of your essay along with the underlying logical links between them.

Our point, perhaps laboriously made, is that the most appropriate rhetorical pattern for answering a question will often be implicit in its wording. Yet it is also clear that not all essay questions can be answered in a pure rhetorical pattern. Consider, for example, this topic:

What did Karl Marx mean when he said, "Freedom is meaningless without equality of opportunity"?

Writing an essay on it will require you to say what Marx meant and also show how the quotation reflects his overall philosophy. And doing so will involve a rhetorical pattern considerably more complex than a clear-cut definition. What we have already said in Chapter 4 bears repeating. Rhetorical modes are intended as an aid to the writer and are not usable in every conceivable assignment. However, the principle of concentrated focus they teach applies to all kinds of writing, even to a paragraph whose organizing pattern is as thoroughly mixed as this one.

Here is a sample question from an actual college essay examination in History of the Americas. First, we supply the question and then we give two student answers, one average and one excellent. Study both answers to see where the second is superior to the first.

Exam question: What was the Rowell-Sirois Commission of 1937–41? What important recommendations did it make concerning federal-provincial relations in Canada? What role did the Depression play in this report?

Average answer: The Rowell–Sirois Commission was appointed by the prime minister of Canada to study what relationship should exist between the federal government and the local provinces. It was particularly important to do so because Canada had suffered some serious fiscal problems during the Depression and a former prime minister had suggested some dramatic social and economic changes that were thought by some Canadians to be unconstitutional because they gave too much power to the provinces. The main idea of the report was to invest the federal government with more power by giving it the right to collect taxes and to be in charge of all welfare programs.

This answer received only an average grade because it did not deal adequately with all three parts of the question. First of all, the essay never fully defines what the commission was. Second, it tells only superficially what role the Depression played, and what little it does tell is not in the required order. Finally, the student offers only minimum facts and details, giving the impression of not having adequately studied for the exam. Now, here is a superior answer to the same question:

Better answer: The Rowell–Sirois Commission was a special task force appointed by Prime Minister William Lyon Mackenzie King to study the role of the federal government in relationship to the local provinces. Two men chaired this commission: First, Newton Wesley Rowell, chief justice of Ontario, and later on, Joseph Sirois. In order to combat problems brought on by the Great Depression of the 1920s, Prime Minister Richard Bedford Bennett had proposed sweeping social and economic changes patterned after Roosevelt's New Deal. Many of these proposals were considered unconstitutional and led to Bennett's ouster. When William Lyon Mackenzie King became prime minister, one of his early tasks was to appoint the Rowell–Sirois Commission to study both the economic as well as the constitutional problems of Canada. Three years after its appointment, the commission submitted its report, focusing on two major points: (1) The higher courts had been reversing the intentions of the founding fathers of the confederation. (2) The powers of the provinces had grown beyond proper limits. In consequence of these two points, the report suggested that a strong central government was needed to guide and control the economy. The following specific recommendations were made:

    1. The federal government take over the debts
       of the provinces.

    2. The federal government collect all taxes.

    3. The federal government provide
       administrative and welfare programs.

    4. The federal government make provisions for
       the unemployed.

Despite the fact that many Canadians objected
to these suggestions and that much of the
report was ultimately rejected, the commission
succeeded in convincing the people that the
government had a responsibility for the social
and economic welfare of the people. The
acceptance of this view gave unity to the
provinces.

This answer is superior because it is comprehensive and deals with the topics in their exact order in the question. It is evident that the student has not only studied but also mastered the subject.

Exercises

1. The questions below were questions actually asked in college exams. Suggest the proper mode(s) of development for each question. If more than one mode applies, list all appropriate modes.

a. From biology:

Discuss the major events that occur in plate tectonics. In your discussion explain how these events are responsible for the major features of the ocean floor seen today, as well as how they explain the formation of some important islands and shallow marine environments. (Use the appropriate terms in your answer and be complete in your explanation.)

b. From history:

What was the Yalta agreement of 1945? Who were the participants? How did the agreement affect China?

c. *From literature:*

In a 500-word essay, define the *nada* philosophy, indicating its source as a dominant theme in Ernest Hemingway's *Farewell to Arms*. Begin with a clear thesis and support this thesis through specific examples from the novel.

d. *From psychology:*

Bruno Bettelheim has made the following statement: "Every child believes at some point in life . . . that because of his secret wishes, if not also his clandestine actions, he deserves to be degraded, banned from the presence of others, relegated to a nether world of smut." In a brief essay, indicate how any one of the case histories studied this semester supports Bettelheim's contention.

Chapter Fourteen

The Research Paper

*R*eading *maketh a full man; conference a ready man; and writing an exact man.*

FRANCIS BACON (1561–1626)

The research paper is aptly named, for it is a scholarly paper based on a systematic search. You search for a topic, for opinions that support your particular treatment of it, and for a narrowed thesis. You search for an organizing pattern for your ideas and for an appropriate style to express them.

From all this searching arise some measurable benefits. You learn to use the library, a skill which will prove useful no matter what your academic major or eventual employment. You learn the rules by which scholars work, the documenting forms they use to cite the works of others, and the standards of style and scholarship that they practice. And you learn these skills in the best and most memorable way of all—by doing.

You also learn to sift through contrary opinion, meld it with your own, and produce an original work. For that is what the research paper should be—your own original views on a topic backed by the supporting opinions of others. In writing the research paper you will play the dual role of editor and writer. As an editor, you find, extract, and edit the ideas and opinions of others that support your thesis. As a writer, you incorporate this material smoothly into the flow of your style and make it part of an original composition.

The Process of Writing a Research Paper

The process involved in writing a research paper is not markedly different from the one you would use to write any essay. You must find your topic, whittle it down to a controlling idea, and then frame it into a thesis statement. Next, you must research and uncover sources that support your thesis, arrange your ideas in their most emphatic order of presentation, and prewrite a formal outline. The rough draft comes after, followed by successive revisions. The conscientious student would follow this agenda for any essay.

For the research paper, this process differs somewhat in degree and complexity. Research papers are longer than ordinary essays and therefore require more legwork, more time spent in writing, and a more formal style. Typically, they will range between a specified length of five to ten pages. Many instructors also require the citation of a minimum number of sources along with submission of note cards, an outline, and a rough draft. The schedule for writing such a paper will vary, but ordinarily it will run over five weeks with submissions made by the student at specified intervals. That is the chronology we assume for the following discussion.

First Week: Finding a Topic

First, the topic you eventually settle on should be complex enough for an essay of some five to ten pages. This is probably as long an essay as you have to write in your first year or two of college, so be sure you base it on an appealing topic. Second, as you search for a topic, remember that instructors have their individual likes and dislikes too, and that it is only common sense for a writer to choose the topic most likely to please his or her reader. Finally, narrow your topic choice down to one that can be researched mainly at your local library. Since the collections found at most college libraries are substantial enough to support all but the most technical topics, this is not a severe limitation. Purely for practical reasons, however, it is smart to write on a topic that is convenient to research.

Using the library

The Card Catalog

The focal point of any search for a topic is the library, and your initial step should be a scan of the card catalog. Usually located in some central part of the lobby, the card catalog consists of alphabetized 3 × 5 cards that index every book in the library's collection. Books are listed separately under author, subject, and title headings. Translators, editors, and illustrators are jointly listed with the author on each card. If you have no idea at all for a topic to write on, rummaging through the card catalog might suggest one.

Microform Indexes

Microform is the name for systems of miniaturized storage. Many libraries store indexes of major periodicals on reels of microfilm that can be read by a special scanner. Others use film mounted on microfiche cards for condensed storage of college catalogs or other published information. Ask the librarian about the systems used in your own library.

Computer Searches

In some libraries, the computer has become a priceless tool for the researcher. Many libraries subscribe to on-line databases that can store and retrieve a vast quantity of information at the touch of a button. For example, the best known database, DIALOG, stores published information on over 100 subjects ranging from government and education to the humanities and physical science. Depending on library policy, students may or may not have free access to the terminals. Ask your librarian about the computer search facility in your own library. If it is there and available, take the time to learn how to call up the various databases. Once mastered, this latest research tool is the fastest and most convenient imaginable.

Periodical Guides

Much of the information you will cite in your paper is likely to be found in periodicals. Guides such at *The Reader's Guide To Periodical Literature* contain alphabetized listings of topics published in general periodicals. Similar guides are available for various subjects—for example, the *Social Sciences Index*, the *Humanities Index*, and the *Education Index*. In some schools, these or like indexes may be part of a computerized database.

The point of this initial visit to the library is to find a topic. You rummage through periodical indexes, scan the card catalog, browse through the book shelves until you find a topic you feel keenly about and would like to make the focus of your paper. By the end of the first week, you usually must have two topics ready for submission to the instructor, who will approve one.

Second Week: Assembling a Bibliography

The working bibliography is a list of promising sources turned up in an initial search. Eventually, this list will be narrowed down to a final bibliography, meaning those works you will actually use in the paper. On your first run through the library, you will most likely find many more sources than you can use and so must play the role of the selective editor. Here are some tips on separating usable from unusable sources:

1. Scan the indexes and tables of contents of books. If a chapter looks promising, leaf to its beginning and scan its thesis.
2. Scan the opening paragraph or two of articles. Finding the writer's thesis should tell whether the article might be useful.
3. Browse through book reviews found in references such as *The Book Review Digest*, whose articles summarize the contents of books.
4. Scan the preface of a book for the author's summary of its contents and emphasis.
5. Pay attention to the card catalog subject entry for any likely looking book. Books are classified on the cards under major headings such as "French Revolution," "Literary Criticism," "Medicine, History of," or "Archaeology."
6. Scan the bibliographical references listed at the end of articles or books for leads to other promising sources.
7. If you are doing a database search, scan the printout that summarizes the subject of an article or book (some databases offer this feature.)

Note that scanning is not the same as reading. You do not have the time to read through every likely source listed in the working bibliography. Scanning means running your eyes over the page, perhaps occasionally reading the initial sentence of a paragraph to grasp what it is about. Determining whether or not a source is usable should take you an average of no more than five minutes. Remember, too, that library workers have an uncanny knack for finding information stored in their collections, and most are eager to help. Get to know one of your friendly librarians and enlist his or her help in assembling a bibliography.

At the end of the second week you should have a working bibliography with each usable source listed on a 3 × 5 card. The card should contain information about where to find each source as well as a note about why it should prove useful. These cards should be submitted to the instructor for approval. Since you are unlikely to use every source in the working bibliography, the number of cards in it should exceed the minimum number of citations required. For example, if your instructor requires you to cite ten sources, your working bibliography should consist of at least fifteen to twenty cards. From this number, you can then choose the ten most applicable sources. Figures 14–1 and 14–2 are examples of bibliography cards.

Figure 14–1 Bibliography Card (personal library)

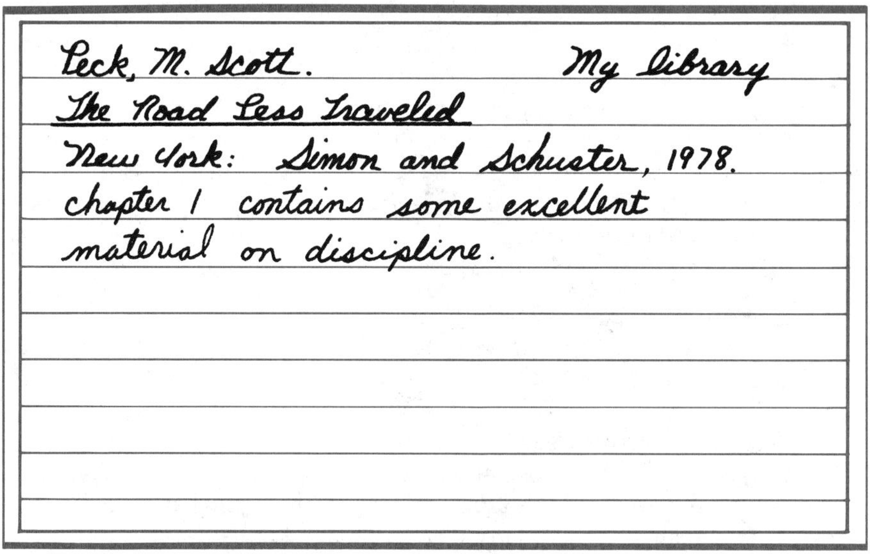
Peck, M. Scott. My library
The Road Less Traveled
New York: Simon and Schuster, 1978.
chapter 1 contains some excellent material on discipline.

Figure 14–2 Bibliography Card (college library)

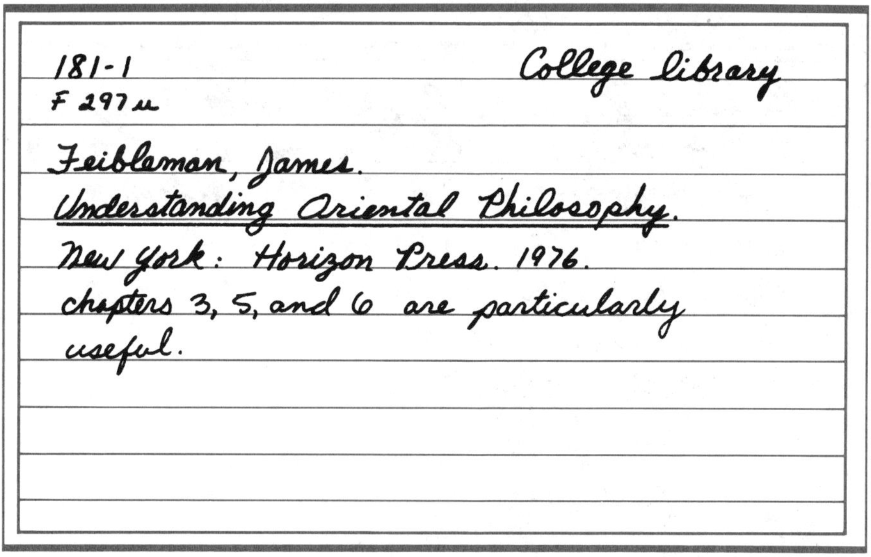
181-1 College library
F 297u
Feibleman, James.
Understanding Oriental Philosophy.
New York: Horizon Press. 1976.
chapters 3, 5, and 6 are particularly useful.

Third Week: Preparing Note Cards, a Thesis Statement, and an Outline

Note Cards

Notes on each source should be made on 4 × 6 cards, written in ink rather than pencil, with only a single idea or quotation on each card. If the quotation takes up two or more cards, staple them together. In the upper left-hand corner of the card, identify the source of the idea or quotation with the author's last name or a key word from the title. In the upper right-hand corner, summarize the information the card contains. The idea is to be able to stack the cards in the order of their appearance in the paper and easily retrieve information from them.

There are four kinds of notes you can make on note cards:

The summary

The summary condenses useful information found in the source. In your own words, you faithfully sum up what is significant about the article or book. You state only major ideas. How much you condense depends on your paper. Some authors may sum up an entire book in one sentence or a chapter in one paragraph. Most student summaries, however, will consist of paragraphs condensed into sentences. Here is an original passage from a book about the ancient Egyptians. The summary of this passage appears in Figure 14–3.

Figure 14–3   Summary Card

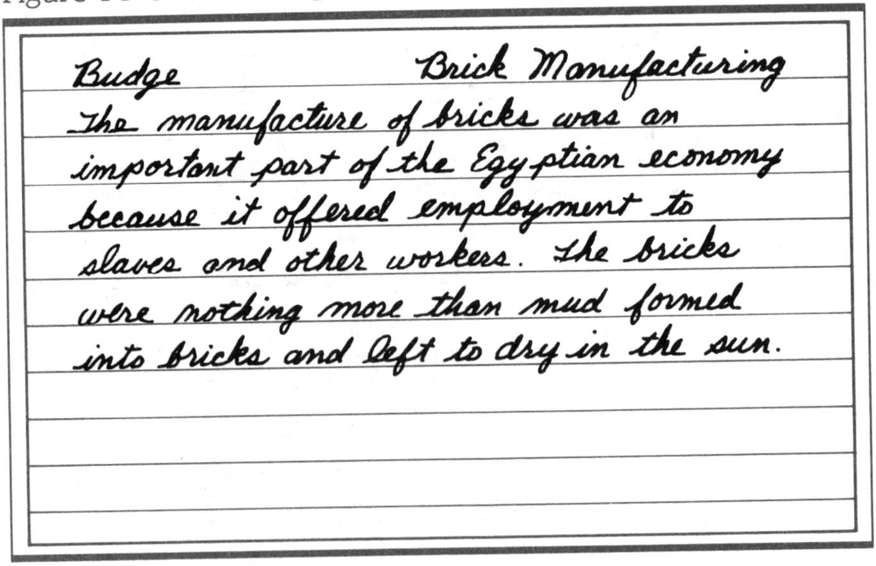

Budge   Brick Manufacturing

The manufacture of bricks was an important part of the Egyptian economy because it offered employment to slaves and other workers. The bricks were nothing more than mud formed into bricks and left to dry in the sun.

> The manufacture of bricks gave employment to a great number of slaves and others, for almost every building in Egypt, with the exception of the temple, which was of stone, was made of unbaked bricks. The muddy soil of Egypt was particularly suitable for brick making, for it was free from stones and could be easily mixed with water and kneaded with the hands into a paste of the necessary consistency. A mass of paste was thrust into a wooden mold of the size of the brick required and the top of it smoothed with a flat stick, and when the brick was dry enough to take out of the mold, it was laid in a row with others on the ground to dry in the sun; in a day or two it was ready for use.
> —William O. Budge, *Dwellers of the Nile.*

The summary gets to the heart of a passage by including only its bare essentials while excluding minor points and details.

The paraphrase

To paraphrase is to put a passage in your own words while remaining faithful to the length of the original. Here is an example. The original passage is below, with the paraphrase reproduced on the card in Figure 14–4.

> The Egyptians of the Neolithic Period believed that their existence would not come to an end with the death of their bodies and they appear to have thought that the renewed life which they

Figure 14–4   Paraphrase Card

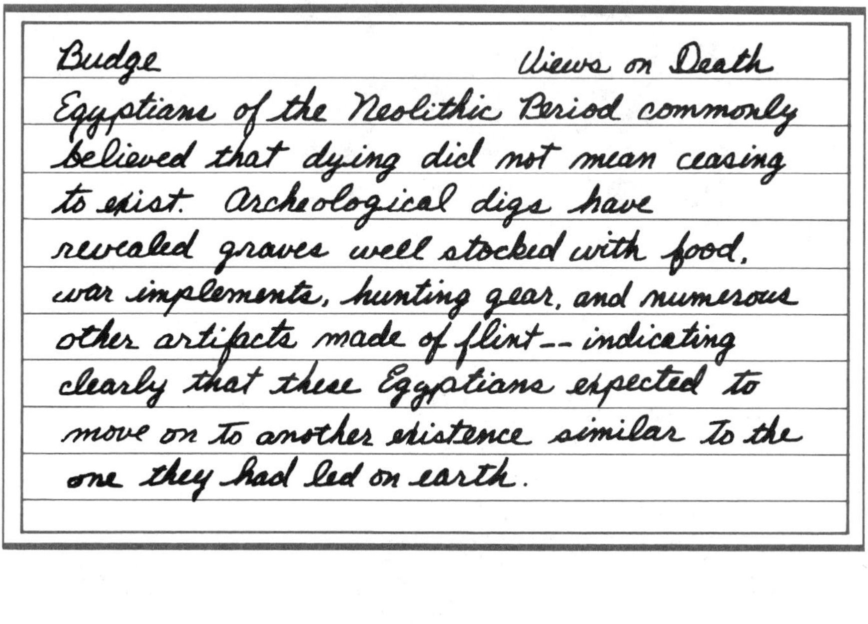

> Budge   Views on Death
> Egyptians of the Neolithic Period commonly believed that dying did not mean ceasing to exist. Archeological digs have revealed graves well stocked with food, war implements, hunting gear, and numerous other artifacts made of flint -- indicating clearly that these Egyptians expected to move on to another existence similar to the one they had led on earth.

would live in some unknown region would closely resemble that which they were accustomed to lead in this world. This is proved by the fact that in the oldest known predynastic graves pots containing food, flint weapons for war and the chase, flint tools, etc. have been found in considerable numbers.
—William O. Budge, *Dwellers of the Nile.*

The paraphrase is useful for incorporating the opinions of different writers into a single consistent style—your own.

The quotation

The quotation is an exact reproduction of an author's words. Slang, misspellings, even oddities of grammar are copied exactly as they appeared in the original. An example is shown in Figure 14–5.

Figure 14–5   Quotation Card

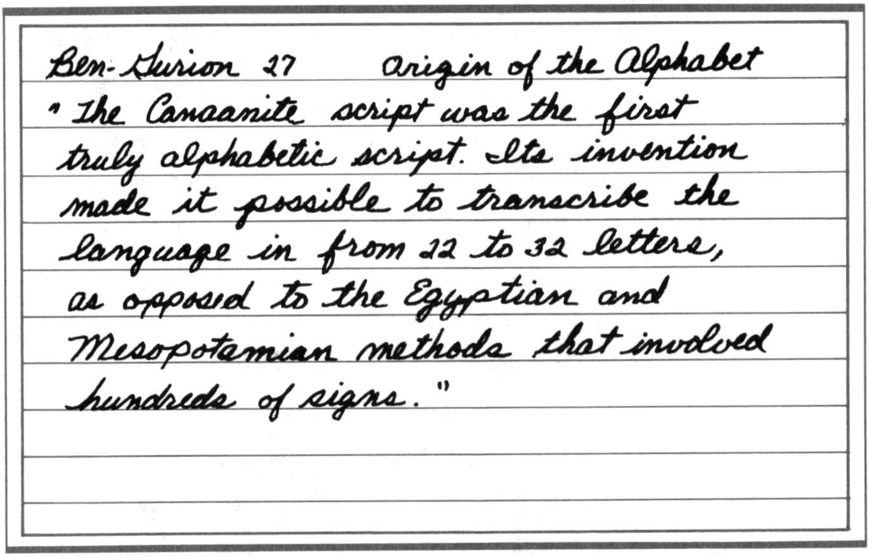

> Ben-Gurion 27   Origin of the Alphabet
> " The Canaanite script was the first truly alphabetic script. Its invention made it possible to transcribe the language in from 22 to 32 letters, as opposed to the Egyptian and Mesopotamian methods that involved hundreds of signs. "

Earlier, we cautioned against the overuse of quotations. Too many quotations cause a choppy style, called the "stringed pearls effect." A good rule to follow is to keep quoted material to under ten percent of the length of the paper.

The personal comment

The place for your own ideas, conclusions, or interpretations is the personal comment card. Use it to jot down any personal remarks about a source. An example is given in Figure 14–6.

Figure 14–6   Personal Comment Card

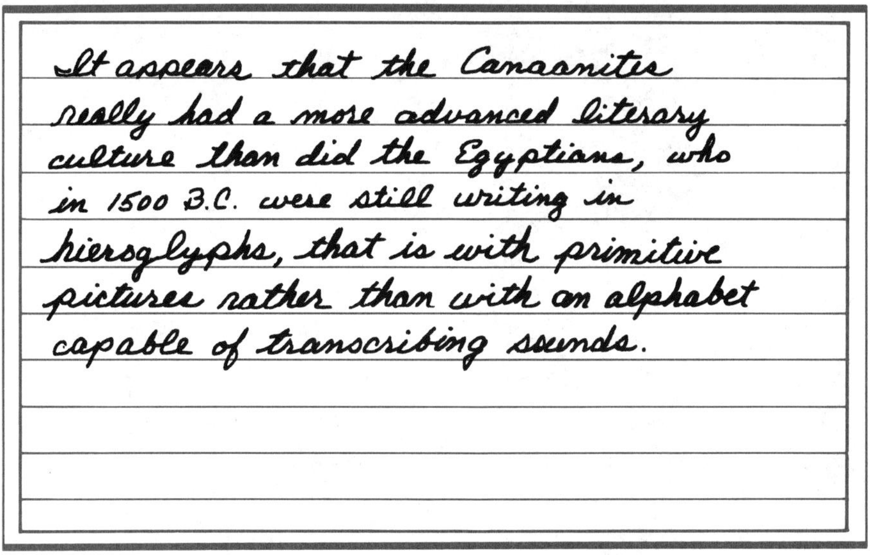

It appears that the Canaanites really had a more advanced literary culture than did the Egyptians, who in 1500 B.C. were still writing in hieroglyphs, that is with primitive pictures rather than with an alphabet capable of transcribing sounds.

Staple the actual source card to the card containing a personal comment about it. That way, you keep the two conveniently together.

The Thesis Statement

In Chapter 3, we explained at length about how to express your topic in a clear thesis statement. Everything we said there applies to the thesis statement of a research paper. There are, however, two main kinds of research papers: the report paper and the thesis paper. The first merely reports the writer's findings on a topic. It neither judges nor evaluates what the writer has found, and it is not argumentative for one point of view over another. Such a paper will contain a statement of purpose rather than a thesis. For example, a report paper on how a law is enacted in Congress might have this statement of purpose:

```
The purpose of this paper is to explain how a
bill is enacted into law by Congress from its
initial reading to final signing by the
president.
```

This is not a thesis in the usual sense. It is a summary of the paper's focus rather than an assertion of the writer's opinion on a debatable issue.

Here are a few more examples of report paper theses:

> Since the fifteenth century, medicine has
> advanced considerably in its knowledge and
> treatment of tuberculosis.
>
> The completion of the first transcontinental
> railroad brought various changes to the American
> population.
>
> The Indian caste system had its origin in
> religion and resulted in an absolutely ordered
> social structure.

On the other hand, if you were writing a research paper arguing against the influence of corporations on the passage of legislation in Congress, you would express that opposition in a thesis, following all the advice already given in Chapter 3. Your thesis might read this way:

> Corporate America wields excessive influence on
> the legislating function of Congress through
> vigorous lobbying, the use of Political Action
> Committees or PACs, and media campaigns.

Here are two more examples of theses for thesis papers:

> Because of his futuristic views on the
> wilderness and the preservation of forests,
> Henry David Thoreau must be viewed as America's
> first pioneer of conservation.
>
> One of the main reasons for child abuse in our
> society is drug abuse on the part of parents.

In both cases, the thesis implies an opposing point of view and therefore requires the writer to *defend* the position taken by the paper.

The Outline

It is nearly a universal practice to require submission of a formal outline in advance of writing a research paper. Instructors can then pore over the student's plan and catch any evident structural flaw while it is easily corrected. But as we discussed earlier in Chapter 2, there are some writers who simply do not work well with an advance plan. If you are among them and your instructor will not exempt you from preparing an outline, you will simply have to make one.

But there are some convincing reasons for writing a research paper from an outline. In a long paper, it is easy for a beginning writer to lose sight of rhetorical purpose. The outline, however, tells you what you must do and guides your hand through successive pages. That a research paper must include material from other sources is another good reason for outlining it. Citing supporting sources at the right place in the paper is easier to do from a prepared outline than during the actual writing.

In preparing your outline, follow the format suggested in Chapter 2. (See also the sample student paper, pages 41–43.) Most likely, you will be required to do a three-level sentence outline such as the example from the student paper on pages 398–99. This detailed and therefore helpful kind of outline is especially useful to a writer for managing the flow of a complex paper.

The note cards, thesis statement, and outline are all due at the end of the third week. By now, you should have a solid grasp of your topic and know exactly what you have to do to write your rough draft.

Fourth Week: Writing the Rough Draft

You are now ready to write the rough draft. Your goal is to write a paper with emphasis on its thesis, to cite supporting opinion where necessary, and to make those citations as seamless and smooth as possible within your text. You must also acknowledge any use you make of the works of others.

In the past, this acknowledgement was given in footnotes or endnotes. Both forms of documentation have now been replaced by a new parenthetical style of documentation adopted recently by the MLA, the Modern Language Association. That style, which is characterized by simplicity and ease of use, is the one we will teach in this text.

Documenting the Paper with Parenthetical Citations

The idea behind documentation is simple. If you borrow from another's ideas or work, you must document the loan and give due credit to the source from which it came. If you don't, you create the false impression that the goods are your own when they were taken from someone else. This kind of theft is known in scholarly circles as **plagiarism**. Since the currency of scholarship is ideas, it is not farfetched to say that stealing a scholar's idea is the moral equivalent of stealing money from a bank. For this reason, if you use the work or idea of another in your paper, you must acknowledge the borrowing through the use of a certain documenting style.

The parenthetical style of documentation features a clean system of citations made within the text. You mention the name of the author whose work you are quoting and/or even the work itself, and you end by citing a page reference in parentheses. For example, let us say that you are quoting from *Literature in Critical Perspective*, a book by a writer named Gordon. This is how you might handle it in your text:

```
Walter Gordon's Literature in Critical

Perspective offers evidence that literary

interpretation depends as much on the

perspective from which the analysis is conducted

as from the actual substance of the work itself

(10-22).
```

OR

```
Walter Gordon offers evidence that literary

interpretation depends as much on the

perspective from which the analysis is conducted

as from the actual substance of the work itself

(10-22).
```

And that's that. Within the text, the citation identifies either the writer and the book or the writer only, then ends with the page numbers in parentheses from which the quoted idea was taken. Complete information about Gordon's book will appear in its alphabetic order on a separate bibliography page titled "Works Cited" (see page 410 for a sample of "Works Cited" entries). On that page it will look like this:

```
Gordon, Walter K., ed. Literature in Critical

Perspective. New York: Appleton, 1968.
```

As you can see, this system has simplicity to recommend it. All actual citations are given within the text itself. A final "Works Cited" page (the new name for bibliography) gives complete publication information about each source.

The rules for using this system are simple to summarize:

1. In the first textual citation, give the full name of the authority:

```
Robert M. Jordon suggests that Chaucer's tales
are held together by seams that are similar to
the exposed beams supporting a Gothic cathedral
(237-38).
```

In subsequent citations, refer to the author by last name:

```
Jordon further suggests that . . . .
```

2. Wherever possible, say why the particular source is important by citing the author's credentials. Doing so is one way to add emphasis and variation to your introduction of a source:

```
Noam Flinker, lecturer in English at the Ben-
Gurion University of the Negev in Israel, an
authority on biblical literature, repeatedly
suggests . . . .
```

3. If you don't introduce the source in your text, list the author's surname in parentheses at the end of the citation along with a page number:

```
Democracy is deemed preferable to monarchy
because it protects the individual's rights
rather than his property (Emerson 372).
```

Note that no comma separates the name from page number.

4. Handle material by up to three authors the same as material by a single author. The form for a textual citation is as follows:

```
Christine E. Wharton and James S. Leonard take

the position that the mythical figure of Ampion

represents a triumph of the spiritual over the

physical (163).
```

If the authors are not cited in the text itself, both should be listed in parentheses along with the page number at the end of the citation:

```
Some have argued that the mythical figure of

Ampion represents a triumph of the spiritual

over the physical (Wharton and Leonard 163).
```

If the work is by more than three authors, use the name of the first author followed by "et al." or "and others" (without a comma after the name).

```
(Smith et al. 51).
```

5. In using two works by the same author, mention the author's name in the text and then separately list each work and page number in parentheses:

```
Feodor Dostoevsky declares that the

"underground" rebel is representative of our

society (Underground 3). He seems to confirm

this view in Raskolnikov's superman speech

(Crime 383–84), where he identifies . . . .
```

Or, if you don't mention the author's name in the text but are citing two works by the same person, make clear in parentheses which title is being cited and give the page number:

```
That the "underground" rebel is representative

of our society is an idea that has its roots in

the work itself (Dostoevsky, Underground 3).

This idea has been echoed in Raskolnikov's

superman speech (Dostoevsky, Crime 383–84.)
```

Note the use of abbreviations. The full title of the first work is *Notes from the Underground,* of the second *Crime and Punishment.* In your parenthetical citation, however, you need use only a key word from the title.

6. To refer to a specific passage in a multivolume work, give the author, volume number followed by colon and a space, and the page reference:

```
Other historians disagree with this view (Durant

2: 25). . . .
```

If the reference is meant to include the entire volume rather than a specific passage in it, give the name of the author followed by a comma, and the abbreviation "vol." followed by the volume number:

```
This view of history has been rejected entirely

by some commentators (Durant, vol. 2).
```

7. For a double reference (a quotation within a cited work) use:

```
As Bernard Baruch pointed out, "Mankind has

always thought to substitute energy for reason"

(as qtd. in Ringer 274).
```

"Works Cited" would contain the following entry:

```
Ringer, Robert J. Restoring the American

     Dream. New York: Harper, 1979.
```

8. In citing a work by a corporate author: if you did not mention the name of the author in your text, the full or shortened name should appear in parentheses at the end of the citation:

```
That peanut butter is a good source of nutrients

is often overlooked by parents. Yet analysis has

shown that it is a rich balance of protein,

carbohydrates, and calories (Consumer Reports 69).
```

9. When quoting a short passage of poetry: if the passage is incorporated into your text, set it off with quotation marks; use a slash (with a space before and after) to mark separate lines; place the documentation in parentheses followed by a period immediately after the quotation. Here is an example:

Byron's profound sense of alienation is echoed

in canto 3 of Childe Harold' Pilgrimage: "I have

not loved the world, nor the World me: / I have

not flattered its rank breath, nor bowed / to

its idolatries a patient knee" (190–91).

10. For quoted material set off from the text: Quotations longer than four lines are indented ten spaces, double spaced, and set off from the text without quotation marks (unless the quotation itself uses quotation marks). Place the parenthetical citation after the last period. Here is an example:

According to an editorial in the May 1, 1981,

issue of Science, the air force, early on, had

designs on the shuttle:

> NASA officials, at least, have no regrets
>
> over redesigning the shuttle to
>
> accommodate military payloads or paying
>
> for the construction of two shuttle
>
> orbiters (out of four) intended for
>
> predominantly military use. (520)

Shorter quotations of four lines or less are introduced in the text and reproduced with quotations marks:

According to Carl Sagan, some researchers

believe that one function of dreams may be "to

wake us up a little, every now and then, to see

if anyone is about to eat us" (151).

11. In citing play by act, scene, and line: use Arabic numerals divided by periods to indicate major divisions in a play. For example, a quotation from Act 1, Scene 1, lines 146–53 of Shakespeare's *King Lear* would be treated as follows:

```
When Lear attempts to divide his kingdom among

his daughters, only the Earl of Kent, his

faithful friend, opposes him:

    Let it fall rather, though the fork invade

    The region of my heart; be Kent

    unmannerly,

    When Lear is mad. What wilt thou do, old

    man?

    Think's thou that duty shall have dread to

    speak,

    When power to flattery bows? To plainness

    honour's bound,

    When majesty stoops to folly. Reverse thy

    doom;

    And, in thy best consideration, check

    This hideous rashness . . .   .

    (Lear 1.1.146–53)
```

12. Use Arabic numerals for books, parts, volumes, and chapters of works; for acts, scenes, and lines of plays; for cantos, stanzas, and lines of poetry.

In-text citations:

Volume 2 of *Civilization Past and Present*
Book 3 of *Paradise Lost*
Part 2 of *Crime and Punishment*
Act 3 of *Hamlet*
Chapter 1 of *The Great Gatsby*

Parenthetical documentation:

(*Tmp.* 2.2.45–50) for Act 2, Scene 2, lines 45–50 of Shakespeare's
  Tempest. Notice that the titles of well-known masterpieces may
  be abbreviated.
(*GT* 2.1.3) for Part 2, Chapter 1, page 3 of *Gulliver's Travels* by
  Jonathan Swift.
(*Jude* 15) for page 15 of the novel *Jude the Obscure* by Thomas
  Hardy.
(*PL* 7.5–10) for Book 7, lines 5–10 of *Paradise Lost* by John Milton.
(*FQ* 1.2.28.1–4) for Book 1, canto 2, stanza 28, lines 1–4 of *The
  Faerie Queene* by Edmund Spenser.

13. Content notes: A content note is used to make a side remark
about some assertion in your text without interrupting the flow of the writing. The note is placed at the bottom of the page and separated from the
last line of the text by four spaces. Its initial line is indented five spaces with
single spacing between the sentences. A superscript numeral in the text indicates the presence of the note. Here is an example from a student paper:

```
The centaur, being half horse and half man,

symbolized both the wild and benign aspect of

nature. Thus the coexistence of nature and

culture was expressed.¹
```

At the bottom of the page appeared the following content note:

```
¹It should be noted that the horse part is
the lower and more animalistic area whereas the
human portion is the upper, including the heart
and head.
```

Interruptions like these are rarely necessary in the typical paper, but when
they are, the place for them is in a content note.

14. Vary your introductions. The parenthetical system is uncomplicated and easy to use. With the exception of the rare content note, superscript numerals have been eliminated along with the tiresome chore of
counting and reserving lines on the bottom of a page for footnotes. But it is
easy to become predictable in the introduction of each source, with the effect of giving the paper a wooden and stilted style. If you therefore cite one
source this way:

```
Neeli Cherkovski argued that in 1958

Ferlinghetti began experimenting with newer

poetic forms and was influenced by the emerging

beat movement (91).
```

use an entirely different introduction for the next. Perhaps you might simply use a parenthetical citation without mentioning the author:

```
This attitude is central to the archetypal

approach used in interpreting poetry (Fiedler 519).
```

Our point is that you should vary the wording of your introductions as conscientiously as you would avoid writing several identically constructed sentences in a row.

Plagiarism

Earlier (see pages 341–42) we defined plagiarism. Citing without an acknowledged source is perhaps the most blatant instance of plagiarism. But there are more venial examples of it that can occur even when a source is cited. Consider, for example, this original passage:

> It is not necessary in a totalitarian dictatorship to be loved by the people. It is enough to be feared, as Stalin was in Soviet Russia. But that Hitler was beloved by the German masses—shocking as that seemed to me and to the outside world—there could be no doubt. Goering was next in their affection. They loved his down-to-earth saltiness, his jovialness, his crude sense of humor, his common touch. To them he was a hail-fellow-well-met. It never seemed to concern them that he was a brutal, ruthless, unscrupulous killer.
> —William L. Shirer, *The Nightmare Years: 1930–1940,* p. 191.

Here is an example of outright plagiarism.

```
There is no question but that Hitler was beloved

by the German people, even though this may seem

shocking to the rest of us. But next to Hitler

in the people's affection, came Goering. They

loved his down-to-earth saltiness, his
```

```
jovialness, his crude sense of humor, his common
touch.  To them he was a hail-fellow-well-met.
It never seemed to concern them that he was a
brutal, ruthless, unscrupulous killer.
```

Altering a word here and there, the writer has lifted this passage nearly intact from the book by William Shirer but given it no credit. This conveys the impression that the idea is the writer's own rather than stolen property.

Plagiarism can also occur even when the reproduced passage is credited to a source. Here is an example:

```
It was well known to the world that the German
people loved Hitler.  What the world did not
know then was that Goering was next in their
affection, that they loved his down-to-earth
saltiness, his jovialness, his sense of humor,
his common touch, and that to them he was a
hail-fellow-well-met (Shirer 191).
```

Even though a source is cited, this passage is still plagiarized because it takes words verbatim from the original without quotation marks to indicate the copying. The theft in this case is one of phrasing and style. Here is how this material should have been handled:

```
It was well known to the world that the German
people loved Hitler.  But after Hitler, they
also loved Goering.  As Shirer put it, they
loved "his down-to-earth saltiness, his
jovialness, his crude sense of humor, his common
touch," and seemed untroubled by the fact that
he "was a brutal, ruthless, unscrupulous killer"
(191).
```

The quotation marks tell us that the writer has gotten these words from someone else.

Exactly what kinds of material do you have to document? The rule of thumb is based on common sense and fairness. If an assertion is repeated by a minimum of five sources, you may regard it as general knowledge and not give credit. But if an idea, no matter how well known, is memorably and cleverly phrased by another writer, you should not repeat it word for word without giving the originator credit. Play fair with your sources, be forthright in presenting your own opinions, and plagiarism will not be an issue in your paper.

Writing the Rough Draft

To write the paper, have your outline and thesis in front of you, arrange your note cards in the order of appearance in the paper, and begin. Remember that it is normal to have to make several stabs at a beginning. With a thorough outline and a stack of note cards to support all your major points, you should have a solid framework for the paper. Now it is merely a matter of bricking it in, word by word, sentence by sentence.

You are expected to write the paper in a formal style, using no colloquialisms or slang unless as part of quoted material. Don't refer to yourself as "I" unless your teacher has consented to your writing on an intensely autobiographical paper (which would be a most peculiar research assignment). Similarly, you should not refer to yourself with the royal "we," and you should never use "you" as a pronoun referring to an unspecified person. In short, you are expected to adopt a scholarly tone—not a pedantic one—and to use words and phrases that reflect your objectivity in dealing with the material. Review the discussion of voice and style in Chapter 2 if any of this is unclear to you.

The rough draft of the paper is due at the end of the fourth week. Happily, you are now almost done. The greatest labor is behind you, and what lies ahead are only the finishing touches.

Fifth Week: the Final Paper Complete with a Bibliography

At the end of the fifth week, you should submit a final paper containing the following: (1) an outline, (2) title page, (3) text of the paper, (4) content notes (if any), and (5) "Works Cited" page (or bibliography). The facsimile on page 402 shows the layout of the title page of a student paper. Notice that no separate title page is necessary. The first page of the paper is the title page. Type the body of the paper double spaced with 1-inch margins. Number each page consecutively in the upper right corner. Number the outline with small Roman numerals; then number the main body of the paper with Arabic numerals. Beginning with page 2, precede the page number with your last name in case a page is misplaced. If your paper contains content notes, place them on a separate page entitled "Notes." Make sure that each content note is numbered and corresponds to the proper superscript in the text (see p. 348).

Mainly, what will be left is to compile a "Works Cited" page in which you cite all the sources paraphrased, summarized, or quoted in the paper. Before we discuss the forms these citations should take, it is useful to summarize some basic conventions that apply to the "Works Cited" page:

1. Cited works must be listed on a separate page.
2. The title "Works Cited" must be centered one inch from the top of the page with two spaces between the title and the first citation.
3. Entries are listed alphabetically by the surname of the first author. Subsequent authors are listed with their names in normal order. Anonymously written works are entered alphabetically by the first word of the title, omitting all articles such as "a," "the," or "an."
4. Subsequent titles by an already listed author are entered in the line below on a separate line beginning with three hyphens and a period:

```
Lewis, Sinclair. Babbitt. New York: Harcourt,

     1922.

---.Main Street. New York: Harcourt, 1920.
```

5. Indent the second line of each entry five spaces.
6. Double space throughout.

I. General order for citations of books in "Works Cited"

Bibliographic references to books list items in the following order:

a. Author

The name of the author comes first, alphabetized by surname. If more than one author is involved, invert the name of only the first and follow it by a comma:

```
Brown, Jim, and John Smith
```

For more than three authors, use the name of the first followed by "et al.":

```
Foreman, Charles, et al.
```

In some cases the name of an editor, translator, or compiler will be cited before the name of an author, especially if the actual editing, translating, or compiling is the subject of discussion.

b. Title

Cite the title in its entirety, including any subtitle, exactly as it appears on the title page. A period follows the title unless the title ends in some other mark, such as a question mark or an exclamation mark. Book titles are underlined; titles of chapters are set off in quotation marks. The initial word and all subsequent words (except for articles and short prepositions) in the title are capitalized. Ignore any unusual typographical style, such as all capital letters, or any peculiar arrangement of capitals and lower-case letters, unless the author is specifically known to insist on such a typography. Separate a subtitle from the title by a colon:

D. H. Lawrence: His Life and Work.

c. Name of Editor, Compiler, or Translator

The name(s) of the editor(s), compiler(s), or translator(s) is given in normal order, preceded by "Ed.," "Comp.," or "Trans.":

Homer. The Iliad. Trans. Richard Lattimore.

However, if the editor, translator, or compiler was listed in your textual citation, then his name should appear first, followed by "ed(s).," "trans.," or "comp(s)." and a period:

TEXTUAL CITATION:

Gordon's Literature in Critical Perspective

offers some . . .

"WORKS CITED" ENTRY:

Gordon, Walter K., ed. Literature in Critical

Perspective. New York: Appleton, 1968.

If you are drawing attention to the translator, use the following format:

TEXTUAL CITATION:

The colloquial English of certain passages is

due to Ciardi's translation.

"WORKS CITED" ENTRY:

> Ciardi, John, trans. <u>The Inferno</u>. By Dante
>
> Alighieri. New York: NAL, 1961.

d. Edition (if Other Than First)

The edition being used is cited if it is other than the first. Cite the edition in Arabic numerals (3rd ed.) without further punctuation. Always use the latest edition of a work, unless you have some specific reason of scholarship for using another.

> Holman, C. Hugh. <u>A Handbook to Literature</u>.   3rd
>
> ed.   Indianapolis: Odyssey, 1972.

e. Series Name and Number

Give the name of the series, without quotation marks and not underlined, followed by the number of the work in the series in Arabic numerals, followed by a period:

> Unger, Leonard. <u>T. S. Eliot</u>. University of
>
> Minnesota Pamphlets on American Writers 8.
>
> Minneapolis: U of Minnesota P, 1961.

f. Volume Numbers

An entry referring to all the volumes of a multivolume work cites the number of volumes *before* the publication facts:

> Durant, Will, and Ariel Durant   <u>The Story of</u>
>
> <u>Civilization</u>.   10 vols.   New York: Simon,
>
> 1968.

An entry for only selected volumes still cites the total number of volumes after the title. The volumes actually used are listed *after* the publication facts:

> Durant, Will, and Ariel Durant.   <u>The Story of</u>
>
> <u>Civilization</u>.   10 vols.   New York: Simon,
>
> 1968. Vols. 2 and 3.

For multivolume works published over a number of years, show the total number of volumes, the range of years, and specific volumes if not all of them were actually used.

```
Froom, LeRoy Edwin.  The Prophetic Faith of Our

    Fathers.  4 vols.  Washington: Review and

    Herald, 1950–54. Vol. 1.
```

g. Publication Facts

Indicate the place, publisher, and date of publication for the work you are citing. A colon follows the place, a comma the publisher, and a period the date unless a page is cited.

You may use a shortened form of the publisher's name as long as it is clear: Doubleday (for Doubleday & Company), McGraw (for McGraw-Hill), Little (for Little, Brown), Scott (for Scott, Foresman), Putnam's (for G. Putnam's Sons), Scarecrow (for Scarecrow Press), Simon (for Simon and Schuster), Wiley (for John Wiley & Sons), Holt (for Holt Rinehart & Winston), Penguin (for Penguin Books), Harper (for Harper & Row). For example:

```
Robb, David M., and Jessie J. Garrison.  Art in

    the Western World.  4th ed.  New York:

    Harper, 1963.
```

But list university presses in full (except for abbreviating "University" and "Press") so as not to confuse the press with the university itself: Oxford UP, Harvard UP, Johns Hopkins UP.

```
Gohdes, Clarence.  Bibliographical Guides to the

    Study of Literature of the U.S.A..  3rd ed.

    Durham: Duke UP, 1970.
```

If more than one place of publication appears, give the city shown first on the book's title page.

If more than one copyright date is given, use the latest unless your study is specifically concerned with an earlier edition. (A new printing does not constitute a new edition. For instance, if the title page bears a 1975 copyright date but a 1978 fourth printing, use 1975.) If no place, publisher, date, or page numbering is provided, insert "n.p.," "n.p.," "n.d.," or "n. pag.," respectively. "N. pag." will explain to the reader why no page numbers were provided in the text citation. If the source contains neither author, title, or publication information, supply in brackets whatever information you have been able to obtain:

> Photographs of Historic Castles. [St. Albans,
>
> England]: N.p., n.d. N. pag.
>
> Farquart, Genevieve. They Gave Us Flowers.
>
> N.p.: n.p., 1886.
>
> Dickens, Charles. Master Humphrey's Clock.
>
> London: Bradbury and Evans, n.d.

h. Page Numbers

Bibliographical entries for books rarely include a page number; however, entries for shorter pieces appearing within a longer work—articles, poems, short stories, and so on, in a collection—should include a page reference. In such a case, supply page numbers for the entire piece, not just for the specific page or pages cited in the text:

> Daiches, David. "Criticism and Sociology."
>
> Literature in Critical Perspective. Ed.
>
> Walter K. Gordon. New York: Appleton, 1968.
>
> 7–18.

II. Sample bibliographic references to books

a. Book with a Single Author

> Brodie, Fawn M. Thomas Jefferson: An Intimate
>
> History. New York: Norton, 1974

b. Book with Two or More Authors

> Bollens, John C., and Grand B. Geyer. Yorty:
>
> Politics of a Constant Candidate. Pacific
>
> Palisades: Palisades Pub., 1973.

Allport, Gordon W., Philip E. Vernon, and

    Gardner Lindzey. Study of Values. New York:

    Houghton, 1951.

Brown, Ruth, et al. Agricultural Education in a

    Technical Society: An Annotated Bibliography

    of Resources. Chicago: American Library

    Assn., 1973.

c. Book with a Corporate Author

American Institute of Physics. Handbook. 3rd

    ed. New York: McGraw, 1972.

NOTE: If the publisher is the same as the author, repeat the information, as shown here:

Defense Language Institute. Academic Policy

    Standards. Monterey: Defense Language

    Institute, 1982.

d. Book with an Anonymous or Pseudonymous Author

No author listed:

Current Biography. New York: Wilson, 1976.

If you are able to research the author's name, supply it in brackets:

[Stauffer, Adlai]. Cloudburst. Knoxville:

    Review and Courier Publishing Assn., 1950.

The name of an author who writes under a pseudonym (or *nom de plume*) may also be given in brackets:

Eliot, George [Mary Ann Evans]. Daniel Deronda.

    London: n.p., 1876.

e. Work in Several Volumes or Parts

When citing the whole multivolume work:

> Wallbank, T. Walter, and Alastair M. Taylor.
> Civilization Past and Present. 2 vols.
> Chicago: Scott, 1949.

When citing a specific volume of a multivolume work:

> Wallbank, T. Walter, and Alastair M. Taylor.
> Civilization Past and Present. 2 vols.
> Chicago: Scott, 1949. Vol. 2.

When citing a multivolume work whose volumes were published over a range of years:

> Froom, LeRoy Edwin. The Prophetic Faith of Our
> Fathers. 4 vols. Washington: Review and
> Herald, 1950–54.

When citing a multivolume work with separate titles:

> Jacobs, Paul, Saul Landen, and Eve Pell.
> Colonials and Sojourners. Vol. 2 of To
> Serve the Devil. 4 vols. New York:
> Random, 1971.

f. Work within a Collection of Pieces, All by the Same Author

> Johnson, Edgar. "The Keel of the New Lugger."
> The Great Unknown. Vol. 2 of Sir Walter
> Scott. 3 vols. New York: Macmillan, 1970.
> 763–76
> Selzer, Richard. "Liver." Mortal Lessons. New
> York: Simon, 1976. 62–77.

NOTE: The MLA no longer recommends the use of the word "In" preceding the title of the collection or anthology.

g. Chapter or Titled Section in a Book

```
Goodrich, Norma Lorre.  "Gilgamesh the

     Wrestler."  Myths of the Hero.  New York:

     Orion, 1960.
```

NOTE: List the chapter or titled section in a book only when it demands special attention.

h. Collections: Anthologies, Casebooks, and Readers

```
Welty, Eudora.  "The Wide Net."  Story: An

     Introduction to Prose Fiction.  Ed. Arthur

     Foff and Daniel Knapp.  Belmont: Wadsworth,

     1966.  159-77.

Cowley, Malcolm. "Sociological Habit Patterns in

     Linguistic Transmogrification." The

     Reporter. 20 Sept. 1956:  257-61. Rpt. in

Readings for Writers.  Ed. Jo Ray McCuen and

     Anthony C. Winkler. 2nd ed.  New York:

     Harcourt, 1977. 489-93.
```

i. Double Reference—a Quotation within a Cited Work

```
As Bernard Baruch pointed out.  "Mankind has

always thought to substitute energy for reason"

(as qtd. in Ringer 274).
```

"Works Cited" would then contain the following entry:

```
Ringer, Robert J. Restoring the American Dream.

     New York: Harper, 1979.
```

j. Reference Works

(i) Encyclopedias

Ballert, Albert George. "Saint Lawrence River."
    Encyclopaedia Britannica. 1963 ed.

"House of David." Encyclopedia Americana. 1974
    ed.

Berger, Morroe, and Dorothy Willner. "Near
    Eastern Society." International
    Encyclopedia of the Social Sciences. 1968
    ed.

(ii) Dictionaries and annuals

"Barsabbas, Joseph." Who's Who in the New
    Testament (1971).

"Telegony." Dictionary of Philosophy and
    Psychology (1902).

k. Work in a Series

(i) A numbered series

Auchincloss, Louis. Edith Wharton. University
    of Minnesota Pamphlets on American Writers
    12. Minneapolis: U of Minnesota P, 1961.

(ii) An unnumbered series

Miller, Sally. The Radical Immigrant. The
    Immigrant Heritage of America Series. New
    York: Twayne, 1974.

l. Reprint

Babson, John J. History of the Town of
    Gloucester, Cape Ann, Including the Town of

> Rockport. 1860. New York: Peter Smith,
>
> 1972.

Thackeray, William Makepeace. Vanity Fair.

> London, 1847—48. New York: Harper, 1968.

m. Edition

Perrin, Porter G., and Jim W. Corder. Handbook

> of Current English. 4th Ed. Glenview:
>
> Scott, 1975.

Craig, Hardin, and David Bevington, eds. The

> Complete Works of Shakespeare. Rev. ed.
>
> Glenview: Scott, 1973.

n. Edited Work

If the work of the editor(s) rather than that of the author(s) is being discussed, place the name of the editor(s) first, followed by a comma, followed by "ed." or "eds.":

> Rowland, Beryl, ed. Companion to Chaucer:
>
> Studies. New York: Oxford UP, 1979.

If you are stressing the text of the author(s), place the author(s) first:

> Clerc, Charles. "Goodbye to All That: Theme,
>
> Character and Symbol in Goodbye, Columbus."
>
> Seven Contemporary Short Novels. Ed.
>
> Charles Clerc and Louis Leiter. Glenview:
>
> Scott, 1969. 106—33.

o. Book Published in a Foreign Country

Vialleton, Louis. L'Origine des êtres vivants.

> Paris: Plon, 1929.

Ransford, Oliver. Livingston's Lake: The Drama
of Nyasa. London: Camelot, 1966.

p. Introduction, Preface, Foreword, or Afterward

Davidson, Marshall B. Introduction. The Age of
Napoleon. By J. Christopher Herold. New
York: American Heritage, 1963.

q. Translation

Symons, John Addington, trans. Autobiography of
Benvenuto Cellini. By Benvenuto Cellini.
New York: Washington Square, 1963.

r. Book of Illustrations

Janson, H. W. History of Art: A Survey of the
Major Visual Arts from the Dawn of History
to the Present. With 928 illustrations,
including 80 color plates. Englewood
Cliffs: Prentice and Abrams, 1962.

s. Foreign Title

Use lower case lettering for foreign titles except for the first word and proper
names:

Vischer, Lukas. Basilius der Grosse. Basel:
Reinhard, 1953.

Supply a translation of the title or city if it seems necessary. Place the English
version in brackets immediately following the original, not underlined:

Bruckberger, R. L. Dieu et la politique [God and
Politics]. Paris: Plon, 1971.

III. General order for bibliographic references to periodicals in "Works Cited"

Bibliographic references to periodicals list items in the following order:

a. Author

List the author's surname first, followed by a comma, followed by the first name or initials. If there is more than one author, follow the same format as for books (see pages 356–57).

b. Title of the Article

List the title in quotation marks, followed by a period inside the quotation marks unless the title itself ends in a question mark or exclamation mark.

c. Publication Information

List the name of the periodical, underlined, with any introductory article omitted, followed by a space and a volume number, followed by a space and the year of publication within parentheses, followed by a colon, a space, and page numbers for the entire article, not just for the specific pages cited:

> Smith, Irwin. "Ariel and the Masque in The
>
> Tempest." Shakespeare Quarterly 21 (1970): 213–
>
> 22.

Journals paginated anew in each issue require the issue number following the volume number, separated by a period:

> Beets, Nicholas. "Historical Actuality and
>
> Bodily Experience." Humanitas 2.1 (1966):
>
> 15–28.

Some journals may use a month or season designation in place of an issue number:

> 2 (Spring 1966): 15–28.

Magazines that are published weekly or monthly require only the date, without a volume number:

> Isaacson, Walter. "After Williamsburg." <u>Time</u> 13
>
> June 1983: 12–14.

Newspapers require the section or part number, followed by the page:

> Rumberger, L. "Our Work, Not Education, Needs
>
> Restructuring." <u>Los Angeles Times</u>, 24 May
>
> 1984, pt. 2: 5.

d. Pages

If the pages of the article are scattered throughout the issue (for example, pages 30, 36, 51, and 52), the following formats can be used:

> 30, 36, 51, 52 (This is the most precise method
>
> and should be used when only three or four pages
>
> are involved.)
>
> 30 and passim (page 30 and here and there
>
> throughout the work)
>
> 30ff. (page 30 and the following pages)
>
> 30+ (beginning on page 30)

IV. Sample bibliographic references to periodicals

a. Anonymous Author

"Elegance Is Out." <u>Fortune</u> 13 Mar. 1978: 18.

b. Single Author

Sidey, Hugh. "In Defense of the Martini." <u>Time</u>

24 Oct. 1977: 38.

c. More Than One Author

Ferguson, Clyde, and William R. Cotter. "South

    Africa—What Is to Be Done." Foreign

    Affairs 56 (1978): 254–74.

If three authors have written the article, place a comma after the second author, followed by "and" and the name of the third author. If more than three authors have collaborated, list the first author's name, inverted, followed by a comma and "et al."

Enright, Frank, et al.

d. Journal with Continuous Pagination Throughout the Annual Volume

Paolucci, Anne. "Comedy and Paradox in

    Pirandello's Plays." Modern Drama 20

    (1977): 321–39.

e. Journal with Separate Pagination for Each Issue

When each issue of a journal is paged separately, include the issue number (or month or season); page numbers alone will not locate the article since every issue begins with page 1.

Cappe, Walter H. "Toward More Effective

    Justice." The Center Magazine 11.2 (1978):

    2–6.

Mangrum, Claude T. "Toward More Effective

    Justice." Crime Prevention Review 5 (Jan.

    1978): 1–9.

Brown, Robert. "Physical Illness and Mental

    Health." Philosophy and Public Affairs 7

    (Fall 1977): 18–19.

f. Monthly Magazine

Miller, Mark Crispin. "The New Wave in Rock."

Horizon Mar. 1978: 76–77.

Davis, Flora, and Julia Orange. "The Strange

Case of the Children Who Invented Their Own

Language." Redbook Mar. 1978: 113, 165–67.

g. Weekly Magazine

Eban, Suzy. "Our Far–Flung Correspondents." The

New Yorker 6 Mar. 1978: 70–81.

"Philadephia's Way of Stopping the

Shoplifter." Business Week 6 Mar. 1972:

57–59.

h. Newspaper

Tanner, James. "Disenchantment Grows in OPEC

Group with Use of U.S. Dollar for Oil

Pricing." Wall Street Journal 9 Mar. 1978: 3.

List the edition and section of the newspaper if specified, as in the examples below:

Southerland, Daniel. "Carter Plans Firm Stand

with Begin." Christian Science Monitor 9

Mar. 1978, western ed.: 1, 9.

Malino, Emily. "A Matter of Placement."

Washington Post 5 Mar. 1978: L 1.

i. Editorial

If the section or part is labeled with a numeral rather than a letter, then the abbreviation "sec." or "pt." must appear before the section number. For example, see the unsigned editorial below.

Signed:

> Futrell, William. "The Inner City Frontier."
> Editorial. <u>Sierra</u> 63.2 (1978): 5.

Unsigned:

> "Criminals in Uniform." Editorial. <u>Los Angeles</u>
> <u>Times</u> 7 Apr. 1978, pt. 2: 6.

j. Letter to the Editor

> Korczyk, Donna. Letter. <u>Time</u> 20 Mar. 1978: 4.

k. Critical Review

> Andrews, Peter. Rev. of <u>The Strange Ride of</u>
> <u>Rudyard Kipling: His Life and Works</u>, by
> Angus Wilson. <u>Saturday Review</u> 4 Mar. 1978:
> 24–25.
>
> Daniels, Robert V. Rev. of <u>Stalinism: Essays in</u>
> <u>Historical Interpretations</u>, ed. Robert C.
> Tucker. <u>The Russian Review</u> 37 (1978): 102–
> 103.
>
> "Soyer Sees Soyer." Rev. of <u>Diary of an Artist</u>,
> by Ralph Soyer. <u>American Artist</u> Mar. 1978:
> 18–19.
>
> Rev. of <u>Charmed Life</u>, by Diane Wynne Jones.
> <u>Booklist</u> 74 (Feb. 1978): 1009

l. Published Interview

> Leonel J. Castillo, Commissioner, Immigration
> and Naturalization Service. Interview. Why
> the Tide of Illegal Aliens Keeps Rising.

U.S. News and World Report 20 Feb. 1978:

33–35.

m. Published Address or Lecture

Trudeau, Pierre E. "Reflections on Peace and

Security." Address to Conference on

Strategies for Peace and Security in the

Nuclear Age, Guelph, Ont., Can., 27 Oct.

1983. Rpt. in Vital Speeches of the Day 1

Dec. 1983: 98–102.

V. Nonprint materials

Since nonprint materials come in many forms and with varied information, the rule to follow when dealing with them is to provide as much information as is available for retrieval.

a. Address or Lecture

O'Banion, Terry. "The Continuing Quest for

Quality." Address to California Assn. of

Community Colleges. Sacramento, 30 Aug.

1983.

Schwilck, Gene L. "The Core and the Community."

Lecture to Danforth Foundation. St. Louis,

16 Mar. 1978.

For how to handle the reprint of an address or lecture appearing in a periodical, see IV.m.

b. Art Work

Angelico, Beato. Madonna dei Linaioli. Museo de

San Marco, Firenze.

Notice that titles of works of art must be underlined.

c. Computer Source

A computer citation will refer to either: (1) a computer program, that is, information received directly from a data bank, or (2) a written publication retrieved by a computer base.

(i) Computer program

First, list the primary creator of the database as the author. Second, give the title of the program underlined, followed by a period. Third, write "Computer software," followed by a period. Fourth, supply the name of the publisher of the program, followed by a comma and the date the program was issued. Finally, give any additional information necessary for identification and retrieval. This additional information should include, for example, the kind of computer for which the software was created, the number of kilobytes (units of memory), the operating system, and the program's form (cartidge, disk, or cassette):

```
Moshell, J. M., and C. E. Hughes. Imagination:

     Picture Programming. Computer software.

     Wiley, 1983. Apple II/IIe, 64KB, disk.
```

(ii) Source retrieved from a database

Entire articles and books are now being stored in huge databases, with companies like ERIC, CompuServe, The Source, Mead Data Control (Nexis, Lexis), and many others providing the access service. These sources should be listed as if they appeared in print, except that you will also list the agency providing the access service. If possible, list any code or file associated with the source:

```
Cohen, Wilbur J. "Lifelong Learning and Public

     Policy." Community Services Catalyst 9

     (Fall 1979): 4–5. ERIC. 1982. Dialog 1,

     EJ218031.
```

d. Film

Film citations should include the director's name, the title of the film (underlined), the name of the leading actor(s), the distributor, and the date of showing. Information on the producer, writer, and size or length of the film may also be supplied, if necessary to your study:

```
Ross, Herbert, dir. The Turning Point. With Anne

     Bancroft, Shirley MacLaine, Mikhail
```

```
Baryshnikov, and Leslie Brown. Twentieth

Century-Fox, 1978.
```

e. Interview

Citations of interviews should specify the kind of interview, the name (and, if pertinent, the title) of the interviewed person, and the date of the interview:

```
Witt, Dr. Charles. Personal interview. 18 Feb.

    1984.

Carpenter, Edward, librarian at the Huntington

    Library, Pasadena. Telephone interview. 2

    Mar. 1978.
```

f. Musical Composition

Whenever possible, cite the title of the composition in your text, as for instance:

```
Bach's Well-Tempered Clavier is a principal

keyboard . . .
```

However, when opus numbers would clutter the text, cite the composition more fully in "Works Cited":

```
Grieg, Edward. Minuet in E minor, op. 7, no. 3.
```

g. Radio or Television Program

Citations should include the title of the program (underlined), the network or local station, and the city and date of broadcast. If appropriate, the title of the episode is listed in quotation marks before the title of the program, while the title of the series, neither underlined nor in quotation marks, comes after the title of the program. The name of the writer, director, narrator, or producer may also be supplied, if significant to your paper:

```
Diving for Roman Plunder. Narr. and dir. Jacques

    Cousteau. KCET, Los Angeles. 14 Mar. 1978.

"Chapter 2." Writ. Wolf Mankowitz. Dickens of

    London. Dir. and prod. Marc Miller.
```

Masterpiece Theater. Introd. Alistair

Cooke. PBS. 28 Aug. 1977.

Dead Wrong. CBS Special. 24 Jan. 1984.

h. Recording (Disk or Tape)

For commercially available recordings, cite the following: composer, conductor, or performer, title of recording or of work(s) on the recording, artist(s), manufacturer, catalog number, and year of issue (if not known, state "n.d."):

Beatles, The. "I Should Have Known Better." The

Beatles Again. Apple Records, SO–385, n.d.

Bach, Johann Sebastian. Toccata and Fugue in D

minor, Toccata, Adagio, and Fugue in C

major, Passacaglia and Fugue in C minor;

Johann Christian Bach. Sinfonia for Double

Orchestra, op. 18, no. 1. Cond. Eugene

Ormandy. Philadelphia Orchestra. Columbia,

MS 6180, n.d.

Eagle, Swift. The Pueblo Indians. Caedmon, TC

1327, n.d.

Shakespeare's Othello. With Paul Robeson, Jose

Ferrer, Uta Hagen, and Edith King.

Columbia, SL–153, n.d.

Dwyer, Michael. Readings from Mark Twain. Rec.

15 Apr. 1968. Humorist Society. San

Bernardino.

Wilgus, D. K. Irish Folksongs. Rec. 9 Mar. 1969.

U of California, Los Angeles, Archives of

Folklore. T7–69–22. 7½ ips.

Burr, Charles. Jacket notes. Grofe: Grand Canyon

Suite. Columbia, MS 6003, n.d.

i. Theatrical Performance

Theatrical performances are cited in the form used for films, with added information on the theater, city, and date of performance. For opera, concert, or dance productions you may also wish to cite the conductor (cond.) or choreographer (chor.). If the author, composer, director, or choreographer should be emphasized, supply that information first.

> Getting Out. Dir. Gordon Davidson. By Marsha
>
> Norman. With Susan Clark. Mark Taper Forum,
>
> Los Angeles. 2 Apr. 1978.

This citation emphasizes the author:

> Durang, Christopher. Beyond Therapy. Dir. John
>
> Madden. With John Lithgow and Dianne Wiest.
>
> Brooks Atkinson Theater, New York. 26 May
>
> 1982.

This citation emphasizes the conductor:

> Conlon, James, cond. La Bohème. With Renata
>
> Scotto. Metropolitan Opera. Metropolitan
>
> Opera House, New York. 30 Oct. 1977.

This citation emphasizes the conductor and the guest performer:

> Commissiona, Sergiu, cond. Baltimore Symphony
>
> Orchestra. With Albert Markov, violin.
>
> Brooklyn College, New York. 8 Nov. 1978.

This citation emphasizes the choreographer:

> Baryshnikov, Mikhail, chor. Swan Lake. American
>
> Ballet Theatre, New York. 24 May 1982.

VI. Special items

No standard form exists for every special item you might use in your paper. Again, as a general rule, arrange the information in your bibliographic entry in the following order: author, title, place of publication, publisher, date, and any other information helpful for retrieval. Some examples of common citations follow.

a. Art Work, Published

Healy, G.P.A. The Meeting on the River Queen.

    White House, Washington, DC. Illus. in

    Lincoln: A Picture Story of His Life. By

    Stefan Lorent. Rev. and enl. ed. New York:

    Harper, 1957.

For how to handle an art work you have actually experienced, see page 368.

b. The Bible

When referring to the Bible, cite the book and chapter within your text (the verse, too, may be cited when necessary):

    The city of Babylon (Rev. 18.2) is used to

    symbolize . . .

OR

    In Rev. 18:2 the city of Babylon is used as a

    symbol of . . .

In "Works Cited" the following citation will suffice if you are using the King James version:

    The Bible

If you are using another version, specify which:

    The Bible, Revised Standard Version

c. Classical Works in General

When referring to classical works that are subdivided into books, parts, cantos, verses, and lines, specify the appropriate subdivisions within your text:

```
Ovid makes claims to immortality in the last

lines of The Metamorphoses (3. Epilogue).

Francesca's speech (5.118–35) is poignant

because  .  .  .
```

In "Works Cited" these references will appear as follows:

```
Ovid. The Metamorphoses. Trans. and introd.

    Horace Gregory. New York: NAL, 1958.

Alighieri, Dante. The Inferno. Trans. John

    Ciardi. New York: NAL, 1954
```

d. Dissertation

Unpublished: The title is placed within quotation marks and the work identified by "Diss.":

```
Cotton, Joyce Raymonde. "Evan Harrington: An

    Analysis of George Meredith's Revisions."

    Diss. U of Southern California, 1968.
```

Published: The dissertation is treated as a book, except that the entry includes the label "Diss." and states where and when the dissertation was originally written:

```
Cortey, Teresa. Le Rêve dans les contes de

    Charles Nodier. Diss. U of California,

    Berkeley, 1975. Washington, DC: UP of

    America, 1977.
```

e. Footnote or Endnote Citation

A bibliographical reference to a footnote or endnote in a source takes the following form:

```
Faber, M. D. The Design Within: Psychoanalytic

    Approaches to Shakespeare. New York:

    Science House, 1970.
```

In other words, no mention is made of the note. However, mention of the note should be made within the text itself:

```
In Schlegel's translation, the meaning is

    changed (Faber 205, n. 9).
The reference is to page 205, note number 9, of

    Faber's book.
```

f. Manuscript or Typescript

A bibliographical reference to a manuscript or typescript from a library collection should provide the following information: the author, the title or a description of the material, the material's form (ms. for manuscript, ts. for typescript), and any identifying number. If possible, give the name and location of the library or institution where the material is kept.

```
Chaucer, Geoffrey. Ellesmere ms., E126C9.

    Huntington Library, Pasadena.
The Wanderer. Ms. Exeter Cathedral, Exeter.

Cotton Vitellius. Ms., A. SV. British Museum,

    London.
```

g. Pamphlet or Brochure

Citations of pamphlets or brochures should conform as nearly as possible to the format used for citations of books. Give as much information about the pamphlet as is necessary to help a reader find it. Underline the title:

```
Calplans Agricultural Fund. An Investment in

    California Agricultural Real Estate.

    Oakland: Calplans Securities, n.d.
```

h. Personal Letter

Published:

```
Wilde, Oscar. "To Mrs. Alfred Hunt." 25 Aug.

    1880. The Letters of Oscar Wilde. Ed.
```

> Rupert Hart—Davis. New York: Harcourt,
>
> 1962. 67—68.

Unpublished:

> Thomas, Dylan. Letter to Trevor Hughes. 12 Jan.
>
> 1934. Dylan Thomas Papers. Lockwood
>
> Memorial Library. Buffalo.

Personally received:

> Highet, Gilbert. Letter to the author. 15 Mar.
>
> 1972.

i. Plays

(i) Classical play

In your text, provide parenthetical references to act, scene, and line(s) of the play:

> Cleopatra's jealousy pierces through her words:
>
> What says the married woman? You may go;
>
> Would she had never given you leave to come:
>
> Let her not say 'tis I that keep you here;
>
> I have no power upon you; hers you are.
>
> (1.3.20—23)

The reference is to Act I, Scene 3, lines 20–23. In "Works Cited" the play will be cited as follows:

> Shakespeare, William. Antony and Cleopatra. The
>
> Complete Works of Shakespeare. Ed. Hardin
>
> Craig and David Bevington. Rev. ed.
>
> Glenview: Scott, 1973. 1073—1108.

NOTE: When the play is part of a collection, list the pages that cover the entire play.

(ii) Modern play

Many modern plays are published as individual books:

> Miller, Arthur. <u>The Crucible</u>. New York: Bantam,
>
>   1952.

However, if published as part of a collection, the play is cited as follows:

> Chekhov, Anton, <u>The Cherry Orchard</u>. 1903. <u>The</u>
>
>   <u>Art of Drama</u>. Ed. R. F. Dietrich, William
>
>   E. Carpenter, and Kevin Kerrane. 2nd ed.
>
>   New York: Holt, 1976. 134–56.

NOTE: The page reference is to the entire play.

j. Poems

(i) Classical poem

Lucretius [Titus Lucretius Carus]. <u>Of the Nature</u>

>   <u>of Things</u>. Trans. William Ellery Leonard.
>
>   <u>Backgrounds of the Modern World</u>. Vol. 1 of
>
>   <u>The World in Literature</u>. Ed. Robert Warnock
>
>   and George K. Anderson. Chicago: Scott,
>
>   1950. 343–53.

Or, if published in one book:

> Dante [Dante Alighieri]. <u>The Inferno</u>. Trans.
>
>   John Ciardi. New York: NAL, 1954.

(ii) Modern poem

Modern poems are usually part of a larger collection:

> Moore, Marianne. "Poetry." <u>Fine Frenzy</u>. Ed.
>
>   Robert Baylor and Brenda Stokes. New York:
>
>   McGraw, 1972. 372–73.

NOTE: Cite pages covered by the poem.

Or, if the poem is long enough to be published as a book, use the following format:

```
Byron, George Gordon, Lord. Don Juan. Ed. Leslie

    A. Marchand. Boston: Houghton, 1958.
```

k. Public Documents

Because of their complicated origins, public documents often seem difficult to cite. As a general rule, follow this order: Government. Body. Subsidiary bodies. Title of document (underlined). Identifying code. Place, publisher, and date of publication. Most publications by the federal government are printed by the Government Printing Office, which is abbreviated as "GPO":

(i) The Congressional Record
A citation to the Congressional Record requires only title, date, and page(s):

```
Cong. Rec. 15 Dec. 1977, 19740.
```

(ii) Congressional publications

```
United States. Cong. Senate. Permanent

    Subcommittee on Investigations of the

    Committee on Government Operations.

    Organized Crime--Stolen Securities. 93rd

    Cong., 1st sess. Washington: GPO, 1973.

United States. Cong. House. Committee on Foreign

    Relations. Hearings on S. 2793,

    Supplemental Foreign Assistance Fiscal Year

    1966--Vietnam. 89th Cong., 2nd sess.

    Washington: GPO, 1966.

United States. Cong. Joint Economic Committee on

    Medical Policies and Costs. Hearings. 93rd

    Cong., 1st sess. Washington: GPO, 1973.
```

(iii) Executive branch publications

```
United States. Office of the President.

    Environmental Trends. Washington: GPO,

    1981.
```

United States Dept. of Defense. <u>Annual Report to</u>

<u>the Congress by the Secretary of Defense</u>.

Washington, GPO, 1984.

United States. Dept. of Education. National

Commission on Excellence in Education. <u>A</u>

<u>Nation at Risk: The Imperative for</u>

<u>Educational Reform</u>. Washington: GPO, 1983.

United States. Dept. of Commerce. Bureau of the

Census. <u>Statistical Abstracts of the United</u>

<u>States</u>. Washington: GPO, 1963.

(iv) Legal documents

When citing a well-known statute or law, a simple format will suffice:

US Const. Art. 1, sec. 2.

15 US Code. Sec. 78j(b). 1964.

US CC Art. 9, pt. 2, par. 9–28.

Federal Trade Commission Act. 1914.

When citing a little-known statute, law, or other legal agreement, provide all the information needed for retrieval:

"Agreement Between the Government of the United

States of America and the Khmer Republic

for Sales of Agricultural Commodities."

<u>Treaties and Other International</u>

<u>Agreements</u>. Vol. 26, pt. 1. TIAS No. 8008.

Washington: GPO, 1976.

Names of court cases are abbreviated and the first important word of each party is spelled out: "Brown v. Board of Ed." stands for "Oliver Brown versus the Board of Education of Topeka, Kansas." Cases, unlike laws, are italicized in the text but not in "Works Cited." Text: *Miranda v. Arizona*. "Works Cited": Miranda v. Arizona. The following information must be supplied in the order listed: (1) name of the first plaintiff and the first defendant, (2) volume, name, and page (in that order) of the law report cited, (3) the place and name of the court that decided the case, (4) the year in which the case was decided:

> Richardson v. J. C. Flood Co. 190 A. 2d 259.
>
> D.C. App. 1963.

Interpreted, the above means that the Richardson v. J. C. Flood Co. case can be found on page 259 of volume 190 of the Second Series of the *Atlantic Reporter*. The case was settled in the District of Columbia Court of Appeals during the year 1963.

For further information on the proper form for legal citations, consult *A Uniform System of Citation*, 12th ed. Cambridge: Harvard Law Rev. Assn., 1976.

l. Quotation in a Book or Article Used as a Source

(i) Quotation in a book

> MacDonald, Dwight. As quoted in John R. Trimble.
>
>   Writing with Style: Conversations on the
>
>   Art of Writing. Englewood Cliffs: Prentice,
>
>   1975.

(ii) Quotation in an article

> Grabar, Oleg. As quoted in Katharine Slater
>
>   Gittes. "The Canterbury Tales and the
>
>   Arabic Frame Tradition." PMLA 98 (1983):
>
>   237–51.

m. Report

Titles of reports in the form of pamphlets or books require underlining. When a report is included within the pages of a larger work, the title is set off in quotation marks. The work must be identified as a report:

> The Churches Survey Their Task. Report of the
>
>   Conference on Church, Community, and State.
>
>   London: Allen & Unwin, 1937.

```
Luxenberg, Stan. "New Life for New York Law."
     Report on New York Law School. Change 10
     (Nov. 1978): 16–18.
```

n. Table, Graph, Chart, or Other Illustration

If the table, graph, or chart has no title, identify it as a table, graph, or chart:

```
National Geographic Cartographic Division. Graph
     on imports drive into U.S. market. National
     Geographic 164 (July 1983): 13.
```

NOTE: The descriptive label is not underlined or set off in quotation marks.

```
Benson, Charles S. "Number of Full-Time
     Equivalent Employees, by Industry, 1929–
     1959." Table. The Economics of Public
     Education. Boston: Houghton, 1961. 208.
```

This time the table has a title, so it is set off in quotation marks.

NOTE: All tables, graphs, charts, and other illustrations should be numbered for easy reference.

o. Thesis

See VI. d., "Dissertation," (page 374).

Sample Student Paper

The following sample research paper graphically illustrates the extent to which a conscientious student must be prepared to rewrite and revise a work. We include a draft of the paper, showing the corrections the student made in her own hand during rewriting. Also included is the finished paper along with the student's outline and "Works Cited" page. The note cards incorporated into the text are reproduced on the facing left-hand pages.

Meticulously researched and written in a clear and unpretentious style, this paper can serve as a model for your own efforts at writing and rewriting a research paper.

Bullard 9   <u>Introduction</u>
Cassatt was born on May 22, 1844, in
Allegheny City, Pennsylvania. Full name:
Mary Stevenson Cassatt.

Bullard 90   <u>Introduction</u>
Cassatt is described as "America's
foremost woman painter," who entered the
male dominated art world "at a time when
most women were still restricted to
household duties and motherhood.

Sweet 154   <u>Introduction</u>
Cassatt received recognition as an
art advisor for prestigious art
collectors in the years after 1889.

Sweet <u>XIV</u>   <u>Childhood Years</u>
As a child she traveled extensively
throughout Europe with her family.

Bullard 11   <u>Childhood Years</u>
In 1851, Cassatt and her family moved
to Europe, settling in Paris, then
Heidelberg then Darmstadt, Germany.
(altogether four years).

Draft:

Annette Mikailian

Professor McCuen

English 101

November 20, 1985

Mary Cassatt and Impressionism

Born on May 22, 1844, in Allegheny City, Pennsylvania, Mary Stevenson Cassatt, "America's foremost woman painter," *daringly* entered the male-dominated art world" at a time when most women were still ~~expected only to aspire~~ *restricted* to household duties and motherhood (Bullard 9, 90). This *liberated and* fascinating ~~liberated~~ woman became accepted as the only American female artist ever to be accepted in the Impressionist group. In addition to her ~~notability~~ *fame* as an artist, Cassatt also received recognition as an art adviser for prestigious art collectors in the years after 1889 (Sweet 154).

~~Being~~ *B*orn the fortunate daughter of a wealthy businessman, Mary Cassatt was ~~fortunate enough~~ *able* to travel extensively, ~~and~~ spending ~~much~~ *weeks and months* of her childhood in Europe ~~with her family~~ (Sweet xiv). Mary was only seven years old when ~~in 1851~~, she and her family moved to Europe, *for a period of four years,* settling first in Paris, then Heidelberg and Darmstadt ~~Germany, for a period of four years~~ (Bullard 11). On their return to America in *the winter of* ~~late~~ 1855, the Cassatt family stopped in Paris

383

Breskin 8   Influences
"The fact that she was taken to live in
Europe during her childhood, was in all
likelihood, important in the formation of her
determination to become an artist."

Bullard 11   Academic Background
In the fall of 1861, Cassatt enrolled at the
Pennsylvania Academy of the Fine Arts for
a period of four frustrating years.

Hale 31   Academic Background
Lack of parental support:
"I would almost rather see you dead" her
father had said to her when she announced
her determination to become a professional
artist.

Bullard 11   Academic Background
Mary, dissatisfied with her studies at the
Pennsylvania Academy, decided to leave for
Europe to conduct an independent study of the
old masters.

Bullard 9   Apprenticeship in France
In the summer of 1866, Mary Cassatt went
to Paris. She attended classes in the workshop
of the prominent French painter Charles Chaplin.

Bullard 12   Apprenticeship in France
Cassatt studied the old masters in the
great museums of Paris.

to see the Exposition Universelle, the art
section of which featured large exhibitions of
such ~~very well-known~~ famous artists as Ingres,
Delacroix, and Gustave Courbet (Bullard 11).
"The fact that she was taken to live in Europe
during her childhood, "declared the art critic
A. D. Breeskin ~~(Graphic Art 8)~~, "was in all
likelihood important in the formation of her
determination to become an artist," (Graphic Art 8).

    Eager to learn, and despite her family's
opposition to her pursuit of the Arts, (young) ~~and~~
ambitious Mary began her extensive artistic
studies ~~when~~ when in the fall of 1861, she enrolled
at the ~~Pennsylvania~~ Academy of ~~the~~ Fine Arts, in Pennsylvania for
~~where she spent~~ trying to adjust to the restrictions of
~~a period of~~ four frustrating years, (Bullard 11) fossilized
teachers.
"I would almost rather see you dead" her father determined
had said to her when she announced her to keep
determination to become a professional artist, trying her mary from
(Hale 31). But Mary, dissatisfied with her own artistic
studies at the Academy, shocked her father even wings.
further when she informed him of her decision to
leave America for Europe in an attempt to study
the old masters independently (Bullard 11).

    Her decision to go to Europe was most
likely based upon the fact that Europe at that
time was the leading art center in the world.
Where else but in the beautiful city of Paris
could Mary find so many large collections of

Bullard 12   Apprenticeship in France
Mary, who possessed an "inquiring mind,"
probably attended the Paris World's Fair of 1867,
where a private collection of Gustave Courbet's
and Edouard Manet's paintings were exhibited.

Bullard 12   Apprenticeship in France
This was an important factor in her development
as an artist, because her works in the years before
1895 were influenced by these two leading exponents
of Realism, who challenged the "artificial" style
of the French Art Academy.

Rugoff 103   Back home in the U.S.
With the outbreak of the Franco-Prussian
War in 1870, Cassatt was forced to return
home. She began selling some of the paintings
she had created in Paris.

Mathews 73   Back home in the U.S.
Cassatt was terribly unhappy in the U.S.:
"I am in such low spirits over my prospects
that although I would prefer Spain, I should
jump at anything in preference to America."

Rugoff 104   Academic Training in Italy
In 1872, Mary returned to Europe, settling
in Parma, Italy, for a period of eight months.
She attended classes at the Art Academy.

Bullard 12   Academic Training in Italy
In Italy, Mary studied Antonio Correggio's
depictions of the Madonna and Child, which
greatly influenced her later impressionistic
works.

masterpieces? ~~in art~~. ^Thus, in the summer of 1866,^ 3

~~With this in mind, she~~
~~embarked~~ the streets of Paris ~~in the summer of~~ ^became Mary's daily^
~~1866, where for a short time~~ she attended ^haunts. There, art historian John Bullard tells us,^

classes in the workshop of the prominent French
^However, these studies did not last long. Mary, too much of a^
painter Charles Chaplin (Bullard 9). ^ ~~But Mary,~~ ^free spirit and^

~~being~~ too independent to be confined to any type

of academic restrictions, decided to conduct

independent studies in the great museums of

Paris, by copying the great works of the old

masters ~~on her own~~ (Bullard 12). Mary, who

possessed an "inquiring mind," must have

attended the Paris World's Fair of 1867, where a

private collection of Gustave Courbet's and

Edouard Manet's paintings were exhibited

(Bullard 12). This was an important factor in

her development as an artist, because Cassatt's

works in the years before 1875 were largely

influenced by these two leading exponents of

Realism, who challenged the "artificial" style

of the French Art Academy (Bullard 12).

   With the beginning of the Franco-Prussian

War in 1870, Cassatt returned home to

Philadelphia where she began selling some of the

paintings she had created in Paris (Rugoff 103).
                   ^dissatisfied^
However, soon ~~frustrated and unhappy~~ with her

accomplishments here in the United States, Mary

decided to return to Europe where she could

truly continue her artistic training free of any

Bullard 12   Growing Success

In the spring of 1872, Cassatt sent her first
acceptable painting to the Paris Salon.
The painting is entitled Before the Carnival.
Due to her parents' opposition, Mary submitted
this painting under the name "Mlle. Mary
Stevenson."

Fine 130   Growing Success

In 1874, Mary sent her second acceptable
salon entry entitled Madame Cortier.
Edgar Degas remarked: "It is true, there
is someone who feels as I do."

Rugoff 104   Success at last

From 1875-1876, Mary exhibited at the
Paris Salon, but her fifth entry in 1877 was
denied because her paintings had become
Impressionistic in style. Degas, however, was
impressed by her 1874 salon entry and asked
her to join the Impressionist group.

Bullard 13   Cassatt joins Impressionist

"I accepted with joy. Now I could work
with absolute independence without considering
the opinion of a jury. I had already recognized
who were my true masters. I admired Manet,
Courbet, and Degas. I took leave of conventional
art. I began to live."
(Cassatt's reply to Degas' offer).

restrictions. ~~In~~ a letter addressed to her

closest friend, Emily Sartain, Cassatt wrote: *reveals Cassatt's enormous disappointment over her artistic career in America:* "I am in such low spirits over my prospects that

although I would prefer Spain I should jump at

anything in preference to America" (Mathews 73).

Hence, in 1872 Mary returned to Europe, only

this time settling in Parma, Italy, where she

attended classes at the Art Academy (Rugoff

104). There she studied Antonio Correggio's

depictions of the Madonna and Child, which

greatly influenced her later Impressionistic

works and led her to develop her own famous

"mother and child" theme (Bullard 12).

As she progressed in her academic studies,

Mary ~~soon began developing~~ *gradually developed* her own artistic

style. In the spring of 1872, ~~Cassatt~~ *she* sent her

first acceptable painting ~~, to the Paris Salon~~,

entitled <u>Before the Carnival</u> *to the Paris Salon* (Bullard 12).

However, due to her family's disapproval of her

artistic career, the painting was submitted

under the name "Mlle. Mary Stevenson" (Bullard

12). A year later, Mary decided to settle in

Paris for the rest of her life. In 1874, she

sent her second acceptable Salon entry. This

painting, entitled <u>Madame Cortier</u>, captured the

attention of the famous Impressionist painter,

Edgar Degas, who, upon seeing the painting,

Bullard 14   Degas and Cassatt
Degas was one of the biggest influences
on Cassatt. This influence caused her to
change her style.

Rugoff 104   Degas and Cassatt
Both Degas and Cassatt exhibited in the
Impressionist exhibitions of 1877, '79, '80,
'81, and '86.

Bullard 24   Degas and Cassatt
Degas' influence is most apparent in the
painting called Little Girl in a Blue
Armchair.
  "extensive use of pattern"
  "brushwork"
  "asymmetrical composition"

Personal Comment   Cassatt's Personal Style
Gradually Cassatt developed her own original
style, free from specific influences. She
focused on a "mother and child" theme —
probably making up for the fact that she
had no children of her own.

remarked: "It is true. There is someone who feels as I do" (Fine 130).

For two consecutive years (1875–76) Mary exhibited at the Paris Salon, but was denied her fifth Salon entry in 1877 because her paintings had become Impressionistic in style (Rugoff 104). In the same year, Degas, who was impressed by her 1874 Salon entry, asked her to join the Impressionist group, and Cassatt accepted the offer (Rugoff 104). According to her first biographer, Achille Segard, Cassatt had said:

> I accepted with joy. Now I could work with absolute independence without considering the opinion of a jury. I had already recognized who were my true masters. I admired Manet, Courbet, and Degas. I took leave of conventional art. I began to live (Bullard 13).

From that moment on, Mary Cassatt's artistic career *took a leap forward* ~~changed for the better~~. As Cassatt and Degas began working together, a close professional and personal relationship developed between the two artists. Together, they participated in the Impressionist exhibitions of 1877, '79, '80, '81, and '86 (Rugoff 104). Cassatt's artistic style also began

Bullard 15   Height of Cassatt's Career
"Her work in the 1870 exhibition was
noticed favorably by several critics, including
Edmond Dusanty and J. K. Huysmans."

Breeskin 16   Japanese Influence
Cassatt visited the great Japanese art
exhibition in 1890, held at the Ecole des
Beaux Arts in Paris. Cassatt's works began
to show a strong Oriental influence.

Bullard 52   Japanese Influence
Techniques used in The Bath:
1) rich patterns
2) strong contours
3) solid forms
The Bath is known for its Japanese
influence.

Bullard 16   Final Success
On June 10th of 1891, Mary held her first
one-woman show at Durand-Ruel's, and was
praised by such famous painters as Pissarro
who referred to her works as "rare" and
"exquisite."

Bullard 20   Cassatt's Final Years
In her final years, Cassatt became inactive
as an artist.
She turned bitter due to the loss of her
closest friends.
She began to lose her eyesight.
Mary Cassatt died of diabetes in 1926, at
Chateau de Beaufresne, her summer
palace in France.

to change, as a result of Degas' influence on her works (Bullard 14): she began to apply paint in a brushy-tonal style, her palette became colorful, and she began drawing subjects from everyday life. One of the best examples, in which Degas's influence is most apparent, is the painting entitled <u>Little Girl in a Blue Armchair</u> (1878). The "extensive use of pattern," "the brushwork," and "the asymmetrical composition" of this painting are largely attributed to Degas' influence on Cassatt (Bullard 24).

However, in the 1880's, Cassatt ~~made obvious advancements~~ *as advanced noticeably* in her career, ~~and~~ her paintings began to show more originality in design, and in ~~depicted~~ *that* subject matter. It was during this period of time ~~when~~ *that* Cassatt developed her famous "mother and child" theme. ~~It is a widely held belief~~ *It seems reasonable to conclude* that because Cassatt never married and was unable to have any children, *of her own, she gratified* her desire to be a mother ~~was in a way gratified~~ through her paintings of mothers with their children.

Cassatt ~~also~~ began to receive ~~considerable~~ *more and more* recognition for her paintings showed at the Impressionist exhibitions. According to E. J. Bullard, "her work in the 1879 exhibition was noticed favorably by several critics, including Edmond Duranty and J. K. Huysmans" (15).

Mary Cassatt reached the height of her career in the years between 1890 and 1900.

Personal Comment   Conclusion

An outstanding artist and an exceptional woman, Mary Stevenson Cassatt died without even knowing she contributed more than just her paintings to the world. She gave birth to new hopes for all the women in the world who were afraid of reaching the horizons beyond the boundaries of their comfortable homes.

After she visited the great Japanese art exhibition in 1890, held at l'Ecole des Beaux Arts in Paris, Cassatt's works began to show a strong Oriental influence (Breeskin, Graphic Art 16). For example, the painting entitled The Bath (1892), wherein compositional devices such as solid forms, "rich patterns," and "strong contours" are highly emphasized, shows the Japanese influence on Cassatt (Bullard 52). On June 10th of 1891, Mary Cassatt held her first one-woman show at Durand-Ruel's and was praised by such famous painters as Pissarro, who referred to her show as being "rare" and "exquisite" (Bullard 16). At last, Mary Stevenson Cassatt received the recognition which she deserved so very much as a true professional artist.

Her final years were ~~The 1900's were~~ not productive for Mary Cassatt. She slowly ~~In her final years, Cassatt~~ became more and more inactive artistically, moribund and turned bitter due to the loss of her closest friends, of and her eyesight (Bullard 20). Mary Cassatt died of diabetes in 1926 at Chateau de Beaufresne, her summer palace in France (Bullard 20). The art world now treasures her work as belonging to the history of art.

An outstanding artist, and an exceptional woman, Mary Stevenson Cassatt died without even

8

knowing that she contributed more than just her

paintings to the world. She ~~gave~~ *had given* birth to new

hopes for all the women in the world who were

afraid of reaching the horizons beyond the

boundaries of their comfortable homes.

Works Cited
~~Bibliography~~

Breeskin, Adelyn D., and Donald H. Karshan. The
Graphic Art of Mary Cassatt. New York:
Smithsonian Institution P, 1967.

Bullard, E. John. Mary Cassatt New York:
Watson—Guptill, 1976.

Fine, Elsa H. Women & Art. Totowa, N.J.:
Rowman and Allanheld, 1978.

Hale, Nancy. Mary Cassatt. New York: Doubleday,
1975.

Matthews, Nancy M. Cassatt and Her Circle. New
York: Abbeville, 1984.

Rugoff, Milton. "Cassatt, Mary." Encyclopedia of
American Art, 1981 ed.

Sweet, Frederick A. Miss Mary Cassatt.
Norman, Okla.: U of Oklahoma P, 1966.

Final version:

Annette Mikailian

Professor McCuen

English 101

November 20, 1985

Mary Cassatt and Impressionism

THESIS: At a time when most women were
still in the kitchen, Mary Cassatt
entered the male—dominated art world and
received recognition as America's
foremost woman painter.

I. The daughter of a prosperous businessman, Mary
Cassatt spent much of her childhood in Europe
with her family.

A. In 1851, the Cassatt family moved to Europe,
settling in Paris and Germany for the next
four years.

1. During her two—year stay in Paris, Cassatt
was exposed to the artistic life of the
French.

2. In 1853, the family moved to Heidelberg and
then Darmstadt, Germany.

B. Late in 1855, the family returned to America,
stopping in Paris to see the Exposition
Universelle.

    1. The art section of this world's fair featured large exhibitions of Ingres, Delacroix, and Gustave Courbet.

    2. Such an experience at the age of eleven could well have aroused Mary's own desire to become an artist.

II. Mary Cassatt's official artistic studies began when she was seventeen.

    A. In the fall of 1861, she enrolled at the Pennsylvania Academy of Fine Arts.

        1. For four years she followed a frustrating academic course of study.

        2. Dissatisfied with her studies at the Pennsylvania Academy, she decided to go to Europe to study the old masters independently.

    B. After overcoming the resistance of her parents, Cassatt left for Paris in the summer of 1866.

        1. For a short period of time, Cassatt studied in the atelier of the academic painter Charles Chaplin.

        2. But she soon left for independent study in the great public art collections of Paris.

    C. As a young student of the Arts, Cassatt was influenced by the many famous artists of that time.

1. In the years before 1875, Manet and Courbet influenced the works of Mary Cassatt.

2. Corregio's depictions of the Madonna and Child influenced Cassatt's later impressionistic works.

3. Degas, the very famous impressionist artist, was the strongest influence on Mary Cassatt.

4. After the Japanese exhibition of 1890, her works began to show the influence of Japanese prints.

III. In 1873 Mary Cassatt decided to settle in Paris for the rest of her life.

A. The decision to settle in Paris proved crucial to Cassatt's development as an artist because Paris was the center of all that was new in art.

1. Mary first met Degas in 1877, at the third Impressionist exhibition, where she was asked to join the Impressionist group.

2. She participated in all five Impressionist exhibitions with Degas.

3. With Degas' influence she developed her Impressionistic style.

B. Cassatt's most famous works are noted for their "mother and child" theme.

1. She developed this theme during the 1880s

as she began developing her own independent style.

    2. It is said that her love for children was immense, but because she never married, she had no children of her own.

C. Cassatt's most productive years were the 1890s.

    1. She developed a new style, influenced by the Japanese prints.

    2. She was praised by many famous art critics.

D. In her last years, Mary Cassatt turned bitter, due to her partial loss of eyesight.

    1. She became inactive and lonely.

    2. Mary Cassatt died a famous artist, at Chateau de Beaufresne on June 14, 1926, at the age of eighty-two.

Annette Mikailian

Professor McCuen

English 101

November 20, 1985

Mary Cassatt and Impressionism

Mary Stevenson Cassatt, "America's foremost
woman painter," daringly entered the male—
dominated art world at a time when most women
were still restricted to household duties and
motherhood (Bullard 9, 90). Born on May 22,
1844, in Allegheny City, Pennsylvania, this
liberated and fascinating woman became
recognized as the only American female artist
ever to be accepted in the Impressionist group.
In addition to fame as an artist, Cassatt also
received recognition as an art adviser for
prestigious art collectors in the years after
1889 (Sweet 154).

Born the fortunate daughter of a wealthy
businessman, Mary Cassatt was able to travel
extensively, spending weeks and months of her
childhood in Europe (Sweet xiv). Mary was only
seven years old when she and her family moved to
Europe for a period of four years, settling
first in Paris, then in Heidelberg and Darmstadt
(Bullard 11). On their return to America in the
winter of 1855, the Cassatt family stopped in

Paris to see the Exposition Universelle, the art
section of which featured large exhibitions of
such famous artists as Ingres, Delacroix, and
Gustave Courbet (Bullard 11). "The fact that she
was taken to live in Europe during her
childhood," declares art critic A. D. Breeskin,
"was in all likelihood important in the
formation of her determination to become an
artist" (Graphic Art 8).

Eager to learn, and despite her family's
opposition to her pursuit of the Arts, ambitious
young Mary began her extensive artistic studies
in the fall of 1861, when she enrolled at the
Academy of Fine Arts in Pennsylvania where she
spent four frustrating years trying to adjust to
the restrictions of fossilized teachers
determined to keep Mary from trying her own
artistic wings (Bullard 11). "I would almost
rather see you dead," her father had warned her
when she announced her determination to become a
professional artist (Hale 31). But Mary,
dissatisfied with her studies at the Academy,
shocked her father even further when she
informed him of her decision to leave America
for Europe in an attempt to study the old
masters independently (Bullard 11).

Her decision to go to Europe was doubtless
based upon the fact that Europe at that time was

the leading art center in the world. Where else but in the beautiful city of Paris could Mary find so many large collections of masterpieces? Thus, in the summer of 1866, the streets of Paris became Mary's daily haunts. There, art historian John Bullard tells us, she attended classes in the workshop of the prominent French painter Charles Chaplin (Bullard 9). However, these studies did not last long. Mary, too much of a free spirit and too independent to be stultified by academic restrictions, decided to conduct her own independent studies in the great museums of Paris by copying the great works of the old masters (Bullard 12). Mary, who possessed an "inquiring mind," must have attended the Paris World's Fair of 1867, where a private collection of Gustave Courbet's and Edouard Manet's pointings was exhibited (Bullard 12). This was an important factor in her development as an artist, because Cassatt's works in the years before 1875 were largely influenced by these two leading exponents of Realism, who challenged the "artificial" style of the French Art Academy (Bullard 12).

With the outbreak of the Franco-Prussian War in 1870, Cassatt returned home to Philadelphia, where she began selling some of the paintings she had created in Paris (Rugoff

103). However, soon dissatisfied with her accomplishments here in the United States, Mary decided to return to Europe, where she could continue her artistic training free of any restrictions. A letter addressed to her closest friend, Emily Sartain, reveals Cassatt's enormous disappointment over her artistic career in America: "I am in such low spirits over my prospects that although I would prefer Spain I should jump at anything in preference to America" (Mathews 73). Hence, in 1872 Mary returned to Europe, only this time settling in Parma, Italy, where she attended classes at the Art Academy (Rugoff 104). There she studied Antonio Correggio's depictions of the Madonna and Child, which greatly influenced her later Impressionistic works and led her to develop her own famous "mother and child" theme (Bullard 12).

As she progressed in her academic studies, Mary gradually developed her own individual artistic style. In the spring of 1872, she sent her first acceptable painting, entitled <u>Before the Carnival</u>, to the Paris Salon (Bullard 12). However, due to her family's disapproval of her artistic career, the painting was submitted under the name "Mlle. Mary Stevenson" (Bullard 12). A year later, Mary decided to settle in

Paris for the rest of her life. In 1874, she
sent her second acceptable Salon entry. This
painting, entitled <u>Madame Cortier</u>, captured the
attention of the famous Impressionist painter,
Edgar Degas, who, upon seeing the painting,
remarked: "It is true. There is someone who
feels as I do" (Fine 130).

For two consecutive years (1875-76) Mary
exhibited at the Paris Salon, but was denied her
fifth Salon entry in 1877 because her paintings
had become Impressionistic in style (Rugoff
104). In the same year, Degas, who was
impressed by her 1874 Salon entry, asked her to
join the Impressionist group, and Cassatt
accepted the offer (Rugoff 104). According to
her first biographer, Achille Segard, Cassatt
had said:

> I accepted with joy. Now I could work
> with absolute independence without
> considering the opinion of a jury. I
> had already recognized who were my
> true masters. I admired Manet,
> Courbet, and Degas. I took leave of
> conventional art. I began to live.
> (quoted in Bullard 13)

From that moment on, Mary Cassatt's
artistic career took a jump upward. As Cassatt

and Degas began working together, a close professional and personal relationship developed between the two artists. Together, they participated in the Impressionist exhibitions of 1877, '79, '80, '81, and '86 (Rugoff 104). Cassatt's artistic style also began to change, as a result of Degas' influence on her works (Bullard 14): She began to apply paint in a brushy-tonal style, her palette became colorful, and she began drawing subjects from everyday life. One of the best examples, in which Degas' influence is most apparent, is the painting entitled <u>Little Girl in a Blue Armchair</u> (1878). The "extensive use of pattern," "the brushwork," and "the asymmetrical composition" of this painting are largely attributed to Degas' influence on Cassatt (Bullard 24).

However, in the 1880's, as Cassatt advanced noticeably in her career, her paintings began to show more originality in design and in subject matter. It was during this period of time that Cassatt developed her famous "mother and child" theme. It seems reasonable to conclude that because Cassatt never married and was unable to have any children of her own, she gratified her desire to be a mother through her paintings of mothers with their children.

Cassatt began to receive more and more recognition for her paintings displayed at the Impressionist exhibitions. According to E. J. Bullard, "her work in the 1879 exhibition was noticed favorably by several critics, including Edmond Duranty and J. K. Huysmans" (15).

Mary Cassatt reached the height of her career in the decade between 1890 and 1900. After she visited the great Japanese art exhibition of 1890, held at l'Ecole des Beaux Arts in Paris, Cassatt's works began to show a strong Oriental influence (Breeskin, Graphic Art 16). For example, the painting entitled The Bath (1892), wherein compositional devices such as solid forms, "rich patterns," and "strong contours" are highly emphasized, shows the Japanese influence on Cassatt (Bullard 52). On June 10, 1891, Mary Cassatt held her first one-woman show at Durand-Ruel's and was praised by such famous painters as Pissarro, who referred to her show as being "rare" and "exquisite" (Bullard 16). At last, Mary Stevenson Cassatt received the recognition she deserved as a true artist.

Her final years were not productive for Mary Cassatt. She became more and more artistically moribund and turned bitter due to the loss of her closest friends and of her eyesight (Bullard 20). Mary Cassatt died of diabetes in 1926 at Chateau de Beaufresne, her summer home in France (Bullard 20). The art world now treasures her work as belonging to the history of art.

An outstanding artist and an exceptional woman, Mary Stevenson Cassatt died without even knowing that she had contributed more than just her paintings to the world. She had given birth to new hopes for all the women in the world who were afraid of reaching the horizons beyond the boundaries of their comfortable homes.

Works Cited

Breeskin, Adelyn D., and Donald H. Karshan.

   The Graphic Art of Mary Cassatt. New York:

   Smithsonian Institution P, 1967.

Bullard, E. John. Mary Cassatt. New York:

   Watson—Guptill, 1976.

Fine, Elsa H. Women & Art. Totowa, N.J.:

   Rowman and Allanheld, 1978.

Hale, Nancy. Mary Cassatt. New York: Doubleday,

   1975.

Matthews, Nancy M. Cassatt and Her Circle. New

   York: Abbeville, 1984.

Rugoff, Milton. "Cassatt, Mary." Encyclopedia of

   American Art, 1981 ed.

Sweet, Frederick A. Miss Mary Cassatt.

   Norman, Okla.: U of Oklahoma P, 1966.

Exercises

1. Write a one-sentence summary of the following passage:

A failure in learning should *never* be punished by blows. Learning is difficult enough. To add fear to it simply makes it more difficult. Fear does not encourage, it drives on blindly. It blocks the movement of the mind. It produces the opposite effect to that of true education, because it makes frightened pupils dull and imitative instead of making them original and eager. And it is useless to object: "Boys don't fear physical punishment, they laugh at it and forget it": for it can always be made tough enough, by a brutal master, to make most of them secretly afraid and some of them paralyzed with terror.
—Gilbert Highet, *The Art of Teaching.*

2. Write a paraphrase of the following passage:

Eventually, a condition of learning any art is a *supreme concern* with the mastery of the art. If the art is not something of supreme importance, the apprentice will remain, at best, a good dilettante, but will never become a master. This condition is as necessary for the art of loving as for any other art. It seems, though, as if the proportion between masters and dilettantes is more heavily weighted in favor of the dilettantes in the art of loving than in the case with other arts.
—Erich Fromm, *The Art of Loving.*

3. Find three different ways to introduce the following quotation by Samuel Johnson about Joseph Addison:

As a describer of life and manners he must be allowed to stand perhaps the first of the first rank.

4. Arrange the following information into the proper form for "Works Cited":
a. The first volume of a work edited by G. B. Harrison and 17 other editors. The title is *Major British Writers*. Published in New York by Harcourt, Brace & World in 1959.
b. "High Spirits in the Twenties," an article in the July 1962 issue of *Horizon*, a magazine. The article is found on pages 33–40 of volume IV, issue number 6. The author is John Mason Brown.
c. A review of the book *The Building*, authored by Thomas Glynn. The reviewer is R. Z. Sheppard, writing for *Time*, Dec. 30, 1985, page 76. *The Building* is published in New York by Alfred A. Knopf, 1985.
d. The Cambridge University Press edition of the Bible.

e. C. S. Lewis's novel *Perelandra,* put out by Macmillan Publishing Company in New York, 1944.

f. An entry from the 1963 edition of the *Encyclopaedia Britannica* under "Pottery and Porcelain." The section referred to is by Sir Edgar John Forsdyke.

Appendix

Practice Essays to Revise, Edit, and Proofread

The following essays, submitted by students exactly as shown, vary in quality as well as subject matter. With revision, editing, and proofreading, each could be markedly improved. Your assignment is to revise each essay until you think it is strong enough to merit an "A." Using the techniques of revising you have learned from this book, tamper with the essays at will, adding, deleting, or rephrasing passages to improve the overall quality. The questions below are intended as guidelines to help you with this task:

1. Is the main point of the essay clear? Is it stated as a thesis somewhere in the first paragraph?
2. Is the pattern of organization obvious and helpful? (For example, progressing by order of importance, by space or time orientation, or by simple logic.)
3. Does each paragraph make a clear point? (Is it unified and coherent?)
4. Do the paragraphs reflect appropriate modes of development?

   Narration: Can the reader instantly tell *when* the action happened, *where* it happened, and *to whom* it happened? Is the narration well paced, stressing the important events while glossing over the unimportant? Are sufficient details included? Is the point of view clear and consistent?

   Description: Are the details focused on a dominant impression? Are the details specific and concrete rather than vague? Does the description come to life through colorful images and figurative language?

413

Examples: Are the writer's examples relevant to the point being made and are they effectively developed? Are the examples clearly introduced so that it is contextually clear what they mean?

Definition: Is it clear what term the writer is defining? Does the definition clearly answer the question "What is it?" Has the writer provided a dictionary-type definition first and then extended it?

Process: Does the writer tell the reader what process is being explained? Are all steps of the process included? Is the order of the steps clear and easy to follow? Can you understand the writer's explanation without confusion?

Comparison/Contrast: What items are being compared or contrasted? Are the bases of the comparison/contrast made clear? Are both sides of the question treated completely? Is the comparison/contrast clearly organized—either within or between paragraphs? Does the writer use plain indicators of comparison or contrast (*like, similarly, however, on the other hand,* and so on) to underscore the essay's purpose?

Causal Analysis: Does the causal connection make sense? Does the writer focus on the nearest rather than the most remote cause? Does the writer avoid circular reasoning about cause? (For example, "Swearing is bad because it means using profane language.") Is the writer's reasoning impartial or is it biased?

Classification: Is it clear what subject the writer is classifying? Is the classification based on a single principle (looks, color, age)? Has the *entire* subject been divided without the omission of any important part? Do the categories overlap or are they clearly separate? Are all of the categories treated with equal emphasis?

5. Does the essay have a strong beginning? Does it grab and hold your attention with a punchy statement, a quotation, an anecdote, a dramatization of the topic, or some other memorable opening?

6. Are clear transitions made between the paragraphs?

7. Does the essay conclude with some finality? (Make sure that it does not weakly peter out, move away from the subject, or abruptly stop, leaving the reader hanging.)

8. Are the individual sentences within the paragraphs clear and concise? (Check for errors of mixed constructions; lack of parallel construction; unreasoned sentences; dangling or squinting constructions; misplaced elements; shifts in person, number, voice, tense, or mood.)

9. Are the individual sentences within the paragraphs concise? (Check for the following errors: repetitiousness, unnecessary words, pretentious overuse of big words.)

10. Are the sentences emphatically written? Are they balanced? Has the writer overused the passive voice? Have multiple *of's* been eliminated? Have fragments and comma splices been corrected? Have jarring sounds, such as unintentional rhyme or alliteration, been avoided? Are the sentences varied in structure and in length?

11. Is the writer's diction effective? Does the language strike you as sincere? Are the writer's images vivid rather than stale?

12. If the essay is a formal argument, is its proposition stated clearly and forcefully? Has the opposing point of view been addressed? Is the evidence persuasive and varied, consisting of facts, witness, experience, and expert testimony?

13. Is the manuscript free from typographical or spelling errors, from grammatical mistakes, from poorly punctuated sentences, and from all other mechanical problems that are the result of careless proofreading?

Student Essay 1

Inner Beauty

The word <u>beauty</u> can be defined as "a beautiful person or thing, especially a beautiful woman." Modern day beauty is described in physical terms— pretty features and a slim figure. But there is a different kind of beauty. An inner beauty that comes from kindness, generosity, courage, and love. Eleanor Roosevelt, wife of Franklin Delano Roosevelt, who was President of the United States during the discordant years of World War II, was a woman who possessed this inner beauty irregardless of the fact that she did not have physical beauty judged by today's standards. She revealed her inner beauty to the world many times.

Mrs. Roosevelt was deeply committed to civil rights and to human dignity. She was the first wife of a President to openly support the civil rights of Blacks. Oftentimes she tried to include Blacks where they would normally not have been included. She invited the National Council of Negro Women to hold meetings at the White House, and unlike other First Ladies allowed herself to be photographed regularly with Blacks. She set a standard for courage in welcoming Blacks to participate at national levels.

Mrs. Roosevelt had an incredable love of humanity. After her husband took office during the Depression, her calling became to give encouragement to the poor and helpless of America. She went everywhere misery could be found. She visited everything from rural slums to the dying mines where men were out of work, to the soup lines in the inner cities. She was avid in combatting poor housing unemployment. She gave many empassioned speeches criticizing the crumbling stairways, grimy kitchens, and rat-infested cellars of New York's tenaments.

Eleanor Roosevelt fought for peace all of her adult life. After her husband died in 1945, President Truman appointed her to the American Delegation of the United Nations General Assenmbly. She is quoted as saying, "We face today a world filled with suspicion and hatred. . . . We can establish no real trust between nations until we acknowledge the power of love above all the other powers. . . . " One of Eleanor's greatest talents, it seems, was the ability to take the arguments of established views and opinions and turn them into human situations that could be discussed in human terms.

She also wrote a immensely popular syndacated column called "My Day."

Student Essay 2

The Sumo Wrestler

I envision the Sumo wrestler as Rueben did his Renaissance women, voluptuous in proportion. The Sumo wrestler exhibitions many corporeally physical deformities and infirmities not ubiquitous on an ordinary figure. Let me illustrate: His steatopygous abundant buttocks, smooth as a fetal pig, glistens under spotlights; his Alpine thighs vibrate with potentiality. The Sumo wrestler's fortification, his elephantine belly, is the epicenter of power.

This Oriental combantant, thick set and squat, is a worthy adversary. He approaches his adversary as if he were walking on broken glass, with great caution. His flatulent limbs reach out to tease the opponent. His pudgy fingers perform calisthenics in anticipation of contact. Beads of sweat adorn his massive brows.

The Sumo wrestler is dressed in unique attire. A loin cloth for him is de rigueur in this sport. Dating back to the Greco—Roman empire and used on through the centuries of professional wrestling, it has been upgraded to its present form. The wrestler's imposing behind is highlighted by the severe lines of the garment draped from his shoulders. The jutting cut of the loin cloth accentuates his spacious hips. To minimize the wrestler's cyclopean girth, a thick belt, made of cloth, is attached to the garment--minimal wear for an apish gargantuan.

I admire the Sumo wrestler's physique, he is so amply endowed. He is one of art's treasures.

Student Essay 3

Female Beauty in Renaissance Paintings

The Renaissance--the rebirth of all that was glorious in ancient Greece and Rome--inaugurated various concepts of beauty portrayed by the painters of that period. The ideal females in Early Renaissance paintings were slim, young beauties on the brink of maturity, and the madonnas and graces of the High and Late Renaissance gradually began to present a more robust figure.

One of the earliest of an Early Renaissance beauty is <u>Venusu</u>, painted by Sandro Botticelli. Fresh, blooming, and young, this vision of beauty stands tall and nude. Her wiry long flowing hair, draped behind her softly rounded thin neck, appearing to be soft yellow color turning brown. Her eyes, tender and a deep blue, exude an tensile gaze, gentle as a zephyr on a summer day. Her lips, a shade of rose, are round and small above a chin with a button in the middle.

Furthermore, in Botticelli's hands this classical seductress takes on a virtuous quality.

Let us take Leonardo Da Vinci's <u>Mona Lisa</u>. Her enigmatic face genuinely reflects the taste of the period. Her hair, as thin as the veil spread on her head, is a dark brown. Her eyelids are round like the vaulted ceilings of a Gothic Cathedral. Her gaze is as soft and delicate as her subtle and mysterious smile. And her nose, long and angular, makes her even more unique. In addition, this astonishing High Renaissance beauty embodies a quality of maternal tenderness, which was to High Renaissance men the essence of virtuous womanhood.

From all the different Neo-Classical concepts of beauty, a new Renaissance ideal evolved. Among the most famous painters representing this Late Renaissance ideal was Michelangelo Buonarroti. The enticing goddesses depicted by Michelangelo are all full-figured women—generously endowed—and displaying muscles a male might be proud of. The bodies of these females are as big as those of the giants in Greek and Roman mythology. And their eyes flash with passion and anger, as if they wanted to pass the last judgment on mankind.

Student Essay 4

Microwave Ovens Versus Conventional Ovens

In terms of time, expense, and convenience, the microwave oven is superior to the conventional oven.

First of all, the microwave oven can save the cook
a great deal of money. Not only does the cook save
money on the initial purchase, but he or she also
saves money while actually using the microwave. The
microwave cooks food two to three times faster than
the conventional oven and requires no preheating,
which saves on the amount of electricity or fuel used
while cooking, and in turn saves money.

Secondly, the microwave can save time. One of the
microwave's biggest assets is the speed at which it
cooks, and of course any time saved in the kitchen can
be applied to liesure. In our world of today, most
people do not have time to prepare meals in the time—
consuming traditional manner. An example of the time
saved when cooking with the microwave can be seen in
baking a potato. The conventional oven requires at
least forty—five minutes to one hour before a potato
is thoroughly baked. The microwave, on the other
hand, requires no more than eighteen minutes. A beef
roast that requires two hours of baking in a
conventional oven will require only one third that
amount of time in a microwave (and will be juicier).
Time can also be saved by warming food or defrosting
frozen foods in the microwave.

Last, the microwave oven offers convenience. It
can be extremely helpful in serving up meals quickly.
Soup, casseroles, vegetables, or hot drinks can be
heated up in a matter of minutes. Water can be boiled
almost instantly. Futhermore, the amount of dishes to
be washed can be reduced when cooking with a microwave

since one can heat several food items in one dish whereas a conventional oven requires that each type of food be placed in a separate piece of cookware. The automatic timer on the microwave rings to alert you when the food is cooked, and then the oven will automatically shut off. Unlike the microwave, the conventional oven goes right on burning your food once the intended time is up. The microwave is also wonderfully easy to clean. One need no longer bother with messy oven cleaners or scraps of steel wool. Most microwave ovens come with a glass plate that protects you from spills and will easily slide out for fast cleaning. Also it has no greasy oven racks to clean.

Student Essay 5

Prison Rehabilitation Does Not Work

In the past, convicted criminals were automatically sentenced to death. Needless to say, crime was not as much of a growing problem then as it is now. As time went on, the punishment of criminals convicted of serious crimes became lighter as a result of compassionate sociologists and psychologists whose research concluded that harsh punishment was no deterrent to crime. These well-intentioned people wanted to focus attention on rehabilitating the criminal rather than on punishing him more and more severely. "Afterall, the human mind is a terrible thing to waste," was their altruistic attitude. Unfortunately, this altruistic attitude has gotten our nation into the grave situation it is now in. Prison rehabilitaion is a lovely idea, but so is a Utopian society. Both are easy to talk about, but difficult to achieve.

The rehabilitation notion implies that the inmate needs to be changed. His whole idea about life, along with his attitudes, his values, and self—concept has to be changed. This is as far—fetched an idea as trying to convince a zebra to be a leopard. Hardened criminals have a whole different concept about how to live life and what it should be lived for.

If the inmates need to change, the prison is the best place for rehabilitation programs. What rubbish! The environment in which these programs are to be instituted——of aggression, fear, totalitarianism, and exploitation——is what makes the idea of rehabilitation so preposterous.

Many studies of inmate treatment programs have reported that they have failed. For four years Dr. Robert Martinson analyzed and researched all of the different data connected with studies made of prison reform programs between 1945 and 1967. A total of 231 programs designed to rehabilitate convicted criminals were examined critically. Martinson writes, "There is very little evidence in these studies that any prevailing mode of correctional treatment has a decisive effect in reducing the recidivism of convicted offenders." (The Public Interest, p. 49.)

Two different studies came to the conclusion that inmates who were not involved in rehabilitative programs actually did better when released than those who remained involved in the programs. In a Florida study, 193 randomly selected inmates were given work release therapy, in which they were released to work in the outside world and then returned at night. At the end of the study, the inmates that had the "benefit" of the experience had less favorable answers to an attitude test than those who did not participate. (Criminology, Vol II, No. 3, pp. 345–381). In another study, 1,252 Florida inmates released from prison due to a decision by the United States Supreme Court concerning "the right of indigent felons to counsel" (Murton, The Dilemma of Prison Reform, p. 64), were observed for 30 months. The 1,252 inmates that had been released under the Supreme Court decision did not complete their treatment programs and went without the supervision of parole officers. Another group of inmates (the same number), who had completed their treatment programs and were released under the supervision of parole officers, were also studied and compared with the control group. The results indicated that of those released with supervision and counseling, 15.4% returned to prison whereas only 13.6% of those released without supervision or counseling returned to prison. To sum it up, those who received rehabilitative treatment were twice as likely to return to prison! (Murton, p. 64.)

This seems to be convincing evidence that rehabilitation efforts are pointless and even detrimental to the prisoners' attitudes. Rehabilitation is a great idea, but next to impossible as far as achieving it is concerned. I agree with the statement that "a mind is a terrible thing to waste," but we're going at it the wrong way. I feel that we must dig into the psychological reasons for this behavior. If we find out what goes wrong early, we may be able to discourage crime.

Student Essay 6

Boat People

The day was coming to an end on a remote island as beautiful as a painting. The brisk clean wind went past me refreshingly as I sat on the earth-colored sand to admire the lovely natural scenery. I could hear the roar of the crashing waves breaking upon the shore, smell the fresh salt in the air, and felt the moisture in the atmosphere. The orange fiery lines from the sun were radiating away from the horizon. Suddenly the appearance of a small sailboat was looming on the horizon.

The white spot appeared far way on a vast, blue sea surface. The tattered sails fluttered. The seacoast became crowded and animated with people. Suddenly the boat was within reach. Together they tried to pull it in. We discovered that it had sailed from a great distance. The boat was very battered, and we wondered how it could have endured a trip.

I saw nine skinny male survivors lying on the planks of the boat. But one of them still have enough strength to speak to our camp leader. His weak voice came out through his parched, cracked lips that barely moved, like those of a person half frozen from the cold. I looked at his big, glassy eyes. They spoke of such endurance and fear. His skin was cold and clammy. He had the look of a sick person who was barely alive. In addition, his sunken cheeks made him look more terrible than the face of a corpse. His clothes were torn and grimy and spotted with dry blood stains. The dirt and sweat mixed together created an unendurable fetid odor which emanated from him so strongly that I was inclined to vomit. The rest of the survivors were in the same awful condition. These nine men were immediately carried to the emergency room in the sick bay of our camp. They now had a chance for life. They had survived.

After a while, I noticed that the seaside became tranquil. The moon came up over the mountain and shone on the sea like a bright new light.

PART FIVE

Handbook
Basic grammar
Punctuation
Mechanics
Effective sentences

Basic grammar

A command of basic grammar is as essential to writers as water is to fish. No matter how clever and creative a writer you are, if you cannot string coherent sentences together, use verbs and nouns properly, and make pronouns agree with their antecedents, your writing will inevitably appear amateurish. Yet the odd thing is that you are likely to receive little, if any, praise for mastering grammar. "Nobody ever admired an orator for using correct grammar," wrote Cicero. "They only laugh at him if his grammar is bad." So it is, too, with writers. They are expected to write grammatically, but get no glory for doing it.

It follows that the explanations of grammar, punctuation, mechanics, and style in this section may not help you to write exceptionally or even well. They will, however, help you to write correctly. To write well, you need to be grammatical and imaginative; to write exceptionally, you need to be grammatical, imaginative, precise, colorful, witty, and inspired. But no matter what level of excellence you hope to achieve in your writing, mastering grammar is an indispensable first step.

1. Parts of speech

Words are the smallest grammatical parts of a sentence. Every word in a sentence performs a particular function by which it can be classified. These functions are carried out by eight parts of speech. Originally devised by Dionysius Thrax, a Greek grammarian, in 100 B.C., these categories have come down to us relatively intact.

The eight parts of speech are *verbs, nouns, adjectives, adverbs, pronouns, prepositions, conjunctions,* and *interjections.* Verbs, nouns, adjectives, and adverbs comprise almost all of the words in the dictionary. But even though the other four account for less than one percent of all words, they are used again and again in sentences.

1a. Verbs

The verb is the most crucial word in the sentence since it expresses an action, a process, or a state of being and since without it no sentence is complete. Verbs express commands, make statements about subjects, or link the subject to some idea about the subject.

Sit }	Verbs express commands.
Stop! }	(The subject *you* is understood.)

God loves }	
Serpents hiss. }	Verbs make statements about the subjects.
Fish swim. }	

John is hungry. }	Verbs link the subject to
The children feel tired. }	some idea about the subject.

Most verbs express action or process. Linking verbs express a state of being. In addition to all forms of the verb *be,* they include *seem, feel, grow, look, sound, taste.*

Action:	The cow *jumped* over the moon.
Process:	The clock *ticked.*
State of being:	He *is* happy.
	We *felt* sick.

The verbs in the examples above are complete in a single word, but others include one or more auxiliary (helping) words, thus forming a verb phrase:

The clouds *had disappeared.* (*had* is an auxiliary word.)
I *should* never *have taken* the money. (*Should* and *have* are auxiliary words.)

NOTE: Neither gerunds nor participles function as complete verbs, but more about them in 2c (2). *Verbal phrases.*

---

(1) Tense

Because actions take place at different times—in the present, past, or future—verbs can be adjusted to reflect this fact. The six tenses are:

Present tense expresses actions that happen now or that seem forever true:

I *am eating* breakfast.
John *likes* to eat.
Roses *are* beautiful.

Past tense expresses an action happening sometime in the past:

Nan *ate* all the cherries.
Jack *sent* me these roses.

Future tense expresses an action that will happen sometime in the future.

Will you *buy* some more cherries?
The roses *will die* soon.

NOTE: It has become popular to use *shall* and *will* interchangeably. Nevertheless, purists of the English language make the following distinctions. To express a future action:

I *shall* eat	We *shall* eat
You *will* eat	You *will* eat
He/she/it *will* eat	They *will* eat

To express determination:

I *will* eat	We *will* eat (We are determined to eat)
You *shall* eat	You *shall* eat
He/she/it *shall* eat	They *shall* eat

In the case of questions in the first person, *will* and *shall* are not interchangeable:

Shall we stay till 9:00 or *shall* we leave now?

but

Tomorrow we *will* (or *shall*) stay till 9:00.

Present perfect tense indicates that the action has taken place in the past but lasted until now.

Nan *has eaten* all the cherries.
The roses *have lasted* ten days.

Past perfect tense indicates that an action in the past took place before another past action:

> Nan *had eaten* all the cherries before the guests arrived.
> The lawyer *had gone* to court before June 15.

The *future perfect tense,* which is not often used, indicates a future action that will take place before another future action:

> Nan *will have eaten* all the cherries by lunch time.
> The roses *will have died* before the gardner arrives.

NOTE: Most verbs form the past tense and past participle by adding *ed* or *d* to the infinitive: *walk, walked, walked; believe, believed, believed.* Many verbs, however, form their principal parts through an internal vowel change *or* a final consonant change (*drink, drank, drunk; build, built, built*) or by not changing at all (*let, let, let*). If you are in doubt, check the dictionary, where you will find the principal parts of verbs listed. The principal parts of the following verbs are commonly misused:

> lie, lay, lain (I *lie* in the sun.)
> lay, laid, laid (He *laid* the book on the table.)
> sit, sat, sat (The baby *sits* in her crib.)
> set, set, set (John *has set* the vase on the shelf.)
> rise, rose, risen (We *rise* for prayer.)
> raise, raised, raised (Two men *raised* the flag.)

---

(2) Voice

Voice indicates who or what is doing the acting and who or what is receiving the action. Voice is either *active* or *passive.* In the active voice the subject always performs the action:

> Helen drank a gallon of water. (*Helen* is the subject.)

In the passive voice the subject always is acted upon:

> A gallon of water was drunk by Helen. (*Gallon* is the subject.)

Sometimes the passive voice omits the doer of an action:

> A gallon of water was drunk.

NOTE: Only transitive verbs (see next section) have voice.

(3) Forms

Verb forms are *transitive* or *intransitive*. A verb is transitive if it requires an object:

> Maria *discovered* an error. (*Error* serves as direct object.)

Occasionally a transitive verb will take a direct, as well as an indirect, object:

> She gave her sister a sandwich. (*Sandwich* is the direct object; *sister* is the indirect object.)

A verb is *intransitive* if it does not need an object to complete its meaning:

> The orchestra *played* beautifully.

NOTE: Some verbs are transitive only (*take, enjoy*), while others are intransitive only (*frown, giggle*). However, many verbs can function either way:

> He sang loudly; he sang an opera.

1b. Nouns

A noun is the name of a person, place, thing, idea, or event:

Persons: Dr. Wells, girl, Becky
Places: Chicago, heaven, school, world, park
Things: table, rice, chess, history, politics
Ideas: love, fear, humility, patriotism, stinginess
Events: war, trip, Christmas, Monday

Common nouns represent the names of general classes of persons, places, or things:

> boxer, state, writer, cereal

Proper nouns are always capitalized and name a particular person, place, or thing:

> Mohammed Ali, Michigan, the Constitution, Lake Tahoe

Compound nouns are proper nouns or common nouns that consist of more than one word and function as a single unit:

> South Africa, exchange rate, sunset, headache

1c. Pronouns

A pronoun is used in place of a noun. It is clearer and more concise to say "The man took off *his* coat" than "The man took off *the man's* coat." The antecedent of a pronoun is the word it replaces. Every pronoun must be in the same gender (masculine or feminine), case (subject of the sentence or object of the verb), and number (singular or plural) as its antecedent. Thus, "We saw the girl" will become "We saw *her*" because *girl* is feminine, object of the verb, and singular.

Pronouns may be grouped into seven categories:

Personal pronouns stand for someone or something specific: *I, you, he, she, it, we, you, they.*

Demonstrative pronouns point to nouns: *this, that, these, those.* They can be used as pronouns or as adjectives.

Pronoun: I reject *this.*
Adjective: I reject *this* idea.

Indefinite pronouns are unspecific: *anyone, everyone, each, someone.*

Interrogative pronouns ask a question: *who? what? which?* (Who destroyed the tree?)

Relative pronouns relate back to an antecedent (the banker *who,* the table *that,* the story *which*): *who, whom, those, which, that.*

Intensive pronouns emphasize: *myself, yourself, himself, ourselves, yourselves, themselves.* (I drove it *myself.*)

Reflexive pronouns function as objects or complements. They always refer to the person or thing named in the subject:

She drives *herself* to work every day.
The hot-water heater blew *itself* to smithereens.
I shall buy myself a car.

To use personal pronouns correctly, it is necessary to distinguish among their *subjective, objective,* and *possessive* cases. (See also 7. *Pronoun Case.*) The following table makes these differences clear:

SUBJECTIVE	OBJECTIVE	POSSESSIVE
I	me	mine
you	you	yours
he, she, it	him, her, it	his, hers, its
we	us	ours
you	you	yours
they	them	theirs

NOTE: A special case is *it* or *their* used as an expletive to postpone the sentence subject:

It is best that John be present.
There will be two books on the shelf.

1d. Adjectives

The adjective describes or limits nouns or pronouns. This describing or limiting is referred to as *modifying*. Generally, adjectives appear next to the nouns they modify:

The *green* sweater cost *twenty-five* dollars.

However, adjectives used with linking verbs (see 1a. *Verbs*) may occur after the noun and verb and are called predicate adjectives:

Dr. Jones is so *competent, thorough,* and *kind.*

Many adjectives are formed by adding suffixes such as *-al, -able, -ible, -ative, -ish, -ous,* or *-ic* to certain verbs or nouns:

VERB	ADJECTIVE
digest	digestible
communicate	communicative

NOUN	ADJECTIVE
fame	famous
penny	penniless

NOTES: 1. *A, an,* and *the* are special kinds of adjectives called articles.
2. Demonstrative pronouns often function as adjectives:

Pass me *that* napkin.
This book is Mary's.

1e. Adverbs

An adverb can modify verbs, adjectives, or other adverbs. Generally, adverbs are formed by adding the suffix *-ly* to an adjective:
The following examples illustrate how adverbs are used:

ADJECTIVE	ADVERB
normal	normally
quick	quickly
animated	animatedly

She moved *swiftly.* (*Swiftly* modifies the verb *moved.*)
It is an *exceptionally* boring game. (*Exceptionally* modifies the adjective *boring.*)
The queen whispered *very* softly. (*Very* modifies the adverb *softly.*)

The usual function of the adverb is to say *when, where, how,* and *to what extent* something happened:

> She came *soon.* (When did she come?)
> He put the book *there.* (Where did he put the book?)
> She fought *furiously.* (How did she fight?)
> Our love will last *forever.* (To what extent will our love last?)

See also 1g. *Conjunctions, conjunctive adverbs.*

NOTE: Both adjectives and adverbs can be used in three forms: *positive, comparative,* and *superlative.* The positive form is the unchanged adjective or adverb; the comparative form indicates *more* or *less;* the superlative form indicates *most* or *least.* Here are some examples:

Positive: He spoke *loudly.* (adverb)
She is a *loud* person. (adjective)
Comparative: He spoke *louder.* (adverb)
She is a *louder* person. (adjective)
Superlative: He spoke *loudest.* (adverb)
She is the *loudest* person. (adjective)

The following forms are irregular:

Adjectives

POSITIVE	COMPARATIVE	SUPERLATIVE
good	better	best
bad	worse	worst

Adverbs

POSITIVE	COMPARATIVE	SUPERLATIVE
well	better	best
badly	worse	worst

Be sure that you distinguish between *good* and *well, bad* and *badly:*

Wrong: He plays tennis *good.* (adjective)
 Right: He plays tennis *well.* (adverb)

Wrong: Sam burned his finger *bad.* (adjective)
 Right: Sam burned his finger *badly.* (adverb)

When discussing health, use *well* and *bad:*

> Jack feels *well.*
> John feels *bad.*

When discussing feelings, use *good* and *bad:*

> I feel *good* about my job.
> He feels *bad* about the misunderstanding.

1f. Prepositions

A preposition shows the relationship between nouns, pronouns, verbs, adjectives, and adverbs:

> John stood *behind* the doors. (*Behind* indicates relationship between John and the doors.)

A less complicated definition of the preposition is any word that describes what an airplane can do when approaching clouds. The airplane can go *by, across, above, below, into, between, over, through, inside, beyond, from, to* the clouds, among other things. However, not all prepositions qualify under this definition. *Concerning, regarding, of, for,* or *during* are examples of prepositions that do not.

A few prepositions consist of more than one word: *in spite of, because of, on account of, instead of, together with, in regard to.*

NOTE: A preposition and its object make up a *prepositional phrase:*

> They strolled *inside* the garden. (prepositional phrase)

1g. Conjunctions

A conjunction connects words, phrases, and clauses. Incoherent or mispunctuated sentences often result from misused conjunctions. There are three kinds of conjunctions: *coordinating, subordinating,* and *conjunctive adverbs* (also called *logical connectives*).

Coordinating conjunctions (*and, but, nor, for*) join words, phrases, and clauses of equal importance:

Words: Silk *and* velvet are my favorite materials.
Phrases: Living in pain *or* dying in peace was his choice.
Clauses: George continued to make money, *but* he was miserable.

NOTE: A special type of coordinating conjunction is the *correlative conjunction,* which also joins elements of equal importance but occurs only in pairs:

> *not only . . . but also*
> *neither . . . nor*
> *both . . . and*

Not only did he buy a Porsche, *but also* he paid cash for it.
Neither she *nor* her husband appeared at the reception.
Both my father *and* my grandfather agree with me.

Subordinating conjunctions (such as *if, because, when, since, where, while, whereas, after, before, until, as if*) are used to join subordinate clauses with independent clauses, as:

Felice studies *because* she is ambitious.
If it rains, we must buy an umbrella.

However, place a subordinating conjunction before an independent clause and you will have a *sentence fragment*—a transformation often overlooked by student writers:

The man stood at the door. (independent clause)
While the man stood at the door. (fragment caused by subordinating conjunction)

Such a fragment can be corrected by attaching it to an independent clause:

While the man stood at the door, the dog barked.
The dog barked *while* the man stood at the door.

See also 3. *Sentence fragments.*

NOTE: Relative pronouns can function as subordinating conjunctions to introduce adjective or noun clauses (see 2d):

We blamed the man *who* was driving without a license.
The house *that* she had just finished paying for burned down.

Conjunctive adverbs (such as however, consequently, moreover, besides, on the other hand, that is to say, yet, furthermore, nevertheless, meanwhile, indeed, anyhow, hence, henceforth, then) are adverbs used to connect independent clauses. Always place a semicolon before and a comma after a conjunctive adverb that connects two independent clauses:

The tickets are three dollars apiece; *however,* members of the club pay only two dollars.
The sky was dark and cloudy; *nevertheless,* we pressed onward.

NOTES: 1. A comma should be used before and after the conjunctive adverb when the conjunctive adverb is parenthetical:

My friend drove her car to the party; I, *however,* took the bus.
The other half of the restaurant, *meanwhile,* stood empty and forsaken.

2. The use of *yet* and *so* as coordinating conjunctions has been more or less accepted in informal writing. However, careful writers use *yet* only as a logical connective, and seldom use the anemic *so.*

1h. Interjections

An interjection is used to indicate emotion. Usually, interjections have no grammatical connection with other words in the sentence. Interjections may be either mild or forceful. If forceful, they are followed by an exclamation point.

Mild: *Ah,* you kept your promise.
Well, let's move ahead.
Forceful: *Oh!* I lost my wallet!
Phew! That's hard work!

We began this discussion by saying that a part of speech can be classified according to the way it functions in a sentence. It follows that the same word may serve as a different part of speech in different sentences. Here are some examples:

The stairway contains one broken *step.* (noun)
Please do not let her *step* in the mud. (verb)

The man accompanied her *inside.* (adverb)
Her *inside* pocket is torn. (adjective)
The teacher disappeared *inside* the room. (preposition)

Exercise keeps a person limber. (noun)
They *exercise* every day. (verb)
We need an *exercise* room. (adjective)

Exercises

Exercise 1: Parts of speech
In the sentences below, name the part of speech of each italicized word.

MODEL: The plum was *overly* ripe.

Answer: **Adverb**

1. The priest picked up the book and *caressed* it.
2. The English tried to find a *northern* route.
3. The people were poor, *but* they wore fur pelts.
4. I don't care for *this.*

5. *If* he is allowed to dominate her, he will.
6. He had come on deck *without* notice.
7. There was not enough *space* for the food.
8. The Breeze *had wafted* a strand of hair into her eyes.
9. In time, he *will explain* himself to all of us.
10. Her name was remembered *because of* her book.
11. My husband has five *living* sisters.
12. Why hurt a human being just to please *someone?*
13. The musket shot was aimed *directly* at the frigate's lower sails.
14. She was asked to stay *exactly* alongside.
15. *Wow!* What a beautiful pair of shoes!
16. *Not only* did he say the word in private, *but* he *also* repeated it in front of the crowd.
17. The *cold* was unbearable to anyone from the south.
18. The ballet dancers made one *final* effort before the curtain went down.
19. Mr. Thornburg swam *for* one hour and felt better.
20. *Proudly* she saluted the flag.
21. He blamed *himself* for all of the year's troubles.
22. The fish was white, slimy, and almost *tasteless.*
23. *Well,* perhaps he should take some Vitamin C.
24. The Japanese lady *had waved* her fan and had smiled encouragingly.
25. You have a terrible temper; *nevertheless,* you will make a good leader.
26. *Perhaps* she would suit another company better than mine.
27. Martha had remained thoughtful and *reserved.*
28. They discussed the *feasibility* of a full-scale war.
29. The old woman looked away *and* scowled.
30. In some countries, *it* is considered polite to sip soup from a bowl.

Exercise 1: Parts of speech

Identify the part of speech of each boldface word in the following paragraph.

It was **evening.** Around the low **fire, inside** the **paramount** chief's hut **sat** the **leading** men of the village, **each** swaying to the **rhythmic** tom-tom of the tribal drum. The wrinkled **witch doctor** squatted **near** the chief, **but** he seemed **totally unafraid as** his cunning, birdlike eyes restlessly **sought** the attention of **each** man. His hands were deftly arranging some tiger teeth **and** chicken bones; **however, he** was obviously **completely aware** of the **solemnity** of the occasion. "**Oh,** witch doctor, **we are listening,**" a voice suddenly murmured. The **wrinkled old** man drew his basket of charms **close to** his crossed legs. He **then** threw some charms on the ground **while** he mumbled a monotonous formula in his untranslatable tribal dialect.

2. Sentences

The parts of speech, when put together in certain ways, constitute a sentence. All sentences have a *subject* and a *predicate*. A working knowledge of these components is useful to both the beginnng and the veteran writer.

2a. Subjects and predicates

The subject is what a speaker or writer makes a statement about; the predicate is what is said about the subject. A *noun,* or group of words functioning as a noun, makes up the core of each subject; a *verb,* or group of words functioning as a verb, makes up the core of each predicate. The essence of a sentence may then be said to consist—in its simplest form—of two words, a noun and a verb:

NOUN/SUBJECT	VERB/PREDICATE
People	think.
Bees	sting.
Dogs	bite.

In all three examples, a verb (predicate) makes an assertion about a noun (subject). This basic division applies even if a sentence is written as a question. *Where is my book?* can be divided into subject and predicate just as readily as the sentence *My book is there.* At the heart of both constructions are a noun and a verb—that is, a part about which something is said and a part that either asks or asserts something about a subject.

The three examples given above illustrate sentences in their most rudimentary form: a *simple subject* and a *simple predicate* with a single word functioning in each role. The *complete subject* and *complete predicate* consist of all those words that are a part of the subject and all those that are part of the predicate. Here are some examples:

SIMPLE SUBJECT	SIMPLE PREDICATE
People	think.

COMPLETE SUBJECT	COMPLETE PREDICATE
People of all creeds, ages and nationalities	think about life, love, and death.
People of all creeds, ages, nationalities, no matter what their life-styles or politics,	think about life, love, death, and other eternal questions.

SIMPLE SUBJECT	SIMPLE PREDICATE
He	ran.

COMPLETE SUBJECT	COMPLETE PREDICATE
Grabbing his overcoat and umbrella, he	ran away from the house as fast as he could.

The ability to recognize the complete subjects and complete predicates of sentences is especially useful in properly punctuating them.

2b. Complements

A complement is a word or group of words that completes the meaning of a verb. Complements are divided into the following categories: direct object, indirect object, subject complement, and object complement.

(1) Direct object

A direct object answers the question *What?* or *Whom?* in connection with a verb. In the following sentences, the direct object is italicized:

> The dog chewed the *rug*. (What did the dog chew?)
> He married *Cynthia*. (Whom did he marry?)

(2) Indirect object

The indirect object usually precedes the direct object, and tells *to whom* or *for whom* (or *to what* or *for what*) the action of a verb is done. In the following sentences, the indirect objects are italicized:

> The salesperson gave the *man* a blank look. (To whom did the salesperson give a blank look?)
> Her parents ordered *her* a Datsun. (From whom did her parents order a Datsun?)

(3) Subject complement

The subject complement completes the sense of the verb by further explaining the subject. The following qualify as linking verbs that can be completed by subject complements:

> Forms of the verb *to be: am, are, is, was, were, been*
> Verbs having to do with the senses: *smell, look, taste, feel, sound,* and so forth
> Certain other verbs: *seem, appear, become, remain, grow, prove,* and so forth

The subject complements are italicized in the following sentences:

> Most Spaniards are *Catholics*.
> That animal seems to be a *wolf*.

In addition to nouns, adjectives and pronouns can serve as subject complements:

> The blanket feels *warm* and *comforting.*
> My perfume smells *exotic.*
> He will not admit that it was *she.*

(4) Object complement

The object complement further explains the direct object. In the following example, the object complements are italicized:

> The mob called the criminal a cold-blooded *murderer.*

An adjective can also serve as an object complement:

> The thought of going home made her *depressed.* (*Depressed* modifies the direct object *her.*)

2c. Phrases

A phrase is a group of words, usually without subject and verb, that expresses a thought but is not a complete statement. Phrases can be classified as: prepositional, verbal, absolute, and appositive.

(1) Prepositional phrases

A prepositional phrase consists of a preposition followed by a noun (or pronoun) and any words that modify that noun (or pronoun). The prepositional phrase usually functions as an *adjective* or *adverb*. In the following sentences, the prepositional phrases are italicized:

> Jane left home *without a jacket.* (The prepositional phrase modified the verb *left* by specifying how Jane left home. It therefore functions as an adverb.)
>
> *Behind the bush* huddled a savage dog. (The prepositonal phrase modifies the verb *huddled* by specifying where the dog huddled. It therefore functions as an adverb.)
>
> The slipper *under the bed* was too big. (The prepositional phrase modifies the noun *slipper* by specifying which slipper was too big—the one *under the bed.* It therefore functions as an adjective.)

(2) Verbal phrases

A verbal phrase consists of a verbal and all the words immediately related to it. Do not confuse verbals with verbs. Verbals are derived from verbs, but make no statement about a subject. They function as *nouns, adjectives,* or *adverbs.* There are three kinds of verbals: *infinitive, gerund,* and *participle.*

An *infinitive* is used as a noun, an adjective, or an adverb and is usually made up of the construction *to* + the present form of the verb.

To study is smart. (noun)
This is the way *to study.* (adjective)
John left *to study.* (adverb)

A *gerund* is used only as a noun and has an *ing* ending:

Skiing is my favorite sport. (noun as subject)
She hates *gardening.* (noun as direct object)
Their goal is *making* money. (noun as subject complement)
Before *stopping* he wants to finish. (noun as object of preposition)

A *participle* is used as an adjective. Participles are either present (ending in *-ing*) or past (commonly ending in *-d, -ed, -n, -en.* In the case of irregular verbs, vowels may change, as in *brought* and *clung.*) Participles and gerunds can be distinguished from one another by their functions in a sentence. The gerund functions as a noun; the participle, as an adjective:

Suffering is a part of life. (gerund)
The *suffering* child was hospitalized. (participle)

Like verbals, verbal phrases are either infinitive, gerund, or participle:

(a) Infinitive An infinitive phrase consists of an infinitive followed by its modifiers. The infinitive phrase may function as an adjective, adverb, or noun. In the following sentences, the infinitive phrases have been italicized:

ADJECTIVE

The comedian used *appropriate* humor.

INFINITIVE PHRASE AS ADJECTIVE

The comedian used humor *to match the occasion.*

ADVERB

The lecturer spoke *informatively.*

INFINITIVE PHRASE AS ADVERB

The lecturer spoke *to inform the audience.*

NOUN

Larceny tempts many people.

INFINITIVE PHRASE AS NOUN

To steal money is a common temptation.

(b) Gerund A gerund phrase consists of a gerund and its modifiers. The gerund phrase functions as a noun. (Although a gerund and a participle may share the same *-ing* ending, the gerund always functions as a noun.) In the following sentences, the gerund phrases have been italicized:

Chewing gum with her mouth open was her worst habit. (The gerund phrase functions as a noun and as subject of the verb *was*. Notice that the entire phrase, like all nouns, may be replaced by a pronoun: *It* was her worst habit.)

The reporter praised *the guitarist's loud and regular twanging.* (The gerund phrase functions as the object of the verb *praised*.)

(c) Participial A participial phrase consists of a participle followed by modifiers. It functions as an adjective. In the following sentences, the participial phrases have been italicized:

Crying in pain, the football player limped away. (The participial phrase modifies the compound noun *football player*.)

The windows of the car *parked in the driveway* were shattered to bits. (The participial phrase modifies the noun *car* by specifying which car was meant—the one *parked in the driveway*.)

Bent by old age, the man struggled on. (The participial phrase modifies the noun *man*.)

(3) Absolute phrases

Absolute phrases stand grammatically independent ("absolutely" alone). They have no identifiable grammatical link to the rest of the sentence. Nor are they linked to an independent clause by a subordinating word. Absolute constructions are therefore difficult to identify and easy to misuse. Here are some examples:

The diver having finished his dive, we left for tea.
All things being equal, tomorrow will be our big day.
Considering the state of the budget, the hearings should be continued.

An absolute construction should not be confused with a dangling participial phrase. Here are some examples to clarify the difference between them:

The meeting having gone as planned, we broke for lunch. (absolute construction)

Wrong: *Having met for five hours,* lunch was then served. (Dangling participle implies "lunch" had met for five hours.)

Right: *Having met for five hours,* we were then served lunch. (Participial phrase modifies "we.")

See also 26. *Dangling modifiers.*

(4) Appositive phrases

An appositive phrase is a word or phrase placed beside another word whose meaning it expands or explains. The appositive must always be syntactically parallel to the word it stands in apposition to—that is, it must be the same part of speech and must fulfill the same grammatical function:

(a) Appositive as subject:

Paul's father, *a wealthy businessman,* was forced into bankruptcy. (*Father* and *businessman* are both subjects.)

(b) Appositive as object:

He rejected his first love, *oil painting.* (*Love* and *oil painting* are both objects.)

(c) Appositive as adjective:

He spoke in a paternalistic, that is, *authoritative,* manner. (*Paternalistic* and *authoritative* are both adjectives.)

(d) Appositive as adverb:

The essay was proofread carefully—*with utmost precision.* (*Carefully* and *with utmost precision* are both adverbials.)

Think of appositives as abbreviated or reduced clauses because they can be expanded into clauses by using some form of the verb *be:*

His father, *who was a wealthy businessman,* was forced into bankruptcy.
He rejected his first love, *which was oil painting.*
He spoke in a paternalistic manner, *which was an authoritative manner.*
The essay was proofread carefully, *meaning that it was proofread with utmost precision.*

2d. Clauses

A clause is a group of words containing a subject and a predicate. If the words make sense by themselves, they are said to constitute an independent clause. A clause that does not make sense by itself is called a dependent clause.

(1) Independent clauses
What makes a clause independent is its ability to stand alone and make complete sense. Here are some examples:

The man had bad breath.
People need to buy health insurance.
Fairy tales are important reading for children.

(2) Dependent clauses
A clause that does not make sense by itself is called a dependent clause since it must "depend" on an independent clause to complete its meaning. Here are some examples:

Who was standing next to me
Even though they have Social Security
That fairy tales teach about good and evil

Attached to appropriate independent clauses, however, these dependent clauses become grammatically complete:

The man who was *standing next to me* had bad breath.
Even though they have Social Security, people need health insurance.
That fairy tales teach about good and evil makes them important reading for children.

Dependent clauses can be recognized by the connectives binding them to independent clauses. These connectives are always subordinating words such as the subordinating conjunctions *although, even though, despite, what, that, who, which, when, since, before, after, if, as, because* that introduce adverbial clauses, or the relative pronouns *who, what, that, which* that introduce noun and adjective clauses. (See also 1g. *Conjunctions.*) Dependent clauses can also function as grammatical units in a sentence, playing the equivalent role of a noun, an adjective, or an adverb.

(a) **Noun clauses** A noun clause is a subordinate clause that acts as a noun.

Noun clause as subject:

What he demanded frightened the pilot. (The noun clause is the subject of the verb *frightened.* As with all nouns, a pronoun—in this case *it, this,* or *that* could be substituted for the entire noun clause.)

Noun clause as direct object:

I request *that you clean up your room.*

Noun clause as indirect object:

The government will give *whoever is hungry* food stamps.

Noun clause as objects of a preposition:

She longs for *whatever is right.*

Noun clause as subject complement:

Rest is *what he needs.*

Noun clause as appositive:

We suspected the object, *whatever it was.*

(b) **Adjective clauses** An adjective clause modifies either a noun or a pronoun in a sentence:

He remembered the place *where they had first kissed.* (The italicized adjective clause modifies the noun *place.*)

Look at the flower *she picked yesterday.* (The italicized adjective clause modifies the noun flower.)

(c) **Adverb clauses** An adverb clause modifies a verb, adjective, or adverb in the sentence. It may occur in various positions in a sentence, at the end, the beginning, or in the middle. An adverb clause is usually introduced by a subordinating conjunction:

ADVERB	ADVERB CLAUSE
She blew the trumpet *loudly.*	She blew the trumpet *so that everyone could hear.*
Later he made tea.	*When the water boiled,* he made tea.

ADVERB	ADVERB CLAUSE
Everyone *here* plays the guitar.	Everyone *where I live* plays the guitar.

As you can see from the above examples, the way to identify the function of a cluase is to see what part of speech may be substituted for it. A noun clause may be replaced by an equivalent noun or by a pronoun; an adjective clause may be replaced by an adjective; and an adverb clause may be replaced by an adverb.

2e. Kinds of sentences

Sentences are grouped into four types according to the number and kinds of clauses involved: simple, compound, complex, and compound-complex. A knowledge of the different sentence types is useful to anyone who aims for sentence variety and correct punctuation.

(1) Simple sentences
A simple sentence has one subject and one predicate:

Jim is getting married.
We will sail tomorrow.

NOTE: A simple sentence may have two or more nouns as subject and two or more verbs as predicate:

The *birds* in the sky and the *fish* in the sea add to life's beauty.
(*Birds* and *fish* form a compound subject.)

The entire town *praised* and *thanked* the mayor. (*Praised* and *thanked* form a compound predicate.)

(2) Compound sentences

A compound sentence consists of at least two independent clauses.

> The houses are tall, but the streets are narrow.
> Behind the fence is a garden, and beyond the garden lies a lake.
> We sang songs and offered prayers, and we waited for rescue.

(3) Complex sentences

A complex sentence consists of one independent clause and one or more dependent clauses. The dependent clauses are italicized in the following examples:

> Everyone arrived *when the sun came out.*
> *If he were to inherit a million dollars,* he would give it all to people *who work on farms.*

(4) Compound-complex sentences

A compound-complex sentence consists of two or more independent clauses and one or more dependent clauses. The independent clauses are in boldface and the dependent clauses are italicized:

> **He refused to enter the house** *unless I went with him;* yet, *while we were inside,* **he showed no fear.**
> *When they pay their gas bill,* **they will be happy** *that they bought the car,* but **they will never thank me for my advice.**

Exercises

Exercise 2a: Complete subjects and complete predicates

In the sentences below, separate the complete subject from the complete predicate by a vertical line.

> MODEL: The country road | stretched into the distance.

1. The traveler, a tall man in his late thirties, stood looking up into the branches of the oak tree.
2. Now old and bent, his father had loved to sit beneath the bridge.
3. Wandering about the campus with Francis, he remembered suddenly a particular summer morning.
4. The pattern of the coming year and of his behavior was set.
5. Like most religious fanatics, she had absolutely no sense of humor.
6. Its remarkable beauty did not lie only in its bright glitter.

7. Mrs. McClosky, a guest of the mayor, refused to ride in a car driven by a chauffeur.
8. Facing each other in front of the fire, two red sofas always waited for us every evening.
9. A hint of anger or coldness in his voice would keep her in the depths of despair for weeks on end.
10. The old man arose hurriedly and disappeared into the woods.

Exercise 2a: Simple subjects and simple predicates

In the following sentences, underline the simple subject once and the simple predicate twice.

MODEL: Moved almost to tears, I whispered back.

1. Perhaps his answer was an assent of the heart rather than of the mind.
2. Next year, too many people will visit the Vatican.
3. According to the Bible, "A prating fool will come to ruin."
4. The pilot was landing the plane during wind, rain, and hail.
5. Beside the president stood the secretary of state.
6. Gentlemen, please take your seats.
7. Did you remember the poem on the wall of the library?
8. John simply could not reject his past.
9. By jumping into the water first, he avoided being pushed by his friends.
10. There are always two sides to a question.

Exercise 2b: Complements

In the sentences below, decide whether the italicized words are direct objects, indirect objects, object complements, or subject complements.

MODEL: More and more, he appeared to be *alone.*

Answer: **Subject complement**

1. She had gone to bring the *eggs* from the henhouse.
2. Spring is a *time* of glorious magic.
3. The children considered him *king* of the block.
4. I had learned a great *principle* of the way grief affects people.
5. Because of its timing, the visit was *oppressive.*
6. Without further thought, Joanne labeled the teacher a *Communist.*
7. We could have simply given *him* a pile of money, but he needed attention and love.
8. To me, her thoughts seemed *nuggets* of gold.
9. Being a respectful man, he gave our *flag* a brisk salute.
10. While singing cheerfully, he stirred the *pot* of soup on the fire.

Exercise 2c: Phrases

In each of the sentences below, indicate what kind of phrase the italicized words are:

MODEL: *To own one's home in California* is extremely expensive.

Answer: **Infinitive phrase**

1. *Hoping not to be called on duty,* I snuggled up in my blanket.
2. *The cub meeting having adjourned,* the students trudged home.
3. He heard the sound *of boots marching down the corridor.*
4. The rain, *little more than a cool mist,* refreshed us immensely.
5. *To say goodbye without hope of seeing one another again* was heartrending.
6. *Cooking from scratch* is becoming a lost art.
7. More than anything else, we wanted *to know our neighbors across the street.*
8. *Playing poker* did not interest him in the least.
9. We looked at Sylvia, *a radiant young woman in her white gown.*
10. We lived *in the community of Whiting Woods.*

Exercise 2d: Independent and dependent clauses

In the sentences below, enclose the dependent clauses in parentheses and underline the independent clauses.

MODEL: (That Carl was not musical) disappointed his parents; however, they bought a piano (because they never lost hope.)

1. He had never doubted that the vessel was westward bound, nor had he ever believed that it would withstand a week of stormy waters.
2. The thought of that wonderful homemade bread conjured up images of a mother who worked day and night so that her family could be well fed.
3. Somehow her parents had instilled in her a clear idea of everything that is honorable.
4. If they wanted to remain allies, they were running a terrible risk.
5. At the same time, we met another friend, Bernard Townsend, witty, intelligent, handsome, who loved the poetry of John Donne.
6. We began, hardly knowing we were doing it, to revise our opinion of the strikers who had suffered so much.
7. Our fundamental assumption, which we had been foolish enough to consider intelligent insight, had been that all Christian church members were rigid and unwilling to think through important issues that affect a citizen's ethical commitments.
8. If they had been asked what they meant when they spoke of life on another planet, they would have answered with pure nonsense.

9. The Benedictine monks built the long, lovely buildings that are still part of one college quadrangle at Oxford University, where John received his degree in 1978.

10. Another reason for not skiing faster was that she was exhausted; however, her companions did not realize her fatigue and kept goading her on until she sat down in the snow and cried with frustration.

Exercise 2d: Identifying types of dependent clauses

In the sentences below, underline each dependent clause and indicate if it is an adjective clause, an adverbial clause, or a noun clause.

> MODEL: We decided to study the painting that had been shipped from New York.
>
> Answer: Adjective clause

1. The truth was that she had heard that tune before.
2. While he loved her desperately, he did not want to give up his job for her.
3. The problem that had been solved yesterday loomed up twice as big today.
4. It has been said that the fourth dimension is time and duration.
5. As a nun, she went where life would be calm and tranquil.
6. The disease, with all of its suffering, would return unless we could find the right specialist.
7. The friend from whom she had received the book never contacted her in the years to come.
8. The job was much more difficult and exhausting that she had expected.
9. The point is to admit candidly what bothers you.
10. Did you spend the entire day looking for the thief who stole your wallet?

Exercise 2e: Kinds of sentences

Identify each sentence below as simple, compound, complex, or compound-complex.

> MODEL: When the great tree came down, it left an empty space against the sky.
>
> Answer: Complex sentence

1. I was conscious of a sort of amazement that a steak could taste so good.
2. They had decided from the beginning to reach out and draw in all of the richness of this great university around them.
3. I did not admit it, but I was beginning to love poetry.

4. She stuck five-dollar bills into the drawer and then she escaped through the front door without leaving a note about where she was going.

5. His grandfather on his mother's side and his grandfather on his father's side were not at all the same, for the former was educated at Princeton whereas the latter had no formal education beyond the fifth grade.

6. When she looked up into those branches filled with rust- and gold-colored autumn leaves, she wanted to stay in New England forever.

7. War was no longer merely a rumor circulated by adventurers and fanatics in an attempt to get some attention.

8. It would seem that a career in the theater requires both an emotional and intellectual commitment.

9. He had not rejected the offer; he merely had not decided yet.

10. Our tacit understanding was that whoever went to the library would pick up the book.

3. Sentence fragments (frag)

A fragment is a phrase or dependent clause capitalized and punctuated as though it were a complete sentence:

> An interesting book from the library.
> Who screamed in a loud voice.

These fragments are incomprehensible by themselves although they are written as if they were complete sentences. The easiest way to correct a fragment in your own writing is to add enough words to make the fragment into an independent clause. In the following examples, words have been added to make each fragment a complete sentence:

> I am reading an interesting book from the library.
> The child who screamed in a loud voice was frightened by a nightmare.

Sometimes, the correction can be made by adding the fragment to a preceding or a following independent clause:

Wrong: Ken might get a job. *If he will contact the manager of the store by Monday.* (The italicized phrase is a fragment.)

Right: Ken might get a job if he will contact the manager of the store by Monday.

In order to avoid sentence fragments in your writing, remember that dependent clauses cannot stand by themselves, and that the addition of any subordinating word to a sentence automatically makes it a fragment. Consider these examples:

Complete sentence: I was tired.
Sentence fragments: Because ⎫
When
Although
Since   ⎬ I was tired.
Whereas
Even though ⎭

Be alert to any construction beginning with a subordinating word. Make sure it is properly joined to an independent clause.

Writers sometimes use fragments for a stylistic effect. In the example below the writer used fragments to make a pair of climactic utterances about bones:

> Bones. Two hundred and eight of them. A whole glory turned and tooled.
> —Richard Selzer, "Bone."

This sort of writing, however, is not recommended for college students. Leave fragments to professional writers, and frame your own thoughts in complete, coherent sentences.

4. Comma splices (cs)

A comma splice occurs when a comma is used to connect two independent clauses not joined by a coordinating conjunciton such as *and, nor, but,* or *for:*

Wrong: The nurse brought in the tray, Mr. Jones began to eat his breakfast.

4a. Correcting comma splices

(1) Comma and coordinating conjunction

Use a comma and a coordinating conjunction to connect independent clauses of equal strength:

> The nurse brought in the tray, <u>and</u> Mr. Jones began to eat his breakfast.

(2) Semicolon

Use a semicolon to connect two independent clauses that are closely related in thought:

> The nurse brought in the tray; Mr. Jones began to eat his breakfast.

(3) Period

Use a period between two independent clauses that require separate emphasis:

> The nurse brought in the tray. Without complaint Mr. Jones began to eat his breakfast.

(4) Subordination

Subordinate one idea to another:

> When the nurse brought in the tray, Mr. Jones knew it was time to eat his breakfast.

5. Run-on sentences (ro)

A run-on or fused sentence, as the name implies, consists of two independent clauses improperly connected, with neither link or break between them.

Wrong: Robert stared at the screen he knew he had seen this fellow before.

5a. Correcting run-on sentences

The same methods of correction used on comma splices can be applied to run-on sentences.

(1) Comma and coordinating conjunction

Use a comma and a coordinating conjunction between clauses of *equal strength:*

> Robert stared at the screen, <u>and</u> he knew he had seen this fellow before.

(2) Semicolon

Use a semicolon between two independent clauses that are closely related in thought.

> Robert stared at the screen; he knew he had seen this fellow before.

(3) Period

Use a period between two independent clauses requiring separate emphasis.

> Robert stared at the screen. He knew he had seen this fellow before.

(4) Subordination

Subordinate one idea to another.

> As Robert stared at the screen, he suddenly realized that he had seen this fellow before.

Exercises

Exercise 3: Sentence fragments

Rewrite the following passages, correcting sentence fragments. If a passage contains no fragments, leave it alone. Add words if needed.

> MODEL: On the surface Jane appears to be a young woman. Struggling
>   between a career and marriage.
>
>   Answer: **On the surface, Jane appears to be a young woman**
>   **struggling between a career and marriage.**

1. Randy is getting more decisive each day. Having promised himself to move in one direction.
2. Among married teenagers, one of the most popular routes out of the locked-in position is divorce. Because it supplies a quick and definite way out.
3. One part of him is searching for freedom. The other part desiring to be rooted and tied down.
4. Whereas the women seemed more mature than the men who entered college.
5. Although some parents offer glamorous opportunities to their children, they usually contaminate these offers with parental rules and values.
6. We each have our own set of ethics. The way we see and interpret right and wrong.
7. The simplest, and what appears to be the safest option, is for Mary to drive the car herself. Then Jack can pick it up from her.
8. On the other hand, if she were to sink all of her money into this publishing company, believing that eventually it would make her rich.
9. To be consigned to a life of boredom just because one wanted to please one's parents.
10. The older we get, the more we become aware of our mortality. Hoping against hope that we shall remain among the lucky few who live to a ripe and contented old age.

Exercises 3, 4, 5: Sentence fragments, comma splices, run-on sentences

Indicate whether the following are complete sentences, fragments, comma splices, or run-on sentences.

> MODEL: Marvin had a difficult time in life, he took himself too seriously.
>
>   Answer: **Comma splice**

1. Three days passed, however, he still did not recognize anyone.
2. While the man was asleep, she had carefully gone through his belongings.

3. Her dresses were made from the most delicate silk her shoes were made from the softest leather.
4. Since the children were playing outside in the blizzard.
5. Of course, it would not pay to make that kind of man angry or jealous.
6. Attempting to make him forget his troublesome past in order to start a new life.
7. He bit his fingernails; his heart was beating rapidly.
8. She wished she could stay with him forever, she could not understand her own feelings about this simple man.
9. Is it possible to calculate the effect of a nuclear attack in our era?
10. Ginger eagerly swallowed her glass of champagne, her face was flushed and hot.
11. I want to be candid, our financial situation does not look good.
12. Jim balanced himself precariously, holding the book high in the air.
13. Confessing to the crowd that he had lied all along.
14. The poor girl is ill; she is not well at all.
15. We listened with great interest after all he was an expert in his field.
16. The message fell on deaf ears, ears that no longer responded to truth.
17. He was not a man to act on the spur of the moment, however, this telegram called for a response.
18. The lawyer called me into his office to explain all of the details involved in signing the papers.
19. While George was completely fascinated by the artist's bizarre use of black polka dots.
20. From now until tomorrow not eating another bite.
21. She felt sick, but the unkind words could not be recalled.
22. Having given directions to the nurse to prepare for the next operation.
23. He had had ten years of pain from the broken bones, ten years of suffering from that spreading ulcer.
24. It was a dark night, the children had walked silently along the dim path.
25. You look healthy you look strong.
26. Then addressing the group of amateur photographers who seemed to need a leader.
27. When he came to our town, he was young and strong.
28. The spots on his body disappeared his skin became healthy again.
29. His raised voice directed to the people who would take the long journey with him.
30. Sylvia Plath wrote depressing poems, she eventually committed suicide.

6. Agreement (agr)

A subject and its verb and a pronoun and its antecedent must agree in number.

6a. Subject-verb agreement

Once you have decided on a subject, it determines what form of verb you will use. For instance, you will write, "A fish swims," not "A fish swim," because *fish* in this instance is third-person singular. On the other hand, you will write, "Most fish swim" because in this instance *fish* is third-person plural. Agreement errors are primarily caused by the unusual word order of a sentence or by words intervening between a verb and its subject.

(1) Unusual word order

Unusual word order in a sentence may confuse you. Consider the following examples:

> The one fruit that I love *is* (not *are*) oranges. (The subject is *fruit*.)
>
> *Have* not (not *has*) the warm days of this lovely summer delighted your heart? (The subject is *days*.)
>
> Too many temper tantrums *were* (not *was*) the reason for their divorce. (The subject is *temper tantrums*.)
>
> Wrapped inside five blankets was (not *were*) a tiny white kitten. (The subject is *kitten*.)
>
> There *are* (not *is*) numerous ways to make good fudge. (The subject is *ways*.)
>
> There *remain* (not *remains*) many unsolved problems. (The subject is *problems*.)

(2) Intervening words

Intervening words may make it difficult to identify the subject. Study the following examples until you recognize the correct subject:

> Several of the students in Professor Smith's course *were* (not *was*) nominated for an award. (The subject is *several*.)
>
> The transportation of diamonds *is* (not *are*) dangerous. (The subject is *transportation*.)
>
> The discussions of that subject *are* (not *is*) necessary. (The subject is *discussions*.)
>
> Hunger, along with inadequate housing, *causes* (not *cause*) riots. (The subject is *hunger*.)
>
> Inner longings, as well as an outward goal, *drive* (not *drives*) ambitious people. (The subject is *longings*.)

(3) Special words and word connectors

To avoid some common agreement errors be alert to certain words and word connectors. Remember the following rules:

(a) A **relative pronoun** usually refers back to, and agrees with, the nearest noun:

Rod Laver is one of the greatest tennis players who *live* (not *lives*) in this country. (*Who* refers back to *players*.)

Tokyo is among those cities that *are* (not *is*) filled with smog. (*That* refers back to *cities*.)

Note the following exception:

This is the only one of the streets that *has* (not *have*) two-way traffic. (*That* refers back to *one*, emphasizing the fact that only one street has two-way traffic; the other streets do not.)

(b) Subjects joined by *and* require a plural verb:

Both his eyesight ad his hearing *have* (not *has*) gone bad.
The boys and Elsa *were* (not *was*) caught up in the drug cult.

but

My best friend and confidante *is* (not *are*) having lunch with me. (*Friend and confidante* refers to the same person.)

(c) Singular subjects joined by *or, either . . . or, neither . . . nor* require a singular verb. However, if one of the subjects is singular and the other is plural, then the verb agrees with the nearer subject:

A large camera or a small computer lies (not *lie*) under that cover.
Neither the chair nor the couch *feels* (not *feel*) comfortable.

but

Neither his money nor his innumerable fans *make* (not *makes*) him happy. (*Make* agrees with the nearer subject, *fans*.)

(d) When used as subjects, **indefinite pronouns** like *either, neither, everyone, no one, anyone, each, everybody,* and *anybody* require singular verbs:

Everybody who is anyone *goes* (not *go*) to the ballet.
Each of the grandmothers *was* (not *were*) given a rose.

NOTE: *All, any, half, none, most,* and *some* are singular or plural, depending on the context:

Singular: Some of the wine *was* (not *were*) sour. (*Wine* is singular.)
Plural: Some of the stairs *were* (not *was*) terribly steep. (*Stairs* is plural.)

(e) Collective nouns (nouns that are singular in form but plural in meaning) require a singular verb unless members are acting individually.

Singular: The crew always *meets* (not *meet*) for a swim at sunrise.
Plural: The crew *are* (not *is*) coming to work in their overalls.

(f) Certain words are **plural in form but singular in meaning** and require a singular verb:

> Physics *is* (not *are*) difficult.
> Mumps *keeps* (not *keep*) children in bed for days.
> The news today *scares* (not *scare*) us all.

NOTE: If in doubt about whether a noun is singular or plural, check your dictionary.

(g) Words denoting **sums of money and measurements** take a singular verb when considered as a single unit, but take a plural verb when considered as separate units:

Singular: One hundred dollars *is* (not *are*) too much money for a wool sweater.
Plural: Three silver dollars *were* (not *was*) stacked on the game table.
Singular: Two miles *is* (not *are*) as far as I can jog.
Plural: Those two miles *stretch* (not *stretches*) into the distance like a snake.

NOTE: Problems in arithmetic can be plural or singular:

> Three and three *is* (or *are*) six.

(h) **Titles** of literary works, whether singular or plural, require singular verbs:

> *The Captains and the King is* (not *are*) Taylor Caldwell's best novel.
> *Myths of the Norsemen tells* (not *tell*) about the twilight of the gods.

6b. Pronoun-antecedent agreement

A pronoun always refers back to an antecedent (the word for which it stands) and must agree in person, number, and gender with that antecedent. The following words are singular and require singular pronouns: *person, each, either, neither, everyone, everybody, someone, somebody, one, anyone, anybody, no one, nobody.*

> The teacher asked, "Did anyone leave *his* (not *their*) workbook on my desk?"

Neither of the students gave *her* (not *their*) correct address to the police officer.

Anyone who loves *his* (not *their*) country must be willing to enlist in the army.

NOTE: Traditional usage has dictated that the masculine pronoun be used for words that include both sexes in order to avoid the awkward use of *he or she, him or her,* and *his or hers.* Many people, however, are offended by what seems an illogical exclusion of women in this construction. Recasting the sentence into the plural to avoid the generic is often possible.

Anyone who has his (not *his or her*) running shoes can use the gym.

All who have running shoes can use the gym.

Collective nouns acting as a single unit require a singular pronoun; those acting as individuals require a plural pronoun:

Singular: The faculty has posted *its* (not *their*) list of demands. (The faculty is acting as a unit.)

Plural: The faculty gave differing responses to *their* (not *its*) heavier teaching loads. (The members of the faculty are acting individually.)

Antecedents joined by *and* require plural pronouns:

Charles and Richard passed *their* (not *his*) exams.

The horse and buggy have had *their* (not *its*) day.

Antecedents joined by *or* or *nor* require a singular pronoun when the antecedents are singular; if one antecedent is singular and the other plural, the pronoun agrees with the nearer antecedent:

Singular: Either the custodian or a guest left *his* (not *their*) coat in the room.

Plural: Neither the guard nor the hostages were happy about *their* (not *his*) situation. (*Their* agrees with the nearer subject, *hostages.*)

but

Singular: Neither the hostages nor the guard was happy about *his* (not *their*) situation. (*His* agrees with the nearer subject, *guard.*)

NOTE: Be sure to use the noun *kind* or *kinds* with the right demonstrative pronoun:

I will not associate with *those kinds* (not *those kind*) of people.

The lecturer suggested *that kind of book* (not *that kind of books*).

Exercises

Exercise 6a: Subject-verb agreement

In the following sentences, choose the correct form of the verb.

> MODEL: The guild of carpenters and blacksmiths (*was, were*) important during the Middle Ages.
>
> Answer: **Was**

1. Americans belong to the nation that (*has, have*) always been vigilant about freedom.
2. A sack of gold coins (*is, are*) far more valuable today than a year ago.
3. There (*is, are*) dozens of rats in that old building.
4. The beautiful maple trees growing along Main Street (*keeps, keep*) the houses cool during summer.
5. Gymnastics (*was, were*) Alex's favorite sport.
6. An umbrella or heavy boots (*is, are*) what he needs.
7. The peasants were indebted to the king for one of the loans that (*was, were*) made.
8. War and peace often (*resides, reside*) side by side in a country.
9. The *Los Angeles Times* (*is, are*) news at a high professional level.
10. The Council of Venice (*was, were*) dogmatic about burial laws.
11. Love, along with strong family roots, (*helps, help*) to create a sense of identity.
12. Organized groups of 200 to 300 and possibly more (*is, are*) marching toward the city.
13. (*Does, Do*) everyone have an umbrella?
14. Measles still (*causes, cause*) permanent damage to some children.
15. Deceptive smiles (*was, were*) the weapon he used most often.

Exercise 6b: Pronoun-antecedent agreement

In the following sentences, choose the correct words in parentheses.

> MODEL: Each of the tenants is complaining about (*his, their*) rent.
>
> Answer: **His**

1. A person can count only on (*himself, themselves*).
2. If anyone gets three "C"s, (*she, they*) will have to resign.
3. A person should not have to worry about (*his, their*) health during adolescence.
4. Everyone spoke (*her, their*) mind.
5. Neither the sky nor the clouds revealed (*its, their*) famous silver lining.
6. Neither a German nor a Frenchman finds it easy to get rid of (*his, their*) accent.

7. Every woman on the staff thinks (*she is, they are*) not paid as well as the men.
8. I hate those (*kind, kinds*) of roving eyes.
9. The genuine belief in fairies and ghosts has seen (*its, their*) heyday.
10. No one who has lived alone in the wilderness for a week can consider (*his, their*) life immortal.
11. Through love and understanding the church wooed back (*its, their*) members.
12. The Chicago police made (*its, their*) legal view quite clear.
13. The long list of names spoke for (*itself, themselves*).
14. The Bible states that one should forgive (*his, their*) enemies.

7. Pronoun case (case)

According to their function in a sentence, personal pronouns can appear in three different case forms: subjective, objective, and possessive.

SUBJECTIVE	OBJECTIVE	POSSESSIVE
I	me	my, mine
you	you	your, yours
he, she, it	him, her, it	his, her, hers, its
we	us	our, ours
they	them	their, theirs
who	whom	whose

The *subjective* case is used for pronouns functioning as subjects and as predicate pronouns:

> *We* own this house.
> Is that Mike standing there? Yes, it is *he.*

The *objective* case is used for pronouns functioning as direct objects, indirect objects, objects of prepositions, and subjects or complements of an infinitive:

> The truck hit *her.*
> He gave *them* a package.
> The laugh came from *him.*
> To see *her* was to love *her.*

The *possessive* case is used for pronouns indicating possession:

> Nothing stood in *its* way.
> The money is *theirs.*
> That watch is *yours.*

Notice that possessive pronouns require no apostrophes.

Wrong: Nothing stood in *it's* way.
The money is *their's*.
That watch is *your's*.

7a. Using the subjective case

Ordinarily we naturally use the correct subjective pronoun. Few of us are tempted to write "Me want to eat" instead of "I want to eat." Nevertheless, some constructions require careful thought.

Treat a clause of comparison introduced by *than* or *as* as if it were written out in full and use the appropriate pronoun case.

Richard is taller than *I* [am].
No one plays as well as *he* [plays].

Pronouns that follow forms of the linking verb *to be* usually are in the subjective case:

I swear it was *she* (not *her*).
We expected that the winners would be *they* (not *them*).

NOTE: An exception is a pronoun functioning as an object complement of the infinitive *to be* (see 2b[4]. *Object complement*):

We expected the president to be *her* (not *she*).

Pronouns used in apposition should be in the same case as the nouns or pronouns to which they refer:

Two runners—*you* and *he*—were seen late at night.
We—John and *I*—did our best.

A pronoun functioning as the subject of a subordinate clause must be in the subjective case even when the entire subordinate clause is used as an object:

The flowers will be presented to *whoever* (not *whomever*) serves as
choreographer of the dance. (*Whoever* is the subject of the verb *serves*.)
They never forgot *who* (not *whom*) had won the war. (*Who* is the subject of
had won.)

When intervening expressions like *I believe, you think, one supposes,* or *he says* come between the verb and its subject pronoun, the pronoun must be in the subjective case:

Who (not *whom*) does he say repaired the light? (*Does he say* is an
intervening expression between *who,* the subject, and *repaired,* the verb.)
The woman *who* (not *whom*) the papers think committed murder has
disappeared. (*The papers think* is an intervening expression between *who*
and *committed murder.*)

NOTE: A noun in the possessive case cannot function as an antecedent for a
pronoun in the subjective case:

Wrong: At the very start of Julie's vacation, she sprained her ankle.
 Right: At the very start of her vacation, Julie sprained her ankle.

7b. Using the objective case

An objective pronoun must be used when a pronoun functions as a direct
or an indirect object, as the object of a preposition, as the subject or as the
object of an infinitive. The following is an example of a pronoun used as a
direct object:

Everyone loved *him* (not *he*).

Special care needs to be taken with compound constructions:

Everyone loved him and *me* (not *I*).

When a pronoun is the object of the verb in a subordinate clause, it requires
the objective case:

He always hurts whomever (not *whoever*) he loves. (*Whomever* is the object
of the verb *loves.*)
but
He always hurts *whoever* loves him. (Now *whoever* is the subject of the verb
loves.)

NOTE: Always treat the *whoever* or *whomever* clause as if it were separate;
then you will use the correct case by judging whether the *whoever/whomever*
is subject or object.

A pronoun can also be used as an indirect object:

Throw *them* (not *they*) a pillow.

Errors of this type by native English speakers are rare.

When a pronoun is used as the object of a preposition, some writers have trouble using the correct case:

The book was given to *him* (not *he*) and *me* (not *I*).

Do not yield to the popular temptation to say "between you and *I*." Although this error is often made by prominent people on television or on the lecture platform, it is ungrammatical. The correct form is "between you and *me*."

Pay special attention to the case of a pronoun combined or in apposition with a noun in the objective case:

Everyone spoke highly of *us* (not *we*) teachers.
The mayor invited two of us—Jack and *me* (not *I*)—to speak.

A pronoun serving as subject or as object of an infinitive is in the objective case:

Subject: They expect *him* (not *he*) to be discharged soon.
Object: We expected to see *him* (not *he*).

Avoid the common confusion of *who* and *whom*. *Who* is always a subject whereas *whom* is always an object:

Who has seen Jim? (subject)
Whom did Jim see? (object)
The girl *who* sold you the ticket is here. (subject)
The man *whom* you recognized has the ticket. (object)
To *whom* are you speaking? (object of preposition)

7c. Using the possessive case

The possessive case should be used before a noun or a gerund:

He will pay *his* son's tuition.
My parents denounce *our* (not *us*) seeing that violent movie.
I appreciate *your* (not *you*) lending me the money.

However, note this exception:

We noticed *him* (not *his*) playing the piano. (The emphasis here is on *him*, not on *playing*, which is a participle.)

NOTES: 1. *My, our, your, her, his, its,* and *their* are classified as adjectives when they modify nouns.
   2. By all means learn the difference between:

it's (for *it is*) and *its* (the pronoun)
who's (for *who is*) and *whose* (the pronoun)

Exercises

Exercise 7: Pronoun case

Underline each pronoun used incorrectly and replace it with the correct form. If the entry is correct, leave it alone.

MODEL: Give the money to the preacher and I.

Answer: Me

1. The fence was taller than him.
2. Does the novel reveal who they killed?
3. The barons built their castles for whoever was within their vassalage.
4. My father gave us boys two dollars in addition to board and room.
5. Tom is certainly far stronger than they.
6. They—the landscaper and him—planted ten rose bushes.
7. Between you and I, the entire project isn't worth a dime.
8. The party was in honor of he and she.
9. The psychologists consider him to be a sociopath.
10. We hoped beyond hope that the victims would not be them.
11. Why doesn't the captain order either Luke or he to play center field?
12. I have just reread the story about them crossing the Rhine River.
13. The accident was caused by him, not I.
14. It was evident that whoever the mob controlled would become the next victim.
15. His father opened the door, expecting that the visitor would be me.
16. The table is ugly because two of it's legs are missing.
17. Regardless of who's wallet this is, the money is gone.
18. Most of the jury members found she to be mentally ill.
19. The community admired both he and she.
20. Whom do they say is the best candidate for the job?

8. Adjectives and adverbs (ad)

Although adjectives and adverbs are both modifiers, they cannot be used interchangeably. Adjectives modify nouns whereas adverbs modify verbs (or adjectives or other adverbs).

Adjective: The pork chop is *good.*
  Adverb: I dance *well.*

Exceptions to this rule are certain linking verbs that require adjectives rather than adverbs because the modifiers following these verbs describe the subject rather than the verb. The most common of these linking verbs are *seem, be, appear, become, look, smell, sound, feel,* and *taste:*

> The fish smells *bad* (not *badly*).
> The patient feels *terrible* (not *terribly*).

8a. Adjectives and adverbs after sense verbs

Verbs of the sense (*look, smell, sound, feel,* and *taste*) are particularly tricky since they require either an adverb or an adjective, depending on their meaning in the sentence:

> The young man looked *eager.* (He is an eager man so an adjective is the appropriate modifier.)
> The young man looked *eagerly* into his lover's eyes. (The act of looking is described so an adverb is the appropriate modifier.)

8b. Don't confuse adjectives and adverbs

Don't use *sure, real,* and *good* when you should use *surely, really,* and *well:*

> The climb was *really* (not *real*) steep.
> I *surely* (not *sure*) enjoyed the concert.

8c. Comparative and superlative forms

See 1e. *Parts of speech.* Also, use the comparative degree when comparing two items and the superlative degree when comparing three or more items:

> Japan is the *stronger* of the two countries.
> Japan is the *strongest* of the Asian countries.
>
> Today I got the *highest* score of anyone in class.
>
> Is this your *best* effort?

Be sure to complete your comparisons:

Wrong: Marie is much healthier.
 Right: Marie is much healthier than she used to be.

8d. Don't convert nouns to adjectives

Don't make awkward conversions of nouns to adjectives. Nouns frequently function as adjectives, as in *torpedo boat, hospital care,* or *fur coat,* but avoid these forms if the resulting words sound confusing, ambiguous, or awkward:

Wrong: president bearing
 Right: presidential bearing

Wrong: jealousy results
 Right: results of jealousy

Exercises

Exercise 8: Adjectives and adverbs

Underline the correct modifier and identify it as an adjective or an adverb.

MODEL: The moon shone (bright, <u>brightly</u>) through the clouds.

Answer: **Adverb**

1. Before a large crowd she was told that she had done (well, good).
2. The apple tasted so (sour, sourly) that I threw it away.
3. The teacher looked (disapproving, disapprovingly) at her.
4. Speaking as (honest, honestly) as ever, he refused to be translated.
5. "He (sure, surely) was betrayed by you," they insisted.
6. "Did you do (well, good) on the final exam?" she asked him.
7. Of the three contestants, she was the (prettiest, prettier).
8. Offer him the (largest, larger) of the two rooms.
9. Most of us consider ourselves (real, really) fortunate if we haven't had surgery by the time we reach middle age.
10. The war continued (steady, steadily) for five years.
11. Drive (slow, slowly); someone is crossing the street.
12. That time he took an (awful, awfully) big chance.
13. She played the violin extremely (soft, softly).
14. I found it difficult to determine which was the (worse, worst) pain of all.
15. At home he felt (capabler, more capable) than at school.

Punctuation

Punctuation marks help to clarify the meaning of sentences. Without punctuation, sentences and paragraphs would not be intelligible to the reader. Some punctuation marks tell when a statement ends, whether it states a fact or asks a question; others form groups of words and ideas for emphasis, or set off material written by someone else. Punctuation marks are not decorative symbols to be used at random. In order to write effectively, you must be familiar with punctuation conventions.

9. The comma (,)

The comma is the most difficult punctuation mark to use. It has so many uses that writers tend to add it everywhere on a page, often incorrectly. Commas are correctly used under the following circumstances.

9a. Commas before coordinating conjunctions

Use a comma before a coordinating conjunction (*and, but, or, nor, for, so, yet*) that links two independent clauses:

> The trees had delicate foliage, but no birds nested in the branches.
> I grew up among these people, and their language was familiar to me.
> The weather was warm, yet the crops failed.

471

NOTES: 1. Do not use a comma to separate a compound predicate:

Wrong: We put on out hats, and opened our umbrellas.
Right: We put on our hats and opened our umbrellas.

2. The comma may be omitted between short independent clauses:

Wrong: It rained, and I wept.
Right: It rained and I wept.

9b. After introductory elements

Use a comma after an introductory subordinate clause and an introductory phrase.

(1) Introductory clause

Before I received my diploma, my father gave me a car.

No comma is needed if the dependent clause *follows* the independent clause:

My father gave me a car before I received my diploma.

(2) Introductory phrase

In the exquisite house of his dreams, all colors of the rainbow would be
  represented.
Speaking of the Devil, there she comes.
To understand the French sense of humor, one needs to be sophisticated.
After paying all of his bills, he invested in an old Chevrolet.

No comma is necessary after short prepositional phrases:

From surgery he was taken to intensive care.

9c. Series

Use a comma after each item in a series except the last.

(1) Words in a series

We shall need ribbons, flowers, and balloons.

NOTE: Careful writers use a comma in front of the final *and* in a series; otherwise, the last two items tend to be taken as a pair:

Confusing: He used different types of conveyances: train, camel, bicycle,
         horse and cart. (Is the horse separate from the cart?)

---

(2) Phrases in a series

We looked under the table, behind the desk, and above the fireplace.

(3) Clauses in a series

He arrived, he moved in, and he took over.

9d. Nonrestrictive clauses or phrases

Use commas to set off a nonrestrictive clause or phrase.

(1) Nonrestrictive clause

A nonrestrictive clause adds descriptive information but is not essential to the meaning of the sentence.

> Harvard, which is one of the most prestigious universities in the United States, has an excellent law school.

In the sentence above, the clause *which is one of the most prestigious universities in the United States* could be deleted without changing the meaning of the rest of the sentence. Consider, however, the following italicized restrictive clause:

> Sarah wants to attend the law school *that her father attended.*

The restrictive clause is essential to the rest of the sentence because it identifies which law school Sarah wants to attend. Therefore, the clause is *not* set off by commas. To decide whether a clause is nonrestrictive or restrictive, leave it out of the sentence. If the meaning of the sentence changes, the clause is restrictive; if the meaning does not change, the clause is nonrestrictive.

Nonrestrictive: The three couples, who all lived on Coldwater Canyon, sued the contractor.

Restrictive: Only the three couples who lived on Coldwater Canyon sued the contractor.

(2) Nonrestrictive phrase

Like the nonrestrictive clause, the nonrestrictive phrase adds descriptive but nonessential information to the sentence, as in the following example:

> Eldon Rogers, dying of cancer, still attends work regularly.

Nonrestrictive: My cousin, employed by the May Company, refuses to buy an insurance policy.

Restrictive: Every person employed by the May Company must buy an insurance policy.

9e. Appositives

Use commas to set off appositives:

> Albert Einstein, one of the most brilliant men of the twentieth century,
>   permitted his brain to be dissected after his death.
> Charles Benjamin Witt, Ph.D., will give a piano recital in March.
> Lone Pine, home of Mt. Whitney, is a popular fisherman's resort.

Appositives are almost always nonrestrictive, but in the following examples they are restrictive and therefore require no commas. The appositives are italicized:

> The movie actor *John Wayne* was on the cover of a magazine.
> I was counting on my cousin *Harry.*
> Edward *the Confessor* died before the Battle of Hastings.

9f. Parenthetical expressions

Use commas to set off parenthetical expressions, which are words or phrases that supply supplementary information and interrupt the flow of the sentence.

> Rembrandt, I suppose, loved his work more than he loved his wife.
> Walking under a ladder, for example, is said to bring bad luck.

Quite often, conjunctive adverbs serve as parenthetical expressions that help make a smooth transition from one sentence to the next. (See 1g. *Conjunctions, conjunctive adverbs.*)

> She did, nevertheless, graduate from nursing school.
> We wondered, furthermore, whether or not he would admit the truth.

9g. Miscellaneous elements

Commas are used to set off a variety of other elements in a sentence. Use commas after *yes* and *no* when they begin a sentence:

> Yes, he did return the sweater.

Use commas to set off words of direct address:

> My dear, he warned you not to touch the water pipe.

Use commas after mild interjections:

> Well, why didn't you say so?

Use commas to set off absolute phrases (see 2c[5]. *Absolute phrases*):

Their prayers recited, they left the mosque to go back to work.

Use commas to set off certain expressions of contrast:

The pillow was embroidered by my aunt, not my sister.

Use commas to introduce brief quotations and to set off quoted material from the rest of the text;

"Then God or Nature calmed the elements," wrote Ovid.
The Bible tells us, "Judge not lest you be judged."

NOTE: When a quotation is interrupted by explanatory words use a comma before and after the interruption. Always place commas inside the quotation marks (see also 16. *Quotation marks*):

"When you have been driven out of your homeland," said Jake, "you feel like a piece of drifting seaweed."

Follow convention in the use of commas for dates, addresses, and places:

Dates: Today is February 25, 1980.
On July 4, 1776, our nation was born.
The company will be solvent by June, 1985.

A comma goes between the day (or month) and the year and after the year if the sentence continues.

Addresses: 1500 North Verdugo Road, Glendale, California 91208 (Do not place a comma between the state and the zip code.)

A comma goes between the city and the state and after the state if the sentence continues.

Use a comma before examples introduced by *such as* or *especially:*

A writer should avoid using trite figures of speech, such as "big as a bear" or "white as a ghost."
Americans love spectator sports, especially football.

Use a comma when it will prevent misreading a sentence:

Confusing: As soon as the airplane lifted the gauges began to fluctuate.
Clear: As soon as the airplane lifted, the gauges began to fluctuate.
Confusing: After Friday afternoon classes will be filled.
Clear: After Friday, afternoon classes will be filled.

NOTE: For fear of omitting commas, many students overuse them. In a number of places commas are not needed:

1. Don't separate a subject from its verb with a comma:

Wrong: All of the elderly people, expected the tax vote to fail.
  Right: All of the elderly people expected the tax vote to fail.

2. Don't separate a verb and its object with a comma:

Wrong: He loudly demanded, all of the money.
  Right: He loudly demanded all of the money.

3. Don't use a comma before the first or after the last item in a series:

Wrong: St. Paul gave Christianity, a theology, a church organization, and a sense of purpose.
  Right: St. Paul gave Christianity a theology, a church organization, and a sence of purpose.

10. The semicolon (;)

The semicolon is a weak period and cannot be replaced by a comma. Use the semicolon between independent clauses to replace the coordinate conjunction:

> The days were dreary; the nights were unbearable.
> The people gathered in the streets and in the market places; they seemed to crawl out of nowhere.

Use the semicolon between independent clauses joined by a conjunctive adverb (*however, consequently, moreover, besides, on the other hand*):

> Everyone demands more and more services from the government; *consequently,* taxes are sky high. (It is customary, although not technically necessary, to place a comma after the conjunctive adverb.)

NOTE: A conjunctive adverb, used parenthetically, is enclosed by commas:

> My sister sings beautifully; my brother, *however,* sounds like a fog horn.

Use semicolons between items in a series when the items contain commas, and between independent clauses joined by a coordinate conjunction if the clauses contain commas:

For our clothing we wore bathing suits, shorts, and overalls; for our shelter we had tents, caves, and sleeping bags; for our food we ate nuts, dates, and bananas.

During the Middle Ages the average person believed in ghosts, magic spells, and omens; but today he believes in television, computers, and stock-market reports.

11. The colon (:)

A colon is used to indicate that something is about to follow. It can be used to introduce a list preceded by *as follows, following, follows:*

The following officers were elected: president, secretary, and treasurer.

NOTE: Use the colon only at the end of an independent clause. Do *not* use it between a verb or preposition and its object:

Wrong: England has produced: Chaucer, Shakespeare, and Milton.
Right: England has produced Chaucer, Shakespeare, and Milton.
Wrong: My three favorite cities are: Paris, London, and Rome.
Right: The following are my three favorite cities: Paris, London, and Rome.
Wrong: Pam had a passion for: reading, writing, and traveling.
Right: Pam had a passion for reading, writing, and traveling.

Use a main clause followed by a colon to introduce quotations of more than three lines:

This is how Sidney J. Harris defines a *jerk:*

A jerk, then, is a man (or woman) who is utterly unable to see himself as he appears to others. He has no grace; he is tactless without meaning to be; he is a bore even to his best friends; he is an egotist without charm.

Use a colon to direct attention to a summary, an explanation, or an appositive:

The entire problem can be summarized in one word: *poverty.*
Two passions have a powerful influence on men: ambition and avarice.
One thing he always remained: a gentleman.

Use a colon to separate the greeting in a letter from the body of the letter:

Dear Sir:

Use a colon to separate a title from a subtitle:

The Masks of God: Oriental Mythology

Use a colon between Bible chapter and verse:

Genesis 3:15

Use a colon between hours and minutes:

4:15 P.M.

Use a colon to separate the name of the speaker in a play from words spoken:

Hamlet: To be or not to be . . .

12. The dash (—)

The dash should not be used for mere visual effect or as a substitute for a comma. Use the dash to show a sudden break in thought:

She was certain that he was dead and she—but no, his body moved.

Use the dash to signal an interrupted or unfinished dialogue:

"I want to be a farmer," he enunciated slowly.
"A farmer? But your father—"
"Don't ever mention my father again. For me, he no longer exists."

Use the dash after a statement, to explain or amplify it:

Barbara began to despise everything associated with the modern world—inflation, revolution, pollution.

Use the dash to emphasize parenthetical elements, particularly when they also contain commas:

She believes that there is nothing—no hell or paradise—after a person dies.
Four planets—Mars, Saturn, Jupiter, and Pluto—were embroidered on silk tapestries.

NOTE: The dash is typed as two hyphens with no space before or after; it is written as an unbroken line the length of two hyphens.

---

13. The period (.)

The period is the first punctuation mark an elementary school student learns. It is most basic because it signals the end of a sentence.

Use the period to end a declarative statement:

The dinner was excellent.

Use a period to end a command:

Don't do that.

Use a period to end an indirect question:

We wondered when the truck would arrive.

Use a period to indicate an abbreviation or a contraction:

Dr.	Fed.	assn.
Mrs.	Co.	secy.
Ms.	M.D.	etc.
Mass.	Inc.	hwy.

NOTE: It is becoming increasingly popular to abbreviate well-known names without periods:

TWA, TV, NATO, HEW, CBS, YMCA

Use a period to indicate decimals:

$60.50   2.5%

A group of three spaced periods is used as an ellipsis to indicate that some words have been omitted from a quotation:

Original passage: "These gods, who do not die, cannot be tragic."
With ellipsis: "These gods . . . cannot be tragic."

NOTE: If the omitted portion of the quotation follows a period, the period is retained, followed by the ellipsis:

Original passage: "The narrative is incomplete. And it may remain so. Nevertheless, it is one of the finest epics from any age."

With ellipsis: "The narrative is incomplete. . . . Nevertheless, it is one of the finest epics from any age."

Ellipses are also used to indicate a pause:

> "Listen to me," she said, trembling with fury. "Don't you ever . . . touch my brother again. If you do . . . I'll shoot you."

14. The question mark (?)

Use a question mark to end a direct question:

> Do you love rain? Why?
> The food was really good? (The question mark cues the reader that what would have been a declarative sentence is functioning as a question.)

NOTE: Do not follow a question mark with a comma or a period:

Wrong: "Do you like red hair?," she asked.
Right: "Do you like red hair?" she asked.

Question marks can indicate uncertainty, especially in historical dating:

> The clay tablets date back to 1750(?) B.C.
> Antiochus II, king of Syria (261?–247 B.C.)

15. The exclamation point (!)

Use an exclamation point to indicate a strong emotion or an emphatic command:

> Whew! You stink!
> What a surprise!
> Quick! Bring me some bandages!

Do *not* use an exclamation point to indicate a mild feeling or to emphasize an idea:

Wrong: I was surprised!
Right: I was surprised.

Wrong: Milton is a better writer than Shakespeare!
Right: Milton is a better writer than Shakespeare.

NOTE: Do not follow an exclamation point with a comma or period:

Wrong: "My God!," screamed the woman.
Right: "My God!" screamed the woman.

---

16. Quotation marks (" ")

The primary use of quotation marks is to set off the exact words of a speaker or writer. Quotation marks are always used in pairs to indicate the beginning and the end of a quotation. Do not enclose any introductory words within the quotation marks:

> He answered sarcastically, "You may be rich, but you're stupid."

Do not use quotation marks for indirect address:

Indirect: He told him that Thursday would be soon enough.
Direct: He told him, "Thursday will be soon enough."

NOTE: Use commas to set off interruptions such as "he said" or "she observed":

> "As far as I am concerned," he said, "she is right."

When the quotation contains a question mark or an exclamation point, the question mark or exclamation point replaces the commas:

> "What does the master wish?" she asked.
> "A kiss at least!" he demanded.

Long quotations (four lines or more) are indented. They do not require quotation marks:

> Alan Simpson offers the following insight into our society:
> The health of society depends on simple virtues like honesty, decency, courage, and public spirit. There are forces in human nature which constantly tend to corrupt them, and every age has its own vices. The worst feature of ours is probably the obsession with violence.

Quoted dialogue requires a separate paragraph for each speaker to stress the change from one speaker to another:

> After a long silence, Kevin muttered, "What's the use? Tomorrow I must leave."
> "But why must you leave?" Rosie asked.
> "Because I need money."

Quoted lines of poetry require no quotation marks since their stanza format already sets them off from the regular text. Quoted poetry should be double-spaced and centered between the left and right margins:

One equal temper of heroic hearts,
Made weak by time and fate but strong in will
To strive, to seek, to find, and not to yield.
—Alfred Lord Tennyson, "Ulysses."

Quotation marks are used to indicate the title of any subdivision in a printed publication: a chapter, an essay, a short story, a poem, a song, a lecture, a newspaper headline.

"Pharaoh and His Subjects" is the title of Chapter 3 in *The Dwellers on the Nile.*
"A New Year's Warning" is a *Time* magazine article on terrorism in Turkey.
"The Flowering Judas" is a short story by Katherine Anne Porter.
Robert Frost's poem "Design" questions God's providence.
"A Mighty Fortress Is Our God" is a marvelous hymn of confidence.
Professor Lang's lecture was entitled, "How to Sell Yourself."
The headline in Part II of the *Los Angeles Times* reads as follows: "FBI May Intervene in Athlete's Fraud Case."

Quotation marks can set off words used in a special sense:

Whenever my grandmother became schizophrenic, Grandpa said she was "exhausted."
What he called "art" had no more merit than did the scribblings of a child.

Quotation marks are used to enclose definitions:

The word *dulcet* means "gently melodious."

Definitions may also appear in italics:

Kinetics is the study of motion.

For a quotation within a quotation, use single quotation marks:

Thoreau once said, "I heartily accept the motto, 'That government is best which governs least.'"

17. The apostrophe (')

Generally speaking, the apostrophe replaces *of* to indicate possession: "the people's choice" rather than "the choice *of* the people." It is also used to form contractions and certain plurals.

To indicate possession, add an apostrophe plus *s* to singular nouns:

Mabel's dress
someone's house

NOTE: Add only an apostrophe to singular words ending in an *s* sound:

> Keats' "Ode to a Nightingale"
> Jesus' words

Add an apostrophe plus *s* to plural nouns to form the possessive:

> the children's hour
> women's clothes

NOTE: Add only an apostrophe to plurals already ending in *s:*

> three tigers' teeth
> several teachers' lecturers

Place an apostrophe plus *s* after the last word in a hyphenated word to form the possessive:

> mother-in-law's hat (not mother's-in-law)
> sisters-in-law's hats (not sisters'-in-law)

Informal English allows writers to shorten words by omitting certain letters. Such shortened words are called contractions:

> can't (cannot)   we're (we are)   In January of '55 (1955)
> won't (will not)   there's (there is)   o'clock (of the clock)
> who's (who is)   it's (it is)   ma'am (madam)

An apostrophe is used to indicate the plural of letters, numbers, symbols, and words referred to as words:

> His *f*'s look like *t*'s.
> Then they were hit by the Depression of the 1930's. (An acceptable
>   alternative is 1930s.)
> +'s and −'s often add nothing to a grade.
> Delete all those innocuous *very*'s.

NOTE: Avoid the possessive apostrophe with inanimate objects:

Awkward: the chair's paint
Better: the paint on the chair

18. The hyphen (−)

Use a hyphen to form certain compound words:

> mother-in-law
> cave-in
> paste-up
> red-handed
> court-martial

Writers frequently construct their own compound words:

> All of us need to get rid of our I-don't-give-a-damn attitudes.

Rules for hyphenating compound words are varied. Check your dictionary to be sure you are following convention.

Use a hyphen to join two or more words used as an adjective before a noun:

> a home-grown tomato
> a well-known song

However, when the compound adjective follows the noun, no hyphen is necessary:

> The tomato is home grown.
> The song is well known.

Do not use a hyphen when the first word of a compound is an adverb ending in *-ly:*

> a dangerously long tunnel
> two badly hurt victims

Suspension hyphens are used in series:

> They ran two-, three-, and four-mile distances.

Use a hyphen after the prefixes *ex, self, cross, all, great;* before the suffix *elect;* between the prefix and a proper name:

> ex-football player
> self-educated
> cross-ventilation
> all-purpose glue
> great-uncle
> president-elect
> pro-Irish

The hyphen is used to avoid ambiguity:

He *recovered* from the shock of losing $10,000.
Mrs. Jones *re-covered* her sofa.

Aerobic dancing is good *recreation.*
The novel was a *re-creation* of his own childhood.

Use a hyphen with compound numbers from twenty-one to ninety-nine and with fractions:

twenty-two
three-fifths

A compound adjective that contains numbers is also hyphenated:

a thirteen-year-old boy

19. Parentheses ( )

Parentheses are used to enclose incidental information:

His home town (Bern, Switzerland) sent flowers to the funeral.
Brigham Young (1801–1877) was once territorial governor of Utah.

NOTES: 1. No capital letter or period is used when a sentence in parentheses is part of a larger sentence:

He believed in the efficacy of yoga (the term means *union*) as a way of uniting the body and the mind.

But a period is placed at the end of a sentence used independently within parentheses:

Earl Kemp Long was the brother of Huey Long and an important political figure in America. (See his biography by A. J. Liebling.)

The comma follows the closing parenthesis in sentences such as the one below:

Despite the emperor's warning (ten days prior to the festival), the soldiers continued the siege.

2. A question mark or exclamation point is placed inside the parentheses if it belongs to the parenthetical material, and outside if it does not:

Inside: She arrived (had she grown older?) once again to captivate him with her beauty.
Outside: Have you read Baker's *Practical Stylist* (latest edition)?

Use parentheses to enclose numerals or letters in enumerations:

> The babysitter was expected to (1) care for the children, (2) cook meals, and (3) wash the dishes.

Parentheses are used around a question mark to indicate uncertainty or doubt:

> In this frieze, the god Osiris (?) is seen seated on a throne.

20. Brackets ([ ])

Use brackets to insert editorial comments in quoted material:

> According to Campbell, "the Bull of Heaven seems to be the storm god [scholars do not clarify his exact identity] controlling the sky."

Use brackets to set off parenthetical material within parentheses:

> (See *The New Columbia Encyclopedia* [New York: Columbia University Press, 1975].)

Exercises

Exercise 9: Punctuation: The comma

Insert commas wherever they are needed. If the sentence is correct, leave it alone.

> MODEL: Try reading the poetry of Chaucer of Donne and of Dryden.
>
> Answer: **Try reading the poetry of Chaucer, of Donne, and of Dryden.**

1. As the proverb says "He that would bring home the wealth of the Indies must carry out the wealth of the Indies."
2. Were those teachers as all teachers before them preoccupied with trivial facts?
3. As Bill saw the case he had simply missed class.
4. There was obviously something missing in me.
5. I wanted to confront that ill-bred woman who hated Germans so much.
6. Yes we did have some moments of delight.
7. She was as efficient as a machine as friendly as a Dalmatian puppy and as beautiful as a movie star.
8. Doctors surgeons in particular have a god complex.
9. I promptly boarded the airplane that he had pointed out.
10. He would stand before us rejoicing in his sinewy body every inch an open air man.

11. We shall reside at 1344 Woodland Drive Detroit Michigan.
12. On March 13, 1950 her first child was born.
13. "But you are prejudiced" she insisted "because you hate him although you don't even know the person."
14. "Take a deep breath" he exhorted us.
15. Man is a gregarious animal but he does not always enjoy harmony with his fellow humans.
16. Hemingway's poignant war novel *A Farewell to Arms* reflects a pessimistic world view.
17. The judge having entered and the audience having risen, the trial began.
18. Because these boys were adolescents, they considered all adults brainless and stultifying.
19. If you set out to climb a mountain no matter how high you climb you have failed if you do not reach the top.
20. He had been on the quest so to speak from the beginning.
21. John Barrymore a member of the famous family of stage actors once played the role of Hamlet while he was drunk.
22. Many infirm lonely people prefer living in a convalescent hospital.
23. Before dying had been an irrelevant mystery to her but now it was a reality.
24. George Orwell said that political writing was often the defense of the indefensible.
25. The great enemy of concise writing one might say is a lack of politeness.
26. Before delving into his personal life let us study his doctrine.
27. Magnificent stately mansions leaned against the hillside.
28. Furthermore the word *science* has the ring of truth and authority.
29. An understanding of art requires that art be evaluated on more than just Aristotelian principles.
30. My little sportscar which has given me nothing but trouble was sold for twice as much as I paid for it.

Exercise 9, 10: Punctuation: The comma and the semicolon

In the following sentences, place a semicolon or a comma or no punctuation within the brackets.

MODEL: The minister asked the audience to rise [ ] everyone stood immediately.

Answer: **The minister asked the audience to rise [;] everyone stood immediately.**

1. I hated him for making so much money [ ] and keeping it all to himself.
2. By sunset the hunters retired [ ] however [ ] at dawn they continued with renewed vigor.

3. Because initiative and trust were sorely lacking [ ] the business went bankrupt within a year.
4. Here are the key people in this venture: Jack Jennings, chairman of the board [ ] Milton Le Cuyer, president of the overseas operation [ ] Dorothy Nibley, marketing supervisor.
5. The nights [ ] however [ ] seem long and cold.
6. Please give her the directions [ ] as soon as she asks for them.
7. As late as 1835 [ ] human sacrifices were performed in India.
8. The community college system in California [ ] without tuition and with open access [ ] is succeeding beyond the wildest and most hopeful dreams of its supporters.
9. All this was unsettling [ ] since I believed in democracy.
10. He had always been short of stature [ ] consequently [ ] he decided to make a success of himself.
11. The stars sparkled [ ] it was a lovely night.
12. Everything was finally in our hands [ ] we were completely in charge.
13. Either these few are considered to be innately superior [ ] or they are selected for special assistance.
14. Give her a telephone call [ ] as soon as you have received the grant money.
15. "It is fortunate that you live in a house [ ]" he stated [ ] "otherwise you might be paying an exorbitant rent."
16. She was a calm woman [ ] not one to be scandalized easily.
17. Ask any of the officials [ ] if you can catch them on duty.
18. The mad elephant had destroyed one of the bamboo huts [ ] it had also turned over the rubbish truck.
19. They stood in line clear around the block [ ] the news having reached the neighborhood that free tickets were being supplied.
20. In the rough [ ] the amethyst was worth $20 [ ] honed and polished [ ] it was worth $200.

Exercise 9–20: All punctuation marks

In the following sentences, supply any missing marks of punctuation. If the sentence is correct, leave it alone.

MODEL: The peoples choice is what counts thats how democracy works

Answer: **The people's choice is what counts; that's how democracy works.**

1. They were asked to supply the following items towels, sheets, and soap
2. He demanded to know when she was going to pay the rent.
3. Do you live in a politically active community he asked.
4. What remains but to spare him all of the unpleasant aspects of keeping house

5. Caroline yelled Fire Get out
6. His cat weighed so much that he called her tons of fun
7. Everybodys a damnable liar he shouted with fury
8. She is a well dressed beautifully groomed woman
9. Our campus bookstore is student owned.
10. Have him read "The Last Ditch," an essay by Robert Coles.
11. Don't write your 7s and 9s so much alike.
12. Albert Schweitzer 1875–1965 was awarded the Nobel Peace Prize
13. He called me a let's see what did he call me
14. The question is this Where do we go from here
15. Poets philosophers hermits all are idealists
16. Jackies bloodstained suit now displayed in the Smithsonian Institution is a horrifying symbol of the vanished Camelot
17. My father in law is a loving grandfather
18. Will you come soon perhaps tomorrow
19. Boston, Massachusetts is his hometown
20. "The Lord is my shepherd. . . . He maketh me to lie down in green pastures."

Mechanics

Students often wonder whether mechanics will count as much toward their grade as content. The answer is that the mechanics of writing are often inseparable from content and therefore must exert a nearly equal influence on the grade. A manuscript that abides by the rules is like a city whose traffic flow is controlled by lights, signs, and regulations; a manuscript that ignores the rules is like a city whose traffic has run amok. You will increase the readability of your writing and make your reader immeasurably happier if you observe proper mechanics.

21. Capitalization (cap)

Capitalization is a way of drawing attention to certain words. Observe the following conventions of capitalization in your writing. Whenever you are in doubt about whether or not a word should be capitalized, consult your dictionary.

21a. First words

Use capitals for the first word in a sentence:

> Above all else, we want peace.
> How did life on our planet begin?

Use capitals for the first word in a line of traditonal poetry:

> The sun does arise,
> And make happy the skies;
> The merry bells ring
> To welcome the spring.
> —William Blake

Much modern poetry is in free verse, and the first word in a line is not always capitalized.

NOTE: If the quotation fits grammatically into a sentence, the first word need *not* be capitalized:

> William Faulkner once said (in a *Paris Review* interview) that "if a writer has to rob his mother, he will not hesitate; the 'Ode on a Grecian Urn' is worth any number of old ladies."

21b. Proper nouns

Capitalize proper nouns, words that are part of proper nouns, and adjectives derived from proper nouns, as well as names of specific people, races, nationalities, languages:

Abraham Lincoln	French
Levite	Asian
Russian	Latin

21c. Names

Capitalize names of continents, countries, states, cities, neighborhoods, streets, buildings, parks, monuments, oceans, lakes, rivers:

Africa	Union Oil Building
Sweden	Central Park
Michigan	Statue of Liberty
London	Atlantic Ocean
Morningside Heights	Lake Louise
Brand Boulevard	Tigris River

21d. Other capitalization rules

The following rules are to be used as guidelines for the use of capitals in your writing.

(1) Specific organizations and institutions

the Lakers
Daughters of the American Revolution
Smithsonian Institution
Federal Reserve
Democratic Party (or Republican)

(2) Historical periods, events, or documents

Middle Ages
Renaissance
Battle of Hastings
Bill of Rights

(3) Members of national, political, or religious groups

Rotarian
Democrat
Methodist

(4) Religions and sacred religious works or terms

Islam	the Virgin
Hinduism	Allah
Catholicism	the Bible
God	the Torah

Some people capitalize pronouns referring to the deity: His, He, Him, Thee, Thou.

(5) Names of days, months, and holidays

Wednesday
August
Thanksgiving
Valentine's Day

(6) Names of academic degrees and specific courses

Ph.D.
Doctor of Jurisprudence
Biology 135
Advanced Typing

Usually if the course is a general course, it is not capitalized: psychology, biology, mathematics.

(7) Names of stars, planets, constellations

Pluto
Mars
North Star
Milky Way

Unless they are personified, *earth*, *sun*, and *moon* are not capitalized.

(8) Names of ships, trains, and aircraft

the Queen Elizabeth II
the Lark
Air Force One

(9) Personifications

Father Time
Mother Nature

(10) Abbreviations indicating time, government divisions, or media stations

A.M., P.M. (also a.m., p.m.)
HEW
FHA
NBC
KNXT

(11) Titles preceding names

Dean Katz	President June Willard
Reverend D. L. Smith	Governor Mario Cuomo
Mr. Eric Reese	Chief Justice Rehnquist

NOTES: 1. Do not capitalize a title when it is not part of the name:

a former senator, Harold Berman
Gail French, director of personnel

2. An abbreviated title, used before or after a name, is capitalized:

Dr. Sigmund Freud
Fernando Garcia, Esq.
Richard Bauer, M.D.

3. Titles of distinction are capitalized when they take the place of the person's name:

The President spoke on TV.
The Archbishop offered the prayer.

---

(12) First word of each outline entry

1. Advantages of credit cards
   A. Instant money
   B. Delayed payment

(13) Titles of literary works

Capitalize all words except articles, conjunctions, and prepositions unless they are the first word in the title:

For Whom the Bell Tolls
"Ode on a Grecian Urn"
The Taming of the Shrew

NOTE: Conjunctions and prepositions of five letters or more are sometimes capitalized:

War Against the King
"Comin' Through the Rye"

---

(14) Points of the compass

Capitalize when they refer to a specific area, but not when they refer to direction:

My aunt lives in the East.

but

Turn west on Broadway.

(15) Titles of relatives

Capitalize when they are not preceded by an article or a pronoun, when they are followed by a name, and in direct address:

Give the rose to Grandmother, my dear.
I owe Aunt Margaret twenty dollars.
Please, Mother, pay no attention.

but

My mother has arrived.
They told us that the aunt was wealthy.

(16) The pronoun *I* and the interjection *O*

As far as I am concerned, he might as well go home.
How many crimes, O Liberty, have been committed in your name?

NOTE: *Oh* is not capitalized unless it appears at the beginning of a sentence.

Exercises

Exercise 21: Capitalization

In the sentences below correct all capitalization. Underline small letters that should be capitalized and strike through capital letters that should be in lower case. If the sentence is correct, leave it alone.

> MODEL: Many Ancient sumerian myths, such as the *epic of gilgamesh,* were found in ashurbanipal's Library at nineveh.

1. If we need money for the First Mortgage, I can always borrow some from uncle charlie.
2. Because dr. Lewis, my English professor, lived in the south for many years, he has remained a baptist.
3. The Monarch butterfly has wings that resemble dead autumn leaves.
4. Anton Chekhov's short story "the new villa" portrays a clash between two cultures, the Aristocracy and the Serfs.
5. When we take our cruise to alaska, we shall go on the olav, a scandinavian Vessel.
6. I am sending grandmother some Violets for her Birthday.
7. The tiv, an african tribe, began their stories, "not yesterday, not yesterday."
8. During the Middle Ages, London had no sewers; consequently, the plague broke out from time to time.
9. After Adam and Eve had eaten of the tree of the knowledge of good and evil, they were expelled from eden.
10. Helen likes to be addressed as "ms. Griffith" rather than "miss Griffith."
11. My grandfather watched Charles Lindbergh land the spirit of St. Louis at orly airport in paris.
12. He will be made a fellow of the royal academy of surgeons next Spring.
13. How many more American Embassies will be attacked by Foreign countries who want to be our enemies?
14. We sat down and listened to the president's state of the union address on tv.
15. The Lincoln Memorial in Washington, D.C. will always remind us that civil war is possible.

22. Italics (ital)

In handwritten or typewritten manuscripts, italics are indicated by underlining. In printing, *italic* type is used.

> Use italics for the titles of books, magazines, and newspapers:

> One of the most thoroughly American books is *Tom Sawyer* by Mark Twain.

Occasionally I don't understand *Time* magazine's choice for "Man of the Year."

He relies on *The Wall Street Journal* for news about economic trends.

NOTES: Copy the title of a newspaper as it appears on the masthead:

Los Angeles Times (not *The Los Angeles Times* or *The Times*)

Use italics for the titles of pamphlets or bulletins, musical compositions, plays, films, television programs, and long poems:

MacDowell Musical Society News Bulletin
Rock Climbing in the Sierras
Verdi's *La Traviata* (opera)
Beethoven's *Concerto No. 2*
My Fair Lady (musical comedy)
Neil Simon's *Chapter Two* (play)
All That Jazz (film)
60 Minutes (TV broadcast)
Byron's *Don Juan* (long poem)

NOTES: 1. Titles of brief musical pieces or songs are usually placed within quotation marks:

"Scaramouche" by Milhaud
"I Could Have Danced All Night" (from *My Fair Lady*)

2. Titles of short poems are placed within quotation marks:

"Journey of the Magi" by T. S. Eliot

Use italics for the names of ships, aircraft, spacecraft, and trains:

USS Missouri (ship)
Spirit of St. Louis (aircraft)
Apollo 17 (spacecraft)
Orient Express (train)

Use italics for titles of visual works of art:

Dicus Thrower by Myron (ancient Roman sculpture)
Girl Pouring Perfume (detail from a wall painting)
Alexander at Issus (second century Greek mosaic)
Leonardo da Vinci's *Mona Lisa* (painting on canvas)

Use italics for foreign words not yet absorbed into the English vocabulary:

Schopenhauer had a gloomy *Weltanschauung*. (world view)
When I entered the room, I had a feeling of *déjà vu*. (already seen)
This day is certainly *bellissimo*. (most beautiful)

Latin abbreviations are not italicized:

etc., i.e., viz., et al., e.g.

Use italics for words, letters, figures, or symbols referred to as such:

Words like *superannuated* instead of *old* sound overblown.
The French have a way of gargling their *r*'s.
Move those *10*'s over to the next column.
Students should avoid using the *&* sign in formal essays.

NOTE: Quotation marks are sometimes used for cases such as those listed above, but we recommend italics.

Use italics for emphasis when it cannot be achieved by choice or placement of words:

Which of the following is *not* a fairytale:
    a. "The Descent of Ishtar into the Netherworld"
    b. "Snow White and the Seven Dwarfs"
    c. "The Frog and the Prince"
    d. "Sleeping Beauty"
(to draw attention to the direction in a multiple-choice examination)

I said that she should com*pli*ment, not com*ple*ment him. (to emphasize the distinction in meaning between the two words)

Exercises

Exercise 22: Italics

In the following sentences underline all words that should be in italics. If the sentence is correct, leave it alone.

MODEL: On my flight to New York, I read Belva Plain's <u>Evergreen</u>, a charming novel.

1. If I had the money, I would subscribe to The New Yorker.
2. When you say you saw Gerald Ford, do you mean the Gerald Ford?
3. My history professor is constantly using the phrase coup d'état.
4. Does it bother you when someone misuses the word disinterested?
5. One television commentator gave the movie The Last Married Couple in America a bad review.

6. My favorite hors d'oeuvre is stuffed mushrooms.
7. The Dome of the Rock in Jerusalem is a holy shrine for both Jews and Moslems.
8. I have Van Gogh's Sunflowers hanging on my office wall.
9. Some of Toulouse-Lautrec's best paintings feature La Goulue, a cabaret dancer whom the artist befriended.
10. Numerous tourists each year take a Mediterranean cruise aboard the Royal Viking Sea, a luxury ship.

Exercise 16, 22: Quotation marks and italics

In the following sentences, underline words that should be in italics, and use quotation marks where needed.

> MODEL: Although poetry has never been my favorite literary genre, I am deeply touched by Edwin Markham's "Man and the Hoe."

1. The chapter entitled China: War and Resistance in Theodore H. White's book In Search of History is informative.
2. Although it has almost become commercialized, Michelangelo's famous David never fails to impress me with its youthful courage and zeal.
3. Ain't Misbehavin' is a zesty, jazzy musical.
4. The literary term used to describe stories that begin in the middle of the action is in medias res.
5. No television show has surpassed the Show of Shows in pure comic effect.
6. The Catbird Seat by James Thurber is a short story about a meek little office clerk who gets even with an overbearing female coworker.
7. In his article Why I Am an Agnostic Clarence Darrow tries to make some Christian beliefs look absurd.
8. John Ciardi's translation of Dante's Inferno keeps the complex gestalt of the original twenty-seven cantos.
9. A tragic loss of lives and property took place when the Titanic sank on April 10, 1912.
10. You Ain't Nothin' But a Hound Dog was one of Elvis Presley's earliest successes.

23. Numbers (nu)

In the following circumstances numbers are usually written out.

Numbers that can be spelled out in two words or less:

> seventy thousand years ago
> forty-five senators
> three fourths of the country

A hyphenated number is considered as one word:

> thirty-five thousand voters

Numbers used as compound adjectives:

> a ten-year-old refrigerator
> a three-wheel electric car

In the following circumstances numbers must be written as figures.

Numbers expressed in more than two words:

> Much had changed in 225 years.
> a list of 3,250 people
> not more than 56¼ inches

Dates:

> November 19, 1929
> 19 Nov. 1929
> 11/19/29
> 55 B.C.
> A.D. 105

"B.C." follows the year, but "A.D." precedes the year. The day of the month may be written out when the year does not follow:

> On the sixth of October

Decades may be written out or expressed as figures:

> In the nineteen sixties
> In the sixties
> In the 1960's (or 1960s)

Centuries are expressed in lower-case letters:

> Following the seventeenth century

Addresses:

> 245 Earlham St.
> Apt. 15
> Pasadena, California 91106

Time of day:

> 4:14 P.M.

If the expression "o'clock" follows, then the hours should be written out:

> three-thirty o'clock

Exact amounts of money:

> $15.98
> $1,350
> $2.5 million (or $2,500,000)

Mathematical scores and statistics:

> 20¼
> ⅝
> 3.5% (or 3.5 percent)
> a median score of 48

Number of books, volumes, pages, acts, scenes, verses, and lines:

> Book 3 (or Book III)
> Volume 4 (or Volume IV)
> page 23 (or p. 23)
> Act 3, Scene 2, lines 15–18 (or Act III, Scene 2, lines 15–18)
> Verse 3

NOTES: 1. The documentation for research papers follows a special format, as explained in Chapter 14 "The Research Paper."

2. Never begin a sentence with a figure. If necessary, rewrite the sentence:

Wrong: 36 was the score.
 Right: The score was 36.

3. If you are writing a paper that contains many numbers, use figures throughout for consistency.

Exercises

Exercise 23: Numbers
Correct all numbers used incorrectly. If the sentence is correct, leave it alone.

> MODEL: That pound of chocolates costs $5.23

1. She swam 3 full miles.
2. Louis XIV was born in 1638.
3. Flapper girls were a product of the nineteen twenties.
4. 1980 was a year of strained relations between the U.S. and Iran.
5. Our flight leaves at three-thirty A.M.
6. The score was 30 to 1.
7. If 48% of the product sells, we shall profit.

8. The bridge cost three million and a half dollars.
9. Volume Three is the most difficult of all.
10. A foot has twelve inches.

24. Abbreviations (abb)

In general, avoid abbreviations. Under the following circumstances abbreviations are correct:

Titles preceding proper names:

>   Dr. Strangelove
>   Mr. Sebastian Peters
>   Mrs. Reinbolt
>   Ms. Balucci
>   St. Theresa

The following titles are written out:

>   President Harding
>   Senator Baker
>   Professor Fiedler
>   The Honorable George Lundquist
>   The Reverend Jesse Jackson

Titles following proper names:

>   Marcel Ford, Jr.
>   Christopher J. Marsh, Esq.
>   Frances Moore, M.D.
>   Henry A. Look, Ph.D.
>   Gilbert Blaine, LL.D.

Names of well-known organizations and a few countries:

FBI	YMCA
CIA	OPEC
HEW	USA
IBM	USSR
CBS	NBC

Words used with dates or figures:

>   23 B.C. (or A.D. 23)
>   8:00 A.M. (or 8:00 P.M.)
>   I answered No. 4 wrong.
>   See Fig. 17.

Incorporated, Company, Brothers, and the ampersand when they are part of the official name of a business:

> Doubleday & Co., Inc.
> Cotton Bros., Inc.

Abbreviations used in footnotes, endnotes, or bibliographies:

e.g.	for example
i.e.	that is
etc.	and so forth
et al.	and others
ed.	edited by, editor, edition
trans.	translated by, translator
p., pp.	page, pages

The English versions of the first four abbreviations above are preferred for writing not related to formal research.

NOTE: Do not abbreviate the following:

1. Names of geographical areas, months, days:

Wrong: The cruise left for the Med. last Wed.
  Right: the cruise left for the Mediterranean last Wednesday.

2. Names of people:

> Will Matthew (not *Matth.*) pay the bill?

3. The words *volume, chapter, page* unless used in research-paper documentation or technical writing:

> He fell asleep after reading three pages (not *pp.*) of the first volume
> (not *vol.*).

4. Names of courses of study:

> She failed chemistry (not *chem.*).

5. The word *Christmas:*

> Christmas (not *Xmas*) will be here soon.

6. The words *street, avenue, road, park, mount, drive, lane, river,* and similar words when they are used as essential parts of proper names:

> Maiden Lane is filled with charming shops.
> The club climbed Mount Whitney.
> Their summer home is on the Colorado River.

Exercises

Exercise 24: Abbreviations

Strike out the version that would be incorrect in formal writing:

MODEL: ~~Give Geo. a call.~~ / Give George a call.

1. Please consult Doctor Smith. / Please consult Dr. Smith.
2. Senator Cranston was interviewed. / Sen. Cranston was interviewed.
3. In the year 55 before Christ's birth, Rome controlled Palestine. / In 55 B.C. Rome controlled Palestine.
4. Terrence Belford, Junior, was in town. / Terrence Belford, Jr., was in town.
5. They returned $3.58. / They returned three dollars and fifty-eight cents.
6. His largest class was Eng. lit. / His largest class was English literature.
7. The Federal Bureau of Investigation was forced to investigate. / The FBI was forced to investigate.
8. Park Ave. is beautiful at Xmas. / Park Avenue is beautiful at Christmas.
9. The first payment is due in Nov. / The first payment is due in November.
10. The men are stationed in Switz. / The men are stationed in Switzerland.

Effective sentences

Now that you have studied basic grammar, punctuation, and mechanics, you are ready to use your knowledge of all these elements to write effective sentences. A study of the principles in this section will help you to write an essay, a research paper, or a report that is made up of clear, concise sentences.

25. Subordination (sub)

Subordination is the use of dependent elements to give focus to a main clause or a kernel sentence. Subordination is one way of combining short, choppy sentences into a longer, smoothly integrated one—a technique that requires an understanding of the different types of phrases and clauses explained at the beginning of this handbook. Consider, for example, the following sentences:

> Caedmon was an ignorant herdsman.
> He believed that his poetic powers came from God.

These two sentences may be combined:

> Caedmon was an ignorant English herdsman who believed that his poetic powers came from God.

The second sentence (or independent clause) has been turned into a dependent clause and subordinated to the first. The result is a sentence that is smoother and longer yet still includes all the original information found in its constituent parts.

505

Many sentences can be subordinated without changing their original sense. Others, however, cannot be subordinated because they express ideas that are equal in value:

> Today, schools provide an education.
> Today, schools do not guarantee jobs.

To subordinate one of these sentences to the other would be to change the original meaning of both:

> Today, schools provide an education because they do not guarantee jobs.

A causal connection, not originally intended, has been established. Sentences such as these should be combined by placing a coordinate conjunction between them:

> Today, schools provide an education, but they do not guarantee jobs.

Subordination can be used only between ideas of unequal importance. Learn to assign the correct value to each sentence and reflect it through a subordinated structure. Consider the following independent clauses:

> 1. Lake Como is a tourist resort.
> 2. It is situated in the foothills of the Alps.
> 3. It is one of the most beautiful spots in Europe.

Through the process of subordination, these three independent clauses can be integrated into one clear and logical sentence:

> Lake Como, a tourist resort situated in the foothills of the Alps, is one of the most beautiful spots in Europe.

The most important independent clauses are 1 and 3, while 2 acquires a less prominent position by becoming a participial phrase and being squeezed into the middle as a parenthetical statement. If we had decided that 1 and 2 were the more important, then the subordinated sentence would have read as follows:

> Lake Como, one of the most beautiful spots in Europe, is a tourist resort situated in the foothills of the Alps.

To subordinate logically as well as coherently, you must decide which ideas are more important and which less, and construct your new subordinated sentence to mirror this decision.

Here are some further examples of subordination. Examine them carefully to see how the combining process works:

Choppy: 1. English architecture evolved in the twelfth century.
               2. It began with the Norman style.

3. It was especially noticeable in the Norman churches.
4. These Norman churches have long naves.
5. They also have rectangular east ends.

Better: English architecture evolved in the twelfth century with the Norman style, which was especially noticeable in the Norman churches with their long naves and rectangular east ends.

Here, sentences 2, 3, 4, and 5 are subordinated to sentence 1. Notice, however, that 4 and 5 are combined with the coordinate conjunction *and* because they express ideas of equal value.

Choppy: 1. In ancient Greece, fire was considered one of the four basic elements.
2. It was considered a substance from which the other elements were composed.
3. The other elements were earth, water, and air.

Better: In ancient Greece, fire was considered one of the four basic elements, a substance from which all other elements—earth, air, and water—were composed.

In this combination, 2 is subordinated to 1, while 3 is inserted parenthetically into 2.

Choppy: 1. The speaker raised his hands to silence the audience.
2. The applause continued.
3. It was punctuated by boos.
4. The boos were isolated.

Better: Although the speaker raised his hands to silence the audience, the applause continued, punctuated by isolated boos.

Here, 1 is subordinated to 2; 4 is merged into 3 as an adjective and then attached to 2 as a participial phrase.

In sum, subordination can be achieved in three ways:

Subordinating a clause:

The beggar played his guitar.
He was hungry.

The beggar played his guitar because he was hungry.

or

The beggar, who was hungry, played his guitar.

Subordinating a phrase:

The mountains reach into the sky.
Their peaks are covered with snow.

Their peaks covered with snow, the mountains reach into the sky.

Subordinating a word:

The atmosphere was damp.
It was marked by darkness.

The atmosphere was damp and dark.

NOTE: Beware of the reverse subordination that results when the less important of two ideas is expressed as an independent clause:

Reverse subordination: Although Alex was accepted into Harvard, her entrance examination showed some weakness in vocabulary. (The fact that Alex was accepted into Harvard is the more important fact and should be expressed in the independent clause.)

Correct subordination: Although her entrance examination showed some weakness in vocabulary, Alex was accepted into Harvard.

Reverse subordiation: His legs paralyzed for life, he was stricken with polio when he was twelve. (The fact that his legs are paralyzed for life is the more important idea and should be placed in the independent clause.)

Correct subordination: Stricken with polio when he was twelve, he suffered paralysis of the legs for life.

Exercises

Exercise 25: Subordination

By careful subordination, combine the ideas in each of the following sets of sentences into one effective sentence.

MODEL: Marcia was highly intelligent.
Nevertheless she suffered from extreme timidity.
She never learned to hide this timidity.

Answer: **Although Marcia was highly intelligent, she suffered from extreme timidity, which she never learned to hide.**

1. My father died.
   We moved into a small town.
   It was outside of Boston.
   It was called Reading.
   There was almost no intellectual life there.

2. Mary Todd Lincoln longed desperately for Willie's presence.
   She longed for him so desperately that one night she awoke.
   It was midnight.
   She had the impression that Willie was standing at the foot of her bed.
3. He was lying on the bare earth.
   He was shoeless, bearded, and half-naked.
   He looked like a beggar or a lunatic.
4. The frightened hawk lay there for a long minute.
   He had no hope.
   He did not move.
   His eyes were still fixed on that blue vault above him.
5. Ulysses S. Grant and Robert E. Lee met on April 9, 1865.
   They met in the parlor of a modest Virginia house.
   They met to work out the terms for the surrender of Lee's Army of Northern Virginia.
   At this meeting a great chapter in American life came to a close and a great chapter began.
6. The mockingbird took a single step into the air.
   His wings were still folded against his sides.
   He accelerated thirty-two feet per second.
   Just a breath before he would have been dashed to the ground, he unfurled his wings.
   He then gracefully floated onto the grass.
7. Cleopatra worked diligently to learn coquettishness and flattery.
   She was the most famous courtesan of the ancient world.
   She reportedly practiced on slaves.
8. It was a cold, bright December morning.
   It was far out in the country.
   An old Negro woman came along a bath through the pinewood.
   Her name was Phoenix Jackson.
   A red tag was tied around her head.
9. The priest nodded.
   Then I surprised the audience.
   I recited a sixteenth century poem about love and commitment.
   The poem caused my bride to burst into tears.
   I was amazed.
10. I refused many prestigious jobs.
    One job I refused was clerking for a judge
    Another job I refused was joining a wealthy law firm.
    I favored the public service sector.
11. Most primitive mythologies contain a flood story.
    In each of these stories the gods decide to destroy all human beings.
    However, they make an exception for one favored family.

This family survives the catastrophe.
Such a family was Noah and his brood.

12. My brother's face remains scarred for life.
When he was a mere baby, he was bitten and scratched by a Siamese cat.

13. There are thousands of marvelous summer resorts in the world.
There is Monte Carlo.
There is Bermuda.
There is Hawaii.
However, I prefer Miami Beach.

14. The highland wind blows steadily from north to northeast.
It is the same wind that blows down on the coasts of Africa and Arabia.
Down there they call it the "monsoon."
"Moonsoon" was the name of King Solomon's favorite horse.

15. I have a vivid picture in mind.
It is a picture of Dr. Albert Schweitzer.
I see him at the age of eighty-four spending most of his time answering his correspondence.
It often consisted of silly questions.

26. Dangling modifiers (dm)

A dangling modifier is a word or a group of words that does not modify anything in the sentence:

> Jogging along the beach, the sun set in a blaze of crimson glory.

A reader who took this sentence literally would think that the setting sun was jogging along the beach. The dangling participle, "jogging along the beach," appears to modify "the sun." Here is one way to correct the sentence:

> As I was jogging along the beach, the sun set in a blaze of crimson glory.

Now *I* is the subject of *jogging* and the phrase becomes a dependent clause. Here are some more examples of dangling modifiers:

Dangling: After our fight, she walked toward me while sitting on a bench. (How can she simultaneously walk and sit?)

Better: After our fight, she walked toward me while I was sitting on a bench.

Dangling: Crying her heart out, I was deeply moved by the sound. (How can the speaker cry another person's heart out?)

Better: I was deeply moved when I heard her crying her heart out.

Dangling: Looking to the far end of the football field, there he was. (The participle *looking* has no logical subject at all.)

Better: Looking to the far end of the football field, they saw him.

Dangling modifiers are usually corrected in two ways: by leaving the dangler as is but recasting the remainder of the sentence; or by expanding the dangling part into a complete dependent clause.

NOTE: Certain absolute constructions are exceptions to these rules (see 2c[3]. *Absolute phrases*):

> *Generally speaking,* men are taller than women.
> *To sum up,* cocktail parties are boring.

Exercises

Exercise 26: Dangling modifiers

Indicate which sentences are correct and which contain dangling modifiers. Rewrite the sentences that contain dangling modifiers.

MODEL: While sneaking into our house through the back door, my father confronted me.

Answer: **While I was sneaking into our house through the back door, my father confronted me.**

1. When looking toward the sky, the enormous white clouds sailing across the deep blue are a breathtaking sight.
2. After complaining in two letters, the client finally received his rebate.
3. By showing respect for my teachers, they respected me in return.
4. After gaining her employer's confidence, doors began to open, and opportunities came her way.
5. Coming from a Persian background, her complexion is a lovely deep olive.
6. To be successful, a person must be willing to persevere despite failures.
7. Barking and snarling, the guests were scared by our big German shepherd dog.
8. Having pimples and lacking self-confidence, my grandmother reassured me that someday I would be beautiful.
9. Realizing that a course in western civilization would broaden his political views, Jack enrolled at UCLA.
10. Grease-stained and covered with dust, Margie rediscovered her diary.
11. The wind began to blow immediately after opening the windows.
12. Never having met the instructor, it seemed foolish of her to be so nervous.

13. Truthfully speaking, Miami, Florida, has a *nouveau riche* atmosphere.
14. Before entering the water, the scuba diving equipment should be checked.
15. Sitting in a sidewalk cafe listening to lovely violin music, San Marco Square seemed utterly romantic.

27. Misplaced parts (mp)

A well-constructed sentence raises no uncertainty about which words belong where. Modifiers should stand as close as possible to the words they modify. Notice how each sentence below takes on a different meaning, depending on where the word *only* is placed:

> *Only* I loved her. (No one else did.)
> I *only* loved her. (I didn't hate, pity, or envy her.)
> I loved *only* her. (I loved no one else.)

A writer must be careful to place modifiers in positions that most clearly convey the meaning intended. The following is an example of a misplaced part:

> The United States has seen its President burned in effigy *on the living room TV.*

The writer has created an absurdity by having the phrase *on the living room TV* modify the verb *burned.* The following version makes clear the writer's intentions:

> *On the living room TV* the United States has seen its President burned in effigy.

Some modifiers, if ambiguously placed between two elements, will seem to modify both:

> The waiter who had served them *swiftly* disappeared.

The meaning of the sentence is unclear because it is impossible to know whether the waiter served swiftly or disappeared swiftly. Here are two clearer versions:

> The waiter who had served them disappeared *swiftly.*

> **or**

> The waiter who had *swiftly* served them disappeared.

Diligent proofreading is a good defense against misplaced parts.

Exercises

Exercise 27: Misplaced parts

Indicate which sentences are correct and which contain misplaced parts. Rewrite the sentences that contain misplaced parts.

MODEL: It only takes Wally ten minutes to clean his room, whereas it takes me one full hour.

Answer: **It takes Wally only ten minutes to clean his room, whereas it takes me one full hour.**

1. Self-esteem is someone's own sense of his value and strength.
2. I almost love everyone of my neighbors.
3. Those men who had snored loudly greeted the morning.
4. Darwin wrote his famous book on the origin of the species in England.
5. All of the old people may be exposed on this trip to diseased water.
6. Because Marie believed in complete abstinence, she ordered merely a bottle of Perrier water.
7. To our amazement, the man almost spent half of his time collecting buttons from all over the world.
8. Some threadbare woman's underwear lay in the middle of the alley.
9. I discovered a sweater knit by my sister under the snow on the roof of our mountain cabin.
10. Last year, our publishing business grossed nearly a million dollars.
11. No one was allowed to use the condominium tennis courts except people living in the Northridge development.
12. A life of luxury was the only kind of life she knew.
13. All students will not be required to register for the draft.
14. One pedestrian got struck down by a truck emerging from the bus.
15. The carpet was laid on the parquet floor, which was made of silk and tied by hand.

28. Parallelism (//)

Parallelism enables a writer to express equal thoughts by using equal grammatical structures. In a parallel sentence, the writer balances noun against noun, adjective against adjective, infinitive against infinitive to emphasize the equality of ideas. Faulty parallelism upsets this balance of ideas in a sentence:

Awkward: My plan was to fish, hunt, and hiking.
  Parallel: My plan was to fish, hunt, and hike.

In short sentences such as the one above the preposition need not be repeated, but in longer sentences it shoud be.

Parallel prepositional phrases:

He talked to us about devotion ‖ to our family,
to our neighborhood, and
to our country.

Parallel subordinate clauses:

All of us knew ‖ that he was petty,
that he was jealous, and
that he was vain.

Parallel gerunds:

What I despised about him was his ‖ drinking,
gambling, and
cursing.

Parallel independent clauses:

‖ We counted our losses;
we cared for the wounded;
we advanced once again.

28a. Basic rules

There are some basic rules to follow when using parallelism. Do not use *and who* or *and which* unless preceded by another *who* or *which* clause.

Awkward: Pope John Paul II is a man with charisma *and who* is admired throughout the world.

Parallel: Pope John Paul II is a man ‖ who has charisma and
who is admired through-
out the world.

When using correlative conjunctions (*either . . . or, neither . . . nor, not only . . . but also, both . . . and*), use parallel constructions to complete the sentence.

Awkward: Either you pay the fine or jail is where you will go. (*Either* is followed by a pronoun, whereas *or* is followed by a noun.)

Parallel: Either ‖ you pay the fine
or   you go to jail.

Awkward: They not only invaded our privacy, but also our time was taken by them. (The *but also* part is in the passive.)

Parallel: They ‖ not only invaded our privacy,
‖ but also wasted our time.

To emphasize parallelism in a sentence, it is sometimes necessary to repeat a preposition, an article, or words in a phrase.

Awkward: She rummaged about in the kitchen, in the basement, and the attic.

Parallel: She rummaged about ‖ *in* the kitchen,
‖ *in* the basement, and
‖ *in* the attic.

(The preposition *in* is repeated.)

Awkward: Love is a gift as well as responsibility.

Parallel: Love is ‖ *a* gift as well as
‖ *a* responsibility.

(The article *a* is repeated.)

Awkward: Where he works and the place he lives are two completely different places.

Parallel: ‖ *Where he* works and
‖ *where he* lives

are two completely different places.
(*Where he* is repeated.)

Exercises

Exercise 28: Parallelism

Indicate which sentences are correct and which have faulty parallelism. Rewrite the sentences with faulty parallelism.

MODEL: Most of the students in my art class are youths of talent and who want to make a living from their art.

Answer: Most of the students in my art class are youths who have talent and who want to make a living form their art.

1. The pleasure of snow skiing comes from the thrill of speeding downhill and that it is out in nature.
2. She told Marie either to clean her fingernails or cut them shorter.
3. His rise had been predicted by astrology, prophecy, and dreams.
4. The crowds at the Olympic games seemed relaxed and enjoying themselves.

5. The father wanted to work rather than have free handouts.
6. He underwrote the cost of the journey, guaranteed revenue to the workers, and promising decent shelter for families with children.
7. My two favorite sports are fishing and to hike.
8. After attending the literature class, Leonard did not feel so much informed on issues as that he had increased his sensitivity to human needs.
9. The assignment was to create a myth about the edges of the universe and read it in class.
10. The bird flew above the tree, beyond the horizon, and into the blue yonder.
11. My salary is not as big as my sister.
12. The king demanded expulsion of the bishops, annihilation of all taxes, and burials.
13. All six of us agreed that we would ride the gondola to the top of the mountain but to hike back.
14. He came; he saw; he conquered.
15. The buildings of our city are black from soot and old age has cracked them.

29. Illogical constructions (ill)

The illogical construction is inexact, confusing, or vague, and may be so for a variety of reasons, a few of which are cataloged below.

29a. Illogical comparisons

Comparisons require that the items being compared be similar and that the comparison be complete. Study the following sentences:

> The rose is prettier than any flower in the world.

Since the *rose* is included in the classification of flower, the sentence is really saying that the rose is prettier than the rose. Here is the comparison logically stated:

> The rose is prettier than any *other* flower in the world.

Another common error is ambiguity resulting from a badly stated comparison:

> He loves me more than his son.

Does he love me more than he loves his son? Or does he love me more than his son loves me? The comparison must be reworded to specify the intended meaning.

Perhaps the most common error in comparisons is incompleteness. Here is a typical example:

> Anacin gives more relief.

More relief than what? Copy writing is replete with this sort of carelessness. Here is an improvement:

> Anacin gives more pain relief than does any other analgesic sold over the counter.

If not marketable, this comparison is at least logically complete. Here are some more examples of comparisons that are illogical and vague because of incompleteness:

Illogical: Women are more aggressive today.
   Better: Women are more aggressive today than they were twenty years ago.

Illogical: French chefs cook better meat sauces.
   Better: French chefs cook better meat sauces than do American chefs.

or

> French chefs cook better meat sauces than they do cream pies.

29b. Mixed constructions

A mixed construction is a sentence that begins in one grammatical pattern but ends in another. Here is an example:

> It was because all members of the firm stood by time-honored moral values that enabled them to survive.

The sentence develops logically until it reaches the word *enabled,* when it takes a sudden lurch into another pattern for which the reader is entirely unprepared. Confusion and misreading will inevitably result. The correct version starts with and ends on the same grammatical pattern thus fulfilling reader anticipation:

> It was because all members of the firm stood by time-honored moral values that they were able to survive.

Here are additional examples of mixed constructions followed by corrected versions. Some of the shifts are subtle variations on the grammatical pattern one would ordinarily anticipate.

Mixed: When the stock market crashed and Sully couldn't get help from anyone, not even Joseph, therefore he committed suicide.

Better: When the stock market crashed and Sully could not get help from anyone, not even Joseph, he committed suicide.

Mixed: As for the effects the large city had on Nancy were typical of what happened to many young people abroad.

Better: As for the effects the large city had on Nancy, they were typical of what happened to many young people abroad.

Mixed: His free will is limited to the circumstances by which his destiny has forced upon him.

Better: His free will is limited by the circumstances his destiny has forced upon him.

Exercises

Exercise 29: Illogical constructions

Indicate which sentences are correct and which contain illogical constructions. Rewrite the sentences that have illogical constructions.

> MODEL: The weather in California is far better than New York.
>
> Answer: **The weather in California is far better than the weather in New York.**

1. The first play concerns the blacks and how they maintained their dignity and facing difficulties caused by the whites.
2. It was in my ability to look past the bad in people to the good that helped me to like my classmates.
3. His mother's judgment of financial investments and real estate values is much sharper than his father.
4. Edmund's job pays better than Mark's.
5. A tragic hero is when a tragic flaw causes his downfall.
6. The reason for the decline of Rome was because the Romans had become morally flabby.
7. Mt. Everest is higher than any mountain in the world.
8. It was not until Antony died before Cleopatra realized how much she loved him.
9. The reason education in the United States seems to have become mediocre is that our schools have been asked to educate more illiterate people than ever before.
10. The emphasis on human rights makes America more democratic.
11. When he dissected a frog in biology lab was the experience he remembered years later.
12. We bought an old cabin which by repairing the roof we could use it for camping in during the summers.

30. Shifts (shift)

It is very important to be consistent in your use of tense, mood, person, voice, and discourse. If you shift your point of view, you will confuse your reader.

30a. Tense (shift/t)

Tense is the form of a verb that expresses the time of its action. The correct tense for a verb is normally dictated by the chronology of the situation being written about. Most of us use the proper tense out of habit. However, here are a few general rules:

Use the present tense to express timeless, general truths or prevailing customs:

> Copernicus pointed out that the world *is* (not *was*) not the center of our universe. (Copernicus' discovery was in the past, but the truth of it still applies today.)

> The rabbi reminded everyone that the Sabbath *begins* (not *began*) Friday at sunset. (The rabbi's warning was given in the past, but the Jewish Sabbath still begins on Friday.)

Indicate differences in time by using different tenses:

Wrong: Eric admitted that he *used* all of the wood.
Right: Eric admitted that he *had* used all of the wood. (Eric must have used up the wood before making the admission.)

Wrong: *Getting* permission from my boss, I will take a day of vacation next week.
Right: *Having gotten* permission from my boss, I will take a day's vacation next week. (The permission has to be granted before the vacation can be taken.)

Indicate simultaneous happenings by using the same tense:

Wrong: Mark waxed his skis while George *gazes* at the mountains.
Right: Mark waxed his skis while George *gazed* at the mountains. (Both the waxing and the gazing happen simultaneously and must therefore be expressed in the same tense.)

Wrong: Because my girlfriend remained at home alone, she *writes* me this melancholy letter.
Right: Because my girlfriend remained home alone, she *wrote* me this melancholy letter. (Both the remaining and the writing took place in the past and therefore require the same past tense.)

Wrong: We had packed our suitcases as well as *ate* our lunch before the train arrived.

Right: We had packed our suitcases as well as *eaten* our lunch before the train arrived. (The packing and eating both took place before the arrival of the train; they therefore require the same past tense.)

30b. Mood (shift/m)

Mood (or mode) indicates under what conditions a statement is being made. In English we have three moods: *indicative, subjunctive,* and *imperative.* The indicative mood is used for the majority of declarations ("The fields are blossoming.") or questions ("Do you feel any better?"). The subjunctive mood is used to express a wish ("I wish I *were* wealthy."), a necessity ("It is necessary that he *see* his children."), or a condition contrary to fact ("If she had taken the medicine, she *would be* alive today."). It is also used for a request or an indirect command ("He insisted that the suitcase *be* checked for drugs."). The imperative mood is used for direct commands (*"Give* me liberty or *give* me death!"*).

When you are writing, make sure you don't shift from one mood to another:

Wrong: They insisted that the money *be* collected and that a receipt *is* given in return. (shift from the subjunctive to the indicative)

Right: They insisted that the money *be* collected and that a receipt *be* given in return.

Wrong: *Pay* your taxes and you *should* also *support* your representatives in Congress. (shift from the imperative to the indicative mood)

Right: *Pay* your taxes and *support* your representatives in Congress.

Don't use *would have* when *had* is sufficient:

Wrong: If I *would have* been born in this country, I *would have* to enlist in the army.

Right: If I *had* been born in this country, I *would have* to enlist in the army. (The *if* clause requires only *had,* not *would have.*)

The subjunctive mood should be used in certain idiomatic expressions:

> *Come* (not *comes*) hell or high water, we'll be there.

NOTES: 1. Study the following rules on how to form the subjunctive.

The present subjunctive of *to be* is invariably *be:*

I demand that he *be* on time.

In all other forms, the subjunctive differs from the indicative only in that in the third person the third-person ending is dropped:

I suggest that she *listen* (not *listens*).

2. *Should* or *would* are often used to indicate suppositions as well as contrary-to-fact conditions:

Should an enemy attack, we *would* go to war.

3. You may prefer to avoid the subjunctive altogether by rewording the sentence:

Subjunctive: Suppose she *were to resign.*
  Rewrite: Suppose she *resigns.*
Subjunctive: Let's require *that he sign.*
  Rewrite: Let's require *him to sign.*
Subjunctive: It is necessary *that we be* kind.
  Rewrite: We *must be* kind.

30c. Person (shift/p)

A writer who doesn't write from a consistent point of view will bewilder the reader. Consider the following:

Basically each individual creates your own psychological self-portrait;
    however, others do contribute factors we use in evaluating oneself.

Like surprise flashes of lightning, the writer has struck from four different points of view: *each, your, we, oneself.* This fractured sentence is easily corrected if a single, consistent point of view is established:

Basically we each create our own psychological self-portrait; however,
    others do contribute factors we use in evaluating ourselves.

Most point of view errors occur when a writer attempts to speak about people in general. Here is a typical example:

Wrong: *Their* first thought is that *you* can't get the job. (The writer has shifted from *they* to *you.*)
Better: *Their* first thought is that *they* can't get the job.

See also 31. *Pronoun reference,* for the use of *one* and *you.*

30d. Voice (shift/v)

The voice of a verb tells you whether or not the subject acts or is acted upon:

> The boy ate the doughnut. (Here the subject *boy* is acting; he is eating the doughnut. Therefore, the voice is *active*.)

Now consider this version of the sentence:

> The doughnut was eaten by the boy. (In this case, *doughtnut* is the subject and it is being acted on by the boy. Therefore, the voice is *passive*.)

The choice between active or passive voice depends on whether you wish to emphasize the actor or the receiver of an action. As a general rule, the active voice is preferable because it is stronger and more direct than the passive. But whichever you use, don't shift unnecessarily from one voice to another:

Wrong: Although the Black Plague killed thousands of anonymous poor, the rich were attacked by it also.

Better: Although the Black Plague killed thousands of anonymous poor, it also attacked the rich.

Wrong: Jerry devoured a steak, and an entire half gallon of ice cream was eaten by him.

Better: Jerry devoured a steak and ate an entire half gallon of ice cream.

30e. Discourse (shift/d)

Discourse means conversation. Discourse can be direct, as:

> The flight attendant told the passengers, "Fasten your seat belts."

Or it can be indirect, as:

> The flight attendant requested that all passengers fasten their seat belts.

In the first example, the exact words of the speaker are used and enclosed in quotation marks. In the second example, the speaker's exact remarks are paraphrased. You may use either direct or indirect discourse, but you must not shift from one to the other:

Wrong: All of us wondered how the highjacker had boarded the plane and why didn't the security guards catch him? (shift from indirect to direct)

Better: All of us wondered how the highjacker had boarded the plane and why the security guards had not caught him.

Wrong: The salesperson informed me that she was collecting money for the blind and would I buy a broom.

Better: The salesperson informed me that she was collecting money for the blind and asked me if I would buy a broom.

or

The salesperson said, "I am collecting money for the blind. Would you buy a broom?"

Exercises

Exercise 30: Shifts in tense, mood, person, voice, discourse

Identify the kind of needless shift in each of the sentences below and then rewrite the sentences from a single point of view.

MODEL: Their first thought is that we will never learn the dance step.

Answer: Shift in person

Their first thought is that they will never learn the dance step.

1. In those early days the primary reason for my happiness lay in the ability I possess to take people for what they are.
2. Henry asked if he could accompany us and would we reserve an airline ticket for him?
3. She swayed back and forth and her body was swung from side to side.
4. When one feels accepted by a peer group, you become a stronger individual.
5. Look for some yeast and you should also pick up a newspaper.
6. His leg was fractured, his face was cut, and he looks like an inflated beach ball.
7. Fine athletes function as role models. If one can measure up, fine; if you can't, you are consigned to the uglies.
8. She held her trophy high, and her medal was worn with pride.
9. As the motorcycle hit the wall, the crowd screams in fear and delight.
10. The crusaders exposed themselves to every peril, and their bodies were given up to the adventure of life in death.
11. The treasurer testified that she just finished her report when the phone rang.
12. Years later she wondered why her youth had been so miserable and how could it have been improved.
13. If he wan't such a monster of conceit, I would admire him for his talent.
14. The young man declared that he was in love and would she please marry him.
15. The corpses are dragged to the courtyard of the palace and were left there for all to see.

31. Pronoun reference (ref)

Every pronoun must have an antecedent. To avoid faulty pronoun reference, make sure that the antecedents of your pronouns are clear.

Do not use a pronoun that could refer to more than one antecedent:

Wrong: The bartender yelled at Harry that *he* could lose his job. (Is it the bartender or Harry who could lose his job?)

Better: The bartender yelled at Harry, "You could lose your job!" (Recasting the sentence is better than creating an awkward repetition, such as "The bartender yelled at Harry that Harry could lose his job.")

Avoid pronouns that refer to entire clauses or sentences:

Wrong: His room is cluttered; his clothes are wrinkled; and even the pages of his books bear stains of grease. *This* really bothers me. (Three full clauses form the antecedent of *this;* the reference is too broad.)

Better: His room is cluttered; his clothes are wrinkled; and even the pages of his books bear stains of grease. *This sloppiness of his* really bothers me.

Avoid pronouns that have no antecedent:

Wrong: In *Oedipus Rex* there is no free will; *it* was predestined by Apollo. (*It* has no antecedent.)

Better: In *Oedipus Rex* there is no free will; *all of the tragic events* were predestined by Apollo.

Avoid pronouns whose antecedents are only implied by context:

Wrong: John lived in Italy during the first eight years of his life; consequently, he speaks *it* fluently. (The antecedent *Italian* is only implied.)

Better: John lived in Italy during the first eight years of his life; consequently, he speaks *Italian* fluently.

Avoid using *it* or *they* without a clear antecedent:

Wrong: In the *Los Angeles Times it* expressed the opposite point of view. (*It* has no antecedent.)

Better: The *Los Angeles Times* expressed the opposite point of view.

Wrong: *They* say that migraine headaches are often caused by repressed anger. (Who are *they*?)

Better: *Some neurologists* say that migraine headaches are caused by repressed anger.

Notice the following correct uses of the impersonal *it* when referring to weather, time, or distance:

> It is foggy today. (weather)
> It is precisely two o'clock. (time)
> Is it much farther to your house? (distance)

Avoid using *you* and *your* except when addressing the reader specifically.

Wrong: If *you* want to be happily married, *you* have to be willing to sacrifice *your* own pleasure.

Better: People who want to be happily married must be willing to sacrifice their own pleasure.

NOTE: To refer to all human beings or people in general, use general terms like *we, one, a person,* or *people*. Notice, however, that throughout this book we often use the pronoun *you* because we are addressing you, our reader, specifically.

Exercises

Exercise 31: Pronoun reference

Indicate which sentences contain a faulty pronoun reference. Then rewrite those sentences to correct the error.

> MODEL: She seemed so young and innocent, which made Helene jealous.
>
> Answer: **Her apparent youth and innocence made Helene jealous.**

1. As serious as our differences may seem, it is a common case of dissimilarities.
2. At midnight the doctor came out and told us that he had survived the surgery.
3. Deprecating comments are made all of the time, and it makes the victim have a low opinion of himself.
4. The nurse's aide lied by writing on the chart that she had been given a bath.
5. She had a house which survived her only three years.
6. The senator squirmed in his seat and avoided the question, which amused the reporters.
7. His best friend warned him that he might get an "F."
8. Many youths feel that their environment is prejudiced against them, and this increases their hostility.

9. If I'm having a boring time, it shows on my face.
10. If a person wants to make money, he must learn how to take risks.
11. Although my brother is taking pre-med courses, I doubt if he will ever be one.
12. How far is it to the main library?
13. In Islam they believe that Jesus was a prophet.
14. I was stood up on two separate occasions, which embarrassed me.
15. Since the children want to make some animals out of apple cores, I need to buy some at the store.

Index

A
Abbreviations, 502–503
Active voice, 253
Ad hominem fallacy, 92–93
Ad populum fallacy, 93–95
Adjectives, 435–36, 467–69
    after sense verbs, 468
    comparative, 436, 468
    positive, 436
    superlative, 436, 468
Adverbs, 435–37, 467–69
    after sense verbs, 468
    comparative, 436–37, 468
    positive, 436–37
    superlative, 436–37, 468
Agreement, 457–63
    pronoun-antecedent, 460–61
    subject-verb, 458–60
Alliteration, 258
Anecdote, 205
Apostrophe, 482–83
Argumentation, 84–88, 127–28, 281–93, 325
    anecdote in, 286–87
    evidence in, 283–303
    example of, 100–109, 128, 281–303
    experience in, 285–86
    facts in, 287–88
    fallacies in, 92–97
    logical links in, 293–303
    proposition of, 281–83
    purpose of, 281
    reasoning in, 290–93
    statistics in, 289–90
    testimonial in, 284–85
Awkward shifts, 238–40

B
Bibliographic references for books, 356–62
    anonymous author, 357
    anthologies, 359
    chapter, 359
    collections, 358–59
    corporate author, 357
    dictionaries, 360
    edited work, 361
    edition, 361
    encyclopedias, 360
    foreign publisher, 361
    foreign title, 362
    of illustrations, 362
    introduction, 362
    preface, 362
    quotation within cited work, 359
    reprint, 360–61
    series, numbered, 360
    series, unnumbered, 360
    in several volumes, 358
    single author, 356
    translation, 362
    two or more authors, 356–57
Bibliographic references for nonprint
    materials, 368–81
    address or lecture, 368
    art work, 368
    computer program, 369
    computer source, 369
    database source, 369
    film, 369–70
    interview, 370
    musical composition, 370
    recording, 371

Bibliographic references for nonprint materials
  (*continued*)
  television or radio programs, 370–71
  theatrical performance, 372
Bibliographic references for periodicals,
  363–68
  author, 363
  page numbers, 364
  publication information, 363–64
  title of article, 363
Bibliographic references for special items,
  372–81
  art work, published, 373
  the Bible, 373
  classical plays, 376
  classical works, 373–74
  congressional publications, 378
  congressional record, 378
  dissertation, 374
  executive branch publications, 378–79
  footnote or endnote citation, 374–75
  legal documents, 379–80
  manuscript or typescript, 375
  modern plays, 377
  pamphlet or brochure, 375
  personal letter, 375–76
  poetry, 377
  public documents, 378
  quotation in article, 380
  quotation in book, 380
  reports, 380–81
  tables, graphs, illustrations, 381
Bibliography, 334–35, 351–81
  example of, 397
Brackets, 486
Brainstorming, 27–29
Bullet lead, 206

C
Capitalization, 491–95
  of first words, 491–92
  of names, 492
  of proper nouns, 492
Card catalog, 332–33
Causal analysis, 127–29, 192–98, 325
  example of, 128, 196–98
Citation of books, 352–56
  author, 352–53
  edition, 354
  editor, compiler, translator, 353–54
  page numbers, 356
  publication facts, 355–56
  series name and number, 354
  title, 353
  volume numbers, 354–55
Citation of periodicals, 364–68
  anonymous author, 364

critical review, 367
editorial, 366–67
journal, continuous pagination, 365
journal, separate pagination, 365
letter to editor, 367
monthly magazine, 366
multiple authors, 365
newspaper, 366
published address or lecture, 368
published interview, 367–68
single author, 364–65
weekly magazine, 366
Classical imitation, 271–74
Classification, 39–40, 127–28, 174–80, 324
  example of, 39–40, 128, 177–80
Clauses, 446–48
  adjective, 447–48
  adverb, 448
  dependent, 446–47
  independent, 446–47
  noun, 447
Clustering, 29–30
  example of, 31, 32
Coherence, 64, 120–24
Colon, 477–78
Comma, 471
  in addresses, 475
  with appositives, 474
  with coordinating conjunctions, 471–72
  in dates, 475
  with introductory elements, 472
  with miscellaneous elements, 474–77
  with nonrestrictive clauses and phrases, 473
  with parenthetical expressions, 474
  in a series, 472–73
Comma splice, 256, 454–55
Comparison/Contrast, 38–39, 127–28, 183–91,
  325
  example of, 38–39, 128, 185–91
Complement, 442–43
  direct object, 442
  indirect object, 442
  object complement, 442–43
  subject complement, 442–43
Computer searches, 333
Conjunctions, 256, 437–38
  conjunctive adverb, 437–38
  coordinating, 437
  correlative, 251, 437
  subordinating, 437–38
Constructions, 232, 234–35, 516–18
  illogical, 516–18
  logical, 235
  mixed, 232, 517–18
  parallel, 234–35
Controlling idea, finding a, 25–37, 59–60
  with brainstorming, 27–29, 30, 32
  with clustering, 29–30, 31–32

with invention, 27
through memories and experiences, 34–35, 61
through observation, 35–36
through research, 36–37
by talking writing, 30–34

D
Dangling modifiers, 510–11
Dash, 478
Definition, 127–28, 151–57, 323–24
  example of, 152
  using etymology in, 153
Description, 127–28, 141–48, 323
  dominant impression in, 142–43
  example of, 128, 141
  specific details in, 143–45
Documentation, 341–51
Dominant impression, 142–43
Draft, 7–10, 69–70, 74–77
  final, 6, 70
  first, 9, 10, 69, 74–77
  second, 8–9, 69
  third, 7–8, 70

E
Editing, 274–75
  definition of, 12
Endnotes, 341
Essay, 38–61, 118, 201–25, 413–26
  anecdote, 205
  bullet lead, 206
  ending the, 217–25
  illustration of, 118
  middle of, 209
  openings in, 201–207
  organization, 38–45
  purpose of, 59–61
  quotation, 207
  spotlight opening, 206–207
  writing, 56–58
Essay exam, 321–28
Etymology, 153
Evidence in developing thesis statement, 84–88
  source of, 85–86
  weight of, 84–85
  worth of, 86
Exactness in word choice, 244–47
Example, 127–29, 158–65, 324
  example of, 128
Exclamation point, 480

F
Faulty alternative, 90–92
Faulty analogy, 98–99
Faulty condition, 90
Figures of speech, 145–46, 267

Footnotes, 341
Fragment, 256–57

H
Hasty generalization, 82–84
Hyphen, 484–85

I
Intensifier, 266
Interjections, 439
Inventive diction, 262–67
Irrelevancies, 92–109
  ad hominem, 92–93
  ad populum, 93–95
  faulty analogy, 98–99
  red herring, 95–97
Italics, 496–98

K
Key words, 122–24, 210–11

L
Literal language, 267
Literary papers, 307–20
  analyzing form in, 315–20

M
Metaphors, 145, 267–68
Microform indexes, 333
Misplaced parts, 512–13
Modifiers, 236–38
  dangling, 236–37
  misplaced, 237–38
  squinting, 238

N
Narration, 51–52, 127–28, 133–37, 323
  example of, 51–52, 127–28, 133–34
  pacing of, 135–36
  point of view in, 134–35
  vivid details of, 136–37
Non sequiturs, 88–92
  faulty alternative, 90–92
  faulty condition, 90
  post hoc ergo propter hoc, 89–90
Note cards, 336, 382–394
Nouns, 433, 459
  collective, 459
  common, 433
  compound, 433
  proper, 433
Numbers, 499–501

O
Observation, 35–36
Organizing an essay, 38–40
  with a model, 38–40
  with an outline, 40–45

Organizing ideas, 38, 71–74
  by logic, 73
  by order of importance, 72
  by simple enumeration, 72
  by space orientation, 72–73
  by time orientation, 73
Outline, 40–45, 168–69, 341, 398–401
  complex, 41–43
  example of, 398–401
  faulty subordination in, 44
  parallelism in, 43
  sentence, 40–43
  simple, 40
  topic, 43

P
Pacing, 135–36
Padding, 66–67
Paragraphs, 115–27, 215–16
  coherence in, 120–24
  constructing from thesis statement, 125–27
  parts of, 116–17
  structure of, 117
  supporting details in, 116–17
  topic sentence of, 116–17
  transitions in, 215–16
  writing unified, 117–19
Parallel structures, 122–24
Parallelism, 43, 513–15
  basic rules of, 514–15
Paraphrase, 337
Paraphrase card, 337–38, 382–94
Paraphrasing, 311–13
Parentheses, 485–86
Parenthetical citations, 341–51
Parts of speech, 429–40
  adjectives, 435–36
  adverbs, 435–37
  conjunctions, 437–38
  interjections, 439
  nouns, 433
  prepositions, 437
  pronouns, 433–34
  verbs, 430–33
Passive voice, 253
Period, 479–80
Periodical guides, 333
Personal comment card, 338–39, 390, 394
Phrase, 243–45
  in place of a word, 243–44
  prefabricated, 243
Phrases, 443–46
  absolute, 445
  appositive, 445–46
  gerund, 444–45
  infinitive, 444
  participial, 445
  prepositional, 255–56, 437, 443

Plagiarism, 342, 349–50
Point of view, 134–35
Post hoc ergo propter hoc fallacy, 89–90
Predicate, 441–42
  complete, 441–42
  simple, 441–42
Prepositional phrases, 255–56, 437, 443
Prepositions, 253, 437
Process, 127–28, 167–74, 324
  basic steps of, 168–69
  correct sequence of, 169–70
  example of, 128, 170–73
Pronoun, cases of, 463–67
  objective, 463, 465–66
  possessive, 463, 466–67
  subjective, 463, 464–65
Pronoun reference, 524–25
Pronouns, 433–34, 458–59
  demonstrative, 434
  indefinite, 434, 459
  intensive, 434
  interrogative, 434
  objective case, 434
  personal, 434
  possessive case, 434
  reflexive, 434
  relative, 434, 458–59
  subjective case, 434
Proofreading, 275–77
  definition of, 12

Q
Question mark, 480
Quotation, 207, 338
Quotation card, 338, 382–94
Quotation marks, 481–82
Quoting, 313–15

R
Recursive nature of writing, 11, 17
Red herring fallacy, 95–97
Redundancy, 241–42
Repetition, 67
Report paper, 339–40
Research, 36–37
Research paper, 331–410
  example of, 381–410
Revising, 12, 62–70, 71–81, 82–109, 231–40
  definition of, 12
  for better organization and structure, 71–81
  for clarity of aim, 62–63, 232–40
  for coherence, 64–65
  for conciseness, 241–48
  for emphasis, 249–69
  for logical progression and thought, 82–109
  for specificity, 65–66
  to suit audience, 68–69
  for unity, 63–64
  to remove wordiness, 66–68

Rewriting, 15–21,
  goals of, 15–16
  procedure and sequence for, 16–21
Rewriting process, 11–12, 16–20
  editing, 12
  proofreading, 12
  revising, 12
Rhetorical mode, 127–30
Rhyming, 257–59
Rough draft, 341–51
Roundaboutness, 67
Run-on sentences, 455

S
Sentences, 249–71, 448–49, 453–54
  balanced, 249–52
  combining, 269–71
  complex, 449
  compound, 449
  compound-complex, 449
  emphatic, 249, 252–59
  inventive diction in, 262–67
  parallel, 249–52
  simple, 448–49
Shifts, 519–23
  in discourse, 522–23
  in mood, 520–21
  in person, 521
  in tense, 519–20
  in voice, 522
Similes, 145, 268–69
Specific details, 143–45
Spotlight opening, 206–207
Statement of purpose, 339
Style, 47–52, 68
  formal, 50
  informal, 50–51
Subject, 441–42
  complete, 441–42
  simple, 441–42
Subordination, 505–508
Summarizing, 309–11
Summary card, 336, 382–94

T
Talking writing, 30–34
Theme, finding a, 308–309
Thesis paper, 339–40
Thesis statement, 25–37, 60–61, 84–88,
  125–27

developing, 25–37, 60
constructing paragraphs from, 125–27
evidence in developing, 84–88
formulating, 25–37
revising, 62–70
Topic, choosing and narrowing, 24
Topic, finding a, 332–33
Topic sentence, 168
Transitions, 122–24, 169–70, 185–86, 209–26
  asking rhetorical questions, 212–13
  phrases, 213–14
  repetition of key words, 210–11
  restating ideas, 211–12
  special paragraphs, 215–16
  summarizing sentence, 214–15
  using phrases, 213–14

U
Unnecessary words, 242–47
Using experiences, 34–35, 61
Using memories, 34–35, 61

V
Verbs, forms of, 433
  intransitive, 433
  transitive, 433
Verbs, tenses of, 430–33
  future, 431
  future perfect, 432
  past, 431
  past perfect, 432
  present, 431
  present perfect, 431
Vivid details, 136–37
Voice, 253–54, 432
  active, 253–54, 432
  passive, 253–54, 432
Voice and style, 47–52

W
Wordiness, causes of, 66–68
  padding, 66–67
  repetition, 67
  roundaboutness, 67
Works cited, 342, 410
  student sample of, 410
Writing process, 10–11
  creative nature of, 10–11
  recursive nature of, 11–17

Proofreading Symbols

Symbol	Meaning
fact*o*ry	Insert a letter
anteced*e*nt	Replace a letter
One *must* make choices	Insert a word
In ~~Peking~~ *Beijing*	Replace a word
in the <u>west</u>	Capitalize
He is a bank /President	Use lowercase
rec*ie*ve	Transpose letters
to ⌐quickly move⌐	Transpose words
a ˅display of (dazzling) light	Move word(s)
the future of#the world	Insert a space
a birth‿mark	Close up the space
dis͜appear	Delete a letter and close up
every ~~last taxable~~ dollar	Delete word(s)
a ~~treacherous~~ enemy	Stet (restore what was deleted)
her own <u>self-esteem.</u>⌐ ⌐Her physical stress	Run the line on (no paragraph)